AMERICAN OLIGARCHY

AMERICAN OLIGARCHY

★ ★ ★ ★ ★

THE PERMANENT POLITICAL CLASS

RON FORMISANO

UNIVERSITY OF
ILLINOIS PRESS
Urbana, Chicago, and Springfield

Library of Congress Control Number: 2017946586
ISBN 978-0-252-04127-3 (hardcover)
ISBN 978-0-252-08282-5 (paperback)
ISBN 978-0-252-09987-8 (e-book)

Proportion . . . would impose on each man burdens corresponding to the power and well-being he enjoys, and corresponding risks in cases of incapacity or neglect. For instance, an employer who is incapable or guilty of an offense against his workman ought to be made to suffer more, both in the spirit and in the flesh, than a workman who is incapable or guilty of an offense against his employer. . . . [I]n criminal law, a conception of punishment in which social rank, as an aggravating circumstance, would necessarily play an important part in deciding what the penalty should be. All the more reason, therefore, why the exercise of important public functions should carry with it serious personal risks.

—Simone Weil, "Equality"

Contents

Preface

In 1994 during a five-month Fulbright lectureship at the University of Bologna at a momentous time in Italian politics, when populist political parties arose to challenge a sclerotic political order that had been in place since World War II, I became familiar with the Italians' *la classe politica*—the political class. Entrenched politicians were under siege, from all sides, left, right, and center. Ordinary Italians as well as journalists and intellectuals had long harbored a culturally ingrained cynicism and disdain for traditional elites. But newly formed populist parties and movements were attracting widespread support and attacking with unprecedented energy established political and economic elites as out of touch and self-serving.[1] Although the upheaval eliminated the Christian Democratic Party that had dominated politics since 1944, the political class eventually did what it always does: survive.

A political class can serve as a convenient scapegoat for popular discontent. But in reality it also possesses very concrete characteristics. In Italy, and increasingly in the United States, many of its members are political professionals for life, *essere sistematica*, "literally to be 'fixed up' for the long pull." Accordingly, the political class tends to be permanent, it continually expands, and it "is relatively immune from outside checks of the kind that elections can provide."[2]

In Italy in 2007 a best-selling book by two journalists, Sergio Rizzo and Gian Antonio Stella, described that immunity: *La casta: Così I politici italiani sono diventati intoccabili* (*The Caste: How Italian Politicians Became Untouchable*). Since then Italians have tended to replace *la classe politica* simply with *la casta*, or *la classe dirigente*, the ruling class.

I began to think seriously about political class in the United States after encountering it later in Joan Didion's scathing essays deconstructing the fictions of American elections and politics, and particularly those created by "that handful of insiders who invent, year in and year out, the narrative of public life." Agreeing to cover the 1988 presidential campaign for the *New York Review of Books*, she discovered that it was clear by then "that those inside the process had congealed into a permanent political class, the defining characteristic of which was its readiness to abandon those not inside the process."

Didion provided a marvelous example of the insider perspective in the commentary of journalist Cokie Roberts following the one-time-only decision by the Supreme Court's five-man Republican majority to hand the 2000 election, on day thirty-five of stalemate, to Republican George W. Bush. In a decision concocted of legalese "limited to the present circumstances," the court decided the case not on general principles or precedents but, in Alan Dershowitz's words, "on a principle that has never been recognized by any court and that will never again be recognized by this court."[3]

Appearing on ABC's *This Week*, Roberts "made the case of the permanent political class for order, for continuity, for the perpetuation of the contract that delivered only to itself: 'I think people do think it's political but they think that's okay. They expect the court to be political and—and they wanted this election to be over.' In the absence of actual evidence to back up this arrestingly constructive reading of what 'people' expected or wanted, she offered the rationale then common among those inside the process. 'At least now, we are beginning to have that post-election coming together.'"[4]

In America evidence abounds of continuing discontent and disgust with the political class, along with a corrosive alienation from government. Indeed, along with rising economic inequality, distrust of governments spans the globe. In 2016 the U.S. electorate, during the primaries and nominating contests for the Democratic and Republican presidential nominations, heard candidates from both parties continuously attack the "political class" or "the establishment." Candidates who were themselves long-term members of the Washington elite condemned it—without blushing—as a dysfunctional entity that large segments of voters had come to view as self-interested or corrupt.

This book describes a broad range of sectors of the American political class, including its corporate and financial sectors, as having acquired "untouchability" and asserts that it has become, increasingly, the ruling class, *la classe dirigente*. Rarely are any of its denizens held accountable for self-dealing or transgressions of the public interest. The "permanent political class" in the United States functions at times as an abstract scapegoat; this book describes many of the ways it acts as a plutocratic oligarchy and contributes not only to the creation of extreme economic inequality, but the creation of an aristocracy of inherited wealth.

American Oligarchy

Introduction

Beyond Plutocracy

Becoming an Aristocracy

In recent decades, challengers to the status quo have relied heavily on the terms *political class* and *permanent political class* to refer to entrenched and self-serving elites. Populist parties and candidates in Europe and North and South America have mobilized to displace them. The currency of these phrases as pejoratives reflects the rise of oligarchies perceived as self-interested and out of touch with ordinary citizens. In the United States the 2016 presidential primaries and general election campaigns produced floods of "antiestablishment" rhetoric directed at politics as usual and career politicians and bureaucrats. *Outsider* and *populist* became accolades.

Across the political spectrum, many observers of Washington, D.C., have recognized the existence of a self-perpetuating and self-aggrandizing political class. But the phenomenon extends well beyond Washington to embrace regional and state political and economic elites occupying a broad array of institutions in and out of government, tied together by ambition, interest, and mutual benefit. But Washington is the epicenter of the permanent political class: Washington, where the median income for white families was $170,364 in 2013, compared to the national median of $58,270; where rapid gentrification has reduced the percentage of low-income African Americans in the population from 60 to 49.5 percent.

This book is a sequel to a study of inequality in the United States. It argues that the permanent political class drives economic and political inequality not only with the policies it has constructed over the past four decades, such as federal and state tax systems rigged to favor corporations and the wealthy; it also increases inequality by its self-dealing, acquisitive behavior as it enables, emulates, and enmeshes itself with the wealthiest One Percent and .01 percent.

The political class bears heavy responsibility for the United States now experiencing economic inequality more extreme than at any time in its history; and it is increasing despite incremental measures to reduce it taken by President Obama (limited by a hostile Republican Congress). Since the 1970s income inequality in the United States has streaked ahead of most European and Latin American countries. Here, the top 1 percent takes home 20 percent of U.S. income, the most since the 1920s; the One Percent's income averages 38 times more than the bottom 90 percent. But that looks puny, compared to the .01 percent taking in 184 times the income of the bottom 90 percent.[1]

In wealth distribution the United States is the *most unequal of all* economically developed countries; here over 75 percent of wealth is owned by the richest 10 percent: by comparison, in the United Kingdom this group owns 53.3 percent. Here, the top .01 percent—the super rich, just 16,000 families—control $6 trillion in assets, as much as the bottom two-thirds of families. The United States had the largest wealth gap of 55 nations according to the Global Wealth Report for 2015 by Allianz (a financial services firm), prompting the report's authors to label the nation the "Unequal States of America."[2]

Most studies of inequality ignore the ways political class behavior creates inequality. The political class's direct creation of economic inequality by channeling the flow of income and wealth to elites has been well documented; less exposed has been how its self-aggrandizement creates a culture of corruption that infects the entire society and that induces many to abuse positions of power to emulate or rise to the One Percent. Most dangerously, its behavior threatens to subject the republic to the hegemony of an aristocracy of inherited wealth.

Directly and indirectly the American permanent political class also contributes to continuing high levels of poverty and disadvantage for millions that exceed almost all advanced nations. Most members of the political class, in and out of government, talk easily and with a veneer of sincerity about the nation's problems: unemployment, lack of good-paying work, crumbling infrastructure, hunger in a country of enormous food production, among others. But the talk does not lead to substantive, radical action to attack and remedy inequality and deprivation suffered by their fellow citizens; the political class avoids above all policy change that might cost it something. Political leaders, especially when campaigning, use populist political rhetoric and embrace a populist style to appeal to "folks" and "everyday Americans." They are the masters, to borrow a phrase from Paul Krugman, of "photo-op populism." But after elections, the "for the people" rhetoric fades along with concern for the res publica.[3]

The permanent political class begins with the three branches of government, above all members of Congress, but I define it broadly as a networked layer of high-income people and those striving for wealth including many politicians in and out of office, lobbyists, consultants, appointed bureaucrats (functionaries of the "regulatory state"), pollsters, television celebrity journalists (but not investigative reporters), and the politically connected in the nation's capital and in the states. Not least are behind-the-scenes billionaires (and some who are highly visible such as Charles and David Koch and Sheldon Adelson) who exert influence with tens of millions to Super PACs and directly to election campaigns and via seemingly nonpolitical giving, such as to universities, mostly hidden from view, that is also "shaping policy influencing opinion, promoting favorite causes, polishing their images—and carefully shielding themselves from public scrutiny."[4]

The political class embraces many other subgroups such as highly compensated university presidents and academic administrators, and the executives of well-funded nonprofit institutions (e.g., hospitals, museums, other cultural institutions). Leaders and those aspiring to leadership in these groups often schmooze and rub elbows with members of the financial and corporate elite; the impulse of the wannabes to emulate the lifestyle and perks of the One Percent sets in motion a powerful imperative to enjoy the highlife, often at public expense.

Over half of the members of Congress are millionaires; their 2013 total worth was $4.3 billion. The high cost of running for office has in part increased the flow of the wealthy into government, but it has resulted also from representatives leveraging their official positions to enrich themselves and their families. The access to campaign funds and the exploiting of loopholes in ethics laws also allow many legislators, even if they are not millionaires, to live like millionaires.

Most members of the political class at all levels of government expect as a matter of course to keep their own interests and those of their families foremost among their priorities. A long time ago while living in Worcester, Massachusetts, and serving on the unpaid board of the public library, I received a call from a candidate running for state representative in my district, who probably over-estimated my influence with other voters. With naked candor he explained his motives in seeking office. Firstly, he said, he intended to look out "for me and mine" (implying I too could be considered "mine"), then the district, then the public welfare, as long as it did not conflict with the first two stated reasons. A political boss of old Tammany Hall put it more directly: "Like a businessman in business, I work for my own pocket all the time."

Looking out for one's own is ingrained in the DNA of a political career. When the distinguished progressive congressman Barney Frank entered politics as the young chief of staff for Boston's new liberal mayor Kevin White, he believed he faced a sensitive situation involving his sister Ann Lewis. "On his own initiative," recalled Frank in his memoir, "White pioneered the appointment of women to high office," including Frank's sister, who he decided to make Frank's deputy. "Sensitive to the charge of nepotism, which was considered a bad thing in the circles I'd previously travelled [liberal academia], I started to explain to City Councilor Fred Langone that it had been entirely White's decision. 'Don't you dare apologize,' he interrupted me. 'If you can't take care of your own in this business, what good are you?'"[5]

A large proportion of the political class excels at "tak[ing] care of their own," above all in Washington and the federal government. As longtime *Washington Post* reporter Robert G. Kaiser put it in his superb book on lobbying and Congress, "in earlier generations enterprising young men came to Washington looking for power and political adventure, often with ambitions to save or reform the country or the world. In the last fourth of the twentieth century such aspirations were supplanted by another familiar American yearning: to get rich."[6]

One sure path to riches in Washington and across the country is lobbying the government on behalf of corporations, banks, special interests, and the wealthy. Tens of thousands of lobbyists ply their trade in the nation's capital, and tens of thousands more in state capitals. The corps of lobbyists in Washington resembles a Fourth Estate, or a fourth unofficial branch of government, as important in making policy as the original three established by the Constitution. Lobbyists also exert influence over electoral campaigns through millions of dollars funneled through Political Action Committees (PACs).

Most denizens of the political class have absorbed the take-what-you-can feather-my-nest ethos that prevails in Wall Street financial institutions and among the corporate elite that works hand in glove with the Capitol political elite and all its hangers-on from K Street lobbyists to media personalities. The political class looks continually for opportunities providing advancement or enrichment; it is hungry, and its appetite when feasting on the commonweal knows few limits.

Some observers of the permanent political class in Washington say that most individuals in it are not corrupt but "decent people" participating in a corrupt system. They maintain this generous view of Congress, for example, even while recognizing that it runs on a system of "legalized bribery," also described technically as a "gift economy," enveloping senators, representatives, and many bureaucrats, the currency of which is usually campaign funding from special interests, taxpayer money, and cost to the good of the republic. Jack Abramoff was the rare uber-lobbyist who went to jail, according to insiders, for doing in excess what other lobbyists and members of Congress do routinely. Kaiser reported that before he went to jail Abramoff was heard to say: "I was participating in a system of legalized bribery. All of it is bribery, every bit of it."[7]

Throughout the political class, shame seems to be an alien emotion. Shameless well describes the political class's unabashed and hidden-in-plain-sight practice of nepotism; its favoritism toward its own ("me and mine") is reaching epic proportions. Nepotism is hardly new. It existed in Britain's North American colonies before there was a United States, and continued to be practiced in government and society throughout the nation's history. But this ruling class, while giving lip service to meritocracy, promotes its children into lucrative positions in government, business, media, and entertainment, along with other relatives, friends, and whoever is in a position to return favors and advantages to the promoters.

Nepotism is so commonplace and obvious that a book has appeared proclaiming it a positive good.[8] It is difficult to reconcile that notion with the United States now experiencing historic levels of inequality of income and wealth. In brief, the rampant nepotism of the political class fuels the galloping socioeconomic inequality of the twenty-first century that shows no signs of abating.

The contemporary political class layered across political, economic, social, and cultural institutions displays more diversity in ethnicity, religion, and, to a lesser degree, gender and race than the white Protestant upper classes of sixty years ago; but its nepotism and self-dealing undercuts any claim to meritocracy.

Sociologist E. Digby Baltzell was born into that upper caste of sixty years ago, an American aristocrat who believed that an upper class should be open to talent and merit. He became an eminent professor at the University of Pennsylvania, best known as a critic of the White Anglo-Saxon Protestant establishment.

Though he may not have coined the term *WASP*, he did as much as any other writer to popularize it. Courtly and accessible to his students, he dressed like an English country gentleman (tweed jackets and bow ties), and rode his old, one-speed bicycle from his home in Philadelphia's upper-crust Delancy Square to the university campus (he owned another home in Wellfleet, Massachusetts). His first book, *Philadelphia Gentlemen: The Making of a National Upper Class* (1958), was a pioneering historical study of the class stratum of his family and associates.[9]

His next book attracted attention among a wider public: *The Protestant Establishment: Aristocracy and Caste in America* (1964) delivered a scathing critique of a closed WASP upper class that had brought on a "crisis in moral authority" because of its "unwillingness, or inability, to share and improve its upper-class traditions by continuously absorbing talented and distinguished members of minority groups into its privileged ranks." Baltzell argued that an upper class could not maintain power or authority, "especially in an opportunitarian and mobile society such as ours," if it remained unrepresentative of society as a whole. In the early 1960s, Baltzell made clear, bastions of WASP exclusivity existed throughout the precincts of economic power and social status, from corporate boardrooms to elite social clubs. Jews, Catholics, and minorities were not welcome, though Baltzell saw reason for optimism in the 1960 election of the first Roman Catholic to the presidency.[10]

Batlzell emphasized then and in later comments that he did not oppose "upper class institutions in the interests of creating a more egalitarian and homogenized society. Quite the contrary." Rather, those institutions must be open to merit and reflect the diversity of American society. Before he died in 1996 Baltzell acknowledged that the American upper class had become more inclusive. Although in the twenty-first century the permanent political class is still impressed by pedigree and "old money," it is more diverse. Yet even as it expands and adapts, it has become an oligarchy blocking opportunity for millions and makes a mockery of Baltzell's ideal.[11]

In her splendid book, *Plutocrats: The Rise of the New Global Super-Rich and the Fall of Everyone Else*, Chrystia Freeland warned that a self-perpetuating oligarchy of wealth that pulls up the ladder of social mobility behind it could "choke off economic growth and become politically unsustainable." She drew upon the example of fourteenth-century Venice, a mercantile powerhouse that was the richest city in Europe. But in 1315 its rulers closed off entry into the commercial class, effectively shutting down social mobility. The Venetians called the oligarchy's action *La Serrata*, or the closure. In the short run the reigning elite kept control over the city's lucrative trade, but in the long term the exclusivity of La Serrata led to the city's decline.[12]

Freeland saw a similar process happening in the United States as the "working rich" are giving way increasingly to a limited number of families who inherit fortunes, a "rentier elite." This "transfer of privilege from one generation to the next is a gradual, cumulative, and very personal process. But as a mechanism for turning an inclusive social and economic order into an exclusive one, it could be as powerful as the more overt Serrata."[13]

In 2014 French economist Thomas Piketty's best-selling book, *Capital in the Twenty-First Century*, identified an economic system steadily concentrating wealth and trending toward aristocracies of wealth in Europe and the United States. Under prevailing conditions "it is almost inevitable that inherited wealth will dominate wealth amassed from a lifetime's labor by a wide margin, and the concentration of capital will attain extremely high levels—levels potentially incompatible with the meritocratic values and principles of social justice fundamental to modern democratic societies." Piketty expressed pessimism that governments possessed the political will to reverse the process. A rentier elite that does not work, produces nothing, and lives off capital assets, he argued, will also accumulate increasing political power.[14]

As wealth has concentrated, the U.S. government has become a plutocracy and less of a representative democracy pursuing the general welfare.[15] The word *plutocracy* has its roots in two Greek words, one meaning "power," the other "wealth." It is not hyperbole to say that we have a government of the rich, by the rich, and for the rich, but it is too simple. By plutocracy I mean a hydra-headed and diverse collection of elites who exert enormous influence to the exclusion of the great mass of citizens: those elites include super-rich families, CEOs of corporations, heads of big banks and other financial institutions, particularly hedge fund managers, and Washington lobbyists, to name a few. They are the beneficiaries and enablers of a concentration of wealth unmatched in other developed countries. The United States is headed beyond oligarchy to an aristocracy of inherited wealth.

Observers of rising inequality warn that American society not only has become beset by extreme inequality but also is acquiring features associated with an aristocracy. Since it became likely that a third member of the Bush family and a second Clinton were preparing to run for president, some observers regarded the prospect as evidence of aristocracy. But political dynasties are nothing new in American politics, along with the tendency of voters to favor familiar family names.[16] It is not evident, however, that the republic will survive the rise of dynasties that constitute an aristocracy of wealth.

The threat posed by an aristocracy of wealth differs from that of a political dynasty such as that of the Kennedys or Bushes. Forebodings of such a development have arisen more plausibly since the Supreme Court's decisions in *Citizens United* and *McCutcheon* equating money with speech and corporations with people, thus enlarging the power of billionaires in elections. (Comedian Stephen Colbert agreed that corporations are legally people: "And it makes sense folks. They do everything people do except breathe, die and go to jail for dumping 1.3 million pounds of PCBs into the Hudson River." Colbert added: "Corporations have free speech. But they can't speak like you and me. They don't have mouths or hands. Just a giant middle finger.")

The watchdog Open Secrets, which tracks money in elections, reported that in 2014 just 31,976 donors—roughly *one percent of one percent* of the entire population—accounted for an estimated $1.18 billion of disclosed political contributions at the federal level. This "Political One Percent of the One Percent" made up 29 percent of all fund-raising that political committees disclosed to the Federal Election Commission, up from 25 percent in 2010. As the gap in income and wealth between the top One Percent and everyone else increases, so too does the gaping disparity in political influence.[17]

Aristocratic attitudes in the shape of a sense of entitlement are increasingly displayed by the very rich, from their expectation that their children deserve admission to the best schools to their rage at the prospect of being deprived of preferential tax treatment. Private equity billionaire and big spender Stephen Schwartzman compared treating carried interest like ordinary income to Hitler's invasion of Poland (he later apologized). Venture capitalist Tom Pickens (estimated worth $8 billion) suggested in a letter to the *Wall Street Journal* that criticism of the One Percent compares with Nazi persecution of the Jews; he proposed that voting be limited to taxpayers, and that the wealthy be given more votes. But the prize for entitled hubris should go to Robert Benmosche, CEO of American International Group, the insurance giant that was a major perpetrator of the economic meltdown of 2007–8, and recipient of about $180 billion of taxpayer bailout money. Post-bailout AIG then awarded $170 million to some 170 employees, including those in the division mostly responsible for the financial wreck. When a predictable backlash to the bonuses followed, Benmosche compared popular outrage to racist lynch mobs in the Deep South.[18]

Recent studies have shown that narcissism and a sense of entitlement rise with wealth, even among the millennial generation. Though it enjoys a reputation for social liberalism, a recent Reason-Rupe survey found that on economic issues "the famed liberalism of young Americans fades as soon as their bank accounts grow."[19]

The entitled attitude of the wealthy is intensified by their ability to increasingly buy privileges, similar to those that first- or business-class airline passengers have long enjoyed: to pay others to stand in line for them; to jump the line at Disney by paying extra; to reserve public parking spaces via an auction; to get last-minute reservations at popular restaurants for a hefty fee; to drive solo in fast lanes restricted to high-occupancy vehicles; as everything becomes for sale, in a market *economy* transforming into a market *society*, as philosopher Michael J. Sandel has pointed out, inequality deepens, and aristocratic entitlement rises.[20]

Well might the children of the wealthy feel entitled: they already outnumber middle-class and low-income cohorts at the most prestigious private and public colleges and universities. The 10 percent and One Percent are pouring resources into enrichment programs to ensure that "No Rich Child [Is] Left Behind." The results show up in wealthier children scoring better grades, higher standardized test scores, and greater rates of participation in extracurricular activities. An expensive prep school education confers social as well as educational advantages; in affluent neighborhoods groups of parents, organizing themselves as nonprofits, raise money to provide their public schools with extra programs and equipment. In short, the American educational system is functioning to increase privilege.

The concentration of wealth accelerates because of federal and many states' tax policies. Although the billionaires who complain of persecution will never admit it, the low tax rates on capital gains and dividends amount to a subsidy for them to enlarge their fortunes. Their preferential taxation has been an engine driving the rate of return on capital—as Piketty argued in *Capital in the Twenty-First Century*—that will continue to exceed the rate of economic growth. And when an investor dies, the capital gains are not taxed at all, further subsidizing wealth concentration in a family dynasty. The propaganda machines of the wealthy complain of government spending on "entitlements" for ordinary

Americans, some of which like Medicare they have actually paid for, while the cost of entitlements for the rich and businesses in the form of nontaxation and subsidies runs into the trillions.[21]

Most of the founders of the United States believed that great wealth and extremes of riches and poverty endangered a republic. Their view of the Old World strongly influenced their view of what kind of society they wanted for the United States: a relatively egalitarian society of opportunity that contrasted with the excess of luxury alongside poverty some had observed on diplomatic missions or visits to Europe. Although many owned slaves and framed a constitution that protected slavery, giving no thought to enfranchising women or people of color, they valued what they called the "general equality of condition" that prevailed among white males as a guarantor of the republic's survival. In contrast to aristocratic displays of luxury, they embraced "republican simplicity," though often as an ideal and not as a reality for themselves.

Thomas Jefferson in particular saw concentration of wealth as a barrier to opportunity and to widely dispersed land ownership necessary to realize his ideal yeoman republic. As the Revolutionary War began, Jefferson, as a member of Virginia's lower legislative chamber, the House of Delegates, immediately targeted two surviving pillars of wealth engrossment, entail and primogeniture. Jefferson wanted to stop the process by which wealth accumulated in "particular families, handed down from generation to generation under the English law of entails." Years later in his private "Autobiography" he explained that repealing entail "would prevent the accumulation and perpetuation of wealth, in select families [by allowing the property owner to require that only family members could inherit his land], and preserve the soil of the country from being daily more and more absorbed in mortmain. The abolition of primogeniture, and equal partition through inheritances, removed the feudal and unnatural distinctions which made one member of every family rich, and all the rest poor." These laws, he earlier wrote to John Adams, "laid the axe to the root of Pseudo-aristocracy."[22]

Jefferson was hardly alone among the generation of nation builders who detested and feared the rise of aristocracy similar to those that lorded over impoverished masses in Europe. During the great national debate over the ratification of the Constitution (1787–89), the opponents of the Constitution, known as Anti-Federalists, believed it conferred dangerous power on a central government and expressed fears repeatedly that it could give rise to an aristocracy. Although Article I of the Constitution contained a clause forbidding the granting of any "title of Nobility," that did not satisfy the critics. Many framers of the Constitution agreed with Jefferson's famous distinction between a "natural aristocracy of virtue and talents," and an "artificial aristocracy, founded on wealth and birth, without either virtue or talents." He considered the natural aristocracy "the most precious gift of nature, for the instruction, the trusts, and government of society."[23]

But some radical critics of the Constitution feared even the power of a natural aristocracy. They believed that men of talent who rose to dominate society would acquire too much power; they preferred that government be controlled by those they styled as "the middling sort." During the great nationwide debate that took place over adoption of the Constitution, both the critics (Anti-Federalists) and proponents (Federalists) feared the rise of an artificial aristocracy of wealth.[24]

John Adams, conventionally regarded as one of the more conservative of the Revolutionary generation, viewed a "natural aristocracy" in a far less positive light than Jefferson. He thought that historically *it* had been the "origin of all artificial Aristocracy, which is the origin of all Monarchy . . . and civil, military, political and hierarchical Despotism, have all grown out of the natural Aristocracy of 'Virtue and Talents.' We, to be sure, are far remote from this. Many hundred years must roll away before We shall be corrupted."[25]

Two hundred years later many critics of meritocracy believe that Baltzell's ideal has devolved into a closing oligarchy, according to the logic inherent in Adams's analysis. Journalist Christopher Hayes, for example, argued in his recent book *Twilight of the Elites* that the presumed meritocracy having replaced the WASP establishment has become an oligarchy that limits opportunity and has accelerated extreme economic inequality. Hayes drew upon changes at the elite Hunter College High School in Manhattan (which he attended) as a prime illustration. Passing one exam and nothing else gets eleven-year-olds accepted at one of the best schools in the nation, tuition free, and a ticket to success for most of its graduates. But its meritocratic ideal, with no legacies, no letters of reference, no subjective assessments, just one test, has been corrupted by developments in the surrounding society beset by inequality. Hunter now draws most of its students from affluent neighborhoods, and admission of blacks and Latinos has dwindled. A test prep industry has arisen in which wealthier parents invest heavily, along with expensive tutoring. Hayes acidly observed that Hunter now "is a near perfect parable for how meritocracies tend to devolve. . . . Its hard-line dependence on a single test is not strong enough to defend against the larger social mechanisms of inequality that churn outside its walls." Hayes observed the Hunter model being replicated at elite universities, as social mobility throughout society declines, with Americans' continuing faith in meritocracy preventing them from recognizing reality.[26]

To be clear, our contemporary permanent political class is not itself an aristocracy; rather it responds to the power of an oligarchy of financial supporters that is becoming an aristocracy of wealth. Most of the political class is satisfied to bask in billionaire approval and to mingle with the One Percent, and occasionally the thrill of schmoozing with the .01 percent.

Chapter 1

Meet the Political Class

Although the *political class* embraces networks, families, and individuals working and living across the country, its hub is Washington, D.C. The nation's capital, workplace of ostensible servants of the American people, is awash, if not inundated, by the political class. Its populace is, as Mark Leibovich described it in *This Town*, "trained to view human interaction through the prism of 'How can this person be helpful to me?'[1] At the head of the class are members of Congress, current, former, and would-be.

How to Know Them

Congress provided a typical example of political class behavior during early 2013 when the draconian federal funding cuts known as the "sequester" kicked in. The sequester was supposed to be an incentive for President Barack Obama and House Republicans to agree on budget issues or have spending reductions automatically begin. In a standoff House Republicans refused to stop the cuts, which soon began to damage the economy and delay recovery. The meat-axe cuts to the federal budget hurt millions of low-income people with reduced money for education, housing, health, and nutrition.

But when Federal Aviation Administration shortfalls forced the agency to furlough air traffic controllers, and for two weeks air traffic backed up with long delays, Congress acted, *just before members themselves would depart for their home districts*, and found money to bring the controllers back to the towers to avoid delays *for them*. By unanimous consent the legislators switched funds from airport improvements to provide funds for the controllers to return full-time to their jobs.[2]

On those trips home members of Congress enjoy an experience unlike the vast majority of ordinary air travelers. Parking? No problem: at Washington's Reagan National Airport they can zip into their own reserved spaces, adjacent to the terminal and free. (The Metropolitan Washington Airport Authority absorbs the loss of $738,760 in revenue it would take in if the people's servants paid their own way.) The airlines allow lawmakers the privilege—unheard of to the rest of us mere mortals—to book themselves on multiple flights, so if they miss an earlier flight they can take a later one.

On the drive to the airport members can ride in style since their passage of the "Cromnibus" budget in December 2014. That legislation already smelled with a rollback of part of Dodd-Frank regulating Wall Street and a campaign finance gift to rich donors letting them increase giving to political parties by ten times the current limit. It also contained a secret provision with a new congressional perk. Hidden on page 982 of the 1,603-page bill members gave themselves $1,000 a month for a luxury car allowance.[3] With reserved airport parking, those who upgraded need not be concerned about their Lexus getting scratched.

Many members who go home frequently (some do not, see below) fly first-class, at taxpayer expense. In typical political class behavior, campaign arms of both Democrats and Republicans have hypocritically played politics with the issue and attacked individual legislators for voting against a ban on first-class travel. Not only is the vote cited misrepresented and not really against such a ban; Congress has not seriously considered depriving itself of any conveniences it has given itself. One exception: the 2016 federal budget banned the perk of members having their portraits painted at taxpayer expense, with the average cost about $25,000.[4]

Representatives also enjoy exercise in their free, on-site gyms with a swimming pool, basketball and paddleball courts, and sauna and steam rooms. During the 2013 government shutdown that lasted sixteen days, the Senate and House deemed their gyms and pools "essential" and kept them open.[5] Senators and House members (and guests) also have access to dining facilities in the Capitol with excellent menu choices at much lower cost than most Washington restaurants. (Many of their servers, however, who bus tables, deliver carryouts, and run cash registers earn less than eleven dollars an hour; cooks who have worked for several years make not much more.)[6]

Although Congress may often disappoint the American people, it excels at taking care of itself. Later in 2013, as millions of Americans encountered hours of delays and frustration in trying to enroll for health insurance under the Affordable Care Act, legislators and their staffs enjoyed smooth sailing. The District of Columbia set up "a special web portal with an expanded menu of health plans, a dedicated toll-free assistance line, and on-site support." DC Health Link provided "special first-class services to help them [members and their staffs] every step of the way."

In 2009 President Obama said that everyone should be able to buy insurance "the same way that federal employees do, same way that members of Congress do." But legislators and their staffs could use a special phone number, compare insurance plans on websites devoted to them, and select from 112 choices offered in the "gold tier" of the DC exchange. Though lawmakers and aides are not eligible for tax credit subsidies, the government pays up to 75 percent of their premiums. By early 2014 more than twelve thousand congressional aides had enrolled in health plans through the exchange. While the ACA required members and aides, like all Americans who enrolled in a new plan, to give up their former insurance coverage, one long-standing perk for Congress was not changed by the new law: they may receive care from a congressional physician, located in the Capitol, for an annual nominal fee.[7]

In addition to their entrenched opposition to the Affordable Care Act, Republican members of Congress have resisted proposals to require employers to provide paid parental leave. In early January 2015 President Obama by executive action granted employees of federal agencies up to six weeks of paid parental leave and urged Congress to extend paid leave to private sector employees. With both houses controlled by Republicans, that was not likely to happen. The existing Family and Medical Leave Act provides up to twelve weeks of *unpaid* leave while protecting the individual's job and existing health benefits.

New York Times reporter Jennifer Senior decided to write to all 100 U.S. Senators asking them how they handled parental leave for their staff. Just 26 replied (15 Democrats, 2 Independents, and 9 Republicans), and virtually all provided paid leave of some kind. It was no surprise that Independent Bernie Sanders from the "Socialist Republic of Vermont" provided generous paid leave, but so too did conservative Republicans Marco Rubio of Florida and Mike Enzi of Wyoming. Mississippi Republican Thad Cochran offers eight paid weeks of leave for both mothers and fathers. Lamar Alexander of Tennessee, chair of the Health, Education, Labor and Pensions Committee, gives twelve paid weeks of maternity leave. These Republican senators may be "philosophically" opposed to requesting private sector employers to treat their employees similarly, but in harmony with political class behavior, "when confronted with the life challenges of their own personnel, these elected officials all believe paid compensation is in order."[8]

Upon retirement from Congress, members who have served at least twenty years receive an average of $59,000 annually in pension benefits. All federal workers including representatives have access to the Thrift Savings Plan, a 401(k) type investment with fees of 0.03 percent, far lower than the fees paid to the average 401(k).

In Washington and environs, life is good for legislators and their staffs. In the Capitol they are likely to breakfast and schmooze with their peers, or wealthy contributors, influential and powerful business executives, celebrities, professional athletes, TV personalities, and Hollywood stars. They dine in the best restaurants and drink in posh cocktail lounges, the bills paid for usually by their personal Political Action Committees (more on this below). They socialize frequently with lobbyists, many of whom are raking in millions in a very short time without much heavy lifting. In 2012 members of Congress enjoyed 239 days off.[9]

Occasionally, Washington becomes a legislator's home, and such members actually lack a residence in their home states. Many live in the Capitol area and reduce their visits "back home" to several a year. What could be more emblematic of political class behavior than a member of Congress not owning a home and not living in the state he or she represents? Sometimes this creates a political backlash and threatens what legislators most cherish: reelection.

In 2014 Senator Pat Roberts's (R-KS) residence became an issue; he arrived in Washington in 1969 and in time made it his home. The seventy-eight-year-old Roberts was virtually born into his state's political class: his great-grandfather had founded Kansas's second oldest newspaper, and his father had served briefly as Republican National Chairman during the Eisenhower years. After service in the Marine Corps and five years as a reporter, he first went to Washington as a congressional staffer. He won election to the House in 1980 and then the Senate in 1996.

Always elected by large majorities, Roberts was expected to easily win re-election in 2014 when it was revealed that he did not live in his own home in Dodge City. Rather, the rent-free house next to a golf course and listed as his voting address belonged to a friend and longtime wealthy donor, C. Duane Ross. Roberts started paying a nominal rent of $300 a month after a Tea Party primary challenger hammered away at Roberts's housing arrangements. In reality, the Roberts owned a home and were longtime residents of Alexandria, Virginia, a suburb of Washington, where his wife Franki worked as a real estate broker, boasting of her "extensive knowledge" of the area. In one interview, Roberts inadvertently said it all: "Every time I get an opponent I go home—I mean every time I get a chance—I'm home."[10] A gaffe, as journalist Michael Kinsey quipped, is when a politician slips and tells the truth.

In the general election Roberts faced stiff opposition from Greg Orman, an independent candidate and wealthy businessman. Orman initially enjoyed a large lead after the Democratic candidate withdrew, but the Republican National Committee and outside PACs rode to Roberts's rescue, outspending Orman by about two to one and raising his unfavorable rating with a barrage of negative advertising. On November 4, 2014, Kansas voters returned the thirty-four-year occupant of Congress to office with 52 percent of the vote, well below his usual winning margin. Where they really "live" aside, other members of Congress also spend little time in their home states and make few trips in the span of a year. Geography and age play a role, of course, but so does the seductive allure of the capital and the perks members of Congress enjoy there.

In an October debate Roberts and Orman disagreed about most issues. At its conclusion the moderator asked both candidates to say something nice about their opponent. Orman praised Roberts for his service in the marines and his sense of humor. The senator's version of something nice differed: "I would say you are a very well-dressed opponent. I admire your accumulation of wealth. I have a little question of how you got there from here, but I think that's the American dream I would hope we could make that possible for everybody up and down every small Kansas community."[11] The irony of Roberts using Orman's wealth against him heightens when viewed in light of the ever-increasing wealth of representatives and senators or their affluent lifestyle experienced by few of their constituents.

Profiles of PC Exemplars

Although many public figures could be selected to typify the political class, I selected a moderate liberal Democrat who has promoted such worthy and progressive causes as a single-payer health care system: Tom Daschle, who served both as U.S. Senate minority and majority leader, and who saw his party's "political challenge" during the Bush administration "to truly help the people who we felt were being left out, and left behind."[12] Daschle, like so many former members of Congress, after being defeated for reelection to the Senate in 2004, went on to make big money as a lobbyist, except that he did not register as a "lobbyist" until 2015. Rather, Daschle and his employers seeking government largesse classified him as a "consultant," or "strategic advisor." As such he quickly made millions of dollars and bought a large mansion in a posh Washington neighborhood.

Why select a liberal Democrat for this honor? Many other Democrats or Republicans who moved from political office to lobbying or other lucrative pursuits in Washington or Wall Street could have been chosen. Liberal Democrats, however, are more appealing because some are such shameless hypocrites. Anointing Daschle for this distinction was not easy, since he faced strong competition from other liberal Democratic former U.S. Senators, notably Richard Gephardt and Evan Bayh. Glenn Greenwald would not be surprised by the choice of Daschle; he observed in 2009, "Even for the most cynical observer of Washington sleaze, Tom and Linda Daschle's exploits are quite striking."[13]

Daschle's career and connections also bring into view other exemplars and glittering facets of the political class. Daschle first entered politics in 1972 to work in the presidential campaign of George McGovern—the World War II bomber pilot, reform senator, and public servant wholly unlike the politicians depicted here. Daschle, the eldest of four brothers in a South Dakota family of Roman Catholics, went to college and then served in the air force, after which he, in an apprenticeship like that of so many members of Congress, landed a job as an aide to a senator, South Dakota's James Abourezk, the first Greek Orthodox Christian of Arab descent to serve in the Senate.

Elected to the House in 1978, Daschle served four terms, then three in the Senate. No important legislation bears Daschle's name, but he relished process and excelled as a party insider. In both chambers the pragmatic Daschle rose quickly to leadership positions; indeed, when he became the Senate's minority leader in 1994, only that noted "political animal" Lyndon B. Johnson had served fewer years before becoming a party leader. In 2001 Daschle became Senate majority leader, but after the Democrats lost the Senate in 2002 he was again minority leader. With an eye to taking his seat, Republicans continually accused him of obstructing the agenda of the Bush administration. Targeted by Republican PACs, he lost reelection in South Dakota by a narrow margin and then entered the private sector working for corporations and law firms to which he brought highly valuable knowledge about how to influence congressional policy.[14]

Though not a lawyer, Daschle moved smoothly into positions outside of government with powerful firms as a "senior policy advisor," while denying that he was a lobbyist and not registering as one. In 2005 he went to work for a private equity firm, InterMedia, headed by Leo Hinderey, a friend and political supporter. As a "policy advisor" also to a large Washington law firm engaged in lobbying, Daschle increased his personal fortune while advising sectors of the health industry, including insurers. He also consulted for the global law firm DLA Piper, which employs over 4,200 lawyers in some thirty countries around the world.

After Daschle's first marriage ended in divorce, in 1984 he married Linda Hall, Miss Kansas of 1976, who had worked in marketing for airlines before marrying Daschle. She then held positions in aviation associations and, after a stint as President Clinton's deputy director of the Federal Aviation Administration, joined a prestigious law firm as a full-time lobbyist.

Characteristic of Washington's revolving door, Linda Hall Daschle's clients came mostly from the airline industry, notably American Airlines, on whose behalf she stoutly opposed stricter safety regulations. After 9/11, when Tom rose to Senate majority leader and considered a run for president, Linda's connection to American loomed as a political liability. The airline had six fatal crashes since 1994, and it was American's planes that terrorists flew into the World Trade Center. Some critics uncharitably suggested that Hall Daschle had lobbied to resist stricter security regulations that might have deterred the 9/11 plot.

Still, one day after the attacks, airline lobbyists, including Hall Daschle, sprang into action to persuade Congress to grant them a massive bailout since the federal government had grounded air traffic for three days, and airline travel was about to plummet. In two weeks Congress forked over a $15 billion bailout with American Airlines getting $583 million in cash grants and absolution of legal liability for the hijackings. Congress and the corporate-friendly Bush administration overlooked the fact that the airlines were already in an economic downturn, laying off thousands of employees before 9/11 and continuing to do so afterward, with none of the $15 billion going to those laid-off workers.[15]

Meanwhile, after 2005, as a "senior policy advisor" Tom Daschle provided "analysis" (his word) to clients seeking federal contracts from businesses involved in health care, ethanol production, Native American gambling casinos, and telecommunications. Daschle succeeded so well in this realm that a *New York Times* reporter concluded that his activities offered "a new window into how Washington works . . . [and] shows how in just four years an influential former senator was able to make $5 million and live a lavish lifestyle by dint of his name, connections and knowledge of the town's inner workings."

Several hundred thousand dollars of Daschle's income came from speeches before interest groups to whom he was also giving advice, including health insurers, medical equipment distributors, and pharmacy boards. One Daschle client, United Health, a huge insurance company, earned about a third of its $81 billion in revenue from federally regulated sales of Medicare Advantage and Medicare supplement and prescription drug plans. Since the company often had been at odds with the Department of Health and Human Services, Daschle served as a valuable intermediary.[16]

During those years and after, Linda Hall Daschle added to the couple's millions by lobbying for the defense, aerospace, and airline industries. In 2014 the *Hill* listed her as one of D.C.'s top-earning lobbyists.[17]

Tom Daschle early on climbed aboard the presidential campaign of Senator Barack Obama, who was making health care reform his signature issue. President Obama took office intent on reforming health care and providing insurance for the millions of uninsured. Because of Daschle's extensive experience advising sectors of the health industry and his knowledge of Congress, the new president offered him the position of secretary of Health and Human Services. Daschle's former chief of staff Pete Rouse became Obama's chief of staff and then senior advisor. But now Daschle's "lavish lifestyle" reared up to bite him.

Leo Hindery, Daschle's multimillionaire friend and patron, had given the former senator the use of his personal chauffeur on his entry into private life. Over three years this car service amounted to over $255,000 of income, on which Daschle had not paid taxes. On January 2, 2009, he submitted a revised accounting to the IRS and paid some $140,000 in back taxes. But the Senate committees charged with vetting the finances of cabinet appointees found this belated response unsatisfying. By early February Daschle, saying he regretted his "mistake" about taxes, withdrew from consideration as a cabinet member. (Timothy Geithner, who was president of the Federal Reserve Bank of New York when the economy collapsed in 2008–9, and whom Obama appointed Treasury secretary, survived his "mistake" of not paying all his taxes and took office. Comedian Stephen Colbert commented that Daschle stepped aside because apparently "the position of not paying your taxes is already filled.")

In a 2010 book about health care reform Daschle portrayed the episode as resulting from Hindery's desire to help his driver have a full-time salary as well as "spend more time with family" (an indispensable phrase for the political class). Thus, Hindery's was "an act of compassion," with the added bonus of making Daschle's reentry into private work easier by not having to hunt for parking spaces ("a completely casual arrangement between friends").[18] [NB: In Washington the fact that some must hunt for parking spaces and some do not tells a great deal about rank and status in the political class.]

Daschle also admitted that he and Linda had mistakenly made payments to directors of two charities in South Dakota rather than the charities themselves and could not count the payments as deductions.

Soon it appeared that tax "mistakes" may have been the tip of an iceberg. The *Wall Street Journal* reported just before Daschle withdrew that the Senate Finance Committee was looking into his involvement with a nonprofit student loan agency, EduCap Inc. The company had footed the bill for Daschle to make at least two trips on its jet, one to the Bahamas and one to the Middle East. (Pause button: a student loan company owns a private jet?) Catherine B. Reynolds, EduCap's CEO, is an "old friend" of Daschle. Moreover, EduCap itself—a purportedly nonprofit private business, was attracting government scrutiny for more than providing expensive trips around the globe to prominent politicians. Government watchdogs also asked why the company was giving tens of millions to "charities" that had nothing to do with student loans.[19]

EduCap came to the attention of the Beltway—if not many Americans—during 2007 when the *Washington Post* ran a series describing the nonprofit as a "financial boon" for Reynolds and her family. Two decades earlier, EduCap had begun as a small student loan company—University Support Services—founded by a Catholic priest to help college and prep school students who did not qualify for government-subsidized aid. In 1988 Reynolds joined the new company as comptroller, soon became president, and developed a model of providing private nonguaranteed loans to students that was quickly adopted by other companies as well as Sallie Mae. By the 1990s the company was generating huge amounts of money and was renamed EduCap. In 2000 Wells Fargo bought a for-profit administrative services company spun off from EduCap for $150 milllion.[20]

By 2007 the company had made 350,000 private student loans that came at higher interest rates than federally backed loans, since they were not guaranteed by the government if the borrower did not repay. Indeed, some students borrowing up to $50,000 a year sometimes paid as high as 18 percent effective interest rates. EduCap's business practices, according to the *Post*, "illustrate how the booming and some say largely unregulated private loan industry is creating tremendous wealth for some lenders." It also showed, as an investigation into the industry that year revealed, that lenders were engaging in extensive conflict-of-interest deals with university financial aid officers.[21]

The corporate jet that carried Daschle cost around $30 million and ferried other prominent persons around the world as well as friends and relatives of Reynolds. (Chicago's Mayor Richard Daley took no less than fifty-eight trips on the jet, which cost thousands of dollars an hour to operate.) This alone attracted the attention of the IRS. The company also paid for luxury trips for friends and family, including one to the Bahamas in 2006 where EduCap paid for accommodations at the Four Seasons Resort and a thirty-seven-person lobster bake.

From an inauspicious start Reynolds established herself as a fixture in Washington through political connections and charitable giving. The Catherine B. Reynolds Foundation has donated more than $100 million to cultural institutions across the country, usually entities with ties to the Reynolds family, including a private school after it accepted her daughter in 2001. The Reynolds Foundation also donated at least $9 million to the Academy of Achievement, a nonprofit run by her husband Wayne Reynolds that sometimes funnels money to a for-profit company he runs. The academy's main purpose is to host summits for young persons and famous successful persons. Critics called the summits an excuse for a party, to which Reynolds countered that "we change people's lives." Although Reynolds's charity appears to give away her personal wealth, the foundation does not exist as a separate legal entity from EduCap. So when the Catherine B. Reynolds Foundation donates money, it is from the tax-exempt lending company.[22]

Student associations and other groups have complained of EduCap's deceptive lending practices. Reynolds, however, steadfastly maintained that she was "doing good." She stuck by that mantra after the *Post* report prompted the Senate Finance Committee to demand documents from EduCap explaining how it functioned as a not-for-profit with tax-exempt status. Soon the company sold its private jet.[23]

Meanwhile Reynolds's "old friend" Daschle came under fire for claiming that he was an "advisor" who was not a lobbyist, even though he worked for one of the most lucrative lobbying law firms in Washington. In 2010 "the Daschle exemption," now being claimed by many lobbyists reclassifying themselves as "advisors," drew the ire of the American League of Lobbyists. The latter formed a strange bedfellows' alliance with the liberal Sunlight Foundation to stem the tide of lobbyists who were resigning—or not registering any longer—as lobbyists. The Sunlight Foundation is a progressive watchdog group created in 2006 to bring greater transparency and accountability to members of Congress and to former officeholders like Daschle now employed essentially as "shadow lobbyists." Daschle kept insisting that "I am not a lobbyist." Meanwhile, some 3,600 lobbyists were de-registering in 2008 alone, many to follow the Daschle example of "not being a lobbyist." They continued to provide analysis and advice worth millions of dollars to interests seeking to shape congressional legislation.[24]

A Note on the Private Student Loan Industry

The private student loan industry has enriched loan industry and loan servicing CEOs, Wall Street firms and investors, for-profit colleges, and even the federal government, and it has poured money into the campaign chests of friendly members of Congress. The $140 billion "student loan industrial complex" with 41 million debtors has exploited current and former students with predatory collection practices and misinformation, made their debts deeper, and lengthened the course of repayment.

In 2012 the Consumer Financial Protection Bureau (CFPB) issued a comprehensive report showing how the private student loan industry, during its boom period from 2001 to 2008, resembled the subprime mortgage market in practices that helped cause the economic meltdown of 2008. The CFPB reported that lenders pushed many students into risky loans they could not afford just as banks, with relaxed mortgage requirements, enticed home seekers into buying houses beyond their means.

In 2009 the Obama administration eliminated private middleman lenders but left intact the loan-servicing industry that turned loan collection into a highly profitable enterprise. In 2015 the CFPB surveyed over thirty thousand borrowers and uncovered widespread, persistent abuses, with the companies not informing debtors of methods they could use to lower payments. The Department of Education, after reviewing twenty-two private collection agencies, decided to end contracts with five, one of which is a Navient subsidiary. In 2016 a coalition of twenty-nine state attorneys general reported that Navient (Sallie Mae up to 2013) rushed borrowers off the phone rather than explaining their options, or steered them into plans that would eventually increase their fees and debt. The Department of Education had previously overlooked these abuses and renewed contracts with Navient. (In 1997 Albert Lord took control of Sallie Mae and made it into a moneymaking machine through fees, interest, and commissions on federally backed student loans. He retired in 2013 as a Washington power broker worth hundreds of millions with wealth enough to start a private equity company and build his own golf course near Chesapeake Bay, often joined there by his friend former House Speaker John Boehner [R-OH].)[25]

Richard Gephardt and Tom Daschle: Wealthy Celebrities

The line between celebrities and politicians, like so many others in American society, has blurred, notably with former members of Congress who have become lobbyists. Hence, Daschle and Gephardt both have been listed on the "Celebrity Net Worth" website, which proudly says of Daschle: "Love them or hate them, Tom Daschle has massed [sic] a larger net worth than most regular people. Because of that you have to give Tom Daschle credit. While they say money is not everything and can't buy you bliss, it sure doesn't hurt to have plenty of it like Tom Daschle."[26] (This is the standard line for all the website's loved or hated "wealthy celebrities.")

These political class members stand out because they have so thoroughly turned their backs on policies they advocated, as well as positioning themselves as progressive populists while preparing the ground for possible presidential campaigns. In Gephardt's case the turnaround is spectacular.

Gephardt served as a Democratic congressman from Missouri from 1977 to 2005, including as House majority leader (1989–95) and minority leader (1995–2003). Gephardt, a former Eagle Scout and son of a milkman, ran unsuccessfully for president in 1988 and 2004 touting his championing of labor unions and working-class folks—his father had been a member of the Teamsters Union. Backed by organized labor and donning a Teamsters' windbreaker to look like a regular guy with street creds, he gave rousing speeches to workers. But when Gephardt left Congress, he joined the lobbying law firm of DLA Piper as a "senior counsel." When he began his own lobbying firm in 2007, he set up an "Atlanta-based labor consultancy" that lobbies for wealthy corporate and Wall Street clients, including Goldman Sachs, Boeing, and Visa.[27]

The former teamster's son, who donned the union jacket to campaign, heads a consulting firm that on behalf of Boeing and Spirit Aerodynamics has mounted aggressive anti-union campaigns. As a presidential hopeful he advocated for universal health care, but in 2009 he worked with Big Pharma to extend patents to prevent the release of less expensive generic medicines (and his allies in opposing extensive health care reform included Tom Daschle). Gephardt even went to Capitol Hill with two Goldman Sachs' executives to lobby against Dodd-Frank; he represented Visa in an effort to kill credit card reform and Peabody Energy to blunt climate change legislation.[28]

Gephardt's activities are fairly well known inside the Beltway, though perhaps less so with his former constituents. Armenian Americans, however, have come to regard Gephardt as an unscrupulous opportunist. By the 1970s this ethnic group had organized an influential lobby to improve U.S. relations with Armenia, block aid to Turkey, and gain recognition of the genocide committed against Armenians. As a U.S. senator Gephardt courted the Armenian lobby, and in the late 1990s he joined other Democrats in advocating a congressional resolution recognizing the 1915 Turkish genocide. But after retiring from the House in 2005 and becoming a lobbyist, by 2007 Gephardt cashed in on the Republic of Turkey's well-funded efforts in Washington to suppress any such resolution. (By then, too, the Bush administration regarded Turkey as a needed ally in the Iraq War.) Turkey initially paid $100,000 to DLA Piper for Gephardt's services, which included a pamphlet circulated in the House titled "An Appeal to Reason," denying that the genocide of 1915 ever happened. By 2014 the Gephardt group had hauled in hundreds of thousands of dollars from the Turkish contract, leading a prominent Armenian website to give Gephardt "the prize for the top hypocrite."[29] But of course his career simply exemplified business as usual for the political class. In 2010 he listed his annual billings at $6.59 million.

Eric Cantor, the former House Republican majority leader, provides a more recent case of what Mark Leibovich in *This Town* called "monetizing one's public service." Indeed, Cantor shines in this cohort for the lightning speed with which he moved to do so. After being upset in a June 2014 primary by an unknown Tea Party opponent, within two months Cantor resigned his seat in Congress, doing so, he said "with tremendous gratitude and a heavy heart." Well, not so heavy perhaps. Urging his supporters to keep fighting for the "many working middle-class families" and "society's most vulnerable," Cantor was assured of falling into neither of those categories.

A well-known friend of Wall Street throughout his career in Congress, Cantor scurried to take a lucrative job with the New York investment bank Moelis & Co., a position that would pay him at least $3.4 million through 2015, beginning with a cash payment of $400,000 plus $1 million in company stock. He and his wife had an estimated net worth—from his last financial disclosure filings—of from $6.2 million to $20 million. And as former U.S. labor secretary in the Clinton administration Robert Reich commented: "The well-worn path from Washington to Wall Street has rarely been as clear, nor the entrenched culture of mutual behind-kissing." In traveling that path Cantor followed dozens of former legislators who, after regulating banks, flock to them or to lobbying firms representing banks, a migration that accelerated in 2010 as Congress began to consider what became Dodd-Frank.[30]

Ivory Towers

The political class includes university presidents and other highly paid administrators at private and public academic institutions. In keeping with the choice of liberal politicians Tom Daschle and Richard Gephardt as exemplars of Washington's political class, the case of the groundbreaking, progressive, and successful president of Brown University from 2001 to 2012, Ruth J. Simmons, illustrates how individuals from the ivory tower are connected to the political class's networks and allows a revealing glimpse into their mentality.

Born in 1945 the twelfth child of a Texas sharecropper, Simmons rose to the top of the academic world. In 1973 she earned a doctorate at Harvard and in 1979 entered the lower rungs of administration, rising to higher positions at several institutions. Sixteen years later (1995) she became president of Smith College, the first African American woman to head a major college. At Smith, still a college for women, she inaugurated an engineering program. At Brown she continued to demonstrate skill as an innovator, as well as a fund-raiser, and very soon became hugely popular with faculty and students.

Aware that Brown's founding had originated in large part from the slave trade, Simmons launched a historical inquiry into the relationship. One outgrowth of that reckoning with the university's past prompted Brown to abolish Columbus Day, a holiday in Rhode Island, in favor of "Fall Weekend," the rationale for the change being Columbus's involvement with enslavement of people of color. The faculty voted for the measure, and 67 percent of students polled approved, but people of Italian American descent protested, including local politicians, Brown graduates, and academics across the country.

In 2009 the student newspaper reported that 80 percent of students approved of Simmons's leadership. But that was before Charles Ferguson's award-winning documentary *Inside Job* appeared describing Wall Street misconduct responsible for the 2008 economic meltdown and revealing (1) that Simmons had served on the board of Goldman Sachs after becoming president of Brown, collecting $323,539 in 2009 on top of her $576,000 Brown salary, and (2) that Simmons was one of ten people who approved Goldman Sachs bonuses the previous year in the middle of a crippling recession for millions of Americans. After these disclosures, Simmons announced that she would not stand for reelection to the Goldman board, though not without leaving with stock worth well over $4 million. Now the Brown community in Providence and abroad was divided about Simmons, with some alumni and students openly critical of what they saw as a conflict of interest.[31] Yet Simmons's position with Goldman Sachs, as *Inside Job* had made clear, was typical of many high-profile academics networked into the financial and political class, some of whom had defended, along with prominent university economists, deregulation of the financial industry.

Even with progressive liberals such as Simmons, the pervasive political class mentality can take over their vision and foreground self-interest, as demonstrated by Simmons's reaction to a question posed by Chrystia Freeland in a 2012 interview at the Davos World Economic Forum. Aware that elite colleges' populations had become increasingly populated by the children of the affluent, Simmons "spoke enthusiastically about helping poor children get into Brown, and supporting them financially after they get there." But when Freeland asked her about whether the legacy system, "which explicitly favors the children of alumni, should be abolished, the conversation turned personal. 'No, I have a granddaughter. It's not time yet,' she said with a laugh."[32]

The Smithsonian:
Have Credit Card, Will Travel

In 2000 Lawrence M. Small became secretary of the Smithsonian Institution and its nineteen museums and research facilities, along with the National Zoo, from a very different route than that traveled by Simmons to Brown. Small spent thirty-five years in banking and corporate management, including eight years at Fannie Mae, and naturally "brought a corporate mentality to an institution that long resembled a university campus."[33] Although Simmons was an excellent steward of Brown's interests, the same cannot be said of Small's care of the Smithsonian.

Controversy began as soon as Small took office. He offended Smithsonian researchers by proposing to rename facilities after wealthy donors and by a 2006 deal with Showtime for semi-exclusive access to the institution's archives for a documentary channel. In 2004 a federal court convicted him of purchasing the feathers of endangered birds for his private collection of Latin American artifacts, while animal sickness and deaths at the National Zoo led to the firing of his chosen zoo director. Meanwhile, Roger W. Sant, chairman of the Smithsonian's board of regents, supported Small because of his fund-raising prowess.

In early 2007, the Smithsonian's inspector general, A. Sprightley Ryan, sent a report to the Smithsonian's Board of Regents Audit and Review Committee criticizing Small's financial transactions that, in words that could qualify as a colossal understatement, "might be considered lavish or extravagant." Ryan, a lawyer with experience in the U.S. Department of Justice, joined the Smithsonian as counsel in 2003. She became inspector general when her predecessor, Debra S. Ritt, who had launched the audit, resigned, and told the *Washington Post* that Small had called her to exclude his compensation from any audit. Ryan, at the urging of Senator Charles E. Grassley (R-IA), ignored Small and sent a full report to the regents.[34]

Although the regents had doubled Small's salary in seven years from $330,000 to $617,672, with a total compensation in the offing of $915,698, that was not enough to satisfy Small's expensive tastes.[35] He began by redecorating his offices in "The Castle" on the Mall at a cost of nearly $160,000, including over $4,000 for two English-made chairs, $13,000 for a custom-built conference table, and $31,000 for Berkeley stripe upholstery. (The previous secretary, I. Michael Heyman (1994–2000), did not find it necessary to change the office "at all.") The renovations made up just part of $846,000 in total office expenses Small ran up between 2000 and 2005. Meanwhile, the physical plant of the institution declined, and Small ordered staff to implement austerity measures; in a 2006 email he urged employees to conserve energy. When Small submitted a $5,700 bill for repairs to his own home, failing roofs at Smithsonian museums and archives went neglected. Leaks forced occupants of the decrepit Arts and Industries building to move out. At the National Air and Space Museum water stained the canvas wing of a pioneering flight design that influenced the Wright Brothers.

Small owned his own home in Washington, and by agreeing to use it for Smithsonian functions, over six years he received $1.15 million in housing allowances. Those expenses included $12,000 for upkeep of his swimming pool and $4,000 to replace the lap pool's heater, along with staggering bills for utilities, housekeeping ($273,000), and maintenance. But Small in fact rarely made his home available for institution fund-raising, entertaining just forty-seven donors at eighteen events from 2000 to 2007, mostly during the early years. Initially Small needed to show receipts for these expenses, but after a few months his friendly board no longer required them. The regents even allowed Small to add $24,000 a month to his housing expenses on the basis of a "hypothetical mortgage." In contrast, Heyman had paid rent for a Washington house and received no housing allowance or reimbursement for several home entertainments.

In late February the *Post* published more details of Small's spending. The inspector general's report had found about $90,000 in unauthorized expenses, including charter jet travel, a "side" trip to Cambodia by his wife, luxury car service, catered staff meals, and expensive gifts, along with $28,000 in expenses that had insufficient or no documentation. Small also decorated his office with artifacts from the Smithsonian's collections. Sant, chairman of the board of regents, defended Small's use of these national treasures, saying it was "only appropriate for a museum director or secretary . . . to have some artifacts in his office. . . . That doesn't mean that there ought to be artifacts withheld from the public." To Senator Grassley, however, who had asked for the audit of Small's accounts, it looked "like the Smithsonian Castle has been turned into Mr. Small's palace." Expressing dismay over the authorized and unauthorized expenses, Grassley commented: "Mr. Small's champagne lifestyle turns out to be Dom Perignon."[36]

In late March, after the Senate voted to freeze a $17 million increase in the institution's proposed 2008 budget, and capped pay for Smithsonian executives at $400,000 (the current salary for the president), Small submitted his resignation alleging that he saw the institution becoming "more bureaucratic and political." Sant, speaking for the regents, regretted Small's departure, saying he had raised more money for the Smithsonian than anyone else in the history of the 161-year old institution.[37]

Unfortunately for Sant, a report by an independent commission that appeared in June contradicted this assertion as well as Sant's generous belief that "I don't think he [Small] does this job for the money." Congress now learned that Small's creation of "an imperialistic and insular culture" enabled him for seven years to take nearly ten weeks of vacation every year and be absent from his job 400 workdays while earning $5.7 million on non-institutional work. His deputy, Sheila P. Burke, the Smithsonian's second in charge, took off 550 days while earning $10 million over six years on outside work on more than a dozen nonprofit boards; her salary in 2006 was $400,000. Burke resigned after this information emerged.[38]

The report concluded that "Mr. Small placed too much emphasis on his compensation and expenses" and "aggressively guarded each and every element of what he viewed as his rightful compensation package." He rejected any suggestion that he modify his contract: "It would represent the highest form of naivete to think . . . I would entertain some form of 'give up.'" (In 2006 a Securities and Exchange Commission investigation into Fannie Mae's business practices found that Small was among senior managers who "manipulated the company's earnings in order to obtain bonuses they otherwise would not have received.") Sant's unrealistic image of Small as sacrificing for the institution can be understood in part as a result of Small's insistence to his executive secretary and the Smithsonian's general counsel that he tightly control the information given to the board and that they pass none of his comments about compensation "along to Roger." Most damaging to the regents' defense of Small was the report's finding that Small had not been as effective a fund-raiser as his predecessor and had become more dependent on federal funding. Indeed, the large donations that had come in during his tenure "originated from the work of others." "Mr. Small's management style—limiting his interaction to a small number of Smithsonian senior executives and discouraging those who disagreed with him—was a significant factor in creating the problems faced by the Smithsonian today."[39]

Those problems did not exist during the tenure of Small's predecessor, I. Michael Heyman (1994–2000), a successful fund-raiser and innovative administrator. Heyman, a law professor and former clerk to Chief Justice Earl Warren, served as chancellor of the University of California from 1980 to 1990. He worked as a lawyer in the Department of the Interior before becoming Smithsonian director in 1994. After weathering a controversy over an exhibit planned before he arrived—commemorating the fiftieth anniversary of the attack on Hiroshima and displaying restored sections of the *Enola Gay* bomber—Heyman raised money to build the National Museum of Indian History, secured a $60 million dollar donation for a National Air and Space Museum annex in Northern Virginia, and oversaw the establishment of a Latino Center. Far from appropriating artifacts for his office, he sent an "America's Smithsonian" exhibit across the country and created other programs to share the Smithsonian's treasures with an ever wider audience.[40]

The Small-Burke era of unmitigated larceny unpunished by law also illuminates the way political class boards charged with oversight allow so much leeway to fellow members of their cohort. It mirrors the way Wall Street and corporate boards reward top executives.

A very small (and very conservative) group of regents hired Small: Chief Justice William Rehnquist, former senator Howard Baker (R-TN), and former representative Barber B. Conable Jr. (R-NY). From then on the regents gave Small enormous trust and latitude to build his kingdom and continued to look the other way when controversy arose. In February 2008 they responded in typical political class mode to the release of the attorney general's report by finding Small's spending "reasonable."

This syndrome embraces liberals as well as conservatives. Roger Sant is a wealthy establishment progressive with a record of charitable work and giving to worthy causes. In his youth he served as a Mormon missionary among Native Americans. After he earned an MBA from Harvard (1960), a career in business and government led to his accumulating a fortune. Several positions in finance and a two-year stint at the Federal Energy Administration led to entrepreneurial activity in electrical energy that eventually made him a billionaire. In the 1990s he supported a wide range of worthy causes, including women's and girls' empowerment, ocean conservation, health, and numerous nonprofits; in 1994 he became chair of the Wildlife Fund. In 2008 Sant donated $15 million, in addition to an earlier $10 million, to the Smithsonian's Sant Ocean Hall, which opened that year; in 2014 he was serving as chair of the Smithsonian board's Governance and Nominations committee.[41] Membership in the political class and the One Percent, however, seems to create myopia in matters related to executive compensation in relation to performance.

Small's scandal, however, did not account for all of the bad publicity for the Smithsonian during the decade (2000–2010) when socioeconomic inequality experienced by ordinary Americans, rising since the late 1970s, increased at a rapid pace. The revelations regarding Small led to further inquiry into expenses incurred by directors in satellite museums supervised by Small, Burke, and Sant's board.

If there is a term that describes travel addiction, it can be applied to W. Richard West Jr., the first director of the National Museum of the American Indian. (Some travel experts say that travel addiction exists and results from depression after returning from a trip—so off again.) In less than four years (2003–7) West spent more than $250,000 in institution funds on first-class airfare, four- and five-star hotels, limousines, and entertainment, while globetrotting to every corner of the world. In the process of taking off 576 days from work, West visited Auckland and Wellington, New Zealand; Athens; Bali and Jakarta, Indonesia; Sydney and Brisbane, Australia; London; Singapore; Florence, Rome, and Venice; Paris (a dozen trips); Gothenberg, Sweden; Seville, Spain; Seoul; Vienna; and Zagreb, Croatia; and that is not a complete list of West's destinations. In 2007 West was away 180 days, and the cost of his trips *averaged* $3,520, five times that of other Smithsonian directors. As an irritated (again) Senator Grassley wrote in a letter to the regents, "Mr. West's itinerary for July-December 2007 alone would make the editors of most travel magazines green with envy."[42]

Grassley did not exaggerate, as a glance at just a couple of West's trips indicates. A February 2005 trip to Paris and a meeting of the International Council of Museums extended to Bali and Jakarta, then Singapore. A twenty-three-day trip the next year took him to Athens, Singapore, Australia, New Zealand, and Peru, for "speeches and presentations" (no further details given), at a cost of $18,000.

Ann Ruttle, a financial specialist at the Smithsonian from 2003 to 2006, unsurprisingly said that "Rick [West] was rarely at the museum. I believe Rick had the most travel of any museum director." West's travel vouchers from 2003 to 2006, obtained by the *Washington Post*, were somehow approved by an official who left the Smithsonian in late 2001. West was at the museum, however, for a variety of farewell celebrations he arranged, including staff lunches in Washington and New York, cocktail parties in Washington and Los Angeles, and a sumptuous dinner at the museum in September that cost $124,000. Roger Sant commented: "It is totally appropriate to thank somebody for public service."

West, a member of the Cheyenne and Arapaho tribes, also spent $48,500 of museum funds to commission a portrait of himself that he had hung in the patron's lounge of the Indian museum. When asked why the portrait painter was of Polish and not Indian descent, Smithsonian spokeswoman Linda St. Thomas replied that "they couldn't find a Native artist who did formal portrait sittings."

Until 2007 top Smithsonian officials enjoyed unlimited leave time with pay but were not supposed to get paid for extracurricular activities. West, however, proved himself as adept at pocketing extra outside money as Small and Burke. The Smithsonian gave him $6,000 for a month-long trip to Eugene, Oregon, and he took $27,765 from the University of Oregon as "visiting chair of law," plus $4,000 for travel. For at least seven other trips West was paid twice for his travel and $869 for a hotel bill that was never incurred. He also collected at least $68,500 in honoraria for twenty-four speeches, a practice the inspector general's report "questioned." For 2006–7 he provided receipts for 60 percent of his travel but no information regarding the purpose of the trips. Overall, the October 28 report to Congress said that West's spending was imprudent and often "lavish," but most of it conformed to institution rules. The inspector general did request that West repay the Smithsonian $9,700. Senator Grassley suggested that the board should consider asking West for more reimbursement.[43]

Additional insight into political class behavior emerges from the mild debate among interested observers regarding West's actions. Brian Henderson, a regent who left the board in early 2008, sharply criticized West's spending as "insensitivity at best and arrogance at worst." Henderson, a Merrill Lynch investment banker of Apache descent, pointed to the efforts to "scrimp and save" among low-income ordinary Indians to raise money for the museum. Other affluent members of the political class in and around Washington and

New York, however, defended West's expenses as necessary to "hob nob" with wealthy donors. Commentary on Native American websites, such as Indianz. com, which provides "American Indians and Native Americans news, information, and entertainment," was divided, with defenders seeming to labor under a politically correct unwillingness to criticize West harshly as a fellow Native American.[44] After 2007 West retired from the Indian Museum, but the controversy over West's travel and expenses amounted to a mild hiccup in his career. Appointed a vice president of the International Board of Museums, he stayed on to 2011 and was then made interim director of the Textile Museum. In 2012 he landed another prestigious job: president and CEO of the Autry National Center of the American West in Los Angeles.

Incredibly, Not the End of It

The next revelation regarding abuse of office at the Smithsonian came out of the other Heyman multicultural initiative, the Latino Center. In February 2008, as reports of West's spending broke in the press and riled Grassley, Pilar O'Leary resigned as its director. In April Washington learned why. Inspector General Ryan had again sent the regents a report detailing the director's "extravagant" expenses: in fact, O'Leary had violated multiple ethical and conflict-of-interest policies.

Appointed by Small in 2005, O'Leary had attended Georgetown University and Georgetown's law center and was reportedly fluent in Spanish, French, and Italian. Her impressive résumé included work at the United Nations, Goldman Sachs, JP Morgan, and Fannie Mae, as an assistant counsel to the CEO. She had shown meanwhile a strong interest in Spanish and Latino cultures. Her husband was then vice president of marketing and communications at Georgetown University, and he had worked also at a real estate auction firm and Citigroup. In 2006 O'Leary had appeared on the cover of *Washington Life* magazine as a winner of its "Style & Substance" award; a couple, it would seem, that had it all, including expensive tastes.

O'Leary's spending did not reach Small's and West's levels, but it came largely after the institution was supposed to be exercising more oversight and included items that suggested a level of insensitivity in spending taxpayer money at least as egregiously as Small and West. She had used her expense account for many personal items, including a visit to a hotel spa and gift shops. She rented limousines frequently, including one that took the Latino Center's board from the Smithsonian Castle to a museum that was a ten-minute walk across the Mall. She sent subordinates to her home to fetch items such as wine, medication, a suitcase, a dress, keys, and her BlackBerry. After a trip to Spain, for which the sponsors had paid $1,028, she submitted a reimbursement voucher to the Smithsonian for $1,242.

The inspector general concluded that O'Leary created "the perception that she is using her position for private gain," especially by soliciting gifts "from outside companies and contractors." From companies doing business with the Smithsonian she avidly sought free (and hard-to-get) tickets to concerts, fashion shows, and events such as the Latin Grammy awards. She awarded two contracts the institution deemed improper, one to a friend. Her hotel stays, with reservations routinely made at the last minute, ran up her travel expenses. On frequent trips to Miami, New York, and Los Angeles, she insisted, according to the report, on bookings "at the Conrad Hilton, Ritz Carlton, or Four Seasons, even if they did not offer a government rate." When an investigator asked her why she made reservations at the last minute, thus driving up the price, she replied that the center's Latino constituency "doesn't operate in the same time frames as everyone else is used to—in many Latin cultures, arrangements are made at the last minute." (Could this be called playing the Latino card?)

O'Leary's transgressions attracted far more outrage and ridicule than Small's or West's more extensive legal plunder, perhaps because she was a beautiful thirty-nine-year old woman well-known on Washington's social scene (or just because she was a woman?). She had grown up in an affluent, well-connected family: her father was a managing director of private equity at the World Bank until 1997 and her mother dean of international programs at Georgetown University.[45] She had risen rapidly in finance and government since getting her law degree in 1996. The associated scandals also likely had a cumulative impact worsening the reaction to hers. Yet one can only marvel at her being oblivious as to how the Small and West affairs might affect her as she used her Smithsonian credit card with abandon.

At bottom, however, she exemplifies the political class, particularly those who believe that doing good works entitles them to reward themselves well above their legitimate compensation. She saw herself, in short, as one of the deserving. In addition, she had worked in circles populated by very wealthy, class-conscious, and on-the-make people—the UN, Wall Street, Fannie Mae.

The storm in print and on the Internet ("Why do yuppies feel the need to abuse power?" protested one blogger) hardly phased her as she sailed smoothly on as the political class usually does.[46] In 2008, gone from the Smithsonian, she basked in limelight as cofounder of a nonprofit devoted to raising children bilingual in Spanish and English, before moving on to other prestigious nonprofits. In 2009 she and her husband bought a six-bedroom house for $1.235 million in a pricey, high-status neighborhood. In self-written biographies on subsequent websites she played down her Smithsonian experience.

Chapter 2

Our One Percent Government, Congress, and Its Adjuncts

The Way to Wealth

Get what you can, and what you get hold.

—Benjamin Franklin, *The Way to Wealth*
(1758)

In early 2014, according to a report from the Center for Responsive Politics, Congress reached a milestone: over half of its members—at least 268 of the 534—qualified as millionaires; the median net worth of Congress had risen to $1.5 million. Meanwhile, America's middle class, on whose behalf the millionaire politicians repeatedly claim to "fight," saw its income and wealth decline. During the first decade of the twenty-first century the middle-income tier of Americans actually shrank in size, the only one to do so, continuing a trend of the last four decades. The economic downturn of 2008 intensified the loss of wealth of middle- and lower-income Americans. But the members of Congress grew wealthier, most of them not battered by the recession.[1]

Indeed, during the Great Recession of 2008–10 the net worth of members of Congress increased by 25 percent. Some did much better: Republican Senate minority leader Mitch McConnell's wealth grew by 29 percent (after the death of his mother-in-law he received gifts from his very wealthy wife's father); Rep. Darrell Issa's worth grew by 37 percent to $220 million; and House Minority Leader Nancy Pelosi's wealth rose by 62 percent. At the same time the net worth of all Americans declined by 23 percent. A few members, an unknown number, became wealthier by insider trading making use of knowledge of pending legislation. One-fifth of both the House and Senate have benefited from "double-dipping." They are collecting pensions from previous government service, usually as state legislators; in the latter service, some took part in writing generous payouts. Although some states and cities prohibit double-dipping, those rules do not apply to members of Congress.[2]

What ordinary citizens fail to realize, however, is that although all members of Congress may not be millionaires, "serving" in Congress enables almost all of them to *live like* millionaires.

The affluence of many members of the political class causes them to lose connection with ordinary Americans. While running for office, however, candidates dwell on whatever parts of their biography suggest humble beginnings or hard times endured by parents or grandparents. Anyone who paid attention to the 2008 Democratic presidential primaries will recall how often Senator John Edwards, super rich from a law career winning personal-injury lawsuits against large companies, reminded voters that his father was a millworker (and his mother a postal employee). During the 2016 Republican presidential primaries, candidates Ben Carson, Ted Cruz, and Marco Rubio, among others, never missed an occasion to mention their parents' or their own humble beginnings (sometimes embellished).

The wealth that many politicians bring to the campaign trail has rendered them, in the words of that acute observer of Washington politics Mark Leibovich, "narrative-challenged." If parents who worked in mills or had immigrant origins are not available, grandparents will do to construct a story to connect with the "hurting" middle class. "In recent years," Leibovich comments, "American politics has been overrun by an adversity-theft epidemic."[3]

Part of the reason for the uptick in millionaires in Congress is also the high cost of political campaigns, giving an advantage to wealthy candidates. But service in Congress (or other public office) leads to more wealth. Access to information about the stock market and insider trading may be part of it, although studies by academic economists disagree as to whether members of Congress's stock portfolios outperform the market average. But there is no doubt that Representatives and Senators enjoy investment advantages not available to ordinary Americans.[4]

Because of that on April 4, 2012, President Obama signed the Stop Trading on Congressional Knowledge Act (STOCK), passed by Congress in response to negative publicity. But Congress then delayed compliance three times and commissioned a study to determine if there were security risks associated with the transparency required by STOCK. The report gave Congress a desired rationale to eliminate the law's critical requirement, gutting it, in April 2013. Appropriately, the Wall Street–savvy House majority leader Eric Cantor pushed the bill through an almost empty chamber with no debate and by "unanimous consent." Although insider trading is still illegal, members of Congress could easily get away with it.[5]

Yet the real payoffs for the people's servants, as illustrated by the celebrity profiles in the last chapter, typically come *after* they leave office. As Chrystia Freeland put it in her *Plutocrats*, "Politicians can't fully monetize their plutocratic networks until they retire."[6] Although the revolving door from Congress to Wall Street or K Street—the honeycomb of lobbyists' offices—does indeed lead to the most lucrative rewards, occupying a seat in Congress, employing staff, and raising campaign funds offers multiple opportunities to enrich oneself and family and friends. Think of it as "perk and pocket."

Profiles in Getting and Holding: "Perk and Pocket"

In 2012 the nonpartisan watchdog organization Citizens for Responsibility and Ethics in Washington (CREW) conducted the "first ever complete study of how members of the House of Representatives use their positions to benefit themselves and their families." CREW found that 248 members of Congress funneled money to family members, friends, and business associates through their congressional offices, campaign committees, and political action committees. For the 2008 and 2010 election cycles 82 members (40 Democrats and 42 Republicans) together paid $5,575,090 in salaries and fees directly to family members. The top five disbursers to "family" included some well-known politicians.

Rep. Alcee Hastings (D-FL), who President Carter in 1979 appointed as the first black federal judge in Florida, was convicted of bribery in 1988, but he survived the scandal and won election to Congress in 1992. By 2015 Hastings was paying his longtime girlfriend, Patricia Williams, the maximum a staffer can earn, $168,411 (perhaps she took him to dinner a few times?). She had served as his lawyer in his impeachment trial, for which he claimed he still owed her substantial legal fees. In 2011–12 Hastings fended off charges of sexual harassment from Winsome Packer (a name you could not make up in this context), who worked with Hastings as a representative to the Helsinki Commission during 2008 to 2010. She charged that he made sexual advances after appointing her to a $165,000-a-year position. Clearly she came up short in the gratitude department. Although a federal judge eventually dismissed Packer's lawsuit, ruling that she should hold the Helsinki Commission responsible, Hastings had acquired notoriety not only for his sexual escapades but also as one of the biggest congressional spenders on expensive trips abroad, usually with a female staff member who preceded Packer, Vanessa Griddine.[7] If Patricia Williams was jealous of these women, it paid to look the other way as her pay as a staffer from 2000 to 2015 totaled over $2.2 million.

Few politicians enriched their family, friends, and businesses in their districts more than Rep. Jerry Lewis (R-CA), who steadfastly milked the nation's treasury while brushing aside FBI investigations and media criticism. CREW calculated that he paid his wife as his chief of staff $512,293 during the cycle it investigated. That was trivial compared to the fabulous wealth that during his thirty-four years in Congress (1979–2013) Lewis directed to relatives, staff members, and notably the lobbying firm of Copeland Lowery. His munificence to his clients could hardly be done justice if it received an entire chapter here. Briefly, from 1985 to 1993 Lewis served with Rep. Bill Lowery on the House Appropriations Committee. The two became friends and figured out how to get aboard the cornucopia of the Washington gravy train. In 1993 Lowery left Congress to form a lobbying firm, and in 1999 Lewis became chair of the Defense Appropriations Subcommittee, which oversees more defense spending than any other congressional subcommittee. In 2005 they hit an even bigger jackpot when Lewis became chair of House Appropriations and steered hundreds of millions of dollars to Lowery's firm. The revolving door between the offices of Lewis and Lowery spun so fast that it operated "almost as a single machine to swap taxpayer dollars for corporate donations." Senior members of Lewis's staff who joined Copeland Lowery soon became multimillionaires. One of them did such a thriving business with her former boss that she became known as "K Street's Queen of Earmarks." Reelected sixteen times from a safe district, usually with 65 percent of the vote, in the years before retiring Lewis sent over a billion in earmarks to his district and inland Southern California.

Another Californian, Rep. Maxine Waters, a liberal, outspoken Democrat, paid her daughter and grandson a combined $495,650. In 2012 Waters was cleared of ethics charges involving her grandson, who serves as her chief of staff, because he had pressured the Treasury Department to give a bailout to a bank in which her husband held stock and served on its board of directors.[8]

Libertarian and Tea Party icon Rep. Ron Paul (R-TX) paid six different relatives a total of $304,599. Although Paul enjoyed a reputation for straight dealing and rectitude, CREW found him to be ethically challenged and listed him among eight members of Congress who received "dishonorable mention" as "most corrupt" for 2012 (eleven House members and one senator appeared on CREW's dishonorific "most corrupt" list). CREW based its choice on House documents and an investigation by the Capitol Hill newspaper *Roll Call* that found Paul had improperly received double reimbursements for travel expenses—reimbursed once by taxpayers and a second time by a libertarian group whose checkbook was managed for most of the incidents of double-dipping by his daughter's mother-in-law. In all, Paul was likely reimbursed twice for fifty-two trips over several years.

Although a strident foe of government spending, Paul directed some $1.5 to $2 billion in taxpayer-funded agricultural subsidies to his district before he retired in 2013. In 2010–11 he requested almost $500,000 in earmarks; he defended such departures from his opposition to "wasteful" spending by comparing them to tax credits and not wishing to leave his constituents out of the game of welfare for agribusiness.[9]

Even in this gallery of bold-faced self-dealers, Rep. Howard "Buck" McKeon stands out as a champion of "perk and pocket." A ten-term Republican from California whose district contains, along with scenic national parks, a number of military bases, McKeon did not make CREW's list of 2012's most corrupt dozen, but did get "dishonorable mention."

From 2002 on he paid his wife Patricia a total of $588,284 to serve as treasurer of his campaigns for reelection, but that is just one slice of how McKeon profited from his position in Congress. Like other legislators, notably former senator Chris Dodd (D-CT), McKeon received a "VIP" mortgage from Countrywide, the subprime lender involved in the 2008 housing bubble, saving him thousands of dollars. Earlier his wife worked as a lobbyist for CSX, a railroad company that benefited materially from her husband's influence. McKeon joined John Boehner in 2006 to grant for-profit colleges unlimited taxpayer assistance. These often predatory institutions spend more on marketing than education, are often charged with fraud, and are responsible for pushing many of their graduates and those students that do not finish into crushing debt. McKeon has invested in and profited from the industry.

Becoming chair of the House Armed Services Committee in 2011, McKeon never encountered a weapons system not worth funding, whether wanted by the Pentagon or not. Earlier he had emerged as a leader of the Unmanned Systems Caucus in Congress, a group set up by an association of military drone manufacturers clamoring for the use of drones within the United States for law enforcement and commercial use. As a warrior for Pentagon pork, McKeon became the top recipient in Congress of funds from Lockheed Martin, Northrop Grumman, General Dynamics, General Atomics, and Boeing.[10]

McKeon and Paul made CREW's "most corrupt" list of eighteen representatives for 2012, but Robert E. "Rob" Andrews (D-NJ) headed the list of "most corrupt" in both 2012 and 2013. Elected for twelve terms (1990–2012), when the fifty-seven-year-old Andrews announced his resignation in February 2014 he said it had nothing to do with the Democrats likely remaining the minority party in the House nor with an ongoing ethics investigation; rather, "I love Congress but I love my family more."

The House Ethics Committee had no doubt about Andrews's regard for his family. The ethics inquiry centered on Andrews using campaign money for personal expenses, often related to his family, and earmarks benefiting institutions that employed family members.

In June 2011 Andrews and his wife and two daughters flew to Scotland to attend a wedding for which he charged his campaign over $30,000, claiming that it was legitimate because the groom was a donor. He refused to identify the "donor." Subsequently it came out that the mystery man had been a consultant and had once given Andrews $250. After the New Jersey *Star-Ledger* ran a story detailing Andrews's Scotland expenses, he repaid his political action committee for the costly trip, including $7,725 for three nights at the five-star Balmoral Hotel in Edinburgh.

That same month "Andrews for Congress" spent $10,000 on a party at his home celebrating his twenty years in Congress and daughter Jacqueline's high school graduation. Meanwhile, for six years before and after that "elegant to carnival fun," Andrews and daughter Josie made many trips to Hollywood ostensibly for political purposes but coincidentally to promote Josie's show business career. His campaign committee spent at least $100,000 on Andrews and Josie's travel to California; Josie, he claimed, was doing campaign work.

In any case, theater companies where Josie performed received thousands of dollars from Daddy's political funds, including more than $100,000 to Philadelphia's Walnut Street Theater. When Josie worked at the Prince Music Theater, the Broadway Theater of Pitman, and the Grand Opera House of Delaware, those venues became lucky recipients of "Andrews for Congress" largess.[11]

Even more fortunate perhaps was Rutgers University School of Law, Camden, where Andrews's wife Camille served as associate dean of admissions; she was also an attorney in a private equity firm. From 2001 on Congressman Andrews directed more than $1.5 million in earmarks to the institution. (In 2012, a total of 38 congressional members—24 Democrats and 14 Republicans—sent earmarks to a family business, employer of a family member, or associated nonprofit.) Andrews's liberality toward the school—with taxpayer money—may help explain why in 2012 its administration defended Camille Andrews when she was accused by the watchdog group "Law School Transparency" of recruiting prospective students with "misleading to plainly false statements" about employment and earnings for Rutgers-Camden graduates; she had touted it as one of the "Best Law Schools for Getting Rich." LST labeled her claims "deceptive" and in violation of American Bar Association standards. One of her superiors termed the charges "unfounded."[12] (Probably no one questioned her expertise on "Getting Rich.")

During 2012 Camille Andrews added an electoral victory to her résumé. Rob decided to challenge incumbent U.S. senator Frank Lautenberg in the Democratic primary, hoping that the eighty-eight-year-old senator was vulnerable (Andrews had made an unsuccessful run for governor in the 1990s). Camille stepped in to run for his seat in the congressional primary and, brushing off allegations that she was merely a "placeholder," won. Of course when Lautenberg drubbed Andrews in the Senate primary, she stepped aside for Rob to run again for what would be his last term.[13] While now free to devote himself to family, Andrews, his wife, and their daughters surely had reason to retain their love for "Congress" and all it had done for them.

Rob Andrews, of Scottish and Scots-Irish descent, claimed among his ancestors American portrait painter Charles Wilson Peale and a Roosevelt. A long-tailed genealogy, however, is not necessary to make one's fortune in Congress, or simply to live the high life. In "The People's House" ethnic minorities enjoy equal opportunity, as evidenced by the cases of Gregory Meeks and Silvestre Reyes.

Gregory Meeks, a nine-term African American representative from New York, has survived redistricting in 2012, numerous scandals, and House ethics inquiries. After representing a mostly minority Sixth Congressional District up until 2012, he took redistricting in stride with 67 percent of the vote in the new Fifth District composed of a diverse constituency of mostly middle-class minority groups. Meeks's durability benefits from a huge campaign funding advantage supplied by the financial industry: in 2014 the Center for Public Integrity included Meeks in what the center labels Congress's "banking caucus" for its efforts to oppose regulation of banks and payday loan operations.[14]

Payday lenders are perhaps the most ubiquitous of predators on the working poor, entrapping them in a cycle of ever-increasing debt. Annual interest rates can rise to 300 to 400 percent. Typical borrowers, often young military personnel, make $25,000 to $35,000 a year, cannot repay the loans on time and still meet other expenses, and get caught in a debt trap for months or years. Meeks and other members heavily funded by the industry claim that payday lenders "replace loan sharks," but payday stores are the loan sharks. The business thrives on ties to large "respectable" banks and campaign cash to allies in Congress.[15]

The payday business regards Meeks as one of its champions. From 2009 to 2013 payday interests contributed at least $50,000 to his campaign funds. In 2013 the congressman signed on as cosponsor of a bill to limit oversight of the industry, and four months later he received a $5,000 contribution from a payday PAC. The next year when a bill introduced in Congress to protect consumers from "Unreasonable Credit Rates," endorsed by thirty-eight organizations including several consumer organizations and the NAACP, Meeks rose to oppose it. By 2015 payday lenders were illegal in New York State (they find ways around state laws by going offshore); Meeks introduced a "reform" bill to limit restrictions on the business.[16]

CREW included Meeks on its exclusive list of "most corrupt" in 2011, 2012, and 2013. The "improper gifts and loans" he has received included paying $830,000 for a McMansion deemed to be worth much more and built by one of his major campaign contributors, and a dizzying tangle of "loans" to Meeks from local businessmen. He has been investigated by federal officials for being part of a possible scam used often by other politicians and entrepreneurs: creating a phantom charity to help victims of Hurricane Katrina that raised tens of thousands and paid out a grand total of $1,392 to actual victims of the storm. Meeks claimed he was not responsible for running the "charity" and has no idea what became of the rest of the money.[17] (Well, he was not elected to be an accountant.)

Meeks's ties to R. Allen Stanford, a banker with interests in South America, have added to his portfolio of ethical challenges. A Stanford-backed nonprofit, the Inter-American Economic Council, paid for at least six of the congressman's trips to luxurious Caribbean resorts and hosted a fund-raiser for him on St. Croix. In 2009 Stanford was charged by the U.S. Securities and Exchange Commission with running a $7 billion Ponzi scheme. Convicted of fraud in March 2012, Stanford was sentenced to one hundred years in a Florida federal penitentiary.[18]

Meeks grew up in Harlem in public housing, went to college and law school, and then entered government work. Elected to the state assembly in 1992, he ran for Congress in 1998 and gained the support of prominent local African American leaders, including Al Sharpton (known for seeking publicity except when it comes to the matter of his unpaid taxes). Meeks has claimed that he is actually "poor," with only a few thousand dollars in a savings account. But the *New York Times* described him in 2010 as living "a life worthy of a jet-setter. When he travels he stays in luxury hotels like the Mondrian South Beach in Miami and the Ritz-Carlton in San Juan, Puerto Rico. He drives a Lexus, leased by the federal government, at a cost of $1,000 a month. He eats expensive meals at BLT Steak in Washington and Docks Oyster Bar in Manhattan, among other trendy spots." Although his known financial holdings may be slim, he raises huge amounts of campaign money—while facing only token opposition—and spends equally large amounts on expensive trips, meals, and personal services. One year his campaign committee shelled out $17,973 for tickets to the Super Bowl in New Orleans. In 2008 he did admit that sums of $6,200 for a personal trainer and $9,800 to lease and repair a Lexus SUV were not related to campaign work and paid fines totaling $63,000.[19]

Meeks's leased Lexus involves one of Congress's lesser known perks. House members (but not senators) enjoy the benefit—at taxpayer expense—of leasing whatever kind of car they choose, and the government picks up the tab for maintenance, insurance, registration, and excess mileage charges. In 2008 the *Times* reported that Meeks's Lexus cost $998 a month, the highest among the 125 members of the House who then used the perk. Meeks, when questioned about the car, said it was reliable but declined to talk more about it saying, "These are never lighthearted stories." But the next year Meeks lost the distinction of leasing the most expensive car when the *Wall Street Journal* reported that during 2008 Alcee Hastings had leased a 2008 Lexus luxury hybrid for $24,730.[20] Of course, since December 2014 Meeks or any other member of Congress has

access to $1,000 a month to pay for a personal luxury car, a detail tucked into—
way into—the notorious "Cromnibus" budget.

The *Journal's* account dealt generally with representatives using their office
expense accounts of $1.3 million a year for a wide range of items, from expensive
electronics to printing specialty calendars for constituents ($84,000 in the latter
case). But other representatives prefer to reimburse themselves from their campaign committee funds. During the 2008 and 2010 election cycles, Congressman
Silvestre Reyes (D-TX) reimbursed himself, handsomely, over $250,000 for travel,
office supplies, and campaign event food. During the same period, for fund-raising
services he reimbursed his niece, Veronica Cintron, $175,550 and $143,125 for travel,
office supplies, campaign gifts, and charitable donations.

Reyes represented Texas's Sixteenth Congressional District, almost 80 percent
Hispanic, from 1997 to 2013. Like Meeks a symbol of how well the "American
Dream" works, he was the oldest of ten children and, after serving in Vietnam,
worked for the Border Patrol for many years. In Congress Reyes continued his former connection to the U.S.-Mexican border by crusading for high-tech electronic
surveillance systems, awarded in no-bid contracts to companies that employed
his daughter Rebecca. By 2004 an audit by the General Services Administration
revealed that some $200 million had been given to contractors who had deliv-
ered "mismanagement," "shoddy work," or "work that was incomplete or never
delivered." Ironically, in November 2012 the House Ethics Committee said that
Reyes was under investigation for possibly violating ethics rules and federal law
in connection with using campaign money for expenses related to his daughter's
house in Washington from 2008 to 2012—a paltry $13,000. In the 2012 Democratic
primary an outside PAC targeting long-term incumbents spent heavily against
Reyes, and he lost to a younger, energetic newcomer who drew votes from independents and Republicans. It is not clear that Reyes's ethical issues had anything
to do with his defeat.[21]

The Burden of Fund-Raising,
or, Livin' Large Continued

In recent decades when members of the House or Senate voluntarily retire from
office without seeking reelection, they cite a number of reasons. Sometimes
they face a tough reelection campaign, but often they tend to invoke personal or
family considerations ("I want to spend more time with my family"); partisan

polarization and gridlock; and the amount of time they must devote to raising money to gain reelection.[22]

Just after the November 2012 election newly elected Democratic members of Congress learned from the Democratic Congressional Campaign Committee that fund-raising calls would take up a large part of their average day. The DCCC proposed this schedule: 1 hour for "Strategic Outreach, Breakfasts, Meet & Greet"; 2 hours Committee/Floor; 1–2 hours Constituent Visits; 4 hours Call Time to raise funds for their next campaign. Rep. John Larson (D-CT) called it "a miserable business. You might as well be putting bamboo shoots under my fingernails." Former Rep. Tom Perriello (D-VA), now at the Center for American Progress, said four hours may be "low-balling so as not to scare the new Members too much."

Fifteen years ago Anthony Corrado, a leading expert on campaign finance, described the "money chase" as far more than phoning. On most mornings while Congress is in session, he wrote, "a number of campaign fund-raising breakfasts are being held, usually sponsored by individual corporations, trade associations, or other lobbying organizations. The evenings are filled with candidate receptions, sometimes as many as a half-dozen or more per evening. . . . In addition are party fund-raising events, political action committee receptions, and even fund-raising efforts conducted by PACs or political committees established by or affiliated with specific members of Congress." A *Huffington Post* report of the specifics of how fund-raising would take up "an obscene portion of a [member's] typical day" bore the title: "Call Time for Congress Shows How Fundraising Dominates Bleak Work Life."[23] Well, not always so bleak.

Recall Rep. Gregory Meeks's trip to St. Croix in the Virgin Islands sponsored by Ponzi scheme architect Stanford: bleak? Indeed, it is typical of many congressional fund-raising trips. Members favor expeditions far from their home states to tony, expensive resorts where as many as fifty to a hundred donors and lobbyists are invited. The Four Seasons Resort in Colorado where legislators ski and party is a popular destination. Others include Park City, Utah; Palm Beach, Islamorada, Longboat Key, and Key Largo, Florida; Kiawah Island, South Carolina; Bermuda; and Dorado, Puerto Rico.

"This is the world of destination fund-raisers," wrote Eric Lipton in the *New York Times*, "where business interests blend with pleasure in exclusive vacation venues. Lobbyists go to build relationships with lawmakers, Democrats and Republicans alike, seeking action—and often inaction—in Washington for their clients and companies, with millions of dollars at stake." These events are legal, though in 2007 Congress prohibited lobbyists from giving any gifts to representatives. Of course, the Beltway freeloaders figured out how to get around the law. Campaign committees and "Leadership PACs" controlled by the legislators now pay their catering and lodging expenses, as do lobbyists and donors who also cover the cost of trips.

So it was that former senator Kelly Ayotte (R-NH), a critic of government spending who in 2010 handily won election by emphasizing Tea Party themes, enjoyed her vacation skiing at Park City, Utah, (she was on the ski team in college) along with a gaggle of corporate executives and lobbyists. "'Anyone who wants to do some runs with me, I would love to,' Ms. Ayotte told her guests, many of them already garbed in ski gear."[24]

Closer to home Washington fund-raisers are a weekly occurrence. Former lobbyist Jack Connaughton described fund-raisers as "simply part of the job. Senators and members of Congress continuously call the heads (and the lieutenants) of almost every lobbying firm in D.C. to ask them to do fundraising events." Some lobbyists, in turn, "are fanatical about fund-raising. They host as many as two or three events each week." Connaughton suspected that the large sums of money involved in these events might come initially from the lobbying firm's employees (a federal crime) who derive their income from their corporate clients, funds that then wind up in "the fundraising coffers of the senators and members they most frequently lobby."[25]

Republican Ed Whitfield represented Kentucky's First Congressional District comprising most of the western part of the state for over two decades. He held fund-raisers from California's posh Beverly Hills Hotel to an expensive Washington steakhouse, as well as the ski resort of Vail, Colorado. In his position as chair of the House Subcommittee on Energy and Power, Whitfield attracted $1.1 million in campaign contributions from electric utilities and oil, gas, and mining companies. The health care and pharmaceutical industries also gave to Whitfield—$340,000 in the 2014 cycle—since he also served as a member of the House Subcommittee on Health. In Congress from 1995 to his resignation in September 2016, Whitfield had not faced a competitive election since 1996.[26]

Whitfield's wife Constance Harriman-Whitfield is a former assistant secretary of the Interior Department and a lobbyist for the Humane Society Legislative Fund. In 2014 the congressional ethics committee opened an investigation into whether Whitfield improperly aided his wife's lobbying work by introducing or cosponsoring bills related to Kentucky's horse industry, particularly laws to prevent the practice of "soring" horses, inflicting pain to have them walk with an unnatural gait (a worthy cause). She reported lobbying on a dozen such bills between 2011 (when she began work for the HSLF) and 2014. Whitfield's office helped arrange "as many as a 100 meetings" for the Humane Society, some of which he conducted. The upshot: in a collegial case of mutual back-scratching the committee decided against a full-scale investigation, at the same time dropping a probe into a Democratic member.[27]

Junkets

According to Answers.com,

> A junket is an organized group of gamblers which is typically organized by a casino to attract players.
>
> A junket, as relates to government, is a trip, usually by an official or legislative committee, paid out of public funds and ostensibly to obtain information.

And the difference is? In government junkets every player wins. Taxpayer-funded trips by members of Congress, often with their spouses, "ostensibly to obtain information" in locales such as Hawaii, the Far East, the Middle East, and wherever, are a lifestyle perk whose use by members has skyrocketed in recent years. The allure of traveling on a military jet with first-class service and a doctor on board, certainly beats commercial coach-class travel. In the first decade of the twenty first century, lawmakers often selected Afghanistan to observe the military situation "on the ground" and "to visit the troops." The troop visit is usually a drive-by affair (legislators are prohibited from staying overnight), followed by a leisurely return with stops in such cities as Vienna, Paris, or London, lodged in swank hotels. In 2009 then House Speaker Nancy Pelosi led an entourage of other members, spouses, and aides to Afghanistan for a day. On the return they recovered from the rigor of Afghanistan by sojourning for eight days in Italy, spending $57,697 on hotels and meals. Other favorite destinations for legislators and spouses include the Galapagos Islands and Australia's Great Barrier Reef, "to study global warming."[28]

Taxpayers foot the bill for a fleet of sixteen passenger jets maintained by the U.S. Air Force for congressional use. The cost for a small group of junketeers to the Middle East is about $150,000. The air force version of the Boeing 757 flies large groups for about $12,000 an hour. The Defense and State Departments pay for most publically funded travel, and nearly two dozen officials work full-time arranging the trips.

At the same time, privately funded junkets by lawmakers have also increased rapidly, despite an ostensible congressional ban against lobbyist-funded trips. In 2006 lobbyist Jack Abramoff's broad range of corrupt practices included financing trips abroad—golf in Scotland most notoriously—for members of Congress. The next year Congress passed legislation prohibiting lobbyist-paid trips, but of course legislators and lobbyists found a loophole that in effect allows them to still trot the globe in style. In 2013 members took more such trips than in any year since the Abramoff-inspired reforms: 1,887 free trips at a cost of almost $6 million. In reality, many of the private sponsors of the trips have close, if not incestuous, ties to lobbying firms. The American Israel Education Foundation, for example, shares an address with the influential lobby the American Israel Public Affairs Committee. In 2013 the foundation spent $1.7 million on congressional junkets.[29]

Lawmakers and lobbyists have found imaginative ways around the 2007 reform. "Indeed, the reality is that lobbyists who can't legally buy lawmakers a sandwich can still escort members on trips all around the world" and arrange to have them paid for by shifting corporate money around. Aside from simply ignoring the rules or feigning ignorance, a major evasion works like this. The U.S. Constitution forbids public officials from accepting any gifts from a foreign government unless explicitly approved by Congress, *but* if a lobbyist (usually working with corporate clients) does so on behalf of a foreign government, under the 1961 Mutual Educational and Cultural Exchange Act, then all is kosher. Currently eighty-six programs for trips are covered under the MECEA.[30]

Turkey is one of the MECEA countries. In April 2013, for example, former Republican Speaker of the House and then lobbyist Dennis Hastert and his old adversary Dick Gephardt, former Democratic House minority leader, accompanied eight members of Congress on an all-expenses paid trip to Turkey. Hastert and Gephardt worked for competing firms that split the $1.4 million the Turkish government pays them to polish its image. Ironically, Hastert served as Speaker when the 2007 Abramoff-inspired reform was enacted.[31] Abramoff himself, now a critic of his former pursuits, thinks of the new rules that "they just reshuffled the deck. . . . They're still playing the same game." For months lobbyists had worked on planning the Turkey trip, exchanging phone calls and emails repeatedly with members' staffers and attending frequent meetings on Capitol Hill.

The members who flew to Turkey, in roomy business-class seats, included two Democrats and six Republicans. Maine Democrat Chellie Pingree, a self-styled reformer, told the *National Journal* that she had not "thought of" her hosts as registered lobbyists, but if they called her (presumably to cash in on their "bonding"—her word—on the trip), she said, "I don't think, personally, it would make a difference."

Perhaps not, but a "codel" (the name for trips by congressional delegations) to Baku, Azerbaijan, apparently made a big difference for that country's interests. In May 2013 ten members of Congress (four were Texans; Gregory Meeks also went along: as the late, great Robin Williams would say, "surprise! surprise!") plus thirty-five staffers attended an energy conference in Baku. At the time Azerbaijan had a vital interest in having Congress exempt an oil field and a $28 billion pipeline project from sanctions against Iran. In response to an investigation by the *Houston Chronicle*, only two members responded, vaguely, to questions regarding the trip's funding. Two months after the "conference," language exempting partners in the Azerbaijan pipeline and oil field was "mysteriously added" to the Iran sanctions bill. All ten congressmen who went to Baku voted for the modified sanctions.

Since 2000 a database, Legis-Storm, created by congressional watchdog Jock Friedly, has kept track of 38,633 privately funded trips costing $90.0 million. But when Friedly filed a Freedom of Information Act request for more detailed information about the trips, "[I] got *bupkes*. I got basically nothing."[32] (If the reader does not know what *bupkes* means, you don't want to know.)

Members of Congress do not need to be rich to live rich. They live like millionaires thanks also to Leadership PACs. Originally created to raise money for campaigns, these PACs have evolved into "a lifestyle subsidy" since they proliferated in the late 1990s.[33]

Representatives have no monopoly on junkets: lavish "conferences," symposia, retreats, and other excuses to party big at resorts are enjoyed often by executive departments and agencies. In 2012 the inspector general reported a General Services Administration 2010 Las Vegas conference that cost $823,000, making headlines and sparking taxpayer outrage. The next year antitax conservatives thrilled at the news that their favorite whipping boy, the IRS, spent $50 million on 225 employee conferences from 2010 to 2012. Other agencies' spending, however, seems to fly under the radar, with rationales for the pricey get-togethers often vague, such as the Defense Department

confab at Pearl Harbor for commanders and spouses to "come together . . .
face-to-face . . . to communicate, collaborate, and learn from the experience
of all the attendees." In fiscal year 2012 the departments of Veterans' Affairs,
Justice, Health and Human Services, and Energy and other agencies each
spent more than the IRS.[34]

Consider the case of Senator Saxby Chambliss (R-GA) highlighted in a
2009 *ProPublica* report. In 2007 and 2008 Chambliss played golf at swank resorts to the tune of a quarter of a million dollars. By Senate standards, Saxby
is not super rich, in 2009 ranking eighty-ninth in wealth (though he easily
qualifies for the top 10 percent). His Leadership PAC picks up the tabs, with
the money coming from lobbyists, political action committees, and corporate donors. In 2009, 70 percent of members had them, and by 2013 "nearly
everybody" had one. Indeed, for the newly elected, setting up a Leadership
PAC is now one of the first things they do. Like Chambliss, other senators
and representatives use these "slush funds" for outings at premier golf courses,
but they also pay for fishing in the Florida Keys, skiing in Colorado, visits to
Disneyworld, major league baseball games, and parties, like the $32,985 Sena-
tor Harry Reid spent at Las Vegas casinos. Sometimes lawmakers organize
expensive events or parties just before they leave office. The routineness of
these expenditures on extravagant entertainment, travel, and self-indulgence
is matched only by the bald-faced, intelligence-insulting rationales for these
activities provided by their hired help. When asked by *ProPublica* how it was
possible for Chambliss to host golf outings at three different California resorts on the same day, his "communications director" declined to answer but
had earlier sent an email replying, "Every fundraising event Sen. Chambliss
has held has been appropriately conducted, all expenses have been closely
scrutinized and all reporting has been accurate." *ProPublica*, however, could
find no evidence of "fundraising" at the events in question.[35] In 2003 at a "golf
fund-raiser" for Chambliss, President George W. Bush joked that the senator
had stopped him on the way to the dais and said, "If you keep it short, we can
get in a round of golf."

The Affluent Voting for the Affluent

It should come as no surprise that members of Congress ignore the policy preferences of lower-income Americans and vote for policies favored by affluent

constituents. Political scientist Larry Bartels conducted a now well-known analysis of voting by Republican and Democratic senators and found that members of both parties "are consistently responsive to the views of affluent constituents but entirely unresponsive to those with low incomes." Democratic senators occasionally supported policies favored by middle-income constituents, while Republicans responded only to the preferences of their well-off constituents. Additional research by Princeton's Martin Gilens, covering several decades, confirmed that the American Congress seldom pays attention to the preferences of poor and middle-class Americans. Legislators know that higher-income constituents have higher rates of voter turnout and political activism, but more importantly wealthy constituents provide them with "the mother's milk of politics": money to fuel their reelection campaigns. And as campaigns have become more expensive, members of Congress have become more dependent on and responsive to large donors.[36]

The annual congressional salary alone of $174,000, as Stephen Lurie pointed out in *The Atlantic*, "qualifies every member as the top 6 percent of earners." Nearly 200 members of Congress are multimillionaires, and one hundred have over $5 million in wealth. Lurie's point was that it mattered a great deal that "politicians have no experience of poverty" and thus are "woefully out of touch with economic reality for those living in poverty." From 1998 to 2008 only 13 out of 783 members of Congress came from a blue-collar background, and those had long left behind that experience. As Duke University's Nicholas Carnes has pointed out, the absence from Congress of working-class Americans, who constitute a substantial part of the population, has resulted in unfavorable policies for the working class. Workplaces are less safe, tax policy favors the rich, the social safety net is anemic, and labor unions have been weakened. "White-collar government" and voting by class, with the wealthy favoring the wealthy, Carnes's research showed, has been remarkably stable since World War II.[37]

The pattern continues, as a recent study of voting in the House of Representatives on legislation that would *increase* current levels of socioeconomic inequality. The researchers examined representatives' status in relation to their voting. Whereas Republicans regardless of their social class favored legislation increasing inequality, Democrats—the presumed party of the middle class and working people—of high status and income also tended to support measures increasing inequality.[38]

The Breakers of the Law Make the Law

George Orwell once observed that the English imperial makers of the law in India became the breakers of the law in Britain. In Washington, D.C., making and breaking the law both occur in Congress. The ninth report on congressional corruption by CREW named seventeen members on its "dishonorable" roll, ten of whom were listed before and six of whom were hitting the trifecta. So CREW wondered: "Why are we still talking about these six?" The answer is that the Department of Justice (DOJ), the House and Senate ethics committees, and the Federal Election Commission (FEC) simply are not doing their jobs. "The glacial pace of investigations into misconduct," commented CREW, "means many cases have dragged on for years and some have been dropped entirely with no explanation, despite strong evidence." Any citizens familiar with CREW's reports could easily conclude that "congressional ethics" is an oxymoron.

In a case involving criminal conduct by Rep. Don Young (R-AK), the House Ethics Committee formed an investigative subcommittee more than two and a half years after the DOJ first brought the case to Congress's attention. Young's practices of earmarking transportation funds to a donor, "rampant personal use of campaign money, and failing to disclose gifts and trips from lobbyists" did not move the Ethics Committee to action.

The committee readily dismisses charges on the simple say-so of the accused. Rep. Gregory Meeks's word that he simply misplaced documents—that never existed—flew right by his peers; in the case of Rep. John Tierney (D-MA), they accepted the word of Tierney's brother-in-law, a convicted felon living as a fugitive from justice in Antigua.[39]

The One Percent Supreme Court

The American public does know there is "so damn much money" in politics. Recently close to 80 percent of Americans have said that corruption is "widespread throughout the government"; in October 2014 Gallup reported that 69 percent believe Congress is "focused on special interests."[40] But the five-man conservative majority of the Supreme Court (Chief Justice John Roberts and Justices Samuel Alito, Anthony Kennedy, the late Antonin Scalia, and Clarence Thomas) showed itself totally out of touch with the American public, as well as political reality, on the subject of money in politics. In *Citizens United*

(2010) the activist five struck down a century of campaign finance law and opened the floodgates of corporate spending on advocacy campaign expenditures (i.e., for or against a candidate). In 2014 the Roberts court pushed even further its perverse reading of the First Amendment that "money is speech" in *McCutcheon*, allowing individual donors to contribute to as many candidates as desired. Although the decision retained the limits on the size of contributions to candidates and political committees, fat-cat donors could now give to as many candidates as they wish, as much as $3.5 million in any election cycle. Chief Justice Roberts's majority opinion stated that money influences politics only when one individual directly bribes an official in exchange for a vote, a "quid pro quo," a naive view of politics astonishing to most average citizens who overwhelmingly know that money corrupts legislators and government in many other ways.[41] The activist five's perspective totally ignores how business is done by the political class in Washington and state capitols.

The justices' lack of political experience—all are lawyers who never ran for political office—helps explain their naïveté regarding money in politics. Nor does the court reflect America's diversity. For starters, all the justices (including Scalia) attended just three Ivy League schools, with eight members from Harvard or Yale; all except Roberts are from the East Coast, four from New York; three are Jewish; six are Roman Catholic; there are no Protestants.

Less remarked upon, however, the Roberts court is not just *for* the One Percent, it is *of* the One Percent. All are millionaires, with Ruth Bader Ginsberg and Stephen Breyer worth $15 to $20 million; John Roberts and Samuel Alito own assets in the $3 to $15 million range; Sonia Sotomayor and Antonin Scalia boosted their wealth into the low millions through book advances and royalties. Elena Kagan, Clarence Thomas, and Anthony Kennedy are the least wealthy, though all three are likely millionaires. Besides those who publish books, all the justices use their positions to make tens of thousands from speaking fees. In 2012 Scalia reported making twenty-eight trips to schools and conservative organizations.[42]

As bona fide members of the political class, some justices shamelessly engage in political activity that violates the court's routinely unobserved Code of Conduct. The code does not discourage "ideological activity" related to the law but does explicitly ask that justices avoid the "appearance of impropriety" by actions that would erode "public confidence in the integrity and impartiality of the judiciary." Thomas, and Scalia during his tenure, attended political strategy conferences arranged by the reactionary billionaires Charles and David Koch, of Koch Industries, who contributed heavily to Tea Party and other organizations in the forefront of opposition to the Affordable Care Act, and who have been inveterate opponents of campaign finance reform. Both Scalia and Thomas appeared at such conferences while issues of health care and campaign finance were pending before the court (Scalia 2007, 2010; Thomas 2008). These events included political planning for a far-right Republican agenda and electoral defeat of Democrats as well as moderate Republicans. In January 2011 Scalia also gave a "constitutional tutorial" to newly elected Tea Party Republican members of Congress shortly after their arrival in Washington. Samuel Alito has spoken at events held to raise money to advance right-wing political movements. Of the liberal bloc, Ginsburg has spoken to groups that are primarily political.[43]

Public appearances and interviews by justices have increased exponentially since the 1960s, according to a study by law professor Richard L. Hasen of members' (recorded) public appearances and interviews. In the 1960s the number was 192, declining in the next decade and then rising steadily thereafter. Since 2000 Hasen observes a number of factors has created "Celebrity Justices," who are engaged with the media and public on an unprecedented scale, with 609 appearances/interviews during 2000 to 2009 and 744 during 2005 to 2014. Nine of the ten justices with the most appearances historically sat on the Roberts court. Scalia did not record the most public engagements, but his more controversial appearances probably stimulated others to venture outside the court. The financial incentive of book deals also played a role. Lacking evidence to tie the justices' increasing "celebrity" to the public's decline in confidence in the court, Hasen does find that political polarization has played a role, since judges "have become public gladiators in a national fight over the Court and its jurisprudence."[44]

Justice Thomas thus far is the only Supreme Court justice who has failed, along with some other members of the political class, to pay all his taxes owed to the U.S. Treasury. For thirteen years Thomas did not report income totaling close to $2 million earned by his wife, Virginia Thomas, checking the "None" box on his tax return regarding his wife's income. When watchdog organizations brought the matter to the attention of Congress (and to Chief Justice Roberts to no effect), Thomas explained that he made an inadvertent mistake "due to misunderstanding the filing instructions." This oversight went on for thirteen years and followed a period of ten years from 1987 to 1997, including his years as judge on the U.S. Court of Appeals for the District of Columbia, when Thomas did report his wife's income.[45]

Virginia Thomas's earnings came from her unreserved political activism, including anointing herself as an "ambassador to the Tea Party." Well before her Tea Party affiliation she worked behind the scenes for right-wing causes and then became a highly visible opponent of President Obama and particularly the Affordable Care Act. In 2009 she founded Liberty Central, a lobby to fight Obamacare that immediately received a $550,000 contribution from Clarence Thomas's good friend Harlan Crow, a billionaire Dallas real estate tycoon. (Seventy-four members of Congress requested that Justice Thomas recuse himself from any decision on the health-care reform.) Crow, the *New York Times* revealed in 2011, already had given the justice expensive gifts: a $15,000 bust of Abraham Lincoln, a $19,000 bible owned by Frederick Douglass, use of his private jet, yacht, and luxurious retreats in the Adirondacks and Bohemian Grove, California. Crow also gave generously at Thomas's urging to memorials to the justice's Georgia roots embracing the history of sea island slaves and free blacks near Savannah: $175,000 to a library honoring Thomas and at least $2 million to a seafood canning museum where the justice's mother worked until he was six years old.[46]

Although the mystique of the black-robed justices and the court's aversion to public scrutiny—it allows no televising of its proceedings—projects an apolitical image, public confidence in the court's impartiality and partisanship has eroded sharply since its 2000 decision in *Bush v. Gore*. Although the justices' "extracurricular" activities signal their membership in the political class, a study by Reuters of the cases the court decides to take revealed how firmly the Supreme Court majority is imbedded in Washington's cozy network of money and power, and illustrates to near perfection how the political class operates.

Each year the justices receive over 10,000 petitions to hear cases. Reuters analyzed some 10,300 petitions submitted during the years from 2004 to 2012 and found that a group of 66 prestigious lawyers had their petitions accepted "at a remarkable rate." This elite cohort's appeals were six times more likely to be accepted than the over 17,000 lawyers submitting cases, while they accounted for less than 1 percent of that total. The Reuters researchers called them "the elite of the elite," who were granted 43 percent of the cases the high court decided to accept in the period studied. Just eight lawyers, all men, accounted for almost 20 percent of the cases.[47]

Almost all are prestigious lawyers who work for big corporations (51 of the 66), and some have clerked for the justices, are friends with them, and socialize with them. "The results: a decided advantage for corporate America, and a growing insularity at the court. Some legal experts contend that the reliance on a small cluster of specialists, most working on behalf of business, has turned the Supreme Court into an echo chamber—a place where an elite group of jurists embraces an elite group of lawyers who reinforce narrow views of how the law should be construed." This tilt did not concern one of the court's liberals, Ruth Bader Ginsburg, who commented: "Business can pay for the best counsel money can buy. The average citizen cannot. That's just the reality."[48]

In an accompanying reality the Roberts court favored corporate America 71 percent of the time between 2008 and 2014 in cases involving the U.S. Chamber of Commerce. The court's conservative majority is the most pro-business since the 1950s. The Roberts court's activism in favor of business and a Republican agenda has contributed to the public's unfavorable perception of the court. In an early 2014 survey commissioned by the Constitutional Accountability Society, 60 percent viewed the court negatively, and 55 percent saw the court favoring corporations more than individuals; only 32 percent believed the court treats individuals and corporations equally. A Gallup Poll shortly afterward found confidence in the Supreme Court at a record low of 30 percent.[49]

Public approval probably matters very little to this court, particularly the reactionary bloc, whose arrogance begins with claims to understand the "original intent" of the framers of the Constitution. Justice William Brennan (1956–90) commented years ago on those who presumed to uncover the intentions of the founders: "It is arrogant to pretend that from our vantage point we can gauge accurately the intent of the framers on application of principle to specific, contemporary questions." More worrisome than the reactionary bloc's arrogance has been its lack of respect for decisions by a Congress that is at least popularly elected by the American people. The court's late foremost anti-democrat, Scalia, best expressed this attitude toward Congress in a discussion of a recent congressional vote on extending Section 5 of the Civil Rights Act (regarding the "preclearance" provision requiring states and localities with a history of discrimination to submit any changes in voting or elections to the Department of Justice). When told that Congress had voted 390 to 35 to extend Section 5, Scalia commented that the Israeli Supreme Court "used to have a rule that if the death penalty was pronounced unanimously, it was invalid, because there must be something wrong there." Although Scalia actually misconstrued what is (not was) a rule that delayed but did not invalidate the process, more importantly his remark showed his contempt for an overwhelming congressional majority and democratic process itself. Scalia's allies on the bench, Stanford law professor Pamela S. Karlan has pointed out, have expressed similar disdain for democratic politics.[50]

The current Supreme Court is the first in U.S. history on which sits not one person who had practical political experience; rather, the court is "populated by academics and appellate court justices, and not by people with experience of power and politics, who understand the ways in which real problems of money and influence manifest themselves." In contrast, the Warren court (1953–69) delivered decisions that enhanced "civic inclusion and democratic decision-making." In addition to Chief Justice Earl Warren, a popular former Republican governor of California, that court contained former senators and representatives, state legislators, a former mayor, and former cabinet ministers. They clearly were members of the political class, but at a time before elective office became all about fund-raising, before extreme polarization, and before the present heights of the revolving door between elective office and lobbying. Thus the Roberts court's reactionary majority sits at the apex of the political class and evinces a "deep distrust of democratic processes."[51]

In turning to lobbyists and the power of the financial sector it will appear that the disdainers of democratic process differ little from those who have hijacked representative government.

Chapter 3

Is the Political Class Corrupt?

Is the permanent political class in Washington, D.C., corrupt? Are most members of Congress corrupted by campaign contributions as well as slush funds and nepotistic practices with their staffs, relatives, donor-friends and others, and by their ability, because of the office they occupy, to enjoy the lifestyle of the very wealthy, thereby becoming addicted to money and reelection?

Many scholars and commentators think so, but some find the word harsh and believe the existence of corruption depends on the definition of the term. Indeed, the word "derives from the Latin *corrumpere,* which can mean to bribe, but also to mar or destroy." And at a minimum we tend to regard corrupt persons as deeply flawed, not merely self-serving but also capable of harmful, destructive actions toward others.

Lawrence Lessig, one of the most ardent critics of campaign cash and lobbying, believes that the people in the system are not corrupt but "decent." They are "good people working in a corrupted system." "The enemy is not evil," he avers, and adds "The enemy is well dressed." Of the latter, at least, we can be sure.[1]

The perception that corruption pervades governments has increased all across the globe. In 2013 Gallup reported that majorities in 108 out of 129 countries see corruption as a widespread problem. In the United States the percentage believing corruption endemic in government rose from 59 percent in 2006 to

79 percent in 2013. In another poll 90 percent of Americans said they would favor tough campaign finance laws to get money out of politics, and when "campaign finance" was changed to "corruption" that figure rose to 97 percent.[2] (Maybe the other 3 percent were not sure of what *corruption* means, or perhaps they work in Washington.)

A 2014 "Corruption Perception Index" published by Transparency International corroborates the poll results, with the United States ranked seventeenth among the least corrupt. "From fraud and embezzlement charges to the failure to uphold ethical standards," TI commented, "there are multiple cases of corruption at the federal, state and local levels."[3]

Interest in the subject has grown dramatically recently, judging by the several dozen organizations that now act as government watchdogs, with Common Cause, Public Interest, and Citizens for Responsibility and Ethics in Washington among the vigilant. Using different measures, several monitors have found corruption rampant in all states, with the "most corrupt" varying according to the measures used. The Center for Public Integrity conducted a months-long study published in 2012 (sponsored also by Global Integrity and National Public Radio) and found not one state government it could give an *A* rating regarding its conduct of public business. Eight states, representing a fair cross-section of America—Georgia, Michigan, Maine, North Dakota, South Carolina, Virginia, and Wyoming—received failing grades. Gift taking and other abuses among public officials went unpunished and even unnoticed by toothless ethics commissions. Another survey that asked several hundred political reporters to rank states by both "legal" and "illegal" corruption came up with a different rogue's gallery consisting of Alabama, Illinois, Kentucky, New Jersey, New Mexico, and Pennsylvania; only Georgia made both lists.[4] The state political classes serve, of course, as the farm teams for Washington.

Large majorities of the American public believe that the Supreme Court's decisions of *Citizens United* (2010) and *McCutcheon* (2014) have worsened the problem of political corruption. As law professor Zephyr Teachout has explained in her superb book *Corruption in America: From Benjamin Franklin's Snuff Box to Citizens United*, the Roberts court's naive understanding that only explicit quid pro quo exchanges, the smoking gun of a documented bribe, "narrows the scope of what is considered corruption to explicit deals." But rarely in Washington's political class and its satellites is anyone stupid enough to engage in overt bribery. Rather, as Teachout describes it, the exchanges between lobbyists, corporations, and representatives is a "gift economy which enables a sophisticated masking" of what is in effect a quid pro quo, a transaction the character of which somehow escaped five lawyers out of touch with reality. The "gift economy" is "so sophisticated that even the people inside it feel it is a culture of goodwill and not the auctioning off of the public welfare."[5]

Jack Abramoff agrees with Teachout that the Supreme Court is clueless about money's influence in politics. Following a unanimous 2016 court decision tossing out the bribery conviction of Bob McDonnell, who as governor of Virginia took valuable gifts from a businessman friend seeking state help, Abramoff found confounding the justices' "lack of understanding . . . that a little bit of money can breed corruption. When somebody petitioning a public servant for action provides any kind of extra resources—money or a gift or anything—that affects the process."[6]

Michael Johnston, author of a cross-national study of contemporary corruption in developing as well as "affluent market societies," defines *corruption* as *"the abuse of public roles or resources for private benefit."* Yet however defined, corruption inevitably "benefits the few at the expense of the many"; in addition, it is "undemocratic and harms economic growth."[7]

Teachout explains how the gift economy renders meaningless the participation of many ordinary citizens by comparing their congressional districts to what in eighteenth-century England were known as "rotten boroughs." These were districts, some "in the possession and gift of the king," inhabited by few voters who were controlled by wealthy gentry or aristocrats, often the same family for generations, men at a remove who often had no interest in or connection to the district itself (as with our members of Congress who take up residence in Washington and forget to maintain a real residence "back home"). With representatives' constant need for money to gain reelection and the ability of the very wealthy to give them unlimited amounts, the Supreme Court "has created the country as one large modern set of rotten boroughs. A few people [big donors] represent a district [not necessarily from that district, she might add], but the rest are gravestones. And money buys the outcome."[8]

The Fourth Estate: Lobbying

The term *Fourth Estate* originally referred to a power outside the established government, usually the print media as an unofficial branch of government. While all forms of media exert enormous influence over society and government, the corps of lobbyists in Washington and across the country now constitute a Fourth Estate, or a fourth unofficial branch of government as important in making policy as the three established by the constitution. This shadow corps can be more influential than the original sectors in determining economic policy because through it, the funders of elected officials often dominate public policy.

Since the 1990s lobbying in Washington has experienced explosive growth. In 2012 the industry spent $3.31 billion, almost seven times the amount spent in 1983. Consistently since 1998 more than three-quarters of the total laid out has been spent by corporations and business associations. In 2012 corporations spent $34 for every $1 spent by public interest, nonbusiness advocacy groups, and unions; they outspent unions alone by $56 to $1. According to political scientist Lee Drutman, the traditional model of a plurality of interest groups competing with and checking one another's influence has been swept away by business dominance, with corporate sectors and individual firms now fighting one another for influence.[9]

Lobbying in the states has enjoyed enormous growth in the past two to three decades, especially as gridlock has risen in Washington. Corporations, lawyers, and lobbyists have poured resources into state capitols where policy decisions

Copyright Joel Pett. Reprinted with permission.

are being made. Not just legislators and bureaucrats but states' attorneys general have attracted so much spending in gifts, parties at conferences, and campaign contributions that a broad coalition, including the National Association of Attorneys General, is taking steps to blunt the efforts of corporate donors and lobbyists to control their decisions.[10]

During the years of the Bush administration the number of registered lobbyists rose rapidly to over fifteen thousand. Since 2007 and passage of the Honest Leadership and Open Government Act following the Abramoff scandal, the number has declined—in 2013 to just over twelve thousand and has gone down steadily since then. Lobbyists' disclosed income has also dropped from its high of $3.55 billion in 2010 to $3.31 billion in 2012. Both declines are misleading, as lobbyists possess more power, and make more money, than ever. Lobbyists are simply unregistering and continuing their work under a different name, while law and lobbying firms are hiring "shadow lobbyists" like former Senator Tom Daschle as "consultants" or "policy advisors" or "historical advisors" (Newt Gingrich's preferred designation as a nonlobbyist) who do not register. The 1995 Lobbying and Disclosure Act, amended in 2006–7, provides a vague definition of lobbying easily circumvented, with no enforcement mechanism nor criminal penalties for violating it. So while lobbying is not withering away, as a comprehensive report by Open Secrets makes clear, what is disappearing is the reporting of lobbyists' activities and income and the public's access to critical information about the operation of government.

The number of shadow lobbyists and their income has become difficult to determine. A study by political scientist Tim LaPira for the Sunlight Foundation discovered that "for every one lobbyist who does the public the favor of disclosing his or her activities, there is a shadow lobbyist listed in the [lobbyist phonebook] who does not." LaPira estimated that in 2012 the amount spent on lobbying by interests seeking to influence government policy was about $6.7 billion, which included "stealth lobbying"; disclosed lobbying totaled $3.31 billion, a decline from 2010's high of $3.55 billion.[11]

Thus the numbers working as lobbyists could be much higher. James A. Thurber has studied and written about Congress for over thirty years, and before holding prestigious academic positions he served as a legislative assistant to Senators Adlai Stevenson, Hubert Humphrey, and William Brock and Representative David Obey. Thurber estimates that all those doing the work of lobbyists amount to about one hundred thousand, a figure nowhere near the number now registered.[12]

Some firms that engage in extensive lobbying are gigantic. WPP, a London-based worldwide marketing and public relations company has 350 subsidiaries; in Washington WPP has acquired Blue State Digital, Benenson Strategy Group, Burson-Marstellar, Direct Impact, Hill+Knowlton Strategies, Dewey Square Group, QG Public Affairs, Palisades Media Ventures, the Glover Park Group, and Wexler and Walker Public Policy Associates. Lobbying of this scope, commented Thomas Edsall, "is now an integral part of a much broader system of corporate leverage and control, a system that has left the federal regulation of this new breed of influence strategists far behind."[13] Lobbyists together with the interests they work for are now the Fourth Estate.

"So Damn Much Money"

Support for Lawrence Lessig's generous assessment of the political class runs k deep in the gift economy comes from the veteran *Washington Post* reporter Robert Kaiser in his book *So Damn Much Money: The Triumph of Lobbying and the Corrosion of American Government.* Kaiser described the origin of earmarks as the innovation of two young lawyers, Gerald S. J. Cassidy and Kenneth Schlossberg, who had set up shop in Washington as lobbyists after working among poor farm laborers in Migrant Legal Services in Florida. Cassidy, though embracing 1960s idealism and a liberal Democrat, had come from a poor family and set his sights on becoming rich from the beginning. In 1976 Schlossberg-Cassidy and Associates teamed up with the ambitious new president of Tufts University, Jean Mayer, to persuade Congress to fund a new nutrition center at Tufts. Schlossberg-Cassidy "had brought something new to an old game by stationing themselves at a key intersection between a supplicant for government assistance, Tufts, and the people who could respond—members of Congress and the executive branch." They realized representatives were all too willing to score points with their constituents, and they carved out a niche acquiring earmarks for other universities. In time, *they* initiated proposals *to* universities after doing some research on institutions' possible needs, and as their reputation grew, the firm also landed hugely profitable corporate clients. Kaiser described Cassidy's rise as emblematic of the industry as he became one of the wealthiest and most powerful lobbyists in Washington; and he regards Cassidy as a decent man.[14]

Lobbyists now earn sums that Cassidy would have regarded as fabulous when he entered the trade. Most lobbying compensation is undisclosed, but some, especially for top dogs in tax-exempt trade associations, is open to public view. In 2012, twelve trade association executives made over $2 million a year. The biggest earners made $6,761,000, $4,761,900, and $4,006,893.[15]

Kaiser ended his book with a chapter titled "A Corrosive Culture," but while granting that the public has long associated lobbying with corruption, Kaiser sees a "very American moral conundrum." Americans "tend to believe that people should not be getting rich by influencing government decisions," but they also believe, "often fervently, in the right to 'petition the government for a redress of grievances.'" Moreover, "many of America's noblest institutions, among them the Red Cross, the United Way, the Kiwanis clubs, and the March of Dimes, pay handsome fees to lobbyists to help them influence government decisions." And he wondered if the country "was [not] well served by the creation, at taxpayer expense, of a top-flight nutrition research center at Tufts?"[16]

Putting aside whether petitioning for taxpayer money as a subsidy, grant, or boondoggle is the same as pleading for a "redress of grievances," Kaiser's narrative provides repeated instances of not so "noble" appropriations that tip the scales against lobbyists obtaining "good" earmarks like a university nutrition center. Firstly, there is the matter just noted of Cassidy's firm (and others who quickly got in on the game) ginning up requests for universities to make; then following the same technique with large corporate clients, many of them not so interested in nutritional health, much less clean air or water.

Kaiser tells of lobbyists getting legislation passed merely to benefit clients and actually harming the public interest: the Housing and Urban Development scam of 1989 making millions for real estate developers and lobbyists; the 2005 Bankruptcy Abuse Prevention and Consumer Protection Act that should have been called the "Bankruptcy Creation (for consumers) and Banker Profits Act"; the unfunded 2003 drug benefit added to Medicare, giving seniors more money for drugs, with huge profits to the pharmaceutical industry, and preventing consumers from importing cheaper generics from Canada, along with refusing to let the federal government negotiate prices (in the 2002 election cycle Big Pharma gave $7.7 million to Republican members; in 2004, $12 million); the defeat of proposals to close the loophole allowing hedge and private equity funds to pay only 15 percent in taxes. Many similar examples could be gleaned from Kaiser and other sources. The for-profit prison industry now employs one of the biggest lobbying enterprises in Washington, which indirectly supports "policies that put more Americans and immigrants behind bars." It advocates for stricter penalties for minor crimes and undocumented immigrants, longer prison sentences, tougher parole standards, and against any decriminalization measures. Profit, not rehabilitation, motivates the industry.[17]

An assessment of Congress's denizens as not so "decent" has come from Peter Schweizer, a conservative fellow at the Hoover Institution at Stanford University. Schweizer concentrated his fire not on earmarks but on legislators' tactics of "milking" or "toll booths," which he characterizes as "extortion": a protection racket comparable to "the Mafia street thug who offers a business 'protection'"—*from him*. "Milker bills" are often introduced with no intention of getting them passed but to prompt campaign-fund contributions from companies or individuals who do not want them passed; they are also called "juicer bills" or "fetcher bills," "because they are introduced largely for the purpose of squeezing money out of the target"; whatever they are called, "these bills are designed not to make good law, but rather to raise money." A "toll booth" is erected by a chair of a powerful legislative committee just before a vote on a bill affecting an industry or company pushing the bill; if the interested parties have not coughed up "tribute," the bill is delayed. "Tom DeLay [when majority whip] made an art of this practice. . . . Speaker of the House John Boehner . . . perfected it."[18]

"You Can't Do Anything without the F*****g Money"

Jack Abramoff owns the distinction of being "the lobbyist who went to jail" for astronomical overcharging of clients (primarily Native American tribes) and other corrupt practices. Twenty-one others, including two White House officials, one member of Congress, nine lobbyists, and nine staffers pleaded guilty or were found to be guilty. Kaiser emphasized that it was not "the nature" of what Abramoff did, but the extremity of it. Abramoff "was an extreme example of the breed, not another breed altogether."[19] As journalist Michael Kinsey famously said, "The scandal isn't what's illegal, the scandal is what's legal."

Abramoff's memoir made clear—as did many lobbyists who spoke to Kaiser—that campaign contributions are directly tied to votes. For years members of Congress have promoted the fiction—while in office—that their votes are not for sale. Money buys *"access,"* they admit, but not their votes. The public no longer believes this dodge and knows that its votes matter far less than the campaign cash contributed to members of Congress. Politicians also say that money has no effect because it comes from competing interests that cancel out one another. Former representative Barney Frank (D-MA) dismissed that rationalization: "People say, 'Oh it doesn't have any effect on me,'" he told National Public Radio. "Well, if that were the case we'd be the only human beings in the history of the world who on a regular basis took significant amounts of money from perfect strangers and sure that it had no effect on our behavior."[20]

Rep. Gregory Meeks and his fellow members of the "banking caucus" provide evidence that campaign contributions do indeed buy votes. Recall how Meeks received a $5,000 campaign contribution four days after cosponsoring a bill to protect payday lenders. In October 2015 a watchdog group asked the Office of Congressional Ethics to investigate eleven members of the "banking caucus" who, like Meeks, repeatedly received cash from payday executives or allied PACs immediately before or just after votes. "The donations," commented the *Nation*'s Joshua Holland, "appear to cross the fuzzy line between routine fundraising and a quid pro quo arrangement—what non-lawyers would see as something approaching outright bribery."[21]

In state capitols, too, lobbyists' money buys more than "access," according to the classic study of lobbyists at the state level by political scientist Alan Rosenthal. Events in New York in recent years dramatically confirmed Rosenthal's twenty-five-year-old study. In July 2013 repeated political scandals and indictments of elected officials prompted Governor Andrew Cuomo to establish a Commission to Investigate Public Corruption (known as the Moreland Commission under the act authorizing investigation of public corruption). Although Cuomo disbanded the commission abruptly in March 2014, to the dismay of government watchdogs, its preliminary report in December 2013 described "an epidemic of public corruption." "In recent years," the report stated, "too many local and state elected officials, staff members, and party leaders have been indicted and convicted for offenses running the gamut of shame: bribery, embezzlement, self-dealing, and fraud. . . . One out of every eleven legislators to leave office since 1999 has done so under a cloud of ethical or criminal violations, and multiple sitting officials are facing indictment on public corruption charges. The list goes on and on." The commission's inquiries led to an explosive scandal in early 2015 when Sheldon Silver, the powerful Democratic speaker of

Copyright Joel Pett. Reprinted with permission.

the New York assembly for two decades, was arrested on charges of mail and wire fraud, extortion, and bribery. Federal agents accused Silver of raking in millions in bribes and kickbacks while claiming he was getting rich from practice as a personal injury lawyer representing ordinary people. Preet Bharara, the U.S. Attorney for the Southern District of New York, found that the law practice did not exist.[22]

After Silver's arrest a classic *political class* wrinkle emerged regarding Silver's longtime friend and chief of staff, Judy Rapfogel, who remained in place earning a salary of $180,503, more than Governor Cuomo. Silver had given her a $10,000 raise shortly before his arrest. In July 2014, Rapfogel's husband, William, Silver's business associate and friend since boyhood, was sentenced to up to ten years in prison for stealing $9 million from the Metropolitan Council on Jewish Poverty of which he was executive director. The Silver-Rapfogel connections had many facets, the juiciest perhaps being that Judy Rapfogel sat in on legislators' meetings headed by Silver in which they decided to direct millions to nonprofits, including William Rapfogel's Met Council. An instance of political class use of power for sex emerged when federal prosecutors revealed that Silver had extramarital affairs with two women, one who lobbied for him and another for whom he had gotten a state job.[23] (Judy Rapfogel, never charged with a crime, retired with a pension of $115,000 and now works for Trump son-in-law Jared Kushner's real estate company.)

Silver and Rapfogel were briefly the face of corruption in New York, but the commission reported that the problem was systemic. In its executive summary it highlighted a secretly recorded conversation involving the exchange of cash for a gubernatorial nomination:

> "That's politics, that's politics, it's all about how much. Not about whether or will, it's about how much, and that's our politicians in New York, they're all like that because of the drive that the money does for everything else. You can't do anything without the f*****g money."

The commission conceded that while many public officials are honest, "the system itself truly is 'all about how much.'" In calling for campaign finance reform, the commission also pointed to "the weakness of our laws related to lobbying, conflicts of interest and public ethics."[24]

New York is hardly the most corrupt of states; it did not even make the two lists of "most corrupt" mentioned above. But the Silver-Rapfogel affair and the Moreland Commission report illustrate how state legislators there and across the country make use of pet nonprofits to engage in profiteering. Opportunity for corruption through nonprofits has increased in recent years as state governments have outsourced many functions to community-based nonprofits to provide social services more effectively than government bureaucrats—that is the rationale. "The function may be outsourced," according to Susan Lerner, executive director of Common Cause of New York, "but a lot of the funding is coming from government." Lawmakers then make it their business, literally, to direct funds to favorite nonprofits that then become shot through with nepotism, favoritism, and conflict of interest. Few states, however, have created clear oversight of lawmakers' financial connections to nonprofits receiving large grants of taxpayer money. In 2006 the Colorado Ethics Board saw nothing wrong with two lawmakers voting on or sponsoring legislation to give funds to nonprofits with which they worked, one as a paid director and the other as an unpaid board member. The general counsel of Florida's House of Representatives has issued similar opinions; in one case the legislator was a paid employee. In Illinois, as in New York, legislators can direct funds to nonprofits without disclosing their sponsorship; not surprisingly, in 2010 a federal grand jury subpoenaed records related to dozens of state grants to nonprofits tied to lawmakers. California is one of the few states requiring disclosure, but according to California Common Cause, the practice of lawmakers directing funds to nonprofits thrives. Indictments of state reps resulting from charity scams occur continuously across the country.[25]

The Revolving Door

"How much" is the grease that oils the hinges of revolving doors at the state and federal levels, sending record numbers of former legislators into lobbying. Why remain a representative or senator—though already lucrative for self, family, and friends—when a move from the Capitol to K Street can bring a starting income of several hundred thousand to millions, without the hassles of raising money for reelection?

In 1976 only 3 percent of members leaving Congress moved into lobbying; now well over half do. In early 2015 a total of 422 former legislators were lobbyists (registered and "stealth"), 75 former senators and 347 former representatives. After the 2007 law designed to slow the flow through the revolving door, 1,650 congressional aides registered to lobby within a year of leaving Capitol Hill, finding it "effortless" to avoid the one-year ban.[26]

As the revolving door spins ever faster, some men and women are running for office or become staffers as a career stepping-stone to lobbying and enormous incomes. Former legislators and their staffers, and other former government officials, earn significantly more as lobbyists than those without government experience, according to the Sunlight Foundation. And former leaders of Congress—majority leaders, chairs of key committees, and their staffers—are avidly sought by lobbying firms and are the biggest winners on K Street.[27]

When Trent Lott was born in 1941 in Grenada, Mississippi, his father was a sharecropper and his mother a schoolteacher. When he was six years old his family's finances improved when his father got work at a shipyard in Pascagoula. After college and law school, and work in the Capitol as a staffer to a prominent congressman, Lott won election to the House in 1972 and the Senate in 1988. When the affable senator and former Republican majority leader abruptly left the Senate in 2007, he candidly admitted to reporters that he intended to make himself rich as a lobbyist and quickly did so. The timing of Lott's departure was prompted by the urgency to take up his new trade before the 2007 reform took effect requiring former members to wait two years before engaging in lobbying (a rule honored more in the breach). In 2010 he earned $6 million; between 1998 and 2012 twenty-five of his former staffers earned a total of $91 million in lobbying revenue—the highest of any member of Congress. Coming in second behind Lott's revolvers were those of former Senator Bill Frist (R-TN), who followed Lott as majority leader from 2003 to 2007. In 2014 Lott worked with former senator John Breaux (D-LA) lobbying on behalf of the Russian Gazprombank, a target of U.S. sanctions levied because of Russia's role in the Ukrainian war.[28] The bank is the third largest in the Russian Federation and closely tied to the Kremlin.

When Jack Abramoff made millions as a lobbyist, his "most powerful move" in getting what he wanted from a legislator was to cultivate the chief of staff who in most offices "is the center of power." After several meetings, and "possibly including meals or rounds of golf," he would utter a few "magic words": "When you are done working for the Congressman, you should come to work for me at my firm."

> With that, assuming the staffer had any interest in leaving Capitol Hill for K Street—and almost 90 percent of them do, I would own him and, consequently, that entire office. . . . Suddenly, every move the staffer made, he made with his future at my firm in mind.[29]

Contemporary Abramoffs no longer need to introduce the prospect of a move to K Street to either staffers or members since it is now often on their minds. As Teachout comments, "The *likely* career path of a congressperson is to become a lobbyist." The revolving door, according to Teachout, resembles "The Problem of Placemen" in Old England and the colonies that the founders of the nation worried about. Their experience with corrupt officials and appointees influenced their constructing a government marked by a separation of powers. Two hundred years later "a different problem of placemen arose . . . when lobbyists started hiring over half the members of Congress and many of their staffers after they left office."[30]

The accelerating exodus of staffers to K Street, as Lee Drutman points out, has had the effect of increasing the power of lobbyists by shortening the overall tenure of staffers; that group is becoming younger and less experienced, creating even more reliance on lobbyists in crafting legislation. The competition among lobbyists to influence policy makes contested laws more complex; a document hundreds of pages long is difficult for new staffers and the public to understand, and it also increases lobbyists' influence.[31]

As a presidential candidate, Senator Barack Obama proclaimed often that he intended to "change the way Washington works," specifically by limiting the influence of lobbyists in his administration and curbing their sway over Congress. In 2007 he promised that "lobbyists won't find a job in my White House." After just two years in office—and subsequently—it was evident that diminishing lobbyists' power was a Sisyphean task. Indeed, even before taking office Obama put lobbyists on his transition team provided they did not work on issues related to their previous jobs.

Yet even that Maginot Line was penetrated, as the case of Mark Patterson, an archetypal member of the political class, illustrated. Since graduating from college in 1984 Patterson had spent most of his life in Washington as a lawyer, a policy director for Senator Tom Daschle, and then went to work as a lobbyist for Goldman Sachs after Daschle's 2004 defeat. In 2003 he married Jennifer Lee, a senior attorney for the Enforcement Division of the Securities and Exchange Commission (SEC) (perhaps of some interest to Goldman). In 2008 incoming Treasury Secretary Geithner tapped Patterson to be his chief of staff. The Daschle connection extended to the new president, as Obama had hired Pete Rouse, Daschle's former chief of staff, to do the same job for him as he entered the Senate in 2004. Rouse, one of the most influential and highly regarded staffers in the Capitol, followed Obama into the White House as a senior policy advisor. In 2014 both Patterson and Rouse left the administration to work for the huge law firm of Perkins Coie (recruited by a former White House counsel), which professed that their new hires would not engage in lobbying since the firm claims not to have a lobbying operation.[32] And so two more high-level Obama appointees joined the ranks of the uncounted "stealth lobbyists."

Obama did refuse to take money from federal lobbyists, corporations, and PACs to help fund the transition. But by 2014 there were at least seventy previously registered corporate, trade association, and for-hire lobbyists in the administration, and the president needed to back off part of the administration's 2010 ban on lobbyists serving on industry trade commissions after a court challenge went against the White House. Many nonregistered "advocates" and "consultants" joined Obama's team; and many of its former members moved immediately into lobbying without waiting a year by not registering as lobbyists. Indeed, Obama's efforts to diminish lobbyists' influence actually increased the number of nonregistered or "stealth lobbyists." It may have been true, according to White House spokesman Eric Schultz, that Obama "has done more . . . to close the revolving door of special interest influence than any president before him"; but as Thurber observed, Obama has found "changing the lobbying industry difficult because of its size, adaptability, and integral part [sic] of pluralist democracy."[33] A Fourth Branch indeed.

The Affordable Care and Patient Protection Act, although designed to provide health insurance for millions of the uninsured, also meant huge profits for sectors of the health care industry and their CEOs. At the same time, legislators, staffers, and hired "experts" who crafted the law exited through the revolving door to K Street even before the botched launching of the program. By late 2013 at least thirty former authors of the law had moved on to lucrative lobbying or "consulting" to help affected health industry companies increase their profits. Previously nonpolitical Dr. Dora Hughes served four years as counselor to Secretary of Health and Human Services Kathleen Sebelius. In 2012 she left that post to work for Sidley Austin, a lobbying firm representing pharmaceutical companies, medical device makers, and insurers. Yvette Fontenot worked on the bill as an aide to the Finance Committee; she later joined Avenue Solutions, "a boutique lobbying shop." Rep. Earl Pomeroy (D-ND), who voted for the ACA, spent nearly two decades in Congress as an advocate for the hospital industry. Defeated for reelection in the Republican comeback of 2010, he moved swiftly into lobbying for long-term care hospitals, finessing the one-year ban on members leaving office by partnering with his former chief of staff, who was not affected by the one-year restriction.[34]

But these monetizers of their public service are small fry compared to the person who actually wrote much of the ACA, Elizabeth Fowler, the chief health policy counsel to Sen. Max Baucus (D-MT), chair of the Senate Finance Committee that had the task of drafting the legislation. When the bill passed, Baucus heaped praise on Fowler as the architect of the law: "She is a lawyer, she is a Ph.D. She is just so decent." Sitting behind him throughout the consideration of the health care bill, Fowler had worked as a high-level executive and lobbyist for Well Point, the nation's largest health insurer. The ACA's mandate that uninsured individuals must purchase from the private market and the immediate rejection of a public alternative meant huge profits for the health-care industry.

Marcy Wheeler of *Politico* said that besides Fowler "we might as well consider Well Point its author as well—the White House brought her in to implement the roll-out, though in typical media blindness to reality her name seldom surfaced during the disaster that followed." In late 2012 Fowler left the administration to take charge of "global health policy" at the pharmaceutical giant Johnson & Johnson. This prompted Glenn Greenwald of the *Guardian* to comment, "It's difficult to find someone who embodies the sleazy, anti-democratic, corporatist revolving door that greases Washington as shamelessly and purely as Liz Fowler."[35]

More charitably, Bill Moyers said that friends of Fowler would call that harsh, that she is devoted to public service and worked to craft a law that would pass. But, Moyers added, that is not the point. Rather, "she's emblematic of the revolving door culture that inevitably means . . . corporate interests will have the upper hand in the close calls that determine public policy. It's how insiders [of the political class] fix the rules of the market."[36] And in Fowler's defense one might point to the person who put her at the fulcrum of the law: the Senate's "Master of the Revolving Door," Max Baucus.

King of K Street, Ambassador to China

It was Obama's bad luck (or his lack of engagement) that allowed Sen. Max Baucus (D-MT), chair of the Senate Finance Committee and a nominal Democrat in bed with business interests, to construct his signature health care reform. Critics later said that Obama took the political capital from his inspirational victory in 2008 and handed it over to Max Baucus.

Elected to the House for two terms (1975–79), and then to the Senate in 1978, Baucus immediately became a creature of Washington. Indeed, Baucus owned no home in Montana after 1974; although he bought half of his mother's house in 2002, he lived in the Capitol district for over four decades. The money he raised from corporate interests protected his seat. In 2007 he ascended to chair of the Senate Finance Committee; few posts in Congress attract more corporate money. But even before that, from 2003 to 2008, he received more than $5 million from the health and financial sectors. Many of his former staffers, meanwhile, had moved to K Street, constituting a powerful network of influential lobbyists. In 2009, when Baucus took over creating what became the ACA, five of his staffers worked for twenty-seven different organizations either in health care or insurance. It was not surprising, then, that he immediately declared that "single payer [is] not on the table," and that the first meeting he called to discuss legislation included representatives from the pharmaceutical and insurance companies, HMOs, and hospital management. Indeed, White House press secretary Robert Gibbs expressed surprise that K Street had a copy of the planned bill before the president or congressional leaders.[37]

Two dozen or more former Baucus staffers also worked as lobbyists for corporations seeking tax breaks from his powerful Finance Committee, functioning as a smooth-running machine that made billions for corporate clients, millions in salary for the lobbyists, and millions in what might be thought of as kickbacks that the lobbyists and PACs plowed into Baucus's reelection campaigns. An investigation by the *New York Times*'s Eric Lipton determined that no other member of Congress had "such a sizeable constellation of former aides working as tax lobbyists, representing blue-chip clients that include telecommunications businesses, oil companies, retailers and financial firms."[38]

In April 2013 the seventy-two-year-old Baucus announced that he would not run for reelection. In December President Obama nominated him as ambassador to China, touting his expertise on trade, and he was easily confirmed by the Senate. Staffers had been important to Baucus in other ways. He met his second wife when she was a staffer for Sen. Paul Tsongas (D-MA), and in 2011 he married his third wife, one of his former staffers.

Baucus's career surely challenges Glenn Greenwald's assessment that "it's difficult to find someone who embodies the sleazy, anti-democratic, corporatist revolving door that greases Washington as shamelessly and purely as Liz Fowler."

Wall Street and the Revolving Door

Perhaps the most lucrative revolving door, as the case of Eric Cantor demonstrated, moves between government and Wall Street, a gilded entryway whose hinges "The Street" lubricates with gobs of money. When bank executives leave finance for government, their firms give them lucrative compensation packages that they would have earned had they stayed in place. The banks do not, however, vote restricted shares and deferred compensation to executives who leave for a nongovernmental job or retire early. Only those who migrate into "public service" get such rewards.

In 2014 the AFL-CIO sent a letter to banks questioning why the firms pay out these packages to departing executives when those rewards were intended to keep them. Union officials wonder if the practice could be a "backdoor way to pay off a newly minted government official to act in Wall Street's private interests rather than the public interest."[39] Wall Street received the letter shortly after revelations that a Goldman Sachs banker, who had worked at the Federal Reserve Bank of New York for seven years as a regulator, had obtained confidential information from a former colleague still working at the government bank. Goldman fired two of its employees involved, but the Fed also fired a regulator who leaked tapes disclosing the conflict of interest and who charged that her attempts to discipline Goldman were blocked by her bosses.[40]

Soon after this incident demonstrating banker-regulator collaboration, President Obama prepared to appoint Antonio Weiss, the global head of investment banking at Lazard Ltd., as undersecretary to U.S. Treasurer Jack Lew. If Weiss succeeded in getting confirmed, Lazard would pay him a $20 million bonus. Democratic senators led by Dick Durbin of Illinois and Elizabeth Warren of Massachusetts raised a firestorm of opposition to Weiss as too close to Wall Street. Weiss withdrew his nomination, and liberal Democrats claimed victory, but one wonders why. Obama then appointed Weiss as counselor to Lew—presumably taking his bonus with him. Appropriately enough, as Lew had come to the administration from Citigroup, a bank bailed out with taxpayer money, and which had given him a bonus in the disastrous year of 2008. When questioned later at his senate hearing about the terms of his departure, he professed he was "not familiar with the records that were kept"—*regarding his compensation.* Bloomberg got hold of his employment contract, which stipulated that any incentive or retention pay would be forfeited unless he left for a "high-level position with the U.S. government." Lew in fact received $250,000 to $500,000 in accelerated restricted Citi stock and $1.1 million in salary and discretionary cash.[41]

The episode of financial espionage involving inside information exchanged between the Fed and Goldman officials pales in comparison to the platoon system by which former federal bank regulators become vociferous lawyer-lobbyists hired by the banks to attack and roll back even the mildest regulation. A reporter attending a Securities Enforcement Forum, a panel discussion involving top regulators and lobbyist-lawyers representing financial firms, observed that the experience felt like a visit to "an alternate universe."

He witnessed the current enforcement director of the SEC, Andrew Ceresney, being browbeaten by five of his predecessors, now lobbyists for banks. "The conference turned into a free-for-all of high-powered and influential white-collar defense lawyers hammering regulators on how unfair they have been to their clients, some of America's largest financial companies." The lawyers included Robert S. Khuzami, Obama's first enforcement director, and George S. Canellos, who had just left the SEC. Ceresney heard complaints ranging from the SEC's prosecution of minor corporate infractions to the severity and politicization of punishments. (Khuzami took over as enforcement director in the midst of the financial crisis and received credit for "reinvigorating" the unit. But he also took fire for not prosecuting bank executives and for levying fines as punishment that one federal judge called "pocket change" and "half-baked justice at best." Khuzami now bites back at the SEC on behalf of the corporate law firm Kirkland & Ellis, which gave him a starting salary of $5 million a year.)[42]

As traffic grew between banks and the upper levels of the Obama administration, that between Congress and lobbying firms representing banks accelerated. Since the passage of the Wall Street Reform and Consumer Protection Act (Dodd-Frank), the banks have put into high gear their hiring of former legislators and staffers. Indeed, even before President Obama signed the bill into law in July 2010, no fewer than 125 former legislators and staffers were working for financial firms to limit federal regulatory power. One senior aide to Rep. Barney Frank (D-MA), Peter S. Roberson, who on Frank's financial services committee helped draft legislation regulating risky over-the-counter derivatives, was hired in early 2010 as a lobbyist for Intercontinental Exchange, the leading clearinghouse for derivatives.[43]

Wall Street also extends its influence over Congress by paying for "access"—if not votes. According to the Center for Responsive Politics, in the 2013–14 election cycle the financial sector's campaign contributions to federal candidates and parties far outstripped any other interest group: just under $500 million. Although the elites of finance have contributed to both Democrats and Republicans, usually giving more to the party controlling Congress, since 2011 the flow of campaign cash from finance to Republicans has exceeded previous amounts and far outdistanced giving to Democrats.[44]

Legislators sitting on Senate and House finance committees derive even greater benefits from Wall Street banks. A study by London Business School economists found that banks substantially enhanced the net worth of members of those committees compared to other representatives. Finance committee members "report greater levels of leverage and new liabilities as a proportion of their net worth. . . .with lower interest rates and longer maturities." As business reporter David Sirota commented, "It is good to be king."[45]

Wall Street's efforts to undo Dodd-Frank began as soon as it passed. The banks' clout in Congress surfaced in October 2013 when the House voted to eliminate Dodd-Frank's restrictions on banks' handling of derivatives, a bill that Citigroup practically wrote for its congressional sponsors. The lobbyists' suggestions appeared in over seventy of the law's eighty-five lines, and two key paragraphs were nearly verbatim. Longtime consumer advocate Sen. Elizabeth Warren, not having been pulled into the vortex of the political class, gave a blunt speech denouncing Congress for allowing "lobbyists for the biggest recipient of bailout money in the history of this country" to write the provision weakening Dodd-Frank to create "even more bailout opportunities." She called instead for breaking up the big banks, noting that the Dodd-Frank provision was "attached to a bill that needs to pass or else the federal government will grind to a halt."[46]

Citigroup had given $503,150 to legislators, the most to Jim Hines (D-CT), a cosponsor and utility-fielder "Republican for a Day." Speaker John Boehner (R-OH), also a cosponsor, received $917,000 from interests behind the bill. In January 2014 congressional Republicans managed to get Democrats to agree to cutting funds for the SEC and other Wall Street regulators by ending demands to cut further the federal food stamp program. So blackmailed Democrats traded less oversight on banksters to keep poor people fed.[47]

The incestuous bonds of the permanent political class in financial Washington are captured by former lobbyist Joe Connaugton's description of "The Blob" ("it's really called that") in his book *The Payoff: Why Wall Street Always Wins*. The Blob "refers to the government entities that regulate the financial industry—like the Banking Committee, Treasury Department, and SEC—and the army of Wall Street representatives and lobbyists that continuously surrounds and permeates them. "The Blob moves together. Its members are in constant contact by email and phone. They dine, drink, and take vacations together. Nor surprisingly they frequently intermarry [see Mark Patterson, above]. Indeed, a good way to maximize your family income in DC is to specialize in financial issues and marry someone in the Blob. . . . What you and your spouse do all the time is share information."[48]

At the Core of Oligarchy:
Who Gets to Jump the Line?

The word *nepotism* was "coined sometime in the fifth century to describe the corrupt practice of appointing papal relatives to office—usually illegitimate sons described as 'nephews.'" Today, although no systematic data seems to have been collected, anyone familiar with the practice of nepotism among America's elites agrees that the promotion of one's offspring, relatives, and friends has enjoyed an "enormous boom." Indeed, Adam Bellow, who titled his 2003 book *In Praise of Nepotism*, observed that "the boom in generational succession is something new in both scope and character" (Bellow is the son of the novelist Saul). Nepotism frequently commands attention in business publications and psychological journals. Studies of its practice in business, where it has been endemic, tend to reflect Bellow's assessment of "good" and "bad" nepotism. "Bad" happens when the boss's son or daughter screws up; otherwise, no big deal.[49]

Bellow convincingly described the practice as inevitable in most areas of life, but he conceded that it is "a threat to opportunity" and that there are "emergent caste tendencies in the American elites. Unchecked nepotism leads to the formation of a caste system." The "transfer of privilege from one generation to the next is a gradual, cumulative, and very personal process. But as a mechanism for turning an inclusive social and economic order into an exclusive one," it can become destructive of the society as a whole and lead to its decline.[50]

Nepotism among the permanent political class in Washington and its satellites has flourished in recent decades. Bellow declared that "no one wants to be accused [of nepotism],"[51] but the reality is that the political class practices nepotism routinely, brazenly, and shamelessly, giving their "nephews" plum jobs, promotions, a place at the head of the line.

An inventory of nepotistic relationships in Washington, according to a 2002 column by Dana Milbank, "reads like a scatterbrained rendition of 'Dem Bones,' with brothers and daughters and sons-in-law all connected in a government body united almost as much by DNA as by political ties." The *Washington Post's* Milbank's description of the George W. Bush administration as "a family matter" is worth quoting at length:

> Two weeks ago, the State Department announced that Elizabeth Cheney, the vice president's daughter, would become a deputy assistant secretary of state. Her husband, Philip Perry, last week left the Justice Department to become

chief counsel of the Office of Management and Budget. There, Cheney's son-in-law will join OMB Director Mitchell E. Daniels, Jr., whose sister, Deborah Daniels, is an assistant attorney general.

That's just the beginning. Among Deborah Daniels's colleagues at Justice is young Chuck James, whose mother, Kay Coles James, is the director of the Office of Personnel Management, and whose father, Charles, Sr., is a top Labor Department official. Charles James, Sr.'s boss, Labor Secretary Elaine L. Chao, knows about having family members in government. Her husband is Sen. Mitch McConnell (R-Ky.), and her department's top lawyer, Labor Solicitor Eugene Scalia, is the son of Supreme Court Justice Antonin Scalia.

Other families populating the Bush administration included the Mehman brothers (Ken and Bruce), McClellans, Powells (Colin L. as secretary of state and son Michael as chair of the Federal Trade Commission), Ted Cruz and wife Heidi.

> Also on the fairgrounds are FCC commissioner Kevin Martin, married to Cheney aide Cathie Martin, and Cheney aide Nina Rees, spouse of White House speechwriter Matthew Rees. The brother of National Economic Council staffer John Ackerly begins work later this year on the president's Council of Economic Advisers. OMB spokesman Chris Ullman served in the administration with his wife, Kris, until the couple's daughter was born 14 weeks ago. 'She's never worked in the administration,' he says of the infant."
> Then there are the inter-branch families. . . .[52]

Paul Krugman commented that what was interesting about this roll call (just partially recounted here) "is how little comment, let alone criticism" it had occasioned. He thought it "symptomatic of a broader phenomenon: inherited status is making a comeback"; he connected it to the rise of inequality of wealth, the stunting of class mobility, and the passing on of inherited privilege. "The official ideology of America's elite remains one of meritocracy, just as our political leadership pretends to be populist." The mantra of family values, he noted, means "the value of coming from the right family."[53]

The Obama administration also engaged in nepotism, though perhaps to a lesser degree. Critics complained most about his bringing loyal associates from Chicago into the administration, as well as ties between the White House and top executives of the news media. "ABC News President Ben Sherwood is the brother of Elizabeth Sherwood-Randall, a top national security adviser. . . . His counterpart at CBS news division, president David Rhodes, is the brother of Benjamin Rhodes, a key foreign-policy specialist. CNN's deputy Washington bureau chief, Virginia Mosley, is married to Tom Nides, who until earlier this year was deputy secretary of state. . . . Further, White House Press secretary Jay Carney's wife is Claire Shipman, veteran reporter for ABC. And NPR's White House correspondent, Ari Shapiro, is married to a lawyer, Michael Gottleib, who joined the White House counsel's office in April [2013]." While these connections feed right-wing paranoia regarding the news media's presumed "liberal bias," they are business as usual among the political class.[54]

During the Obama presidency watchdogs of nepotism have focused on offspring and wives of former legislators and governors winning election to the same seats their parents occupied, or in the case of Lisa Murkowski of Alaska, being appointed to a Senate seat vacated by her father, governor Frank Murkowski (R-AK). The favoritism shown to the daughters and sons of Congress has also attracted attention. Among the more egregious cases, Heather Bresch, Sen. Joe Manchin's (D-WV) daughter—whose M.A. on her résumé was not earned—in 2012 became CEO of Mylan Inc., a Fortune 500 pharmaceuticals company that benefited from millions in tax breaks while Manchin was governor of West Virginia. (In 2016 Bresch was in the middle of a Martin Shkreli–like scandal and congressional investigation because the firm, no stranger to scandal and self-dealing, had raised the price of EpiPen, an emergency anti-allergy injector, 500 percent to $600.) Senator Ron Wyden's (D-OR) son graduated from Columbia and moved right into management of his own hedge fund, "no doubt capitalizing on contacts he made interning at the $19-billion hedge fund of one of his father's supporters, David Shaw." A former manager of the Shaw fund commented: "Not many college kids get to intern on a D.E. Shaw portfolio for the summer." Nathan Daschle, son of our old friend Tom, went from Harvard Law to a stint at a Washington law firm that quickly qualified him to move to executive director of the Democratic Governors Association, then to vice-president for Clear Channel Media. The children of members of Congress also populate the ranks of well-paid lobbyists.[55]

Then there is the rampant nepotism in the media, no discussion of which is complete without mention of Chelsea Clinton, hired by NBC in 2011 as a television journalist (while her mother was secretary of state), at a salary of $600,000 annually. When she left that post in August 2014, *New York* magazine commented that Clinton "will no longer pretend to be a reporter," noting that she was being paid about $26,724 for every minute she was televised. Before leaving she switched to a month-to-month contract, "not because she was being paid an insane amount of money *to do almost nothing*" but because of her pregnancy and her mother's probable run for the presidency. Executives at NBC praised Clinton for bringing attention to stories involving good causes associated with her charity work.[56]

Chelsea Clinton symbolizes a celebrity made into a faux journalist, but television is now inundated with what media critic William McGowan calls "media legacies." As early as 2003, well before *l'affaire Chelsea*, McGowan pointed to CNN's Andrea Koppel, daughter of Ted, Anderson Cooper, son of Gloria Vanderbilt, Jeffrey Toobin, whose mother Marlene Sanders was at CBS and father Jerry Toobin at NBC for many years. Mario Cuomo's son Chris with no journalistic training went to ABC, then CNN; NBC hired John Seigenthaler, son of a prominent editor, and Fox took on Douglas Kennedy, son of RFK, and Chris Wallace, son of Mike. Jackie Kucinich, daughter of Dennis, former congressman and presidential candidate, joined the *Hill* at age twenty-four, launching a stellar career in journalism and television. There are many others: Bill Kristol; two sons of Ronald Reagan; Serena Altschul of MTV News and CBS News, daughter of Social Register parents; Fox's Peter Doocy, son of Steve of *Fox and Friends*, and still more.[57]

NBC, referred to by many media critics as the Nepotism Broadcasting Company, leads in media legacies and hiring children of media big shots with famous names (e.g., Mark Halperin, Willie Geist, Mika Brzezinski, Ronan Farrow, Abby Huntsman). When Chelsea arrived she joined Jenna Bush, daughter of George; Meghan McCain, daughter of John; Cody Gifford, son of Kathy Lee; and Luke Russett, son of Tim, hired at age twenty-two right out of college immediately after his father's death. This led the *Guardian's* Glenn Greenwald to release this tweet: "I really want to see a Meet the Press roundtable with Luke Russett, Chelsea Clinton, Jeanna Bush, and Megan McCain." When NBC began promoting its 2014 production of *Peter Pan* featuring anchor Brian Williams's twenty-six-year-old daughter Allison, who had zero experience in musical theater, one media critic gave the company another label: "tackiest house on the street."[58]

Echoing Bellow's comment that "no one wants to be accused of nepotism," against all evidence to the contrary, the *Daily Beast's* Clare Moran concluded her scathing report of Washington nepotism by recommending that "American children born with silver spoons in their mouths looking to use the family name ought to be given a hair shirt and a Rodney Dangerfield DVD on their 18th birthdays—they'll spend the rest of their lives alternatively seeking absolution for their privilege and getting no respect on account of it." Really? Does Moran see any of the beneficiaries of nepotism seeking absolution? Is Moran not aware that we live in The Age of Luke Russert, whom young journalists in Washington reportedly love to hate "as a bloodsport," in part because of his effortless ascent and in part from their resentment at a Capitol awash in nepotism. Luke Russert, who inherited his father's confidence and swagger, has responded to the hatred by saying he could care less. Whether the field is literature, television, entertainment, or politics, the hallmark of this New Gilded Age of Inequality is "naked, unabashed favoritism," and the shameless effrontery of those who give and receive it.[59]

Media critic William McGowan, noting the belated coverage news organizations gave to the excesses of the One Percent that visited recession and hardship on countless millions, attributed media myopia to legacies favoring "the kids of this self-dealing elite." "It's not just about inherited privilege at a time of increasing class stratification, shrinking opportunities and the corruption of the ideal of meritocracy." It's also about scant newsroom dollars paying "media brats far more than they are worth for journalism that is often insular and out of touch." They are ill-equipped, he believes, to understand two of the country's most pressing problems: "social distance and social trust, especially between the elite and the middle." Children of privilege who have moved to the head of the line might not be in the best position, for example, to cover admissions in higher education, increasingly competitive and with elite universities dominated by the affluent. How might "media legacies" honestly and without embarrassment cover "alumni legacies"?[60]

McGowan argues that not only do these privileged members of the "Lucky Sperm Club" increase the public's distrust of the media, but in an age of extreme economic inequality they bring a narrow vision born of their privilege. "Class has long been a press weakness," he writes, "and represents one of its most significant blind spots—encouraging socio-economic obliviousness." Despite talk of "media diversity, class is still given short shrift." And the "faces and names associated with the 'media legacies' inevitably help reinforce the widely-held impression of a journalistic elite that is increasingly out of touch" with average people in everyday life.[61]

New York Times columnist David Brooks and others have observed that the media's distance from ordinary people not in the income bracket of a *Times* columnist led to their failure to connect to the sense of economic dispossession rampant among Trump voters. "Many in the media, especially me, did not understand how they would express their alienation. We expected Trump to fizzle because we were not socially intermingled with his supporters and did not listen carefully enough."[62]

Brooks's paper itself participates in oligarchical favoritism, regularly reviewing books by members of its staff while hundreds of thousands of authors across the country wonder what they need to do to get a review in the "Gray Lady." In an egregious case involving the admittedly talented son of former contributor Frank Rich, in April 2013 the paper gave extraordinary coverage to a novel by Nathaniel Rich (whose mother is Gail Winston, an executive editor at Harper-Collins). The paper first reviewed Nathaniel's novel in the Arts section, then in Sunday's book review; the "Editor's Choice" section of the review listed Rich's novel second. In January Nathaniel and brother Simon, a *New Yorker* contributor and one of the youngest writers ever hired by *Saturday Night Live*, had been the subject of a *Times* feature story about literary families.[63]

One critic of this episode rightly called it a case of "mild nepotism" illustrating the "illusion of meritocracy." It also exemplifies a cross-institutional oligarchy whose social capital blocks opportunity for others. From government to the literary world across every field of endeavor, nepotism promotes the children of the successful and wealthy.

Copyright 2014 Newsday and amNEWYORK.
Reprinted by permission of Jimmy Margulies.

Chapter 4

The Permanent Campaign
and the Permanent Political Class

In 1976 as Jimmy Carter prepared to assume the presidency, a twenty-six-year-old aide, Patrick Caddell, gave him what became a historic memo, that "governing with public approval requires a continuing political campaign." In 1980 journalist Sidney Blumenthal, who later worked for President Bill Clinton, published *The Permanent Campaign: Inside the World of Elite Political Operatives*, a prescient book that described the rise in American politics of governing as campaigning, a strategy already well established.[1]

Blumenthal attributed this development to the decline of political parties and the ascent of television as the principal means by which candidates connected with voters. Political consultants, the key players in the permanent campaign, had replaced the old party bosses and shaped candidates' images and messages in ways party leaders had never done. Pragmatic consultants pursued no "idealistic social goals," just winning.[2]

"The permanent campaign" has a second meaning, referring to members of Congress becoming preoccupied with raising money immediately after one election to prepare for the next. By the mid-1980s members devoted themselves to stoking their campaign war chests throughout the cycle. In the Senate, what *Slate*'s Dave Levinthal described as a "desperate, hungry, and even uncouth hunt for [campaign] cash" has often influenced senators' decisions to retire—along with the pull of the millions to be made lobbying.[3] In both senses the permanent campaign has led to the maintenance, expansion, and entrenchment of the permanent political class.

Blumenthal described the permanent campaign without much attention to assessing its consequences. Twenty years later two prominent political scientists, Norman J. Ornstein and Thomas E. Mann, published a collection of essays weighing the costs and benefits of the permanent campaign and came down on the side of its costs. A winning campaign for the presidency morphs seamlessly into governing. Consultants move into the White House and begin to shape "policy messages and frame issues for advantage in the next campaign." The legislative agenda is tested in polls and focus groups, while partisan allies and adversaries conduct advertising campaigns "indistinguishable from electioneering."

Any politically attentive citizen would agree with the authors that reporters tend to cover elections as "horse races" and policy battles in Washington "with the focus on who is winning and who is losing . . . and not on the stakes involved."[4] Ornstein and Mann concluded that the permanent campaign does too little to inform voters and has contributed to the rise of public cynicism and disengagement.[5]

What the historian Daniel Boorstin in 1960 labeled *pseudoevents* now dominate the twenty-four-hour cable news cycle. "They are not spontaneous real events," as political scientist Hugh Heclo described them, "but orchestrated happenings that occur because someone has planned, incited, or otherwise brought them into being for the purpose of being observed and swaying opinion." To explain them, political consultants appear continuously on cable news programs.[6] But beyond "celebrity" such highly visible consultants like James Carville, Mary Matalin, Dick Morris, Caddell, Frank Luntz, Karl Rove, Paul Begala, and others, the ranks of the permanent campaign have clearly widened. Its operatives now include lobbyists, journalists, television correspondents, fund-raisers, political action committees, wealthy donors, corporate executives, staffers, members of the executive and legislative branches, and "bundlers."

Bundlers, Billionaires, and Super PACs

Bundlers are partisan activists who are in business, corporate CEOs, lobbyists, hedge-fund managers, or campaign staffers, not necessarily wealthy themselves, who raise funds for their favored candidate and "bundle" the checks and channel them to the campaign. In 2000 George W. Bush had a network of bundlers known as "Pioneers" who each pledged to raise $100,000; in 2005 his "Rangers" promised to raise $200,000 each. In 2008 Hilary Clinton's "Hillraisers" aimed to raise $100,000, while Barack Obama recruited dozens of bundlers for his National Finance Committee, each committed to delivering at least $250,000. Although candidate and then president Obama declared his commitment to "transparency," he was slow to identify his bundlers and later provided ranges of their dollar amounts rather than specific figures. In this way, too, Obama turned out to be less different from Washington's political class: his cadre of bundlers included prominent lobbyists.[7]

Bundlers work for presidential candidates for various reasons: some out of partisan loyalty; some from ideological motivations, as with Hollywood gays and lesbians who raised more money for Obama's 2012 campaign than celebrities organized by George Clooney. Bundlers act also for more pragmatic considerations. The Center for Public Integrity determined that dozens of Obama's elite donors—"many of them wealthy business figures—[were] appointed to advisory panels and commissions that can play a role in setting government policy. . . . And some have snagged lucrative government contracts that benefit their business interests or investment portfolios." Many had access to exclusive White House parties and gala social events.[8] This reward system is routine for any administration.

The real prize for a bundler is an ambassadorship. Like his predecessors, Obama appointed former bundlers to "plum diplomatic posts." In 2014 twenty-three of them—nearly 80 percent of the biggest fund-raisers—occupied postings that included Singapore; New Zealand and Samoa; the Netherlands; Germany; France and Monaco; and Belgium. Telecom executive Donald H. Gips, a friend of the president who bundled more than $500,000 for Obama in 2008, not only became ambassador to South Africa, but his company, Level 3 Communications, in which he retained stock, received federal stimulus contracts worth millions. (Gips said he was "unaware" of those grants.)[9]

Some professional bundlers usually receive monthly retainers, which can go as high as $25,000 a month during a campaign. But a new kind of highly paid fund-raiser has emerged sparking controversy, modeled on "donor-advised funds" that have grown spectacularly in the realm of charitable giving. These funds provide clients a profitable way to give to their favorite causes and to offset capital gains taxes, a mechanism that has become increasingly popular since passage of the American Taxpayer Relief Act of 2012. In early 2015 Mary Pat Bonner's fund-raising firm was raising money for Hillary Clinton's as yet undeclared campaign when a *New York Times* report revealed that she took a commission of 12.5 percent on the millions flowing in. Many fund-raisers believe this practice unethical, and some donors want all their money to go directly to the candidate and not to a middleman.[10]

Since *Citizens United* and *McCutcheon*, the importance of bundlers who collect checks from many individuals is declining, at least in the early stages of a presidential campaign. As the 2016 campaign got underway Super PACs started to displace bundlers, with corporations and independent billionaires able to give unlimited amounts. Sheldon Adelson, the billionaire entrepreneur and casino owner, spent $100 million supporting Republican candidates in the 2012 election, and the Koch brothers announced their intention to raise close to a billion dollars for 2016. Other billionaires who give to Republicans include oil moguls Robert Rowling and Harold Simmons and his wife Annette; Paul Singer, hedge fund manager; and Peter Theil, PayPal founder and early Facebook investor. Liberal billionaire George Soros supports many progressive causes and Democrats, and hedge fund manager Tom Steyer gives to Democrats and environmentally friendly Republicans.[11]

Billionaires with ideological agendas masked by charitable giving—now called "philanthrocapitalists"—engage continuously in permanent campaigns parallel to elections but designed to influence voters and policy. Robert Mercer, CEO of Renaissance Technologies, gives to PACs and also to research groups sniffing out "liberal bias" in the media and to the Heartland Institute, a hotbed of climate change denial. John D. Arnold, a former Enron executive, set up a foundation to campaign against public employee pension benefits, spending over $50 million in states across the country to roll back pensions. (Enron, the seventh largest company when it collapsed, wiped out $1.5 billion in public pension assets as thousands of its employees lost their pensions.) Arnold has extended his reach into such institutions as the Public Broadcast System, giving $3.5 million to New York's WNET to do a one-sided series on pensions (the station gave back the money after criticism) and an "education grant" to Brookings (probably $500,000) that eventually produced a report on the "unsustainability" of public pensions.[12]

The Laura and John Arnold Foundation has even donated to support independent investigative journalism centers such as ProPublica and the Center for Public Integrity. The CPI's grant of $2.8 million went to support the role of money in state politics, like the millions John has spread around in battles over state pension funds. So many have reasonably asked, can the CPI be impartial as it investigates PACs and money men like him who swoop in to any state of their choice?[13]

Paul Singer gave millions to pro-Israel groups to lobby against the Iran nuclear deal and led a group of other hedge fund executives in donating heavily to elect Republicans to the New York Senate who would increase funds to charter schools. Singer also chairs the board of the American Enterprise Institute, the think tank that the website *Inside Philanthropy* labeled "The Billionaire's Favorite Think Tank."[14]

Perhaps none of the "philanthrocapitalists" have penetrated as many institutions as the Koch brothers. Their campaign to spread the gospel of free enterprise, anti-regulation, and low taxes throughout universities and colleges alone astounds. Charles Koch's foundation gave $108 million to 366 colleges and universities from 2005 to 2014—and additional tens of millions since then. Often strings are attached, often denied by the educators accepting the money.[15]

Incumbents for Life

In his 2016 State of the Union Address, President Obama stated,

> We also need benefits and protections that provide a basic measure of security. After all, it's not much of a stretch to say that some of the only people in America who are going to work the same job, in the same place, with a health and retirement package, for 30 years, are sitting in this chamber.[16]

Election to Congress buys a ticket into the permanent political class for the great majority of winners, either by moving into lobbying or another government post or through long, gerrymandered incumbency. Incumbents are reelected at consistently overwhelming rates. As every midterm election approaches, the media gives the impression that a real contest looms, instead of what is mostly a pseudoevent. For decades candidates seeking reelection have succeeded at rates usually exceeding 90 percent; even in years when control of the House of Representatives shifted from one party to the other—1994, 2006, 2010—over 85 percent of incumbents won reelection. In 2014, as Republicans gained a majority in the Senate and an overwhelming majority in the House, 96.4 percent of House incumbents seeking reelection held on to their seats.[17]

Incumbency equals reelection begins with the partisan drawing of congressional district lines to create safe seats: gerrymandering, otherwise known as the incumbency protection racket. Both Democrats and Republicans occupy safe sinecures, though recently Republicans, through a concerted campaign to take over state legislatures, now hold more of them. Gerrymanders insure noncompetitive elections won by more than 55 percent or more of the vote; winning percentages often exceed 60 and 70 percent.[18]

Incumbents retain their seats for other reasons. Their office budgets provide them with staff in Washington and their districts, personnel whose jobs depend on the legislator staying in office, so they are motivated campaign workers. Members have travel allowances enabling trips "back home," more frequent during election season, and free postage for mailings to constituents informing them of the terrific job their representative is doing on their behalf.

More importantly, once attained incumbency confers a significant financial advantage over challengers, on average, about $500,000. A study of narrowly won elections from 1990 to 2010 found that whether a Democrat or Republican won the election, in the next election the winner (and now incumbent) received a boost from "access-oriented interest groups." These donors differed from "ideological" investors who stuck with one party or the other; rather, they wanted payback. They accounted for about two-thirds of incumbents' financial advantage and were making a large one-time investment to insure "long-standing connections." In the August 2015 Republican primary presidential debate Donald Trump's boast of getting what he wanted from elected officials illustrated the point: "When they call, I give. And you know what? When I need something from them, two years later, three years later, I call them, and they are there for me. That's a broken system." Not one of his nine rivals on stage took issue with him.[19]

In the early 1990s a movement gathered momentum across the country focused on limiting terms of members in state legislatures and Congress. Although generated in large part by Republicans weary of long decades of Democrats' control of the House of Representatives, it drew popular support from across partisan lines and from independents. By 1994 many states had limited the terms of state legislators, and twenty-three had placed limits on their congressional representatives. But the next year the Supreme Court held that states could not set limits on federal offices, and the "Republican revolution" in the 1994 midterms gave them control of both houses of Congress for the first time in forty years, taking most of the steam out of the effort. Aside from occasional retirements and upsets, the absence of term limits for Congress allows many legislators to remain in office for decades, unless they migrate to the big salaries on K Street.

"Think Tanks": The Shadow Branch

Washington's think tanks can claim to have created an immense amount of change that has reshaped our nation and the world. . . . Think tanks have a quiet power that government either lacks or is unwilling to use. They bring together leaders and experts who should meet but whom government can't convene publically.[20]

Although many think tanks produce useful research and policy papers, the benign view just quoted from a think tank scholar is not shared by all who study them, and some purported research centers are nothing more than shills for corporate America. Both ad hoc as well as some long-established, self-described "independent" think tanks engage in propaganda on behalf of industries that fund them. Some dispense made-up "science" to deny climate change and attack global warming experts and environmental regulations; some have defended the tobacco industry and pollution by agribusiness, or mounted public relations campaigns to whitewash flawed products.[21]

Across a wide range of advocacy Washington's think tanks constitute another overlapping network within the political class, and their policy "experts" routinely participate in the permanent campaign. Former legislators and government officials, journalists, corporate officials, and lobbyists frequently move into them, joining policy-minded academics. The directors, board members, and staffs of such well-known and prestigious think tanks as the center-liberal Brookings Institution and the conservative Heritage Foundation, American Enterprise Institute (AEI), and Hoover Foundation (among others) move through a revolving door between them and the executive branch. Since the 1970s right-wing think tanks have waged a permanent ideological campaign to diminish government and promote a "free market," the latter meaning anything that increases corporate profits and the income of the wealthy.

Considerable overlap exists between lobbying firms and the advocacy practiced by the top think tanks. Most American citizens are perhaps unaware of the extensive influence of these institutions whose denizens are unelected, though many perhaps read opinion pieces written by their members in major newspapers or see their policy experts interviewed on television programs.

Some think tanks often generate reports in the public interest, even those that are explicitly focused on advocacy. But for many of the best known, the reality is quite different. In addition to administrations, think tanks are intertwined with political parties, corporate elites, and interest groups. During Barack Obama's presidency some right-wing think tanks functioned virtually as part of the Republican opposition.

Industrial magnate and philanthropist Andrew Carnegie founded the Carnegie Endowment for International Peace in 1910; it was followed by the Brookings Institution in 1916. Globally there are now hundreds of think tanks, but Washington, D.C., contains the most, with 396 in 2014, and many more nearby in Virginia. Most of the roughly two dozen top think tanks try to balance their claims to independence with their ideological and partisan frames of reference. Sociologist Thomas Medvetz pointed to the Republican-aligned Heritage Foundation to argue that think tanks *"blur the boundaries"* between partisanship and independence.[22] Critics see less "blurring" and more partisanship.

The reason for quote marks around "Think Tanks" in the heading of this section obtains from a skeptical comment by the late journalist Jonathan Rowe of the *Washington Monthly* who earlier served as an aide to Senator Byron Dorgan (D-NE): the name *think tanks*, he wrote, is a misnomer: "they don't think, they justify."[23]

The long rise of conservative think tanks has been well told by Kim Phillips-Fein in her excellent book *Invisible Hands: The Making of the Conservative Movement from the New Deal to Reagan*. Conservative reaction to the New Deal planted the seeds of the ideological campaign to extol the free market and attack liberalism. When the many protest movements of the 1960s inspired by the civil rights movement proliferated and seemed to threaten the free enterprise system itself, corporate elites and increasingly reactionary billionaires stole a march on progressives and began to prevail in a war of ideas by pouring money into institutes, journals, foundations, and university campuses to propagate a corporate- and business-friendly viewpoint calling for lower taxes and less regulation. One result was an enormous growth of conservative think tanks in the 1970s and 1980s; progressives were late in getting into the game.[24]

By the 1990s conservative centers enjoyed an entrenched media presence, as well as an aura of neutrality, usually referenced by reporters without a label. From 1995 to 1997, one survey found, right-leaning think tanks "provided more than half of major media's think-tank citations . . . 53 percent of citations, while progressive or left-leaning think tanks received just 16 percent of total citations." In a random sample of the top four institutions, three of them conservative along with the centrist Brookings, none were labeled. (Brookings has often been labeled "liberal," but its political orientation at times has shifted to the center.) In a sample of 229 citations, Brookings escaped labels 78 percent of the time. The Heritage Foundation was not identified as right-wing in 68 percent of 182 cases.[25] The many conservative tanks have benefited most from the media's lack of labeling.[26]

Presidential candidates at least since Jimmy Carter have relied heavily on think tanks, a now common occurrence. Carter, a one-term governor of Georgia, moved to establish his foreign policy and national security credentials by accepting the invitation of David Rockefeller and Zbigniew Brzezinski to join the prestigious Trilateral Commission, founded in 1973 "to bring together leaders from the private sector" to discuss matters of global concern. Brzezinski, the commission's first director and later national security advisor to President Carter, claimed that "all the key foreign policy decision makers of the Carter administration had served" in the organization. Carter also recruited fifty-four members of the Council on Foreign Relations as well as several from Brookings. Candidate Ronald Reagan relied heavily on the Hoover Institution, the Center for Strategic and International Study, the Committee on the Present Danger (CPD), and AEI, eventually bringing dozens of their staff and associates into his administration. The CPD is virtually a lobby for the defense industry, which received huge outlays of federal money during the 1980s. With Reagan's ascension, too, the Heritage Foundation entered "into the big leagues," according to Medvetz, and became the preeminent conservative think tank.[27]

President George H. W. Bush distanced himself generally from think tanks and specifically from Reagan's advisors because he wanted to get out from under his predecessor's shadow. But think tank personnel populated Bill Clinton's campaign and administration, notably the centrist Democratic Leadership Council and the liberal Progressive Policy Institute. President George W. Bush drew heavily from the ranks of former Reagan advisors, including AEI, Project for the New American Century, and Hoover.[28]

A small think tank founded in 2007 by former Clinton advisors, the Center for New American Security, became a key player in the new Obama administration, providing many of its initial national security officials. But most intertwined with the Obama administration was the Center for American Progress, founded in 2003 by centrist Democrats and liberal billionaires. Increasingly throughout his two terms, President Obama relied on CAP for high-level appointments, especially in the environmental and energy fields.[29]

John Podesta, known as "the most powerful unelected Democrat," served as the first chair of CAP. His résumé reflects the interconnections between think tanks, Democratic administrations, lobbyists, and corporations. While holding many prestigious staff positions on Capitol Hill, including counselor to Senate Majority Leader Tom Daschle (1995–96), Podesta and his brother Tony founded the Podesta Group, perhaps the most influential Democratic lobbying firm in Washington. Its clients include some of the nation's largest corporations, including Walmart, BP, and Lockheed Martin. A valued advisor to President Clinton, he steadied the ship during the storm of Clinton's sex scandal. In January 2014 Podesta left CAP and joined the Obama White House as an advisor on environmental issues, pushing the president to act aggressively with executive orders to protect the environment. A year later he left to become chief of Hillary Clinton's presidential campaign. While Podesta was the most high profile of CAP's staff to work in Obama's administration, the revolving door between it and CAP was "spinning furiously" throughout Obama's time in office.[30]

For years now "researchers" have traveled back and forth between think tanks and lobbying firms. One study found at least forty-nine individuals "who have simultaneously worked as lobbyists for outside entities while serving as top staff, directors or trustees of 20 of the 2 most influential think tanks . . .as ranked by the Think Tanks and Civil Societies Program at the University of Pennsylvania." The CAP, for example, has registered lobbyists on its staff, including senior fellow Scott Lilly, a national security analyst, who lobbied for Lockheed Martin for six years up to 2011.[31]

A 2016 series in the *New York Times* revealed the results of its investigation of seventy-five think tanks. Dozens of scholars conducted research at think tanks while "corporations were paying them to help shape government policy," and many "simultaneously worked as registered lobbyists, members of corporate boards or outside consultants in litigation or regulatory disputes," seldom disclosing their dual roles. Thus think tanks have operated as another valuable extension of corporate power over government policy.[32]

Think tanks, real and otherwise, have advocated for the numerous for-profit colleges that the Obama administration sought to regulate more tightly. But in and out of Congress the for-profits have powerful allies.[33] These ubiquitous institutions—like payday loan shops, but with much more pretentious come-ons—cover the nation's landscape. They have grown rapidly in the last two decades because they offer the promise of good-paying careers to low-income students and veterans. From 1998 to 2008 their enrollment increased by 225 percent, accounting for 10–13 percent of all college students. As the for-profits' revenue stream topped $30 billion a year it came from largely taxpayer money financing student loans. Numerous studies have shown most of them to be predatory, to little regulatory effect, because the for-profits are entwined with the political class and make hefty campaign contributions to federal and state legislators. Some members of Congress and other government officials are investors and profiteers.[34]

The recent failure of Corinthian Colleges, one of the most corrupt for-profits, revealed an extensive web of relationships between lobbyists, think tanks, Republican PACs, government officials, and members of Congress. Corinthian, a publically traded for-profit with 74,000 students at over a hundred campuses, went bankrupt in June 2014; most of its $1.6 billion in annual revenue came from federal student aid. The Consumer Financial Protection Bureau charged the institution with pressuring students to enroll using predatory loan tactics, by defining job placement as any employment lasting one day and paying employers to hire students temporarily, and falsifying job-placement data. Corinthian's tuition and fees for a bachelor's degree totaled from $60,000 to $75,000, higher than most public alternatives. Once students fell into debt, they were harassed by debt-collection agencies.[35]

Corinthian cultivated support from the political class with contributions to Karl Rove's Crossroads PAC and hired two lobbying firms and two "public affairs" companies (one founded by an Obama advisor and the other by a former Reagan administration official). Its creditors included groups that have fought regulation of the for-profit industry: the U.S. Chamber of Commerce, and the American Legislative Exchange Council (ALEC), a faux think tank and right-wing author of state laws favoring corporations and notorious for pushing "stand your ground" gun laws through many state chambers. Among Corinthian's creditors, too, was the American Enterprise Institute, which repeatedly criticized the Obama administration's "bloodlust" for trying to regulate for-profits, and which defended Corinthian specifically.[36]

Corinthian's bankruptcy reveals the political class in its full mode of masked quid pro quo through the gift economy, its influence reaching into some unexpected places. Corinthian made payments to such shadow supporters as former defense secretary Leon Panetta, Urban League President Marc Morial, and Sharon Robinson, CEO of the nonprofit American Association of Colleges for Teacher Education. Robinson, like Morial an African American, appears as a board member on the website of Jobs for America's Graduates, which includes her connection with Corinthian and describes her as a "lifelong civil rights activist."[37] The Urban League's Morial has denounced ALEC for its advocacy of "stand your ground" and "despicable" voter ID laws and as "the shadow author of numerous pieces of legislation aimed at boosting corporate power and profits, reducing worker rights, weakening environmental protections, and restricting voter rights." Yet Morial, perhaps unaware of ALEC's ties to Corinthian, had no hesitation accepting a $1 million gift to the Urban League from Jack Massimino, the school's CEO. Morial not only praised Corinthian for its "long history of preparing students for careers that are in demand," but also wrote an op ed in the *Washington Post* attacking the Obama administration's proposed regulations. Somehow he missed the criticism of Corinthian by other civil rights groups, including the NAACP, National Council of La Raza, and the Leadership Conference.[38]

Even as Corinthian declared bankruptcy in 2015, the nation's largest accrediting organization decided that Corinthian was maintaining standards—not surprising since the Accrediting Council for Independent Colleges and Schools has been riddled with conflicts of interest. Some two-thirds of its board worked as executives at for-profit colleges, including ITT, also accredited during years of fraud investigations. In 2015 the ACICS gave its seal of approval to over 240 institutions receiving $4.7 billion in taxpayer money. One of those, Education Management Corporation, which runs 110 trade schools and was investigated or sued by prosecutors in twelve states, received over $1.25 billion of that sum. In September 2016 the Education Department finally decided to take away its authority to accredit. Meanwhile, as for-profit colleges have been put on the defensive, despite their clout with Congress and the permanent political class, owners of for-profits are switching their schools to nonprofits, "freeing them from the regulatory burdens of for-profit colleges, while continuing to reap the personal financial benefits of for-profit ownership." They become, in effect, covert for-profits.[39]

Attorneys general in more than thirty states are cooperating in an effort to end the abuses of the for-profits, but the industry's resources are formidable. It also has strong allies on Wall Street, where the biggest are publically traded.[40] Quad Partners, a New York private equity firm, has invested heavily, and its founder, who opposes any regulation, has acquired a controlling stake in a major educational publication, *Inside Higher Ed*. Another aggressive defender of the industry has been Donald Graham, formerly of the *Washington Post*, who wrote editorials attacking the Obama administration's attempt at regulation without disclosing the Post Company's ownership of Kaplan, Inc., a huge for-profit chain. Before Graham sold the *Post* to Jeff Bezos of Amazon, Kaplan accounted for 55 percent of the Post Company's revenue. In 2012 Kaplan joined ALEC for a year, along with other for-profits, because of the "think tank's" aggressive defense of for-profit colleges and its opposition to government regulation. Among the "model laws" that ALEC's board of corporate officials and legislators sent out to states was a resolution claiming for-profits were "open-access systems, that serve students at the least expense." By then at least four state attorneys general were investigating Kaplan, 68 percent of whose students drop out before graduating. Graham argued vehemently in editorials that holding for-profits accountable would harm low-income students.[41]

Republicans, once critical of for-profit colleges as debt traps, have become their staunch defenders. ALEC functions as a politically active, highly partisan lobbying organization whose corporate flacks recruit state legislators to introduce "model" bills churned out by the businessmen. It is a creation of some of the most reactionary corporations and billionaires, including David and Charles Koch, a key component of the ideological warfare the Kochs have waged for more than three decades—for example, to deny global warming and defend their right to pollute the air and water. They have specialized in "astroturf" entities with deceptive names suggesting they are grassroots organizations. Their main lobbying arm, Americans for Prosperity (AFP), has evolved from an energizer of the Tea Party movement in 2009–11 into a full-fledged campaign organization with hundreds of operatives in fifty states that backed Republicans in the 2016 election.[42]

Some of the work of AFP's predecessor, Citizens for a Sound Economy (CSE), illustrates the symbiotic relationship between fake-grassroots or astroturf nonprofits and corporate interests. In 1998 CSE launched an eventually successful campaign opposing a multibillion-dollar federal plan to restore the Florida Everglades. Shortly after, CSE received $700,000 in contributions from

Florida's three biggest sugar companies. Rewarded by corporate funding, CSE took on many other causes: denying global warming (Exxon Corp.), opposing higher cigarette taxes (Philip Morris Cos.), maintaining car rental companies' limited liability in Florida (Hertz and Huisenga Holdings), phone deregulation benefiting US West Inc. ($1 million contribution), and many more. The *National Journal* described CSE's "grass roots" activities as "a fig leaf for corporate lobbying efforts." Gary Ruskin of the Congressional Accountability Project said, "It's part of a rent-a-mouthpiece phenomenon."[43]

AFP succeeded CSE in 2003 and has continued to launch deceptive "citizens'" campaigns to benefit big business. Registered under the IRS code as a 501(c)(4), it is a tax-free nonprofit and does not need to disclose its donors. AFP has ramped up its political spending: $122 million to defeat Obama in 2012, $129 million in 2014; and after attracting a media storm of attention with plans to spend close to $1 billion in 2016, it drew back after Trump's nomination to lay out $122 million. Of course, the Kochs' network of allied PACs and billionaires spent additional tens of millions. In early 2017 the Kochs announced plans to spend $300 to $400 million for the 2018 congressional and state elections. AFP manufactures the appearance of grassroots activism by instructing its paid demonstrators to carry handmade signs.[44]

Conservative think tanks are not the only ones with ties to large corporations and Wall Street. Until recently, the liberal Center for American Progress, which scolded conservative counterparts for not disclosing donors, was itself reluctant to reveal its backers, which in fact included big banks, lobbying firms, and corporations. Contributions from the health care industry poured in to CAP while it supported the Affordable Care Act. Further, CAP also did a favor for a corporate ally, praising an alternative energy company, First Solar, after the company received a $3.73 billion federal loan guarantee; CAP strongly advocates alternative energy. Critics have accused CAP of having tailored some of its research and policy reports to favor the Obama administration.[45]

Ken Silverstein, a progressive journalist and sharp critic of think tanks, concedes that "there are plenty of well-respected scholars at prominent Beltway think-tank positions." But he points out that as with politicians, they are caught up in a perpetual cycle of fund-raising. Donors have become more result-oriented, and if they disapprove of the results they get, they move on. "Think tanks are competing with consulting firms, law firms, Super PACS, lobbyists and advocacy groups," observed James McGann, director of the Think Tanks and

Civil Societies Program at the University of Pennsylvania. "That puts pressure on [them] to be more responsive to donors." Thus, they move further toward public relations, special pleading, and lobbying.[46]

Even the prestigious Brookings Institution, perhaps the most disinterested of the bunch, had its reputation stained by the revelation that it accepted money from foreign governments while advocating policies that benefit the donor governments. Brookings was hardly alone among Washington think tanks in accepting tens of millions for essentially lobbying for foreign governments. Routinely the recipients host forums and organize private briefings for senior U.S. policy makers and produce papers reflecting the foreign governments' agendas. Exactly how much foreign money has flowed to think tanks is not known, but since 2011 at least sixty-four foreign governments or their agents have contributed to twenty-eight major U.S. research organizations. Most of the countries involved are in Europe, the Middle East, and Asia, among them many oil-producing nations. The United Arab Emirates gave the Center for Strategic and International Studies over $1 million to help build its new headquarters; in 2013 Qatar, another oil producer, made a $14.8 million, four-year donation to Brookings, helping to fund an affiliate in Qatar and a project on U.S. relations with the Islamic world. Indeed, journalist Jeffrey Goldberg reported that he heard an Obama administration official refer to Massachusetts Avenue, where many Arab-funded tanks are located, as "Arab-occupied territory."[47]

Brookings also developed a new interest in legalizing marijuana after a 2012 visit from a lawyer representing billionaire Peter B. Lewis, who had late in life embraced decriminalization and, before he died in 2013, gave the institute $500,000. Subsequently, the *Washington Post* reported that the think tank "emerged as a hub of research" supporting legalization, organizing seminars and churning out research papers and op-eds.[48]

Executives at Washington think tanks firmly defend their neutrality, arguing that overlap with donors' views and those of their scholars is coincidental. "Our currency is our credibility," said Frederick Kempe, head of the Atlantic Council, which "promotes constructive leadership and engagement in foreign affairs" and has taken in money from at least twenty-five countries since 2008. An internal report of the Norwegian Foreign Affairs Ministry, however, observed that "it is difficult for a small country to gain access to powerful politicians, bureaucrats, and experts" in the Capitol: "Funding powerful think tanks is one way to gain such access, and some think tanks ... are openly conveying that they can service only those foreign governments that provide funding."[49]

In their relationships with donors, whether foreign countries or hedge fund billionaires, think tanks too mirror the gift economy that exists between Congress and business and lobbyists.

Bruce Bartlett is a historian and former advisor to President Reagan who served in the Treasury Department during the George W. Bush administration. A critic of how far to the right the Republican Party has moved, he recently condemned "The Alarming Corruption of the Think Tanks." For Bartlett and others the move of Jim DeMint (R-SC) from the Senate to become president of the Heritage Foundation symbolized the near complete turn to partisan activism of many think tanks, a shift already underway for years. DeMint, however, dropped all pretense of neutrality; he immediately set up a political arm called Heritage Action and launched a nine-city "Defund Obamacare Town Hall Tour." Although the foundation had taken on a partisan edge in the 1980s, DeMint's ascension marked its further evolution into the Tea Party Era. DeMint, of course, perhaps more than any other senator, had flaunted his association with the Tea Party movement.[50]

DeMint's new post likely boosted his $174,000 annual salary as a senator to well over $1 million: his lesser-known Heritage predecessor had made nearly $1.2 million in 2011. Drawing on increased donations from the likes of Chevron, Boeing, and conservative foundations that amounted to $174 million, at least nineteen other Heritage Foundation officials received salaries of over $200,000.

Top think tank executives routinely receive generous salaries: Arthur Brooks of AEI made $645,000 in 2011. Dick Cheney, no friend of heavy lifting, made $200,000 for allegedly serving on the board of trustees one hour per week. The Center for Strategic and International Studies, flush with Emirates money, paid former deputy secretary of defense John Hamre $402,000. Centrist and liberal think tanks also paid their leaders and board members very well. With assets of $410 million and $87 million in grants, Brookings paid its president Strobe Talbott, a former state department official, $476,000. Vice president Martin Indyk, former ambassador to Israel, made $336,000, and William Gale, a tax and retirement expert, took home $358,000.[51]

One "think tank," however, pays its creator nothing, because the Harding Institute for Freedom and Democracy does not exist. After the 2008 Republican presidential ticket of McCain and Palin went down to defeat, criticism of the former Alaska governor flowed freely from McCain aides. Fox News reported that one of them—unnamed—said that Sarah Palin did not know that Africa was a continent. Who made this claim? David Schuster, an MSNBC anchor, identified McCain policy advisor Martin Eisenstadt, who had "come forward" as the author of the claim. Unfortunately, Martin Eisenstadt did not exist either: he was a hoax that had been taking in reporters for months. *New York Times* reporter Richard Perez-Pena labeled him "A Senior Fellow at the Institute of Nonexistence."[52]

The Charitable-Industrial Complex: "The Revolution Will Not Be Funded"[53]

Many philanthropic foundations and nonprofits constitute an integral part of the permanent political class and are intertwined with present and former legislators and bureaucrats, lobbying firms, and think tanks. For the most part these organizations profess their aim of making the world a better place and in fact do improve the lives of millions of people. There are over thirty thousand such entities in the United States, and the largest are recipients of billions of dollars of federal grants (taxpayer money) and corporate donations. These economic giants wield enormous social and political power, and to a great extent, critics say, they use that power like other sectors of the political class to perpetuate themselves, to award themselves large salaries, and in effect to maintain the status quo.

"The Charitable-Industrial Complex" has grown rapidly in recent years, as Peter Buffett, son of Warren, pointed out in a provocative opinion piece in the *New York Times*. From 2001 to 2011 nonprofits increased by 25 percent, a rate faster than that of business or government. "It's a massive business, with approximately $316 billion given away in 2012 in the United States alone and more than 9.4 million employed."[54] Buffett's work with large, liberal foundations to which his father had given generously, however, made him skeptical of what appeared to be a gap between intended and actual results.

Buffet criticized "Philanthropic Colonialism," a concept not original with him, of donors applying solutions to local problems of which they had little knowledge. Further, at meetings with high government officials, investment managers, and corporate leaders he came to observe that all were "searching for answers with the right hand to problems that others in the room had created with their left." As vast amounts of wealth are being created for the few, he observed, some of the super rich engage in "conscience laundering." They feel better about themselves, but "this just keeps the existing structure of inequality in its place. The rich sleep better at night, while others get just enough to keep the pot from boiling over." The end result, he believes, is "a perpetual poverty machine."

Buffet's critique echoed equally trenchant analyses of philanthropy going back to the early twentieth-century Progressive Era when the super rich began setting up philanthropic foundations for both altruistic and pragmatic reasons. For decades, and especially since the 1980s and the Right's assault on government programs and funding, historians, social scientists, and locally based social activists have challenged the effectiveness and function of philanthropic foundations and the "Nonprofit Industrial Complex."

In dealing with the environment, for example, foundations have tended to bypass litigious and confrontational organizations such as Greenpeace and the Native Forest Council in favor of groups that tend to negotiate compromises with polluters. Across the philanthropic spectrum, the pattern has been repeated, according to Mark Dowie. (As an investigative reporter Dowie broke the stories of the defects in the Dalkon Shield and Ford Pinto in the 1970s.) Dowie says they are "indisputably plutocratic" and generally support middle-class rather than lower-class social movements.[55]

Many contemporary scholars who study foundations agree that they perpetuate inequality by funding safe activists and treating symptoms rather than causes. (Older readers will remember Tom Wolfe's 1970 blistering satirical treatment of guilty white celebrities in New York meeting with Black Panthers and besieged bureaucrats in poverty programs accommodating radical protesters but doing little to deal with poverty in *Radical Chic & Mau-Mauing the Flak Catchers*.) The editors of a wide-ranging collection of essays on nonprofits agreed with Dowie that the richest and most powerful foundations "channel the bulk of their resources toward elite class-based institutions [leaving] little money for those organizations serving the neediest members of society." They also point to the slashing of government budgets since the 1980s and right-wing think tanks' and foundations' relentless assault on federal programs. Conservatives insist that private philanthropy will fill the gap created by the rollback of New Deal and Great Society programs, but nonprofit spending does not come close to making up the difference. Meanwhile, reactionary corporations have spent millions to elect politicians who vote to defund social programs.[56]

Since at least the 1930s progressive critics have asserted that philanthropic programs have protected capitalism and maintained inequality. Radical critics continue to point to nonprofits' "co-optation" of social activists by "the ruling class," giving them professional jobs, diverting them from leadership roles in their communities, and orienting them to "the governmental and non-profit bureaucracies that employ them."[57]

Political scientist Jane Roelofs argues that foundations "buffer" social movements and protect the status quo, by absorbing "rising social power" and by essentially promoting and buying off effective activists "while diverting systemic challenges." The major liberal foundations "do this best, as they act in the long-range interests of the corporate world. Their trustees and staff are typical members of the power elite [or *the political class*], but they have added blacks, women, Hispanics, and others using a veneer of "diversity" to appear progressive and to deflect criticism."[58]

For years local activists have experienced what Roelofs describes, having become aware that in competing for nonprofit grants while professionalizing, social movements become separated from social justice. Thus unbought grassroots community organizers self-consciously distance themselves from foundations and nonprofits as well as from the political class. Their salaries and workplaces, not in some gleaming building in Washington, place them at a far remove from those of the executives of wealthy nonprofits. The salaries of the latter, along with their ties to government officials and politicians, place them in the top tier of the political class.

In 2011 the six highest paid nonprofit executives took in princely salaries worthy of Wall Street: Laurance Hoagland Jr., William and Flora Hewett Foundation, $2.5 million, not including $65,311 in medical coverage plus retirement benefits; John Seffrin, American Cancer Society, $2.1 million; Roxanne Spillett, Boys and Girls Clubs of America, $1.8 million; Reynold Levy, Lincoln Center for the Performing Arts, $1.4 million; and Michael Kaiser, JFK Center for the Performing Arts, $1.348 million. Of the four hundred charities the *Chronicle of Philanthropy* surveyed, in 2010 one-third provided bonuses to their executives, with $50,000 the median bonus. In 2012 thirty-four top executives of big charities earned $1 million or more. In the second tier almost seventy nonprofit CEOs earned between $500,000 and $1 million.[59]

Critics see these pay packages as "outrageously high." Defenders say they are needed to keep "top talent" and argue that these executives run complex multimillion-dollar enterprises. But the Charity Navigator website bristles with complaints from donors about over-the-top executive pay. The group's president, Ken Berger, says excessive salaries are *not* necessary to attract competent officials and declares that "arguing that those working for the benefit of the neediest people in our society should make millions and multimillions like corporate leaders defies common sense."

As the economy tanked in 2008–10 and budgets everywhere suffered, members of Congress and some state legislatures agreed with Berger. In 2010 four Republican senators held up a $425 million package of federal grants for the Boys and Girls Clubs of America after staff discovered the extraordinary compensation for head Roxanne Spillett and other executives. Such a package, said Senator Tom Coburn (R-OK) "is not only questionable on its face, but also raises questions about how the organization manages its finances in other areas." Forty percent of Boys and Girls Clubs' funds came from taxpayer money.[60]

After questioning by senators, Spillett said it was the worst day of her life and denied that her thirty-two-year career with the charity was motivated by money. She told board members—already defending her—to stop putting money into her very large retirement fund. Beyond Spillett's current compensation the senators wanted to know about the organization posting a loss of $13.6 million in 2008 while racking up travel expenses for executives of $4.3 million, $1.6 million on conferences, and $544,000 in lobbying fees. The latter aroused interest because the lobbying firm, recipient of $200,000 that could be confirmed, the rest in a black hole, did no documented lobbying, and the person receiving the money was not registered as a lobbyist. The senators also asked for an accounting of $54 million invested offshore and $53 million in private equity funds—while local clubs were closing.[61]

Spillett left the Boys and Girls Clubs the next year, her generous retirement package intact. The true measure of membership in the political class is what happens after a forced retirement: movement into a sinecure, good pay, and praise. The Mendoza College of Business at Notre Dame University hired Spillett to teach graduate students, and Scholarship America, a prestigious nonprofit, appointed her to its board. The websites of both organizations posted biographies fulsome in praise for her accomplishments at the Boys and Girls Clubs.

Although Spillett's salary and spending sparked the senators' ire, neither she nor any of the Clubs' top officials were accused of embezzlement. During her watch and after, however, local directors of Boys and Girls Clubs across the country were charged with stealing money—in places as diverse as Waterbury, Connecticut, La Habre, California, Franklin, Kentucky, Bay City, Michigan, Springfield, Missouri, and the Bronx, New York. Most embezzlers paid fines and did jail time. The sums involved, usually over a period of years, ranged from under $10,000 to over $400,000. This kind of graft seems endemic in a large, decentralized nonprofit organization and increased in the hard times of 2008–11.

But these local scandals pale in comparison to the hundreds of millions of dollars the central offices of major nonprofits lose routinely from embezzlement, fraud, or other wrongdoing. These enormous losses were recently revealed by a 2013 *Washington Post* investigation making use of the recent addition to IRS forms of a question asking philanthropic groups if they had experienced "diversion" of funds in excess of $250,000.

The *Post* analysis of filings from 2008 to 2012 found more than a thousand nonprofit organizations that reported "significant diversion" of assets, a twenty-first-century-century euphemism meaning fraud, embezzlement, theft, and other misappropriation of money. Some nonprofits, embarrassed by their lack of oversight, released incomplete or inaccurate data and details regarding losses.[62]

Several of the *Post*'s egregious cases occupied headquarters in imposing buildings in and near Washington. The American Legacy Foundation, which has managed hundreds of millions of dollars from government settlements with Big Tobacco, conducts health research and informs the public about the deadly effects of tobacco use. Its imposing new building sits a few blocks from the White House. On its 2011 form Legacy reported a diversion in excess of $250,000 stolen by a former employee. But the *Post* learned what Legacy did not say: that the loss was actually $3.4 million, that officers waited three years to investigate, and that the entrepreneurial thief now ran a video emporium in Nigeria.

Not far from Legacy's office on Massachusetts Avenue is the Youth Service America building, which discovered in 2011 a "misappropriation" by a former employee in 2009 of about $2 million. The Alliance for Excellent Education is a few blocks away in the other direction. In 2009 it disclosed that Bernard L. Madoff's Ponzi scheme had taken $7 million out of its accounts: Alliance told the *Post* that this was a "paper" loss. In the same D.C. area even AARP disclosed two incidents of embezzlement totaling $230,000.

These and other "diversions," according to the *Post*, had not been reported in the media. But in December 2014 the Government Accountability Office took notice of the mismanagement of charitable organizations and issued a report recommending greater IRS oversight to prevent fraud and theft. Gary Snyder, an independent watchdog of charities and author of two books addressing the crisis in nonprofits, maintains a website, Nonprofit Imperative, publishing continuing reports of money illegally draining out of charities and suggesting needed reforms. In March 2015, for example, he reported on NeighborWorks America—chartered by Congress in 1978 to aid counseling groups that give mortgage advice and financial aid—as an organization that has leaked out billions of dollars of taxpayer money. NA executives gave out large contracts without bidding and with no regard for conflict of interest. In one year it paid out $900,000 to Quantum, a company run by a former employee, whose address was a one-bedroom apartment in Washington owned by a former NeighborWorks software developer.[63]

Charitable foundations are hardly the only nonprofits that pay salaries and compensation helping to drive extreme inequality in the United States and drain away needed resources. Since the recession of 2008–12, salaries in health care, museums, the performing arts, and higher education have prompted critics to ask if the "core values of nonprofits" have been forgotten. The pay packages of presidents of private *and* public universities have ballooned in the last two to three decades, even as the budgets of most state universities have been cut by their legislatures, and student debt has gone well over $1 trillion. In 2004 no university president made over $1 million: in 2011 forty-two did, with University of Chicago president Robert Zimmer leading the ivory tower millionaires with $3.4 million in total compensation.

As the corporate, Wall Street model has taken over academia, lavish, expensive perks accompany the CEO salaries. New York University gave a $1 million low-interest loan to president John Sexton to buy a summer home on Fire Island; as Johns Hopkins University president Bill Brody left office, Hopkins paid him $3.3 million in retirement benefits; Penn State University fired Graham Spanier during the Sandusky child sex-abuse scandal, sending him off with $2.9 million, and a $600,000-a-year salary while on paid leave just after; Ohio State cushioned highly paid E. Gordon Gee's departure with a compensation package valued at $5.8 million over five years before taxes along with office and parking space, reduced after he accepted the presidency at West Virginia University; Harry Jacobson, former chancellor of Vanderbilt's medical school, raked in $6 million two years after he retired. But the biggest winner in this partial galaxy of university CEOs leaving office with "platinum pay" was Richard Levin, who left Yale University with an $8.5 million payout.[64]

At the City College of New York state funding has declined dramatically while enrollments climbed; classrooms filled, and tuition and student debt soared. Yet its president, Lisa S. Coico, with a salary of $300,000, rode to work in a chauffeur-driven car. In 2015 she oversaw the awarding of $7.25 million in pay to college "executives," up 45 percent from 2008 when "austerity" began; eleven of the biggest salary increases, by percentage, came in 2015 as Coico expanded the administration. She also used university foundation funds for personal expenses, such as food, housekeeping services, and rugs.[65]

University foundations are sometimes used virtually as slush funds for big payouts that provoke public protest, as in the case of the University of Louisville's foundation that President James Ramsey used to disburse millions in deferred payments to himself and his chief of staff, Kathleen Smith, and Provost Shirley Willihnganz. In 2012–13 alone Ramsey received $1.8 million in deferred compensation and Smith and Willihnganz $1.3 and $2.4 million, respectively. In 2015 Ramsey's compensation rose to $2.53 million, more than two to three times that of presidents at dozens of similar institutions. Meanwhile the university, which caters to low-income students, has raised tuition and cut budgets, and from 2008 to 2014 two high-level administrators embezzled nearly $8 million. At Northern Kentucky's state community college its foundation stirred outrage when it gave the outgoing president of Gateway Community and Technical College a $348,000 parting gift. Yet lucky recipient G. Edward Hughes presided over budget cuts, declining enrollment, and high student default rates; critics also accused him of excess spending and self-dealing.[66]

Wall Street–level compensations at academic institutions, assessed by many observers as "out of line with the ostensible mission of academia," often come on the backs of student debtors and underpaid part-time faculty. A report from the Institute of Policy Studies found that from 2005 to 2012, student debt and the number of low-wage faculty rose fastest at the twenty-five universities with the highest-compensated presidents. As student debt increased, "administrative spending outstripped scholarship spending by more than two to one at [such] schools." Meanwhile, adjuncts swelled the faculty at these institutions at a rate 22 percent faster than the average at all universities; permanent faculty declined "dramatically."[67]

As distant from the mission of colleges and universities that executive pay has become (along with the bloated size of university and college administrations), the compensation of CEOs at nonprofit hospitals makes the high-flying academic institutions look like pikers. Between 2011 and 2012 pay for 147 nonprofit hospital heads rose by over 24 percent; for 21 heads it rose by over 50 percent. At the top, compensation packages were stunning: Joseph Trunfio of three-hospital Atlantic Health System in Morristown, New Jersey, took home $10.7 million in 2012; Ronald Del Mauro of Barnabas Health, with multiple hospitals in New Jersey, received $21.6 million in deferred benefits even though he no longer worked in the system (only $8 million were employer contributions, said a financial advisor); George Halverson of Kaiser Permanente in his last year as CEO hauled in $9.9 million in total compensation in 2011, up 25 percent from 2010. The average for the top earners was $2.2 million. *The average worker in nonprofit hospitals in recent years collected paychecks with raises averaging less than 2 percent.*[68]

This quick survey of nonprofit executive salaries demonstrates what has been evident throughout, that the political class and its most fortunate beneficiaries are not confined to Washington, D.C., but can be found throughout the country. A common denominator linking many members of the political class is that their princely compensations are not tied to performance. The highest paid public university presidents have presided over rising tuition, mounting student debt, and the hiring of part-time contingent faculty. The compensation of CEOs of nonprofit hospitals, similarly, does not necessarily reflect the quality of care at those facilities and "do[es] not tend to be associated with obvious measures of success."[69]

Thomas Piketty attributed the enormous rise of income and wealth inequality primarily to the phenomenal increase in wage disparity, with ordinary workers getting less income from their production. As Wall Street levels of compensation have spread across America's institutions, profit and nonprofit, the permanent campaign might be given a third meaning: the drive of top managers to acquire, in Piketty's words, "the power to set their own remuneration."

Chapter 5

Political Class Adaptation
and Expansion

As an entrenched permanent political class presides over an unprecedented gap between the richest 1 percent and everybody else, it has morphed into a nepotistic oligarchy of wealth and privilege blocking opportunity for the great majority of Americans. The oligarchy has spread across multiple institutions and has proved itself adept at co-opting activist organizations and individuals working for fundamental change in the political economy.

The permanent political class protects itself and adapts also by addressing "the American people" with populist rhetoric and assuring them that it has their interests at heart. Neither major political party, however, has protected adequately the vast majority of citizens, and especially the most vulnerable, from economic shocks damaging millions of ordinary citizens. While the Republican Party has become the champion of policies that maintain the status quo or continue to shift wealth upward, the Democrats have moved away from economic progressivism, becoming more pro-business, passively watching labor unions decline. The rise of "citizen interest groups" focused on quality of life concerns also helped shift Democrats' and liberals' focus from economic equality to "post-materialist" issues. Simultaneously a reactionary corporate offensive to weaken or destroy labor unions and convert congressional Democrats to business-friendly policies pushed the political agenda away from economic fairness and social justice. The rise of identity politics also helped fracture the

New Deal coalition and led to greater social liberalism, while extreme inequality of income and wealth outdistanced almost all putatively democratic and economically advanced nations.[1]

Adaptation

The distinguished political scientist Theda Skocpol has described political class adaptation, as well as its blunting of real change in the power structure. Her *Diminished Democracy* offered a convincing explanation of how civic life in the United States has changed from having large numbers of citizens involved in voluntary associations to citizen disengagement and activism by top-down interest groups staffed by professional advocates.

Civic life in the nineteenth century, in contrast to what developed in the late twentieth century, consisted of hundreds of voluntary associations with mass memberships. Contrary to conservatives' wishful thinking, these organizations were not localized but were national and political and flourished in tandem with the federal government. Liberals err in assuming, Skocpol argued, that since the 1960s the country is more democratic; instead, a healthy civic life has withered as Americans are organizing more at the top but joining less.[2]

In an analysis paralleling the discussion above of foundations and nonprofits, Skocpol described the rapid demise of movement activism after the 1960s and the rise of professional advocacy managers who focus on fund-raising. The nation has made gains in "social equality," but meanwhile "cross-class fellowship and inclusive social activism" have disappeared. "Despite the multiplicity of voices raised within it, America's new civic universe is remarkably oligarchic."[3]

That new civic life is dominated by what her colleague Marshall Gans has called "heads without bodies." In describing the transition from membership to management, from the pursuit of activist members to raising money, from "trustees of community to specialized experts," from organizing to communicating, from *doing with* to *doing for*, Skocpol in effect has described the expansion of the political class.[4]

In the 1970s and 1980s public interest advocacy groups proliferated, with many based in Washington focused on lobbying Congress. At the same time "segments of the business world formed more specialized associations, and new groups appeared to do battle with citizen groups. . . . Many corporations and preexisting business associations opened offices for the first time in Washington, D.C., the better to monitor government and counter the newly mobilized rights groups and citizen associations." Though sometimes at odds, the business lob-bies and public interest advocacy groups exist side by side, and the latter have come to resemble the former. The CEOs of the largest civic groups, as noted earlier, earn huge salaries comparable to lobbyists and trade representatives. Their staffs are predominantly upper middle class and rarely interact with local citizens' groups rooted in the middle and working classes.[5]

Skocpol echoed the critics of foundations in recognizing that their philan-thropy often works to blunt radical activism. She recognized too that the policy outcomes routine in the top-heavy civic world limit popular mobilization, pro-mote polarization in politics, and "[skew] national politics and public policy toward the values and interests of the privileged."[6]

The evolution of the environmental movement that began in the early 1970s with sweeping goals for ending the earth's degradation offers a case study of pro-fessionalization, retreat and compromise—as well as expansion of the political class and its co-opting of radical change. The derailment of a movement with an all-encompassing definition of the environment and maximum goals resulted in part from a powerful anti-environmental backlash in the Reagan 1980s, but also from the transition of mainstream "green" organizations into top-down advocacy and their adoption of a strategy of negotiation and compromise with polluters. Mainstream environmentalism responded to Reagan, according to Mark Dowie, "by forming the harmless and stubbornly elitist Group of 10 (later renamed the Green Group), creating its own irrelevance by remaining middle class and white, pursuing 'designer issues' expedient to fundraising, focusing on Washington, lobbying the wrong committees, failing to move women and minorities into top jobs, building ephemeral memberships with direct mail, ignoring the voice of vast constituencies and, eventually—under the rubric of third-wave environmentalism—cozying up to America's worst environmental violators."[7]

The "nationals," as Dowie labeled them, see regional and local grassroots activists as a distraction or "politically unrealistic." When the Reagan adminis-tration launched an all-out assault on the environmental movement, as well as the environment itself, the nationals moved to work with corporate polluters instead of fighting back. "We're not selling out, we're buying in," said Jay Dee Hair of the National Wildlife Federation. Fatally, however (literally, for example, in the case of Los Angeles or Cleveland residents who die from bad air), the compromising "third-wave environmentalists" accepted a "market based incentive" to toxic emissions by creating a pollution credit system. But instead of incrementally reducing pollution, a valuable financial commodity got bought and sold, and incentives to pollute actually increased.[8]

Dowie sees reason for hope in what he called "the rise of environmental ad hocracy," locally and regionally targeted movements, especially those focused on antitoxicity. Although grassroots citizen NIMBY (not in my backyard) interventions continue to have success, assessments of the state of mainstream environmental advocacy in the twenty-first century echo or go beyond Dowie's pessimism. A provocative paper by Michael Shellenberger and Ted Nordhaus, "The Death of Environmentalism: Global Warming Politics in a Post-Environmental World," initially presented at a 2004 meeting of the Environmental Grantmakers Association, no doubt set on edge the teeth of the executives of foundations gathered there who give large amounts of money to the mainstream environmentalists. The two authors, then in their thirties, argued that environmentalism had become "just another special interest," and it should die "so that something new can live." The paper elicited both outrage (from the Sierra Club's executive director) to grudging admiration (from the likes of the respected author and activist Bill McKibben).[9]

In describing environmentalism as a special interest, Shellenberger and Nordhaus did not mention the mainstream's movement in and out of government. But if anything shows that an organization has arrived in Washington's permanent political class it is passage in and out of a revolving door. The right-wing blogosphere is filled with conservative rants regarding exchanges of personnel between the Obama administration and the Environmental Protection Agency.[10]

Another door, however, ushers top EPA officials who leave the agency into high-paying jobs in the industries they once—ahem—regulated. William Ruckelshaus, the first head of the EPA, set the pattern when, two years after leaving government in 1973, he took on a high-level position in Weyerhauser, a huge timber and paper products company. Meanwhile, his law firm was hired by the Society of the Plastics Industry to defend its use of toxic chemicals. Two other heads of the EPA, who, like Ruckelshaus, served with Republican presidents, Russell Train (1973–77) and Lee Thomas (1985–89), also migrated after the EPA to polluting industries, Union Carbide and Georgia Pacific. Ruckelshaus went back to the EPA for Reagan's first term and then left to become CEO of the notorious polluter Browning-Ferris, the nation's second-largest waste management company, a serial offender with known criminal connections. The revolving door from the EPA and environmental organizations is invaluable to polluting industries because it helps "business interests gain unearned environmental credibility." Consequently, leaders of environmental groups are "continuously courted and seduced by lucrative future positions in polluting corporations."[11]

In the case of The Nature Conservancy, by far the wealthiest green group with well over $6 billion in assets, no revolving door is necessary. The Nature Conservancy (TNC) has essentially formed a working alliance with corporate America, including its biggest polluters, which it calls "compatible development." In 2003 TNC controlled assets of about $3.5 billion, employed 3,200 in 528 offices in every state and thirty countries, all overseen from its eight-story, $28 million building in Arlington, Virginia. In that year, however, its well-polished image on which it has spent heavily received a serious setback when, after a two-year investigation, the *Washington Post* ran a series exposing a range of unethical if not unlawful practices. The *Post* articles revealed the extent to which this biggest of the "greens" compromised with industry and misused its vast resources to benefit some donors and trustees as well as its executives. TNC's many breaches of fiduciary trust prompted investigations by the IRS and senators already suspicious of high pay and financial mismanagement at big nonprofits.[12]

On its governing board and advisory committees sat—and sit—senior executives of oil and chemical companies, auto manufacturers, mining and logging operations, and coal-burning electric utilities, payers of millions in environmental fines. These corporate executives, according to some former and present TNC officials, gained undue influence over policy. Indeed, and this should hardly be surprising, the Conservancy's "pragmatism" and boasted policy of compromise had established, in effect, a mirror image of the Capitol's gift economy.

So while preserving millions of acres, TNC also logged forests, engineered a $64 million deal paving the way for opulent houses on fragile grasslands, and drilled for natural gas under the last breeding ground of an endangered bird species.[13]

It bought high and resold at bargain prices prime scenic properties through its "conservation buyers" program favoring its trustees, executives, and insiders who then donated the difference in price to the nonprofit for a big tax deduction. These land sales have been sweetheart deals all around.

In one, TNC bought $2.1 million of shoreline on New York's Shelter Island at the eastern end of Long Island. Weeks later, it resold the ten acres to the former chair of its regional chapter and his wife, a TNC trustee, for $500,000. The new owners then donated more than $1.5 million to the Conservancy to make up the difference, thus giving them a generous tax deduction. Another of TNC's many land sales to insiders involved one to David Letterman, a trustee, who bought part of a 215-acre plot on Martha's Vineyard.

Another prime stretch of coastline in Texas had a different fate: in 1995 Mobil Oil gave the charity a stretch of coastline that supported the almost extinct Attwater's Prairie Chicken. Drilling for oil had already taken place on the new preserve, but the Conservancy decided to increase revenue and sink a gas well fairly close to the bird's habitat. Sued by another charity, TNC lost $10 million. That episode and TNC's drilling was first exposed by the *Los Angeles Times* in 2002. Recently the writer Naomi Klein, an acute critic of corporate scams, revealed in her book *This Changes Everything: Capitalism vs. the Climate*, that TNC was still raking in millions in profit from drilling oil on the land that it controls in Texas—the same property from which the endangered Attwater's Prairie Chicken has disappeared. That sad fact, Klein conceded, could have resulted from several causes. But Klein added that the Conservancy "has been in the oil and gas business for a decade and a half." She also asked why TNC and other green groups own heavy investments in energy companies, and why most do not have policies "prohibiting them from investing their endowments in fossil fuel companies." TNC has over $25 million in "energy" holdings. "The hypocrisy," she observed, "is staggering: these organizations raise mountains of cash every year on the promise that the funds will be spent on work that is preserving wildlife and attempting to prevent catastrophic global warming."[14]

TNC's equivalent of a "shameless commerce division" (to borrow a phrase popularized on the NPR talk show *Car Talk*) sold its name and logo to companies who then claim undeserved credit for being green—known as *greenwashing*. (Greenwashing should not be confused with *pinkwashing*, the most notorious case of which involved the breast cancer charity Susan G. Komen partnering with Baker Hughes, the fifth-largest fracking company. For two years [2013–14] the Houston oil services company donated $100,000 to Komen while selling a thousand pink-painted drill bits used in fracking, which injects probable and known carcinogens into the environment.)[15] TNC allowed S.C. Johnson & Sons, Inc., whose chair sat on the Conservancy board, to use its logo in ads for a toilet cleaner and other toxic products for a payoff of $100,000. General

Motors, called "Global Warmer Number One" by the Environmental Defense Fund (itself no stranger to deals), spearheaded a $1 billion fund-raising campaign for TNC, and in the decade before 2003 gave it cash and vehicles worth $22 million. Coincidentally, TNC was among the last environmental groups to declare global warming a problem. Others of its corporate sponsors, including Exxon Mobil, have spent heavily on propaganda denying that greenhouse gas emissions cause climate change.

Recurring blows to its reputation have not induced TNC to change its methods, despite a blog devoted to recording "The Nature Conservancy Scandals." In response, in 2009 the organization paid Media Strategies $1,251,150 to enhance its image, but the next year as millions of barrels of crude oil leaked from a blown-out BP well in the Gulf of Mexico, the *Washington Post* revealed that TNC had enjoyed a long-standing partnership with BP. The oil company had contributed generously to help TNC protect Bolivian forests and had cultivated an earth-friendly image with help from the Conservancy.[16]

The Nature Conservancy originated in 1951 as a small nonprofit devoting itself to buying land to protect it, well before the environment became a post–World War II cause, even before the publication of Rachel Carson's *Silent Spring* in 1962, and before baby boomers discovered environmentalism, leading to the first Earth Day in 1970. Growing slowly thereafter, in the 1980s its nonconfrontational approach blended perfectly with the anti-environment backlash engineered by the Reagan administration and polluting industries; corporate and even government funds rolled in, along with many small donations, and it became the behemoth it is today.

TNC is hardly the only big green group taking funds from some of the worst polluters and scofflaws. As environmental groups adopted the "market-based" approach to conservation, they provided, observed Klein, "an invaluable service to the fossil fuel sector as a whole."[17] Hardly any of the big environmental nonprofits have escaped some kind of scandal in recent years, usually for being too close to corporate polluters. The World Wildlife Federation has been criticized for having a cozy relationship with Monsanto as well as the "rainforest destroying palm oil company Wilmer."[18]

Big green officials also engage in the nepotism characteristic of the political class. Christine MacDonald, a former media manager at Conservancy International (CI), in a 2008 book sharply critical of environmental groups, wrote that at CI "the children, spouses, and close personal friends of executives, donors, and board members held posts ranging from interns to senior staff." She claimed it "is by no means unique to CI. Instances [of nepotism] at the Conservancy and other conservation organizations are common knowledge in the close-knit conservation world."[19]

MacDonald acidly described how green executives with the "highest salaries in the nonprofit world ... speak the gospel of environmental sustainability [but] live like carbon junkies, burning many times more greenhouse gases responsible for global warming than the average American. They have grown accustomed to celebrity lifestyles and lavish working vacations to places most people won't see in a lifetime." In private jets "they explore the Galapagos Islands, safari in Botswana, and dive the Great Barrier Reef off Indonesia, often with a rock star, famous actor, or corporate scion in tow."[20]

The Populism of the Political/Ruling Class

The members of the permanent political class who run for office appeal for votes with populist rhetoric, and once elected they declare that they govern in the best interests of all. Many claim to be exactly what they are not: nonpoliticians independent of interest groups and unbeholden to the money power, anti-Washington and antiestablishment mavericks.

Senator Paul Wellstone (1944–2002), a Minnesota Democrat, was a rarity in Washington, a genuine populist. He led the progressive wing of Democratic senators, strongly supported labor unions, advocated protecting the environment and expanded federal health care, opposed repeal of the estate tax that would benefit primarily the wealthy, and was "the Senate's reigning crusader against corporate influence over public policy." When he died in 2002 in a plane crash just weeks before his likely reelection, Paul Krugman in the *New York Times* titled his eulogy for Wellstone "For the People" and lauded him as a courageous risk-taker who had always cared for the vulnerable and stood against "powerful interest groups," supporting instead "the interests of ordinary Americans against the growing power of our emerging plutocracy."[21]

In his appreciation of Wellstone Krugman sardonically observed, "Almost every politician in modern America pretends to be a populist; indeed, it's a general rule that the more slavishly a politician supports the interests of wealthy individuals and big corporations, the folksier his manner." An essential ingredient of such a manner for our politicians, as political satirist Mark Leibovich observed, is the frequent use of the word *folks*, which lets the rest of us know they "are real folks who care about real folks because they are always using the word 'folks': city folks, country folks, hardworking folks, younger folks, older folks, black folks, white folks." To win elections, Leibovich continued, they believe they must project the sense that they "identify with 'real' people while expending great time, soul and sycophancy on the millionaires and billionaires who tantalize [their] campaign dreams." *Folk* is a rhetorical "softener" that suggests a mode of kinship and self-conscious informality that politicians increasingly default to. "The last thing a politician wants is to be seen as 'elite,' someone 'out of touch' with the tastes and routines of the voters they need to consider him or her to be 'one of us.'"[22]

Even the Wall Street gentry have employed rhetoric that ethnographer Karen Ho called "market populism," with *Fortune* magazine in 1999 proclaiming the U.S. a "Trader Nation" with everybody wanting a "a piece of the stock market." Thomas Frank pointed out that the online broker E-Trade for a time appropriated the "the language and imagery of the civil rights and feminist movements." Behind the populist rhetoric, as many disclosed private emails among traders have revealed, is a mocking contempt for ordinary people and clients and investors.[23]

Style vs. Substance

In the spring of 2015 Hillary Clinton began her campaign for the Democratic nomination for president with a populist message stressing economic inequality and a rigged system. Soon she needed to reevaluate where to spend her summer vacation. For the past few summers the Clintons had rented very expensive mansions in the Hamptons of Long Island, mingling with the likes of good friend and donor Harvey Weinstein and wealthy celebrities. These "folks" did not qualify as the "Everyday Americans" to whom Clinton was now addressing her speeches.[24] As political consultants stress, "optics" matter.

Clinton had sounded populist themes in her previous campaign for the Democratic nomination. In the 2008 presidential primary general election campaigns, in the throes of a severe national economic downturn, populist themes and rhetoric proliferated. Populist appeals shaped the strategies of even some early Republican candidates. In the Democratic primaries, John Edwards, former senator and 2004 vice presidential candidate, fashioned himself as a populist fighter of poverty, but as he said ruefully in a debate after Obama and Clinton had graciously observed the historic nature of each other's candidacy: "I'm the white guy."[25]

After Edwards left the competition in January, Clinton and Obama waged a long struggle to claim the populist mantle, with each attracting an outpouring of passionate supporters and unprecedented primary turnouts. With no large policy differences between them, both responded to the economic malaise with fiery populist appeals. Both Clinton and Obama denounced oil company profits and "special interests" and promised infrastructure spending to create jobs. With outrage growing over Wall Street's financial risk-taking at taxpayers' expense, Clinton criticized hedge fund managers, drug company subsidies, and "the two oil men [Bush and Cheney] in the White House." Obama charged that Bush-Cheney favored the wealthy who "made out like Bandits." He proposed ending tax breaks for corporations that shipped jobs overseas, and he slammed trade agreements giving "perks for big corporations but no protections for American workers."

The candidates mingled often with ordinary "folks": Clinton downed shots of whiskey with beer in a suburban Chicago bar, while Obama tried his hand at a neighborhood bowling alley, badly. Clinton immediately tweeted a call for "an end to gutter politics." Meanwhile, both candidates benefited from large campaign contributions from Wall Street firms, Obama more than Clinton. Despite Obama's plunge into populist rhetoric, reporters often commented on its restraint. As he explained to a *Washington Post* reporter, "When you hear me talk about people versus the powerful, my populism is built most powerfully around the sense that government is nonresponsive to these folks. They're probably less angry at Wall Street for making money and angrier at Washington for not just setting up some basic rules of the road."

Meanwhile, Republican nominee Senator John McCain injected a strong strain of right-wing cultural populism into the campaign with his choice of former Alaska governor Sarah Palin as his running mate. In the end, however, the downward slide of the economy and voters' judgment that Bush administration policies had failed led economic populism to trump cultural populism.

As president, Obama did not govern as a populist but as a moderate progressive. He did give highest priority to health insurance reform, which contained redistributive provisions, and the first piece of legislation he signed was the Lily Ledbetter Fair Pay Act to promote wage equality for women.

During his first term the president paid infrequent attention to economic inequality, but after being reelected he vowed to make reducing it a major effort of his second term.[26] He acted on his promises by taking several executive initiatives, such as raising the minimum wage for workers on new federal contracts to $10.10 an hour, and in early January 2015 giving federal workers up to six weeks of paid maternity leave and asking Congress to extend this to private workers. Yet in other critical areas Obama did not act as an economic populist.

In 2010 Obama signed into law the Dodd-Frank Wall Street Reform and Consumer Protection Act, an attempt to reign in financial abuses and establish the people-friendly Consumer Financial Protection Bureau. But even before he took office, Obama assembled a team of economic advisors blessed by Wall Street, some of the same men who had played critical roles in bringing on the financial crisis. He appointed as attorney general Eric Holder and as deputy attorney general Lanny Breuer, corporate lawyers whose expertise was defending the misconduct of financial firms and corporations. Not surprisingly, as Wall Street resumed its reckless gambling, the Justice Department refused to prosecute individuals and routinely fined but did not indict bankers who committed fraud; the companies regarded large fines as part of the cost of doing business. Felons at banks "too big to fail" became executives "too big to jail."[27]

In 2015, the president who as a candidate denounced trade agreements that do not protect American workers negotiated a multination trade agreement, the Trans-Pacific Partnership (TPP), fiercely opposed by unions and most of his own party. Senate Republicans joined by a few Democratic "Republicans for a Day" gave him "fast track" approval. Opponents of TPP, now dead with the Trump administration, charged that key provisions written by multinational corporations were being kept secret from the public. Indeed, the draft of the deal was classified, and the public could not have seen its contents for four years. Critics predicted it would lead to the offshoring of more American jobs, claims Obama brushed off.[28]

Former New York governor Mario Cuomo famously stated that candidates campaign in poetry and govern in prose. Obama, though far from a thoroughgoing populist in the mode of Bernie Sanders, should not be put down as a "faker." Rather, he illustrates the truth of Cuomo's observation, and to his credit, Obama both advocated and initiated policies to reduce inequality and help the vulnerable. Too many other members of the political class exhibit a far greater gap between their populist rhetoric and their actions.

Faux Populists

The media quickly anoints politicians as "populist" if they are macho tough talkers. A prime example: New Jersey Republican governor Chris Christie, who won election twice in the normally Democratic state of New Jersey as a "straight-talking, even swaggering leader." Like many so christened he often uses blunt, even insulting language when speaking to the media or critics. He suggested that reporters "take the bat" to a Democratic opponent (who happened to be a widowed grandmother) and called teachers' union leaders "political thugs" who were "using students like drug mules" to carry political messages. In his 2013 campaign for reelection he held over one hundred town-hall style meetings, often face-to-face with voters. On February 26, 2015, at the Conservative Political Action Conference he donned his populist persona "railing against everything." His slogan for his presidential campaign website was "tell it like it is." Many critics have pointed out that Christie's straight talk on issues is frequently anything but accurate: as one observer put it, "People prefer directness to detail." Like other faux populists, he was "adept at getting the public to believe what he says."[29]

Christie's lifestyle, however, is more One Percent than populist. On a "trade mission" to Israel in 2012 Christie and his entourage (wife, father, three of his four children, stepmother, four staffers, his former law partner, and a state trooper) flew on a private plane provided by billionaire Sheldon Adelson, a luxurious aircraft on which Christie has his own bedroom. The accommodations for the group hardly diminished with rooms at posh Kempinski hotels costing about $30,000. The junket wound up with three parties footed by King Abdullah of Jordan.[30]

Letting others pick up the tab is a Christie hallmark. He has boasted of his desire to "squeeze all the juice out of the orange." He brings to mind a passage from Cat Stevens's "Hard-Headed Woman":

> I know many fine feathered friends
> But their friendliness depends on how you do
> They know many sure fired ways
> To find out the one who pays and how you do.

Christie's trips on private planes to see his favorite NFL team the Dallas Cowboys, in Texas and Green Bay, paid for by owner Jerry Jones, raised ethical questions since Jones has a business relationship with the Port Authority of New York and New Jersey. Closer to home, Christie spent big at concession stands at New York Jets and Giants games, using a state debit card to buy $82,594 of refreshments during the 2010 and 2011 seasons; concerned about the spree, the state Republican Committee reimbursed the treasury. That sum pales next to the total of $360,000 he spent from his state allowance over his first five years in office on groceries, snacks, alcohol, sweets, tents, and office supplies. He did not provide receipts or information as to how the spending benefited New Jersey. Indeed, Christie stonewalled at least two dozen public records requests for his spending on out-of-state travel. A New Jersey watchdog commented that this was typical of the governor, "who talks like a cost cutter, yet has a history as a high roller when someone else pays the bills for his first-class travel and four-star hotels."[31]

In his 2009 campaign Christie vowed to protect public employees' "sacred" pensions. Four months after taking office he discussed pensions at the conservative Manhattan Institute, run by one of his money men, hedge fund manager Paul Singer: "Our benefits are too rich," he said, "and our employees aren't contributing enough either." During that campaign, too, he attacked Democratic incumbent Jon Corzine for unethically investing retiree money on Wall Street. In office, Christie awarded pension management contracts to his own Wall Street friends; in 2011 Singer's hedge fund, Elliott Associates, received a contract to manage $200 million in state public pension funds. Then in 2014 Christie, facing a fiscal crisis, put $696 million into the pension fund instead of $1.58 billion, and the next year $681 million instead of $2.25 billion. Meanwhile, he increased taxes on the working poor and vetoed a bill to raise the minimum wage to $8.50. No wonder when Christie delivered a speech at a secret meeting held by the Koch brothers, David Koch, whom no one would mistake for a populist, introduced him as "my kind of guy."[32]

After Christie dropped out of the 2016 presidential primaries, he stunned many Republican allies by endorsing Donald Trump, whom he previously had sharply criticized. His former campaign manager, Hewlett Packard's Meg Whitman, quickly denounced his "astonishing display of political opportunism." South Carolina governor Nikki Haley said he was a "dear friend," but "none of us know why he did that." Clearly she has never had to pick up the check after having dinner with Christie. By endorsing Trump he flew around the country in Trump luxury with the Donald paying all expenses. The cherry on the sundae was the real estate mogul holding a fund-raiser to help Christie pay off his campaign debt.[33]

The two men in fact had been friends since 2002, when Trump's sister, Maryanne Trump Berry, then a federal judge, introduced them. Since then they have frequently double-dated at posh New York restaurants. When Christie became governor the relationship paid off quickly for Trump. The state auditors for several years had been trying to get Trump to pay $30 million in overdue taxes on his casinos. Christie's administration quickly offered a settlement, and Trump paid $5 million, about 17 cents on the dollar. Christie enjoyed Trump's generosity by way of contributions to improvements to the governor's mansion and to the Republican Governors Association when Christie became its honorary chair.[34]

The freshman U.S. senator from Texas, Ted Cruz, has been labeled a populist by both admirers and critics: "The Populist Egghead," *Slate's* John Dickerson called him, "a rare political species—a supposed man of the people who is attacked for his elite credentials and lack of common sense." His "cultural populism" has been compared to the thoroughgoing economic populism of Senator Bernie Sanders. Cruz's foreign policy stances have been described as "hawkish populism," and he has been labeled (mockingly) a "self-styled populist superman" and, with tongue far in cheek, a "humble populist."[35]

First to enter the race for the Republican 2016 presidential nomination, Cruz quickly transformed himself from the Senate's leading gadfly—critics would say obstructionist—to a crusading populist running against the "establishment." His mantra: "It's between Washington and the rest of us." His campaign book, *A Time for Truth: Reigniting the Promise of America,* is touted as an exposé "of the inner working of Washington.... Cruz pointedly identifies the underlying fundamental [*sic*] corruption of Washington's power players, or as he has described them, 'The Washington Cartel.' Cruz convincingly explains how the rigged game works for D.C. insiders at the expense of the American people." In his speeches Cruz also plays up his "hardship narrative," in Cruz's case the "remarkable [success] story" of the son of immigrants, "a working-class Irish-Italian mother and a Cuban father who came to this country with almost nothing."[36]

At the time of his announcement this graduate of Princeton and Harvard Law School let it be known that the 9/11 attacks had made him a convert to country music, because he did not like the way rock music responded to the attacks. He had, he said, a gut reaction to country music: "These are my people," he told CBS News, but neglected to name a single country artist or band.[37]

With both Democratic and Republican rivals addressing economic inequality and a "rigged" economic system and packaging themselves as fighters for "the people," Cruz sought to distance himself from the pack with fiery populist rhetoric. Addressing the friendly Heritage Club in late June, he raised the bar for presidential hopefuls seeking the populist aura. In a forty-minute "stemwinder" Cruz inveighed against Washington's "corrupt alignment of corporate and political power" of "lobbyists and career politicians."[38] Cruz has also used the gambit, popular with the Republican base, of attacking the alleged elite liberal media, though many of his more extreme actions, unpopular even with fellow Republican senators, are designed to attract attention from that same media.[39]

As is often the case with populists-come-lately, ironies can be found abundantly in Cruz's connections to the political class and to "the establishment" he excoriates. While at Harvard Law he proposed to form a study group of classmates consisting of only those who had attended Harvard, Yale, or Princeton as undergrads. That and his belief in his superior intelligence prompted the observation that "someone who's spent his life insisting that he was above everyone around him is asking us to vote for him" as a guy who is on "our side." During his second year he contacted a fellow student he did not know who had just won a prestigious award for a ride from New York to Cambridge. She told the *Boston Globe* later that they had hardly left the city when he asked about her IQ. She didn't know it, so then he asked, "So what's your SAT score?" A fellow classmate of Cruz's at Harvard noted that his academic snobbery marked him as "a pompous a—hole . . . an amazing accomplishment since the competition there for that description is *intense*."[40]

The conservative writer Eliana Johnson observed of Cruz, "The man who boasts of his own ideological purity is perhaps the most obviously tactical candidate." From the moment he arrived at Harvard Law Cruz had set the goal of obtaining a clerkship with Supreme Court Justice William Rehnquist. Knowing that Rehnquist played tennis with his clerks, Cruz took up tennis. Cruz's first-rate intelligence and debater's skills assisted his rise through Republican ranks, overcoming the dislike, even hatred, he inspired among almost everyone he has worked with. Ever the tactician, Cruz has boasted of being "the most hated man in Washington," turning his unpopularity with his peers into an advantage.[41]

In September 2013 Cruz spoke for twenty-one hours on the Senate floor on the need to defund the Affordable Care Act and then forced a government shutdown, angering even many Republican colleagues. Democrats began to ask Cruz pointedly about his own health insurance, since the Texas senator enjoyed a $20,000 a year plan provided by his wife's employer, Goldman Sachs. Heidi Nelson Cruz, talented and ambitious but not as ideological as her husband, had worked for the Wall Street banking firm for eight years in its investment management division. A solid member of the political class, she previously served in the Bush administration in the U.S. trade representative's office, then the Treasury Department, and on the National Security Council. When Cruz began his campaign, she took a leave from Goldman, and Ted no longer received its health coverage. So Cruz, with alternatives available to him and his wife, got it through HealthCare.gov.[42]

As Cruz stepped up his attacks on "crony capitalism" in Washington, his wife's connection to one of the biggest players in the 2008 economic meltdown provided additional ammunition for his critics. But in an interview with Bloomberg News, Cruz met the issue head on, charging that Wall Street banks like Goldman get too many "special favors" from government. With Cruz, the best defense is all-out offense, so he boasted that his wife's experience, abilities and charm provided a huge asset to his campaign.[43]

The Goldman connection indeed is fortuitous, as the firm contributes heavily to Cruz's treasury. Open Secrets reported that "much of his personal wealth is tied up in Goldman as well," and in 2011 he revealed that he borrowed between $100,000 and $250,000 from his wife's employer, an amount that in his 2012 report rose to between $250,000 and $500,000. That low-interest loan and another from Citibank provided $1.2 million for his campaign, a fact at odds with Cruz's claim at the time that it was financed by the couple agreeing "to liquidate our entire net worth . . .and put it into the campaign."[44]

Another Cruz asset was his relationship with his biggest campaign contributor, billionaire Robert Mercer, whose hedge fund, Renaissance Technologies, has been under investigation for six years by a Senate subcommittee for avoiding $36 billion in taxes between 2000 and 2013. Mercer made his money by using computer patterns to outsmart the stock market, proving once again, in writer John Cassidy's words, that very little useful social activity takes place on Wall Street. Besides backing Cruz, Mercer has spent heavily to try to defeat members of Congress who demand accountability from financial firms. In 2012 Rep. Peter DeFazio (D-OR) weathered $650,000 in attack ads paid for by Mercer because he promotes a tax on high-frequency transactions. Cruz, of course, sees no conflict between taking Mercer's money and his attack on "crony capitalism."

Indeed, Cruz's 2012 election to the Senate depended also on the billionaire's money funneled through the Club For Growth, the Senate Conservatives Fund, and Tea Party groups funded by the Kochs. In contrast to several of his rivals for the Republican nomination, Cruz's donor base relied less on small donors and heavily on wealthy capitalists, such as the managing director of Goldman Sachs, Joseph Konzelman, who hosted fund-raisers for Cruz.[45] Capitalist cronyism, it seems, is in the eye of the beholder.

Cruz also oozes inconsistencies as a culture warrior. He presents himself to evangelical voters as an unyielding opponent of same-sex marriage, but in courting wealthy donors he has proved flexible, suggesting it should be decided by each state. When seeking the backing of hedge fund billionaire Peter Singer, who has a gay son, he said if New York state wanted to legalize same-sex marriage, that was fine with him (Singer supported Marco Rubio). At a December 2015 fund-raiser in Manhattan, when asked by a Republican gay-rights supporter if fighting gay marriage would be a "top-three priority" for him as president, Cruz said no.[46]

In February 2016 Cruz won the Iowa Republican primary campaigning against the "Washington cartel" and with an evangelical fervor comparable to that of a televangelist, stressing that *his* campaign would be God-fearing, principled, and conducted with integrity unmatched by his rivals. Yet he had hired a campaign manager with a reputation "for scorching earth, stretching truth, and winning elections." Within weeks he had fired a top campaign spokesman for spreading misinformation about Senator Marco Rubio. But that would not be the last instance of his campaign being accused of dirty tricks. As columnist Frank Bruni commented, "He directs you to his halo as he surreptitiously grabs a pitchfork."[47]

In the 2014 midterm elections a new Republican star emerged from Iowa, Joni Ernst, a former county auditor who had served in the state senate since 2011. In 2013, to her surprise according to Ernst, she received an invitation to attend a meeting of wealthy donors connected to the Kochs at a luxurious Albuquerque resort. Throughout her campaign to win the Republican primary in an upset and through the general election for U.S. senator for the seat formerly held by populist Democrat Tom Harkin, the billionaires' backing for Ernst remained a carefully hidden secret.[48]

Her senatorial campaign began with a $9,000 commercial in which the attractive forty-four-year-old smiled into the camera and said: "I'm Jodi Ernst. I grew up castrating hogs on an Iowa farm, so when I get to Washington I'll know how to get rid of pork and wasteful spending. My parents taught me how to live within our means." Regarding the big spenders in Congress: "Let's make 'em squeal."[49] Her next spot featured her climbing off a Harley-Davidson and firing multiple times at a shooting range target. Ernst milked a populist style, but nothing else about her suggests concern for ordinary people.

Despite Ernst's holding extremely conservative views, even for today's Republican Party, its leadership selected her to respond to President Obama's 2015 State of the Union speech. But her new prominence fixed attention on some glaring contradictions in the "within our means" part of her narrative, as well as her Tea Party small government campaign.

Between 1995 and 2009 members of her family collected $463,000 in federal farm subsidies, most of it, $367,000, going to her uncle Dallas Culver, with $38,665 collected by her father, Richard Culver. Her father also benefited from the two years she spent as Montgomery County auditor, winning contracts for his construction company totaling $215,665. His daughter's funneling those contracts to him violated Iowa's strict code of ethics. Ernst fits "squarely in the camp of GOP office holders who think that government assistance is shameful and debilitating when it goes to anyone but them."[50]

Ernst seems to have a dissociative personality when it comes to government generally. In a talk given before her primary campaign she recalled how the town of Red Oak, the county seat of Montgomery, responded to the economic downtown in 2008–9 when unemployment increased: "It took local investors and local ingenuity [such as building contracts?] to start up new industry in town. It wasn't the federal government that came in and helped our community. . . . What we needed, was for government to get out of the way." In 2009 Montgomery County received nearly $9 million in federal farm aid, $12 million in 2010, and another $9 million the next year. But Ernst is in Washington now taking "a good hard look at entitlement programs," especially the Supplemental Nutrition Assistance Program (food stamps) that aids the poor and hungry: she believes it's necessary "to do a better job of educating the American people that they can be self-sufficient."[51]

In some of her wackier views, Ernst recalls earlier midwestern populists who occupied the fringes. She would dissolve the Department of Education and the EPA and thinks that states can nullify any federal law they choose, and she has mused about United Nations plots to take over Iowa farmland. But Ernst is not any kind of populist; rather, she fits the mold of those that I have elsewhere labeled "libertarians with benefits."[52]

By mid-2015 the flock of Republicans seeking the presidency as well as the fewer Democrats were crafting populist messages to advance their candidacies. Even that hard-right culture warrior, former senator and 2012 candidate Rick Santorum rebranded himself as a conservative working-class populist, announcing his opposition to "big business" as well as big government.[53] Other Republican hopefuls chimed in as professed champions of "hardworking Americans" and the middle class. Some also began to add a critique of *legal immigration* to their mantra of protecting our borders from illegals. Admitting too many foreign-born, they argued, lowers the wages of Americans and has caused the contraction of the middle class. Wisconsin governor Scott Walker declared that our immigration system "ultimately has to protect American workers and make sure American wages are going up." Although considerably less extreme in tone than Trump's anti-immigrant talk, this Republican turn, in the making for several years, reversed Republican policy as recently as the George W. Bush presidency.[54]

The Democrats' move to economic populism began with the postmortems to their crushing defeat in the 2014 midterms, and it gained an unlikely ally: Sen. Chuck Schumer (D-NY), often dubbed "Wall Street's Senator." Schumer, a moderate urban progressive, claims often to represent middle-class working Americans against "special interests," but his close ties to the financial industry are well known. In Congress since 1981 and the Senate since 1999, Schumer "has been the New York financial industry's principal go-to guy in Washington" and "one of the biggest beneficiaries of Wall Street money that Congress has ever seen." Since the economic collapse of 2008, Schumer has needed to balance his behind-the-scenes protection of the big banks' interests while advertising his commitment to Main Street.[55]

In a speech to the National Press Club on November 25, 2014, Schumer burnished his progressive image while prescribing a populist platform for his recently thrashed party. In 2009, he said, Obama and a Democratic Congress should have first tackled the economic concerns of a depressed middle class, focused on jobs and wages, and then pushed health care reform. He stressed that in recent elections defections of white voters from the Democrats had increased, and to recapture them the "first step is to convince voters that we are on their side, and not in the grip of special interests." The man whose closest friends include Wall Street executives suggested the prosecution of bankers for "what seems, on its face, blatant fraud" and tax reform to ensure that CEOs paid higher rates "than their secretaries." He urged that for Democrats, "an element of populism, even for those of us who don't consider ourselves populists, is necessary to open the door before we can rally people to the view that a strong government program must be implemented."[56]

Schumer's remarks brought on an immediate debate among Democrats; former House majority leader Nancy Pelosi disagreed and shot back, "we were elected to do a job, not to get re-elected." Although the argument over the past quickly subsided, divisions among Democrats over how to deal with persisting inequality continued. As Zoë Carpenter, a contributor to *The Nation* and *Rolling Stone*, pointed out, Democratic differences in explaining the causes of persistent and rising inequality are rooted in centrist elements of the party remaining "inextricably tied to some of the elites responsible for the underlying problems."[57]

Silicon Valley billionaires, most of whom are donors to Democrats and cultural liberals, are comfortable with an economy that delivers huge rewards to superstars. A report based on dozens of interviews with tech founders and several billionaires found them to reflect the passive populism and emphasis on equality of opportunity of Democratic centrists. Comfortable with an oligarchic meritocracy, they opposed unions and regulations on their ability to make money. For them, "inequality is a feature, not a bug."[58]

The majority of political class Democrats avoid an analysis of structural causes of inequality, such as the war on unions and workers' stagnant or declining wages, and instead point to exogenous forces such as technology or globalization. They avoid solutions calling for those at the top to pay their fair share and tend to stress the need for better education, for greater "opportunity" for low-income people to move up into the middle class. Robert Borosage, co-director of the progressive think tank Institute for America's Future, calls this "passive voice populism." Regarding the soft panaceas of education and job training, Paul Krugman has commented that "soaring inequality isn't about education; it's about power."

Senator Elizabeth Warren (D-MA), with well-established populist credentials, speaks for the few genuine Democratic progressives and attributes inequality and stunted opportunity to a rigged system that favors corporations and the wealthy. It's about an accumulation of policy choices (and nondecisions) by government over three to four decades as described in Jacob S. Hacker and Paul Pierson's *Winner-Take-All Politics: How Washington Made the Rich Richer—And Turned Its Back on the Middle Class*; it's about the egregiously excessive compensation of CEOs who set their own compensation, making four hundred times the average of what their employees make; it's about the class warfare against unions, their decline, and the decoupling of wages and productivity; it's about the shift of the federal tax burden away from corporations and the wealthy and onto the middle class and poor; and it's about all the other elements of an economic infrastructure that has created plutocratic government.[59]

Hillary Clinton embraced populist rhetoric early during the presidential primary season and told an April 2015 audience in Iowa that it was wrong that "hedge fund managers pay lower taxes than nurses or the truckers I saw on I-80 when I was driving here over the last two days." Told of her intention to close the carried-interest loophole, major Wall Street donors to her campaign had a blasé reaction. "It's just politics," said one hedge fund manager and Clinton supporter.[60]

During the early Democratic primaries, Bernie Sanders, an authentic populist, launched a challenge to Clinton by making inequality of income and wealth his central message and attacking Wall Street in uninhibited fashion. He drew enormous crowds dwarfing those of Clinton in numbers and enthusiasm and nearly won the Iowa caucuses. Clinton soon emulated his rhetoric and echoed his pledge to end the coddling of Wall Street executives who commit felonies and to send them to jail. Sanders, who began his campaign by promising not to attack Clinton but to highlight their differences, soon criticized her for ties to Wall Street and receiving over $1 million for speeches to Goldman Sachs and other firms the Democratic base regards as villains.

Clinton repeatedly countered Sanders by promising to be tough on Wall Street, but amid all the threats Wall Street money poured continuously into her campaign, raising doubts among critics about what she would do in office. One telling difference with Sanders regarded eliminating the capital interest tax loophole and taxing gains as earned income and not at 15 percent. Sanders proposed to abolish it outright, but Clinton preferred to do so in stages, an approach suggested by Laurence D. Fink, chairman of BlackRock, the largest asset management firm overseeing $5 trillion, and mentioned as a possible treasury secretary in a Clinton administration. Wall Street critic Matt Taibbi wondered, not fully tongue-in-cheek, if promising, then failing, to repeal the carried interest tax loophole is a Democratic tradition "designed to ensure that Democrats always have something to run on in election seasons."[61]

Tellingly, once Sanders had dropped out, Clinton began talking more about "opportunity" and less about punishing Wall Street felons or raising taxes on the rich.

The gift economy of the overwhelming majority of the political class ultimately precludes it from a realistic populist analysis of inequality's origins, much less proposals and actions that would cut the flow of wealth to the top. In the 2015–16 election campaign, candidates inundated the air waves with populist rhetoric, including Donald Trump. Since his election, business-as-usual on steroids has continued for the political class.

Chapter 6

The Political Class in a Poor State

Multiple studies of economic and physical well-being consistently rank Kentucky as one of the poorest and unhealthiest states in the nation. Its poverty rate in 2014–15 reached 19–20 percent and had been rising steadily since the 2008 economic downturn. Just over 25 percent of Kentucky's children under age eighteen live in poverty, compared to the U.S. rate of 22.2 percent; just five states have higher rates of children in poverty. Kentucky ranks second in its rate of abused children, double the national average. More residents receive food stamps (18 percent) than in all but three other states. Although the U.S. Census Bureau's 2015 data showed that income across rural America was rising,[1] the state's average weekly wage, adjusted for inflation, is not much different from what it was in 2007. In 2012 it had the nation's third-highest three-year default rate on student loans. Although the 2015 Economic Report from the University of Kentucky business school found the state in some measures to possess "community strength" equal to or above the national average, in the 2014 and 2015 Gallup-Healthways surveys the state ranked forty-ninth in well-being. No state had dirtier air. Kentucky leads the nation in toxic air pollution from power plants, and not surprisingly one in ten Kentuckians suffers from asthma; the state ranks number one in lung cancer and has the highest death rate from lower respiratory disease. People in Kentucky who are unhealthy are in poor health mostly because they are poor, and because of where they live.[2]

Kentucky's *political class* and the business-corporate interests it caters to, however, do very well and have for a long time. From the late 1990s to 2006, income gaps in Kentucky widened more than in just three other states. Other measures of inequality began to level off and improve after the state made a commitment to reducing wide disparities in school funding, but since 2008 those measures have turned in the wrong direction for low-income and rural Kentuckians. During the "recovery" a disproportionate share of income has gone to the top 1 percent. Kentucky is in step with the national trend toward high income inequality. Recently the incomes of the poorest 20 percent of households declined by 17.1 percent and those of the middle 20 percent by 6.2 percent, while the "incomes of Kentucky's richest households dwarf those of its poorest."[3]

Throughout Kentucky there are many conscientious individuals and civic organizations that devote themselves to improving the lives of their fellow citizens; some have done so for decades. They too are part of the state's diverse political class, and they come from all walks of life: they are lawyers, journalists, physicians, social workers, religious, artists, academics, farmers, architects, union officials, workers in charitable agencies, even some elected officials. They usually work in and with the political class and have succeeded over time in bringing improvements in education, health care, social services, crime, and drug abuse, in moving the state away from dying industries such as coal, and in promoting entrepreneurship and innovation. But in the twenty-first century they are laboring uphill because of declining federal and state financing and the inertia of the self-serving and self-aggrandizing sector of the political class satisfied with the status quo.[4]

Although Kentucky's unemployment rate has fallen since the recession to its lowest since 2004 and below the national average (5.1 percent in 2015), the state contains too many low-wage jobs. In the first quarter of 2014 average weekly wages of $811 stood well below the U.S. average of $1,027. In many small rural counties weekly wages were even lower, in the $500–600 range; in three counties a week's wages fell below $500. In hunger and food insecurity, meaning that at some point during the year a household experienced difficulty providing enough food due to lack of money or resources, Kentucky ranked 42nd among the states; its teen birth rate is 44th; a wide gender wage gap persists;

and 46 percent of single-parent households with related children were below the poverty line.[5]

The Way Out: Education

For decades University of Kentucky economists and scholars of Appalachia have advocated investment in education to improve the state's overall quality of life. As the coal industry declined and manufacturing jobs left, reformers looked to education as the way out. In 2007 the authors of the "Kentucky Annual Economic Report" said that the state needed "to increase the stock of knowledge ... by increasing the amount of innovative research ... and by significantly increasing the educational level of workers, and, in particular, increasing the number of college educated workers." Unless the state improved its infrastructure and placed greater emphasis on urbanization and innovative industries, "Kentucky will continue to be one of the poorest states in the Union."[6]

Unfortunately the state legislature responded to the recession by defunding education at all levels; by 2013 the state was spending $4 million less on preschool and ending child-care subsidies for thousands of working poor. A sharp decline in state aid for higher education began to drive up tuition at state universities, and the congressional sequester that entailed meat-axe cuts added to the decline in education funding. In 2013 Kentucky experienced the largest cut per student in the country ($179), and since 2008 it ranks tenth worst in cuts to K–12 education. Since 2008 the state reduced funding for higher education 25.4 percent, a decrease of $2,649 per student. In 2016 a newly elected Tea Party governor attempted to cut state universities' budgets by $18 million, but the state Supreme Court prevented him from doing so.[7]

The withdrawal of support for education has taken place in the context of an "obsolete tax system" filled with "exemptions, deductions, credits and various other breaks" to businesses and corporations. In 2015 "tax expenditures" amounted to $12.9 billion against $10.9 billion in the General Revenue Fund. Projected state revenue for 2016 was not enough to fund the state's infrastructure or maintain levels for police, universities, parks, courts, and prisons. The benefits of the tax breaks to business are often assumed rather than proven. The state's workers making poverty-level wages ($11.29 an hour) grew from one-fourth of the workforce in 2001 to one-third in 2012.[8]

In addition, many county clerks fail to collect delinquent taxes owed by residents and profitable businesses in their borders, directly reducing school funding. In 2015 clerks in two poor counties, Owsley and Boyle, neglected to collect bills amounting, respectively, to nearly $400,000 and $500,000. In five eastern counties coal companies controlled by West Virginia billionaire Jim Justice have mined hundreds of millions of dollars of coal. But as of October 2016 Justice owed a total of $4.2 million in back taxes, depriving local school districts, health departments, and other agencies of funds in some of the neediest counties. Tax delinquency falls heavily on those poor, rural counties, particularly those in eastern Kentucky that already suffer from narrow tax bases. In 2015–16 Justice, with a net worth of $1.56 billion, ran for governor of West Virginia while still owing a total of $15 million in all states with his mines. Yet he had the resources to loan his campaign $2.6 million and to renovate and maintain the Greenbriar, a posh resort in his state frequented by the region's political class. Former Kentucky governor Steve Beshear, a Democratic ally, earlier allowed him to pay just $1.5 million of the $4.5 million he owed in environmental fines.[9]

Even in urban-commercial Lexington and Fayette County the tax system underfunds the schools by an obsolete law intended to protect farmers but gives a large tax break to big developers and owners of houses on ten-acre lots. A *Herald-Leader* investigation found that land and lots still classified as "agricultural" enjoyed extremely low taxes compared to neighbors in modest dwellings who paid higher property taxes: a $10 million development was taxed at $1,755. There are 718 working farms in the county, one-third less than the number getting the land preservation tax break.[10] This amounts to socialism for the affluent.

One of Appalachia's premier scholars, Ronald D Eller, has shown that the underpayment of taxes by mining companies and large multinational corporations that have owned large areas of land is a long-standing problem in eastern Kentucky. "Studies of land ownership and taxation in Appalachia found a direct correlation between the poverty of a county and the percentage of property owned by mineral companies."[11]

Funding for universities has declined steadily, students have experienced rising tuition, and need-based aid for low-income applicants has also declined. The nonpartisan Kentucky Center for Economic Research observed that the state's failure to reinvest in education "will make it harder for the state to grow and attract businesses that rely on a well-educated workforce." Although the numbers of degrees granted rose, the state has suffered "a big drop in graduation rates" and after several earlier years of higher enrollments and degree completions now ranks forty-first among the states. Minority graduation went from 37 percent in 2009–10 to 33 percent in 2013; more than 107,550 qualified low-income students did not receive grants, up from 68,259 three years before.[12]

The priorities of Kentucky's political class emerged in stark relief when the head of the Kentucky Community and Technical College System (KCTCS) retired in 2014. Michael McCall's total compensation of $641,699 (including an automobile allowance of $43,000) made him one of the highest paid community college administrators in the nation (in several years the highest). The KCTCS board, chaired by P. G. Peoples, awarded McCall $324,321 for the following year during which he retired to South Carolina. Meanwhile, tuition and student debt soared, and full-time faculty inflation-adjusted salaries declined.[13]

"Not the Most Corrupt"

Asking why the Kentucky legislature year after year fails to reform the tax system to increase revenue and fund education would seem to be a rhetorical question, given the reluctance generally of American politicians to tackle inefficient and unfair tax codes. Charges of "raising taxes" are threats to staying in office. The Institute on Taxation and Economic Policy judged "virtually every state tax system [to be] fundamentally unfair, taking a much greater share of income from low- and middle-income families than from wealthy families." Kentucky's tax code has several progressive features, including a graduated personal income tax and a tax credit for child care and another linked to the federal poverty level, but resembles almost all other systems by relying heavily on sales and excise taxes.

Combining all state and local income taxes, property, sales, and excise taxes in 2015, the lowest 20 percent of families taking in $16,000 or less paid out 9 percent of their income; the next two lowest cohorts (under $30,0000 and $50,0000) shelled out 10.6 and 10.8 percent of their income to taxes overall, and the $50,000 to $81,000 earners parted with 9.9 percent of their income.

But the share of income paid by families in the higher-income groups fell as their earnings rose, and the lowest amount is contributed by those at $330,000 and up, just 6 percent.[14]

Although Kentucky's tax system is "the 33rd most unfair in the country," its state government does qualify as "one of the most corrupt in the country." A study by Harvard University's Center for Ethics distinguished between illegal corruption and the much more common "legal corruption" (or "legalized bribery"), which in the states mirror the gift economy in Washington, D.C.[15]

The researchers found the Kentucky legislature's illegal corruption to be comparable to other states, but the state was "second to none when it comes to the 'legal corruption' of political favors in exchange for campaign contributions." Some of those "political favors" involve tax loopholes draining money from the state budget. Kentucky's executive branch ranked "moderately high" (3.5 on a 5-point scale) in illegal corruption.

In the twenty-first century the stakes in the state capitol are much higher than in the early 1990s when an FBI investigation known as Operation BOPTROT ended with the conviction of over a dozen legislators for bribery. It resulted from a legal battle between the harness racing industry and thoroughbred racing, and as legislators trotted off to jail, "Kentuckians [Were] Amazed That $400 Can Buy a Lawmaker."[16] Now, much more green stuff is floating around Frankfort.

The findings of the 2014 Harvard center's study of corruption coincided serendipitously with record-breaking spending by lobbyists directed at Kentucky's lawmakers. During 2013 when the legislature met for just thirty days, businesses, organizations, and lobbyists spent $16.4 million to gain "access" on hundreds of bills.[17] In 2014's sixty-day session a bill to prevent large brewers—specifically Anheuser-Busch—from holding distributorships drove lobbyists' spending to a new level: $18 million. Since then, with or without highly contested bills in play, in early 2016 the Ethics Commission reported lobbyists' spending continuing on a record-breaking pace.[18]

Two years earlier, appropriately, at the invitation of the Kentucky Legislative Ethics Commission, "disgraced Washington lobbyist Jack Abramoff explained political corruption . . . to rapt members of the Kentucky General Assembly." Abramoff was a popular choice for an ethics class required of Kentucky lawmakers every winter, but Howard Marlowe, president of the American League of Lobbyists, protested that the state Ethics Commission, which paid Abramoff $5,000 plus expenses, was sending "the wrong message about the Kentucky legislature."[19]

In Frankfort the lobbying business may not deliver paychecks on a par with the mega salaries in Washington, but in a state where the average worker earns about $38,000, it pays quite nicely. In 2014 the biggest earner was Bob Babbage at $816,533 (formerly secretary of state); Sean Cutter at number two came in with $678,480, John McCarthy was third at $612,127; Ronny Pryor fourth at $562,387; the incomes of the next six topped $400,000.[20]

For the state legislators who are the focus of all that money typically, as in most other states and Congress, incumbent rates of reelection are high.[21] The state's representatives also resemble the political class elsewhere in taking care of themselves first, particularly with regard to retirement benefits. Retirement systems exist for teachers, judges, public employees, county employees, and state police, all set up by 1958. Once the lawmakers established theirs in 1980, representatives and governors periodically enhanced benefits in all systems across the board, but in 2005 the legislators created a "super" pension system by which many of them could double- and triple-dip. The key element in a complex formula that allows them to calculate their pensions not solely on the basis of their part-time salary as a legislator, but to include any full-time salary in another state or local government job held either before, during, or after they left the legislature. This "reciprocity" feature has given many former legislators "gold-plated pensions" running into tens of thousands of extra money.

A few examples: Former Rep. Harry Moberly served in the legislature for thirty years; when he left in 2010 he was earning $168,686 a year as a vice president at Eastern Kentucky University, a salary that became his yearly pension, "an estimated lifetime windfall of a least $2.6 million." Former Sen. David Boswell, who served in the House, then as commissioner of agriculture, then in the Senate, has a lifetime pension of an estimated $275,000 from the combined payoffs. Greg Stumbo served in the House, then as attorney general, and then as House Speaker: he could receive an estimated $1,244,694 over his lifetime, not counting a possible compound COLA increase that would add close to $380,000. An outside antitax group estimated that forty-six individuals will receive yearly pensions of $200,000 or higher. The amounts are estimates because Kentucky law requires that public pension information be kept confidential.[22]

As with most states, Kentucky's public system is underfunded—in fact, one of the most underfunded—the second worst in 2013 and the third worst in 2015. Meanwhile, the Kentucky Legislators' Retirement Plan improved from 57 percent in 2013 to 62 percent and is currently 85 percent funded; but the KERS plan covering 81,000 active and retired employees has a funding level of 17 percent needed for the next three decades, the most underfunded in the country. The teachers' retirement plan has racked up $14 billion in unfunded liability, with 54 percent of the money needed for future benefits. The legislature has failed to adequately fund the retirement system (other than their own), but the Kentucky Retirement System board also created the crisis. For years it relied on erroneous projections of investment returns, state and local payroll growth, and the inflation rate. KRS's unfunded liability might be far worse. Kentucky is one of four states not likely to meet its financial obligations.[23]

But while public employees' pensions are at risk, some very wealthy money managers are raking in millions. Hedge funds and investment and private equity firms that manage KRS's $16 billion in assets are earning investment costs 9.2 percent higher than those of pension funds of similar size. In 2010 the public learned that placement agents—middlemen—were paid $12 million over five years to line up the KRS fund as a client, with $5 million going to one agent. Placement agents had recently come under scrutiny after New York State retirement fund officers had colluded with them in kickback schemes involving tens of millions and were on their way to jail. The Security and Exchange Commission reacted by proposing a ban on placement agents, but then it backtracked to new rules aimed at preventing kickback schemes. Chris Tobe, a former KRS trustee and public pension consultant and watchdog, believes that over time millions have been exchanged in "backroom deals." In 2013 Kentucky auditor Adam Edelen found nineteen deficiencies in internal controls and, although he issued a "clean opinion," expressed concern that there was no monitoring of contracts.[24]

Critics on the Left and Right have decried the "state-pension-industrial complex" and Wall Street's ability to siphon off millions that belong to the pensioners. Scandals persist: in 2016 the head of California's retirement fund was sentenced to four years in prison for taking tens of thousands in bribes. In Kentucky, the senate passed two bills bringing transparency to KRS that did not get voted on in the House.[25]

Along with "gold plated pensions," Kentucky's legislators, like past and present members of Congress, enjoy superior health care coverage. In the state's case once legislators attain twenty years of service, their retirement benefits pay 100 percent of premiums for the representatives and their immediate family, except when Medicare starts at age sixty-five—then the plan pays only supplemental insurance premiums. Since the passage of the Affordable Care Act, a half million or more low-income Kentuckians have gained health insurance, primarily because of an executive order of Governor Steve Beshear. The new Tea Party governor has set out to replace the extension of Medicaid with something oriented to the market.[26]

Chapter 6

The Travail of Eastern Kentucky

"The published story of Eastern Kentucky has been one of
unrelieved gloom."

—Harry M. Caudill, *Theirs Be the Power*

Kentucky's status as a poor state endures because it contains the poorest region
in the nation: thirty Appalachian counties in eastern Kentucky where geography, the decline of coal mining, and loss of manufacturing and other jobs have
combined to create persistent poverty. During the twentieth century even while
coal drove the region's economy, people seeking lives outside the mines left for
industrial centers to the north and west. As coal production fell since its peak
in 1990, the population remained stagnant but since 2010 has declined with
out-migration and births outpacing deaths; many ambitious young people left
for education and opportunities for a better life in Lexington, Louisville, and
other nearby cities. People are still entering the region but are mostly poorly
educated, low-wage earners and not in the labor force.[27]

Sixteen of those mountain counties make the list of the one hundred poorest in the country. Although just over 25 percent of the state's children live in
poverty, in eastern Kentucky the rate is about 40 percent. Life expectancy for
males is 70.3 years, three years lower than the state's average and 6.5 years below
the national average.

Across all of rural Kentucky poverty has been rising steadily in recent years.
In 2013, of 120 counties in the state 60 had more than 20 percent of their people
living below U.S. poverty guidelines.[28]

But the coal country of eastern Kentucky, which has bled thousands of mining jobs over the past decade, has fared the worst. By 2015 coal production in
eastern Kentucky fell to its lowest level since the Great Depression of the 1930s,
and two thousand more jobs in that year left the region. In 2014 eastern Kentucky produced just 4 percent of the nation's coal, down from 13 percent in 1984.
The ripple effect undercuts local social services and businesses and increases
poverty. A *New York Times* investigation of the poorest counties in the nation
found six Appalachian counties—Breathitt, Clay, Jackson, Lee, Leslie, and Ma-
goffin—dwelling in the bottom ten for quality and longevity of life, educational
attainment, household income, joblessness, disability rate, life expectancy, and
obesity. Clay County's median household income of $22,296 barely cleared the
poverty line; nearly half of its population is obese, and life expectancy is six
years shorter than average.[29]

140

Repeated federal and state efforts to develop eastern Kentucky, beginning with the War on Poverty, which minimally had the salutary effect of awakening civic action by citizens within the region, have failed to spread prosperity and uplift evenly throughout the region. As Eller observed in *Uneven Ground*, although some peripheral counties with growth centers have seen improvement, a group of ten interior counties "contained some of the highest concentrations of America's persistently poor people." Eller described how many well-intended projects were sidetracked by the traditional local political class, who diverted funds to their purposes and away from dealing with the structural inequities causing poverty. The *comprador* class that collaborated with powerful external economic interests found it useful to blame problems on "outside agitators." In the twenty-first century, an inadequate tax base, a low-wage economy, environmental abuse, civic fraud, absentee landowner-ship, and corporate irresponsibility continued to weaken the region and to limit the lives of its residents.[30]

Most of those interior counties are part of Kentucky's Fifth Congressional District, which encompasses much of eastern and southern Kentucky's depressed area. The Fifth, not surprisingly, has ranked at the bottom in recent surveys of well-being in all U.S. congressional districts. In the 2013 Gallup-Healthways survey the Fifth came in last with its high rates of poverty, tobacco use, uninsured, depression, drug use, obesity, lack of access to healthy food and exercise facilities, and disability. A similar Social Science Research Council report released in 2015 found Kentucky's Fifth District second to last on measures of life expectancy, education, school enrollment, and median earnings.[31]

The district presents a stunning paradox that only the political class can create. Its poverty persists while its seventeen-term powerful member of Congress, Hal Rogers, the longest-serving Republican in Kentucky history, has brought hundreds of millions in taxpayer dollars into the district during his thirty-five-year career.

Rogers's empire consists of a complicated web of nonprofits, commercial enterprises, campaign donors, and family and friends who benefit directly from federal largesse. Known for decades as one of the most prolific users of earmarks in Congress, and nicknamed the "Prince of Pork" by the *Lexington Herald-Leader*, Rogers endorsed the 2010 Tea Party–led ban on the flow of pork-barrel projects to members' districts. But legislators, including Rogers, have found ways to get around the suspension of earmarks by going directly to federal agencies for grants. Between 2000 and 2010 the seven nonprofits

Rogers helped found, to promote the well-being of his constituents, received more than $236 million in federal funds, with more than $173 million from earmarks and $62 million from direct federal grants. Several of the nonprofits aimed at promoting economic development (e.g., Center for Rural Development, Southeast Kentucky Economic Development Corporation, Inc.), and one focused on fighting drug use.[32]

Yet unemployment in the Fifth District remains stubbornly over 10 percent; the median household income is $31,348; 22 percent of all families and 31.6 percent of families with related children under eighteen are below the poverty level; one in three people in the district receive food stamps; in some counties 10 to 20 percent of the population draws at least one disability check; and for years a prescription drug abuse epidemic has produced record numbers of deaths from overdoses. Although part of a national trend, the deaths in Kentucky during that decade were among the highest in the country (more on this topic below).[33]

To Rogers's credit, he has persistently drawn attention to Kentucky's drug abuse problem and has taken action to combat it on a variety of fronts: national, state, and local. He helped create a community-based drug-fighting organization, UNITE, focused on law enforcement investigations, substance abuse treatment, and education of the young. With other members of the Congressional Caucus on Prescription Drug Abuse he has pressured the Federal Drug Administration and other agencies to do more to prevent abuse. Speaking out repeatedly in national forums devoted to tackling the problem, he can fairly be called one of the national leaders in that effort.[34]

Rogers's position as chair of the appropriations subcommittee has given him control over the purse strings of twenty-two agencies under the Department of Homeland Security, amounting to an open spigot of federal funds flowing into the Fifth District and beyond. After 9/11 2001 Rogers sent to the district the production of a tamperproof identification card for airport, rail, and maritime workers. But by 2006 about $4 million had been spent on a study insisted on by Rogers, with some of the work diverted to a small start-up that employed his son John. Meanwhile, one organization involved paid-for trips to Hawaii, California, and Ireland for the congressman and his wife.[35]

Three state universities received $1.5 million in earmarks to develop an electronic monitoring system to ensure the safe delivery of milk. An official in Laurel County directed $530,000 worth of contracts to a woman with whom he had an undisclosed private relationship and who later became his wife. Her company ran up a cost overrun of $220,000 in supplying emergency response trailers, generators, and other gear to several counties; an audit found that charges for the generators were $900 in excess for each and the trailers were "inferior in quality" and smaller than promised. Hundreds of thousands of FEMA disaster aid dollars sent to Carter and Leslie Counties simply disappeared into black holes. State money has also fed the "security" gravy train as Kentucky officials spent $36,000 to determine whether terrorists were embezzling money from . . .*bingo halls.*[36]

Rogers's interference in the identification card project to benefit his contributor friends and family led the conservative magazine *National Review* to label him "an exemplary figure of Congressional disgrace. Private Companies have courted his favor with political donations, golf excursions, and exotic vacations, and he in turn channeled millions of taxpayer dollars in their direction." Both the *National Review* on the right and *Rolling Stone* on the left regarded Rogers's abuse of Homeland Security funds as "not just a financial scandal" but also "a matter of national security." Thereafter, from 2007 through 2013 Citizens for Responsibility and Ethics in Washington repeatedly named Rogers as one of the ten "Most Corrupt Members of Congress," a distinction that hardly put a crimp in his style.[37]

In 2012 a Rogers earmark gained national attention when the *New York Times* reported that he had succeeded in giving a company in his district, Phoenix Products, a contract to produce drip pans for Black Hawk helicopters. By 2011 the U.S. Army had purchased at least 374 of the drip pans at an average cost of $17,000. A similar pan from a company elsewhere cost $2,500. The owners of Phoenix, Thomas and Peggy Wilson, along with their employees, had contributed $37,000 to Rogers's campaign fund; since 2005 they paid $600,000 to a Washington lobbying firm, Martin, Fisher Thompson and Associates, to help secure them federal contracts. In 2006 they added a Kentucky-based lobbying company with a strong connection to Rogers: firm partner Jeffrey Speaks had worked in Rogers's office as projects director for ten years. But in 2012 a rare event took place as the $17,000 drip pans finally became too much for a cost-cutting Congress to swallow: a coalition of most Democrats and eighty-nine Republicans voted to block more funds going to Rogers's boondoggle, with more than $17 million already spent.[38]

Phoenix Products is hardly the only enterprise in the Fifth District that benefited from Rogers's earmarks. From 2008 to 2010 Rogers secured over $250 million in federal largesse before the "earmark ban" for businesses, nonprofits, and projects in his otherwise depressed region. Several landed close to home: $7 million went to paving and upgrading an area of Rogers's hometown of Somerset, including a strip along commercial properties in which he has investments, and a half mile of a residential street with sixty houses including the congressman's. In 2010 Rogers even succeeded in getting $5 million a year to go to conservation groups that protected big cats overseas; one group that could apply for the funds would be a Namibia-based cheetah conservation fund for which his daughter, who lived in Versailles, Kentucky, worked at the time.[39]

The many earmarks have not filtered through to Owsley County, the poorest in the district and in 2012 in the United States. Its population of five thousand has a median household income of $19,351, the lowest outside Puerto Rico. Owsley's profile defies the stereotype of poverty's association with the urban African American and Hispanic poor: Owsley is 99 percent white; over 41 percent of residents fall below the poverty line; over 50 percent receive food stamps; obesity tops 50 percent; its residents' life expectancy of 71.4 years is more than seven years below the national standard.[40]

Owsley, in step with the rest of the Fifth District, routinely votes to return Hal Rogers to office. Rogers won reelection over the last four cycles by margins ranging from 78 to 84 percent. Owsley also typifies "food-stamp counties" that tend to vote Republican nationally. Between 2007 and 2011, as the economy tanked, food stamp recipients doubled in 254 counties: in 2012 Republican Mitt Romney won 213 of them. Owsley County gave Romney 81 percent of its vote. Clay County (see above), with 40 percent or more receiving food stamps, also went heavily for Romney. Congressional Republicans, who cut food stamps, pay little or no price for such actions from their constituents.[41]

Food stamp and other recipients of welfare, "people on the draw" (mountain vernacular for welfare), most likely do not vote. In the 2015 gubernatorial election counties with the greatest number of people on Medicaid voted for a Tea Party Republican who promised to take away Democratic Governor Beshear's expansion of the program to 400,000 needy Kentuckians. But *ProPublica* reporter Alec MacGillis pointed out that the Republican votes come more from "those who are a notch or two up the economic ladder," and their growing attachment to Republicans "is, in part, a reaction against what they perceive, among those below them . . . as a growing dependence on the safety net."[42] Ironically, those "a notch or two up" very likely also receive federal benefits, such as the mortgage interest deduction and Medicare.

While Rogers's network contributes to his political longevity, with votes and campaign contributions, in poor counties other impulses help produce Republican majorities. Much of the Fifth District and other parts of eastern Kentucky have been strongly Republican since the Civil War. But in 2008 many formerly Democratic Appalachian counties—that voted for Gore in 2000 and Kerry in 2004—flipped strongly over to Republican John McCain. Knott County, for example, gave Gore 61 percent and Kerry 63 percent of the vote, but Obama just 45 percent. The Democrat's "otherness" played a role in areas 99 percent white and rural. That Obama intended a "War on Coal" was part propaganda and part the reality of his environmental policy in relation to a declining industry. Obama hurt himself in Appalachia when remarks he made privately were released about rural people losing jobs, becoming frustrated, and clinging to their guns and religion, and the NRA campaigned intensely against him.[43]

The roots of eastern Kentucky's distress and poverty go deep into its past as a region where absentee landlords and outside corporations extracted much of the region's wealth, leaving its inhabitants, once profits were made and exported, to fend for themselves. As Eller explained in *Uneven Ground*, when jobs disappeared, mountain families' "dependence shifted to the state and federal governments as public welfare programs stepped in to prevent starvation and destitution." Without hope of finding work in the region, "increasing number[s] reluctantly turned to public assistance for survival. . . . The new welfare system became a way of life for some mountain residents, who felt powerless to change their situation." As a result, local officials' control over scarce jobs and welfare gave them enormous power over their constituents.[44]

A culture of dependence spread unevenly through the region. In the 1950s manufacturing in eastern Kentucky was failing to keep pace with its growth elsewhere, but the coal industry had not entered its sharp decline. Clay County, for example, averaged over 1,500 mine workers from 1975 to 1990, but then mechanization and other causes steadily reduced Clay's miners to barely 50. By 1996 over half of the employment pool had no jobs, and most were on "the draw." By then, too, Clay stood foremost in the ranks of eastern Kentucky counties corrupted by vote buying and criminal drug gangs.

Earlier, during their heyday the coal companies had set the template for corruption and vote buying. After the late 1990s the number of criminal networks began to diminish when Congress designated eastern Kentucky a High Intensity Drug Trafficking Area and federal prosecutions took effect. Still, local vote buying has continued, and from 2002 to 2011 no fewer than 237 public corruption convictions occurred in the east compared with 65 in the western region. As recently as 2010 a jury convicted eight prominent Clay County officials, including a former circuit judge and former school superintendent. In the spring elections of 2014 reports of vote buying came from Clay and eighteen other counties.[45]

The marriage of dependence and political corruption in eastern Kentucky also preceded Hal Rogers entering Congress in 1981. It was perhaps inevitable, Eller concluded, that the welfare system "would feed the already corrupt and feudal political structure in the mountains." In more detail than can be related here, Eller described how the region's "poverty and dependence . . . choked efforts at long-range planning and community development." After the large corporations withdrew from interference in local matters—"except to maintain low taxes on their land and mineral resources—local leaders had little incentive to change existing economic and political relationships." Indeed, local machines expanded their power over public funds and programs.[46]

Mountain professionals—physicians, bankers, land developers, real estate brokers, and lawyers—often allied with outside capitalists to dominate the economy. Physicians played a critical role in expanding the culture of dependence. As more people became unemployed, they collaborated with county judge executives to provide certification of disability and easily convinced the Department of Social Welfare to cut a monthly check for the "disabled" local claimant who was now obligated to the local political machine.[47]

Disability checks, deserved and not, continue to be a mainstay of eastern Kentucky's economy. Coal mining, of course, can be hazardous to health, with black lung disease and workplace injuries long imbedded in the industry. In 2014 Kentucky's population of 4,339,367 contained 944,041 recipients of Social Security benefits. Of these, 261,032 were receiving disability insurance, and the Fifth Congressional District had by far the most recipients of Social Security Disability Insurance (SSDI).[48]

But legitimate disability claims have been accompanied by manipulation of the system, as revealed by a scandal involving fraud over a period of years perpetrated by a lawyer, bribed doctors, a judge, and the chief judge in the Social Security Office and Disability Adjudication and Review in Huntington, West Virginia. Between 2001 and 2011 the lawyer, Eric C. Conn, of Floyd County, Kentucky, collected $22.5 million in fees by getting disability checks approved for hundreds of clients. Earlier, false claims for benefits had eventually stained the black lung benefits program enacted in 1973; but in recent decades the disease experienced a resurgence, and new federal regulations ensued to prevent coal companies from denying claims by bribing doctors.[49]

Since the recession of 2008–9, and with baby boomers aging, disability claims and benefits have been surging nationally, with pressure growing on the federal Disability Trust Fund. Although Conn is the poster child for corruption, unfounded claims have risen across the country. Over the past twenty-five years the number of people enrolled in SSDI has grown by several million, especially in the five years before 2013. In 1988 there were 2.4 disabled workers on SSDI for every 100 workers in the United States, compared to 6.2 disabled workers for every 100 in 2013. Sen. Tom Coburn (R-OK), a physician, had his staff randomly select hundreds of disability files; they found 25 percent should never have been approved and another 20 percent were questionable. In Conn's Floyd and nearby counties, over 10 percent of the population receives disability checks in contrast to 5 percent nationally. West Virginia and Kentucky, the site of Conn's activities, are the number one and three states receiving disability checks.[50]

In 2011 a *Wall Street Journal* article called attention to David Daugherty (Conn's chief accomplice), an administrative law judge who accepted every disability claim that came his way. That year, too, a civil lawsuit had been filed by two SSA employees accusing Conn and Daugherty of manipulating the system to make money, and the U.S. Senate Committee on Homeland Security and Governmental Affairs began a two-year investigation into Conn's activities. In October 2013 it released a report uncovering "a raft of improper practices" by Conn to obtain disability benefits and fees.

Beginning in a small trailer near his home, Conn became, at the height of his success in 2010, an employer of nearly forty people and the third-highest paid disability lawyer in the country, pulling in $3.9 million that year in fees. Eventually the practice grew to a string of trailers he called the "Eric Conn Law Complex," while living in a $1.5 million 7,500-square-foot mansion in a gated neighborhood near his office. Marketing his services on billboards, television, radio, and online commercials, Conn worked closely with Daugherty to process claims in "assembly-line fashion," with Daugherty scheduling twenty hearings a day in contrast to most judges holding fifteen to twenty hearings a week. His approval rate overall could be rounded up to 100 percent, in contrast to a national approval rate of 60 percent. Daugherty awarded SSDI benefits to 8,413 individuals, for total federal lifetime cash benefits of an estimated $2.5 billion.[51]

The doctors who signed off automatically on medical assessments always found for disability. Conn recruited them after searching the Internet to find those whose licenses had been revoked or who had been sanctioned for ethical problems or linked to malpractice suits. He referred to them as "whore doctors," who obliged him by usually signing forms filled out ahead of time by Conn's office, with many of them containing exactly the same information. Conn paid them well, over six years nearly $2 million. His "go-to doctor" was Frederick Huffnagle who had been the subject of several malpractice suits and who, before his death in 2010, received almost $1 million from Conn. The stable of "whore doctors" included David P. Herr of Ohio and A. Bradley Atkins and Srinivas Ammsetty of Kentucky.[52]

Before the 2011 appearance of the *WSJ* article, the chief judge in the Huntington office, Charles Paul Andrus, had ignored warnings from the SSA staff, and once the story appeared he retaliated against those he suspected of leaking information about Daugherty to the paper. Officials in the SSA office not only smothered complaints about Daugherty but intimidated potential whistle-blowers, since they were benefiting from the high volume of approved claimants in raises and bonuses. The agency removed Andrus as chief judge and quickly placed on leave Daugherty, who then retired. The other judges and supervisors at the Huntington office who enabled Conn and Daugherty faced no serious consequences. Charles Andrus eventually retired with a pension.[53]

Conn's reaction to exposure came swiftly: he refused to speak to the Senate committee, bought several prepaid disposable phones to allow him to confer with Daugherty, destroyed the hard drives in his office, and hired a company to shred over 26,000 pounds of documents. At the Senate hearing, Senator Carl Levin (D-MI) said Conn was "still going strong, representing thousands of disability claimants" and opening a new office in Beverly Hills, California.[54]

In 2012 "Mr. Social Security," as he referred to himself, had been charged with a felony for violating campaign finance laws by illegally funneling campaign cash for the successful reelection of Supreme Court Justice Will T. Scott. He got off pleading guilty to a lesser misdemeanor charge. In May 2015, however, the Social Security Administration suddenly suspended disability payments for nine hundred of his clients, claiming fraudulent evidence had been provided. Some of those clients panicked; two committed suicide.[55] The nine hundred checks did not remain in abeyance very long. Congressman Rogers intervened with the SSA and persuaded the agency to resume payments.

In July U.S. District Judge Amal Thapar dismissed much of the 2013 suit brought against Conn by the SSA whistle-blowers, allowing part of it to continue. In August a judge dismissed one of the wrongful death lawsuits filed after the suicides. By then Conn's defense team included former federal prosecutor Kent Wicker and former Kentucky chief justice Joseph Lambert.[56]

Lambert's presence indicates how the hill country lawyer used the big money made from his disability practice to tie himself into Kentucky's political class. Lambert, a staunch Republican, was first elected to the bench in 1986 and elevated to chief justice in 1998. When he retired in 2008, he had acquired a reputation for partisanship and left behind a controversial $900 million courthouse building spree that added to the state's debt in the midst of a devastating economic recession.

In 2000 Lambert had launched a program to build new courthouses in all 120 Kentucky counties. Some courthouses needed to be replaced, but political opponents criticized the project as both unnecessary and politically motivated. By 2008 some 70 courthouses were being built, but after the recession hit, the court system wound up starved of money; the next year it laid off forty-seven people, and when 38 new courthouses opened in 2011, the cash-strapped state needed to begin paying off the bonds used by counties for their construction.[57]

Controversy arose over several of the projects; critics questioned $900 million spent without competitive bidding and pointed to ties between Lambert, his family, and the construction and finance companies that built most of the courthouses. Codell Construction managed some 60 percent of the courthouse jobs, while the brokerage and investment firm Ross Sinclair & Associates, based in Louisville, worked as financial advisor on almost 70 percent of the projects. The Codell family contributed campaign cash to many county judge executives and other local officials deciding on the building contracts, as well as over $3,000 to the campaigns of Lambert's wife, Debra, for family court judge and circuit court judge. A few months before Lambert retired, Ross Sinclair hired his son, Joseph P. Lambert Jr., and when critics mentioned the word *nepotism*, Sinclair responded, "His Dad, whom I don't know, had nothing to do with it." As Joseph Jr. and his girlfriend moved from Texas to Louisville to join Ross Sinclair, the state Administrative Office of the Courts (AOC), which oversaw the projects, awarded the girlfriend a human resources job that was not advertised. The chief justice supervises the AOC, which is not subject to Kentucky's open records law. A blogger at the *Louisville*

Courier-Journal commented that the courthouse project "may have been one of the most overblown, least disciplined sprees in recent Kentucky history, but at least those in charge seem to have done their best to keep things all in the family."[58]

As Conn's lawyer in June 2015, Lambert alleged that the Social Security agency and not Conn victimized disability recipients in eastern Kentucky. "Mr. Conn's done nothing wrong," he said.[59]

Finally, however, after an inexplicable decade of delay, federal authorities decided that Conn did do "something wrong," and acted before the statute of limitations expired. In April 2016 a federal grand jury charged Conn, Daugherty (arrested in Florida), and a Pikeville psychologist, Alfred Bradley Adkins, with mail fraud, conspiracy to retaliate against a witness, destruction of evidence, making false statements, and money laundering. The judge released Conn on a $1.25 million bond, imposed home incarceration, and posted Conn's mansion to secure the bond.[60]

On March 24, 2017, Conn pleaded guilty to fraud for stealing from the SSA and one count of paying illegal gratuities to a federal judge. He admitted to, among other crimes, submitting "well over" 1,700 false documents. His plea agreement required him to pay the government at least $5.7 million and $46.5 million to the SSA. Ten days later U.S. District Judge Amul Thapar ordered Conn to pay an additional $31 million to the government and the two SSA whistle-blowers who had called attention to the ongoing disability fraud. The next day, fifteen years after evidence of Conn's activities surfaced, the Bar Association suspended Conn's license to practice law in Kentucky.[61]

The years-long bonanza of fraud in the Huntington office occurred in a context of an agency overwhelmed with caseloads, an "emphasis on high volume adjudications over quality decision making," and hundreds of other ALJs (administrative law judges) across the country approving disability claims at rates that agency watchdogs regarded as "red flags." A June 10, 2014, staff report by the U.S. House Committee on Oversight and Government Reform found that the overall allowance rate for ALJs from 2005 to 2013 was 68.5 percent, with ALJs deciding claims already denied, generally twice. Daugherty was not the only rubber-stamper, and Appalachia not the only region where disability claims won near-automatic approval. During 2013 *60 Minutes* devoted a segment to the abuse in the Huntington office, and during that program Marilyn Zahn, the vice president of the Association of Administrative Law Judges, said that "if the American public knew what was going on in our system, half would be outraged and the other half would apply for benefits."[62]

Hal Rogers's Fifth Congressional District can be said to be layered with *two cultures of dependence* essential to the economy of the district: an affluent strata of employed middle- and upper-middle-class people who benefit directly or indirectly from Rogers's prodigious success in earmarking federal funds into the region, boosting politically connected enterprises; and a lower-income layer of recipients of federal safety-net programs including SSI, SSDI, Medicaid, and SNAP (Supplemental Nutrition Assistance Program).

In the 1990s a new extractive industry entered eastern Kentucky, the pharmaceutical, and with aggressive marketing of powerful pain-killing opioids it exported millions of dollars from an already desolated region. Congressman Rogers later described the invasion: "Local hospitals were experiencing more than an overdose per week, families had been overrun by pain pills. . . . These powerful drugs intended to manage pain were suddenly creating pain . . . crime and uncontrollable addiction." The new scourge of opioids, just a few molecules removed from heroin, built on the ills and stunted lives ravaged by earlier exploitations.[63]

When the FDA approved OxyContin for pain management in 1995–96, prescription drug abuse had already taken hold in eastern Kentucky. But by the late 1990s OxyContin—pure oxycodone with a time release—flooded in and soon became known as "hillbilly heroin." The manufacturer, Purdue Pharma, was selling it to mountain doctors "hand over fist." In 2001 law enforcement conducted "Operation Oxyfest," arresting over two hundred people, but soon pipelines opened in Florida and Mexico bringing new supplies as drug dealers rented vans and booked cheap flights from Florida creating what police called the "OxyContin Express." Carloads of Kentuckians drove to "pill mills" in Florida where doctors readily wrote and filled prescriptions. From 2000 to 2009 overdose deaths among men doubled and among women tripled.[64]

In the states most affected by the drug's abuse, elected officials, federal regulators, and police called attention to the dangers of the pill; personal injury lawyers began seeking clients injured by the drug; and lawsuits against the manufacturer began, initiated by individuals, state officials, and U.S. attorneys. Purdue Pharma's lawyers, however, could draw upon political influence to help them defend the company's $1 billion annual sales of the drug.[65]

The pharmaceutical industry had long enjoyed influence in Washington and state capitols through its lobbying and campaign contributions. During the 1990s the industry underwent consolidation, and its political influence grew even more powerful.[66] As actions against the drug mounted, the industry used its clout with Washington's political class.

In 2001 West Virginia's attorney general, Daniel McGraw Jr., filed a civil suit against Purdue accusing it of "coercive and deceptive" tactics, pointing out that while the firm's annual revenue from OxyContin sales exceeded $1 billion, the state bore the cost of treating the addicted. In 2004, just before the case went to trial, President Obama's first attorney general, Eric Holder, then working for the law firm of Covington and Burling in Washington (a firm specializing in defending corporations accused of crimes), negotiated a settlement in which Purdue paid the state $10 million and admitted no wrongdoing.

In Virginia an investigation initiated by U.S. Attorney John Brownlee resulted in a 2007 guilty plea by three Purdue Pharma executives, Michael Friedman, Howard Udell, and Paul Goldenheim. The firm agreed to pay fines of $634.5 million (plus $34.5 million owed by the executives) for pushing what Brownlee described as "a fraudulent marketing campaign that promoted OxyContin as less addictive, less subject to abuse, and less likely to cause withdrawal. In the process, scores died as a result of OxyContin abuse and an even greater number became addicted." Brownlee did his job and made the company pay, even though Purdue flexed its muscle with the George W. Bush administration and threatened his job.[67]

The Virginia case came in the midst of a campaign, led by presidential advisor Karl Rove, to purge some dozen U.S. attorneys who were not responding to Attorney General Alberto Gonzalez's pressure to follow up on Republican allegations of voter fraud. In 2006 several were fired, leading to a hearing into the removals by the Senate Judiciary Committee, now controlled by Democrats following their sweep in the midterm elections. Brownlee testified before the committee that he too had been put on the "hit list" after receiving a call at home from Michael J. Elston, then chief of staff to the deputy attorney general. The call came just before the Purdue settlement, and Elston asked Brownlee to slow down. Brownlee, a Republican, asked Elston if he was calling at the behest of his superior, and when the answer was negative it was clear the call came at the prompting of Purdue Pharma. Brownleee told Elston to leave him alone

Copyright Ed Gamble. Reprinted with permission.

and settled the case the next day. Eight days later Brownlee's name appeared on Gonzalez's "hit list." He kept his job, however, until he left office on his own in 2008.[68]

Part of the Virginia settlement went to reimburse state Medicaid programs, but Kentucky refused an offer to settle for $500,000 and filed its own lawsuit in Pike Circuit Court. Purdue succeeded in having the suit transferred out of Pike County, where a jury might have levied an enormous penalty. With the case back in federal court in December 2015, the company agreed to pay the state $24 million for misleading doctors and patients in its marketing of OxyContin, but admitted no wrongdoing.[69]

In 2012, with the prescription drug abuse epidemic still raging, the Kentucky legislature placed new restrictions on pain clinics and on the prescribing of controlled substances. Known as the "pill mill bill," it mandated a tracking system for all such prescriptions, KASPER (Kentucky All Schedule Prescription Electronic Reporting). After the legislature revised it to accommodate hospitals, long-term care facilities, and approved researchers, one study showed that by 2015 the new system was having effect. At the same time, however, the scourge of heroin was on the rise in both eastern and northern Kentucky.[70]

Chapter 6

The Making of an Epidemic

"The richest newcomer to the Forbes 2015 list of America's Richest Families comes in at a stunning $14 billion. The Sackler family, which owns the Stamford, Conn.–based Purdue Pharma, flew under the radar when Forbes launched its initial list of wealthiest families in July 2014, but this year they crack the top-20, edging out storied families like the Busches, Mellons and Rockefellers.

"How did the Sacklers build the 16th-largest fortune in the country? The short answer: making the most popular and controversial opioid of the 21st century—OxyContin."[71]

Alex Morrell, "The OxyContin Clan"

The ravaging of regions of rural America by OxyContin abuse from Maine to Mississippi—and especially Appalachian Kentucky, West Virginia, Ohio, Maine, and Virginia—did not happen by accident. The Sacklers and Purdue Pharma targeted them.

Three brothers created OxyContin, Arthur, Mortimer, and Raymond Sackler, born to European immigrants who ran a grocery store. They all became psychiatrists, and at a small mental hospital in Queens they produced important research in the biology of mental illness that opened the door to drug treatments. In 1952 they bought a small drug factory in New York City and eventually branched out from producing laxatives to more profitable painkillers. They first took an old drug for cancer pain, morphine sulphate, added a time-release formula, and sold it as MS Contin; in the next decade sales rose to $475 million. Next they took oxycodone, invented in Germany in World War I to send exhausted soldiers back into battle, and added a time-release mechanism that they claimed would prevent its abuse.

Earlier, the elder brother, Arthur, a "brilliant polymath" working for a small advertising firm, became a pioneer of medical advertising and promoted Valium into the first $100 million drug. He was the first to cultivate relationships with doctors, courting them with expensive dinners and junkets and lucrative speaking fees, "an approach so effective that the entire industry adopted it." (*ProPublica*'s "Dollars for Doctors" database now tracks the flow of industry money to physicians, including those with disciplinary records.)[72]

By 1995 when the FDA approved OxyContin, Arthur was dead, but his siblings adopted his aggressive marketing strategy to the selling of OxyContin. All accounts of the success of that strategy, of Purdue Pharma, and the explosive demand for OxyContin agree that the breakthrough depended on marketing and not medicine. Purdue sold the drug not primarily as a cancer pain treatment but as effective and safe for anything from backaches to arthritis. In 1998 it circulated a video asserting that the potential for addiction to OxyContin was less than 1 percent. But drug abusers seeking a fix discovered that they could crush the pill into powder for an immediate high.

From 1996 to 2001 Purdue launched an "extraordinary" campaign to market OxyContin. More than five thousand physicians, pharmacists, and nurses attended over forty pain-management and speaker-training conferences at resorts in Florida, Arizona, and California, all expenses paid. It increased its internal sales force from 318 to 671 representatives. Promotional items such as fishing hats and toys flooded into doctors' offices. The company compiled files of physicians who tended to be the highest prescribers of opioids and with the most chronic-pain patients. It was "unprecedented," according to an article in the *American Journal of Public Health,* in the amount of money spent on this sales campaign. Spending six to twelve times more than on any other drug's promotion, or than competitors spent on similar products, Purdue funded directly or through grants over twenty thousand pain-related "educational programs" to influence what physicians prescribed. In 2001 it paid out $40 million in bonuses to its sales representatives. By 2002 sales of OxyContin brought in $1.5 billion; soon revenue from OxyContin worldwide exceeded $2 billion and in 2010 reached $3.1 billion.[73]

Purdue Pharma targeted primary care physicians in rural areas, knowing that poor people on Medicaid are prescribed painkillers at twice the rate of non-Medicaid patients and are six times at risk for taking overdoses. A recent Washington State study found that deaths from overdoses were 2.5 times higher among people living in areas where 20 percent or more of the population live below the federal poverty level compared to where fewer than 5 percent are in poverty.[74]

In rural America, from Maine to Alabama, prescriptions for OxyContin shot up. From 1995 to 2001 in eastern Kentucky the number of patients entering methodone maintenance clinics rose 500 percent; about 75 percent of them were OxyContin dependent; in West Virginia such clinics reported an influx of hundreds of new patients. By 2002 a quarter of the deaths nationally linked to OxyContin abuse took place in Kentucky.[75]

Compared to its profits, fines paid by the firm have been chump change. In 2010 Purdue made a significant modification in OxyContin, selling a new version that resists abuse; it breaks into chunks, not powder, and when mixed with water becomes a slimy goo, with the result that the street price has dropped. Since 2010, too, Purdue has burnished its image, stressing its concern about abuse, and waging its own "drug war," by holding seminars for law enforcement personnel to educate them regarding drug abuse.[76] More than one public official fighting the opioid epidemic in Kentucky and elsewhere asked: Why did it take them so long to modify the drug?

"The Sacklers were never charged." That sentence appeared in almost every account of the marketing of OxyContin and its ravages across America. Arthur Sackler died in 1987, before OxyContin brought in billions to his brothers and well before the marketing campaign that launched an epidemic. Mortimer died in 2010, just as sales of OxyContin peaked. Raymond has lived into his nineties, and in the formal photo *Forbes* used for the story that began this section, he stood smiling, trim and dapper, with his attractive wife, Beverly, seated beside him.

Wikipedia describes the couple as "international philanthropists," and they have indeed bestowed gifts across continents, to the British Museum, the Louvre, and the Metropolitan Museum of New York, where the Sackler Wing houses the Egyptian Temple of Dendur. Prestigious universities across America have received funds for museums, galleries, fellowships, and support for research in medicine and the sciences; there have been similar gifts to Tel Aviv University. The Wikipedia entry for Raymond mentions briefly that he is "closely associated with the global reach of Purdue Pharma." It does not mention OxyContin.

By 2015 Kentucky still ranked fifth worst in the nation for drug overdose deaths, in part because of increased use of heroin and illicit synthetic opioids, notably fentanyl. One poll found that although prescription drug overdose deaths declined during 2013–14 by 10 percent, deaths from heroin use rose 55 percent. And a new term had been coined to describe drug abusers in Appalachia: *pillbillies*.[77]

Although the pill mill bill brought greater transparency to prescriptions of controlled substances, Kentucky's 2014 expansion of Medicaid (under Obamacare) may have made cheap opioids more available, while at the same time providing greater access to treatment for abuse. In early 2017 in the town of Manchester (pop. 1,500) in Clay County, in an otherwise depressed shopping area, eleven pharmacies continuously fill prescriptions and sell few over-the-counter items. In the twelve-month period ending September 2016, area residents filled prescriptions for 2.2 million doses of hydrocodone and almost 617,000 doses of oxycodone. Whatever Medicaid's recent role, a community health specialist observed that before its expansion uninsured people "were pretty resourceful when it came to finding drugs." Doctors and pharmacists, whose role is not to be enforcers, have continually faced unremitting pressure to keep writing and filling prescriptions.[78]

Fifth in drug overdose deaths but first in homeless children: an analysis of federal education data by the *Herald-Leader* revealed Kentucky to have the highest rate of student homelessness in the nation, the number being over thirty thousand, having doubled in about five to six years. These kids understandably lag well behind other students in learning and are more likely not to finish high school. The recent spurt in their numbers is in part due to improved methods of identifying homeless young people. But the major causes of the increase of recent years are families broken by lack of income to stay together, especially in the former coal counties, and Kentucky's high rate of drug addition after years of a prescription drug epidemic. Not surprisingly, according to a recent report, addiction and the crime it breeds have given the state the highest percentage of children with incarcerated parents: 13 percent of children in 2011–12 reported having a parent in jail at some time.[79]

Kentucky's opioid epidemic arose from conditions specific to Kentucky, but the national political class enabled Purdue Pharma to become the new irresponsible extractive industry with billions in profit build on addiction and ruined lives. "Appalachian problems," wrote Eller, "were fundamentally those of the rest of America."

Across America an epidemic of deaths from opioid, heroin, and fentanyl overdoses continues, originating from economic, social, and community decline, and the complicity of Congress, the FDA, and the national political class.[80] Consider how members of the political class, earning millions as lawyers defending corporate wrongdoing, came forward to protect Purdue Pharma in the prosecutions most threatening to its ongoing business.

In the 2007 Virginia case, the firm's defense team included Rudolph Giuliani and Mary Jo White, typical members of the permanent political class. They succeeded in getting the U.S. Attorney's office to drop a dozen charges against the firm, including Medicaid fraud, unjust enrichment, and false advertising; the firm pleaded guilty to just one, misbranding and misleading. After becoming "America's Mayor" in response to the 9/11 attacks, Giuliani formed a "crisis management" and "security consulting" firm leading to profitable deals with companies attracted to his still glowing 9/11 aura. In 2005 he became a partner of a Houston-based law firm, Bracewell & Patterson, that specialized in defending energy companies accused of polluting and their lead counsel in the Virginia case against Purdue. Mary Jo White argued on behalf of one of the defendants that he was the "moral compass" of the firm. She came from the firm Debevoise & Plimpton, another specialist in defending corporate wrongdoing. Firms like Debevoise eagerly hire former federal prosecutors—White was the U.S. Attorney for the Southern District of New York from 1993 to 2002 before joining Debevoise. In 1994 she worked out one of the first "deferred prosecution agreements" allowing a corporation and individuals to avoid criminal charges, so at Debevoise she naturally specialized in defending corporations accused of breaking laws. In 2013 President Obama appointed her chair of the Securities and Exchange Commission, where she presided over a board heavily criticized for its lax approach to financial fraud. The 2010 Dodd-Frank legislation required publically traded companies to publish the ratio of CEO pay to the average pay of their employees, but this rule was yet to be implemented after her five years in office.[81]

Yet Eric Holder's 2004 work defending Purdue Pharma in West Virginia was far more consequential. The morning of the trial Holder went into the judge's chambers and negotiated the settlement, with the firm paying $10 million over ten years for drug education and treatment and admitting no wrongdoing. By averting a trial, Holder prevented the release of documents and testimony— federal officials had issued six hundred subpoenas for company records since 2002—relating to the firm's criminal activities.[82]

In 2016 those court documents—and many related to Kentucky's case— came to light due to dogged investigative work by STAT, the online health and medical journal published by Boston Globe Media. The litigation had produced some seventeen thousand pages related to the company's activities. Kentucky's attorney general as part of its settlement destroyed its copies, but other key papers were sealed and kept in West Virginia. They demonstrated unequivocally how Purdue Pharma and Abbott Laboratories pressured medical agencies and misled prescribers to keep unrestricted access to opioids flowing and, in effect, bribed pharmacy benefits managers to ease availability and lower co-pays.[83]

In the past decade, Big Pharma spent nearly $900 million to lobby against laws that would limit availability of opioids such as OxyContin, Viocodin, and fentanyl. The money is often laundered through groups like the American Cancer Society and other advocacy groups that represent patients with chronic pain or cancer. Big Pharma's big profits funneled into lobbying explains why pharmaceutical companies have a "stranglehold" on Congress, recently leveraged in passage of the Republican-sponsored Ensuring Patient Access and Effective Drug Enforcement Act. Critics, including Joseph Rannazzisi, former head of the Drug Enforcement Administration's Diversion Control Division, assert that it actually limits the DEA's ability to go after wholesalers, pharmacists, and doctors who engage in illegal activity. Rannazzisi called it "a gift to the industry." Lobbyists for the bill included manufacturers, distributors, and pharmacy chains, some of which were targeted by the DEA in recent years for failure to keep drugs off the black market. Democratic senators criticized a companion bill, the Comprehensive Addiction and Recovery Act, for giving the appearance of supporting treatment but neglecting to provide funding: "using a piece of chewing gum to patch a cracked dam."[84] As treatment funding has dwindled, Congress hamstrung the DEA's ability to lessen the flow of illegal opioids.

Wholesalers constitute as large a source of the opioid epidemic as manufacturers. Three companies, AmerisourceBergen, McKesson, and Cardinal Health, together are as big as Walmart and control 85 percent of the market. When the government asked the distributors to police their shipments, the big three and ten others ignored the DEA, even after warnings and evidence that their shipments fell into the wrong hands. West Virginia, for example, has suffered more than any other state from opioid abuse. Without hesitation wholesalers from 2007 through 2012 shipped 780 million hydrocodone and oxycodone pills, and in ever higher doses, while 1,728 West Virginians fatally overdosed. In 2015 the CEOs of the big three made collectively $450 million.[85]

The wholesalers aggressively lobbied the Justice Department, hired dozens of officials from the DEA to get the agency to back off, and fought investigators to keep their sales secret. In 2013, mysteriously, after Clifford Lee Reeves II took over approval of enforcement, DEA cases suddenly plummeted—"came to a grinding halt," said one DEA field supervisor. After a *Washington Post* report exposing the shift, Democratic senators Ron Wyden and Patrick Leahy have been asking the Justice Department why.[86]

This account barely scratches the surface of the degree to which Congress, the FDA, and agencies such as the Interagency Pain Research Coordinating Committee (IPRCC) enable the sectors of the supply chain to continue and expand

America's opioid epidemic. The FDA, IPRCC, and the medical profession are shot through with conflicts of interest. In 2012, 84 percent of doctors reported receiving payments, free travel, drug samples, or gifts from drug companies. One member of the IPRCC typifies the operation of the national permanent political class: she also sits on the board of the American Chronic Pain Association, a lobbying firm funded mostly by opioid makers. Front groups for Big Pharma continually try to influence the Centers for Disease Control and Prevention (CDC) and other regulatory agencies.[87]

Profiteering from drug abuse is woven into every fabric of government and society, from billionaire CEOs to small online distributors, to doctors and pharmacists, respectable and rogue, to myriad forms of criminal activity, from top to bottom. America's epidemic is on the threshold of becoming a pandemic, as prescription drug abuse spreads to several developed countries, such as Canada, Australia, and China, and to Europe and the Middle East. But for now the permanent political class has made the United States the "reigning champion" of opioid abuse.[88]

Chapter 7

The Profitable World of Nonprofits

The corporate sector has no monopoly on greed.

—Deborah L. Rhode and Amanda K. Packel,
"Ethics and Nonprofits"

Charities and other nonprofit organizations have often been rocked by scandal. One of the most memorable involved the prestigious United Way of America in 1992 when its CEO for over twenty years, William Aramony, resigned amid allegations of diverting over a million dollars to his personal use to support an extravagant lifestyle, including expenses for an affair with a young woman who was seventeen when the fifty-nine-year-old Aramony began courting her. In 1995 he was sentenced to seven years in prison. Although sensational scandals involving charities episodically attract media attention, the roll call of "CharityWatch's Hall of Shame" indicates that fraud and theft occurs almost continuously in the world of giving. The scandals of the nonprofit sector have regularly paralleled those in finance and business, and enterprising con artists and criminals continually invent new ways to bilk charitable organizations and the donating public.[1]

The Aramony case, however, no longer typifies executives exploiting a nonprofit for personal benefit: he went to jail. That rarely happens now, in part because boards of wealthy nonprofits have emulated the corporate model of excess compensation combined with lax oversight. Increasingly, executives of nonprofit organizations with healthy cash flow interact with and become embedded in the political class and adopt the lifestyle of the One Percent. The corrupt interaction of the financial and business sectors with the permanent political class has drawn widespread attention in the media for its contribution to increasing inequality of wealth and income. But the media have paid less attention to the nonprofit sector's promotion of inequality of income and a One Percent lifestyle among the wealthiest organizations that rely on donations as well as taxpayer-funded government grants.

The temptations are huge. The nonprofit sector overall employs 10 percent of the U.S. workforce, and in 2010 corporations, government, and individuals donated $300 billion to charitable enterprises; of the total, at least $40 billion a year is lost to fraud, theft, personal enrichment of executives, and misappropriation. Low-interest, sweetheart loans given to insiders permeate hundreds of large nonprofits. More importantly, its culture became that of the permanent political class in the capital.[2]

Recently charities and other nonprofits have come under increasing scrutiny from independent monitors such as Charity Navigator, American Institute of Philanthropy, and CharityWatch as well as federal and state governments. After 2001 the U.S. Senate Finance Committee began to investigate the loss of revenue to the Treasury due to fraudulent claims regarding charitable giving for large tax breaks. In 2005 tax commissioner Mark W. Everson told the committee that billions of dollars of lost revenue resulted from inflated valuations of donated property, deductions for gifts never given, the use of proceeds from tax-exempt bonds to underwrite for-profit enterprises, and businesses using affiliated nonprofits to lower their tax payments. As chair of that committee from 2003 through 2006 that inveterate watchdog Sen. Charles Grassley (R-IA) sought to curb such tax shelter schemes and also advocated "transparent reporting of high salaries, generous allowances, and loans given to executives of [tax] exempt organizations." His Democratic successor Max Baucus (MT) did not follow Grassley's lead.[3]

Trust in charities had been declining since 9/11, when some of the billions in private aid raised from the public never reached the victims. In 2005–6 the dispersal by FEMA (Federal Emergency Management Agency) of billions in aid in the wake of Hurricane Katrina resulted in "one of the most extraordinary displays of scams, schemes and stupefying bureaucratic bungles in modern history, costing taxpayers up to $2 billion." Both the American Red Cross and the Humane Society of the United States came under investigation for misuse of funds, and trust in charities took another hit. A 2006 investigation of fraud in nonprofit organizations by the Hauser Center at Harvard University found fraud in nonprofits to be endemic and not a case of a few "bad apples." The number of Americans who think that nonprofits are honest and ethical in their use of funds is steadily dwindling.[4]

Scrutiny of nonprofit salaries became even more intense as the country plunged into a recession in 2008–9 created largely by excessively compensated executives at financial institutions who engaged in fraudulent activities involving billions of dollars. After these institutions were rescued by the federal government's infusion of billions of taxpayer dollars, revelations that the perpetrators of the Wall Street debacle subsequently enjoyed generous compensation and bonuses sparked public outrage and focused attention on increasing economic inequality. That backlash engulfed a nonprofit sector already shaken by a decade of negative publicity and growing public distrust.

State attorneys general throughout the country stepped up investigations of nonprofits with prosecutions of fraud and criminal activity. A few officials took an interest in exorbitant salaries. In 2011 Massachusetts attorney general Martha Coakley published an investigative report finding that compensation for board members of the state's four major charitable health insurers was unjustified. The overwhelming majority of other charities' board members received no compensation, in contrast to those of Blue Cross Blue Shield, Fallon Community Health Plan, Harvard Pilgrim Health Care, and Tufts Health Plan. Coakley also criticized a severance package of $11 million for Blue Cross CEO Cleve Killingsworth as symptomatic of excessive pay in the sector. When Blue Cross responded to a storm of negative publicity by rebating $4.2 million to its customers—amounting to about $2 per person, without clawing back anything from Killingsworth—many of those receiving the rebate derided it as a "joke" that underlined inequality in the economy.[5]

Amid a growing sentiment among charity watchers that "nonprofit CEOs who want for-profit salaries should work at for-profit companies," Coakley next took on CEO compensation at twenty-five large nonprofits—health insurers, universities, and charitable organizations—and reported that rich nonprofits "are paying their chief executives huge amounts of money and giving them lavish perks unavailable to most workers." Salaries ranged from $487,000 to $8.8 million, and perks included bonuses, deferred compensation, auto allowances, financial planning, life insurance, and other benefits. The highest paid were university presidents and hospital CEOs. Her report challenged the defense that large packages are necessary "to attract and retain talent," but did not recommend salary caps, rather that boards reconsider their mission and look at how executive pay compares to other workers' salaries.[6]

The next year New York governor Cuomo proposed salary caps on certain nonprofits, acting after learning that two brothers (Philip and Joel Levy), who ran a disabilities development home funded almost entirely with Medicaid, gave themselves salaries of $1 million. If an organization received more than $500,000 from the state in a year and with state funding at 30 percent or more of their annual income, its executives must earn less than $199,000 in compensation. Challenged in court, conflicting decisions stalled the cap. Although both Maine and New Hampshire looked into excess compensation for nonprofit managers, neither took action.[7]

Executives of nonprofits that receive tax money often enjoy private sector perks as well as salaries. From 2000 to 2013 the San Diego Opera received $1.1 million in discretionary grants and over $700,000 in National Endowment for the Arts grants. Its top executive, Ian Campbell, was paid over $500,000 in 2012, a year in which the opera put on four productions and sixteen performances in its four-month season. In San Diego, too, Scripps Research Institute's $423.9 million in revenues included $290 million in government grants—the majority of its income—and paid its president $980,000 and a housing allowance. On the other hand, Feeding America San Diego, which says it helps 73,000 needy people in a given week, with revenue of $32.5 million in 2012, paid its executive director about $105,000 annually.[8]

The Great Recession buffeted nonprofits in another way. Cities across the country struggling with historically low budgets turned to nonprofits for voluntary tax contributions or PILOTs (Payments in Lieu of Taxes). In 2011 Boston sent letters to its largest nonprofits asking for annual payments that would rise to a quarter of what they would owe if they paid property taxes. By 2013 at least 420 nonprofits paid PILOTs to cities, though most in small sums. The Northeast, especially Massachusetts and Pennsylvania, accounted for 75 to 80 percent of payments, and most of the revenue came from ten large organizations led by Harvard University.[9]

Crunched by the recession, some cities began taxing nonprofits outright. With the IRS requiring nonprofit hospitals to disclose specifics of their charity care, community benefits, and executive compensation, the Illinois Department of Revenue revoked the tax-exempt status of three nonprofit hospitals for insufficient free or discounted care. The Tacoma, Washington, City Council simply decided to charge two large nonprofit health systems the fullest possible business-and-occupation rate. Many cities nationwide saw their tax bases shrink with the recession, the bursting of the housing bubble, and wealthy hospitals and universities buying property and removing it from the tax rolls. "In 16 of the 20 most populous cities," according to a *Governing* analysis, "tax-exempt properties today [2012] account for a higher share of total assessed value than they did five years ago." In 2011 as the recession deepened, the IRS revoked the tax-exempt status of 275,000 organizations that had failed to file informational tax forms within three years.[10]

Even before the recession, critics had questioned nonprofit hospitals' privileged tax-exempt status as a "historical relic" on the grounds that the benefits to the community did not balance off the cost to federal and state taxpayers. A 2006 study by the Congressional Budget Office found insignificant (if difficult to measure) differences between the charity work of nonprofits and for-profits. Later studies validated the critics by revealing that two-thirds of nonprofit hospitals, which constitute about 60 percent of all hospitals, devoted less than 2 percent to charity. Perhaps that explains why one survey found that most nonprofits failed to advertise the amount of pro bono care they dispensed.[11]

While CEOs of nonprofits collect One Percent salaries, their hospitals in several states—including Kansas, Oklahoma, Nebraska, Ohio, and Alabama have launched thousands of lawsuits against low-income patients unable to pay their bills. In the small city of St. Joseph, Missouri, its only hospital, Heartland Regional/Mosaic Life Care, has sued and garnished the wages of hundreds of poor patients, many of them workers at McDonalds, Walmart, and a pig slaughterhouse employing 2,800. A debt collection company working for Heartland/Mosaic (which filed over a thousand suits in 2013) seizes patients' wages; the money taken is applied to interest, and debts can grow much larger.[12]

Although not all nonprofit hospitals sue patients, in 2003 the *Wall Street Journal* ran a series of articles by Lucette Lagnado revealing that in several states nonprofit hospitals not only initiated hundreds of lawsuits, garnished wages, and seized tax refunds, but they also routinely had arrest warrants issued and jailed debtors who they claimed ignored requests for payment. Lagnado began by profiling a seventy-seven-year-old retired dry-cleaning worker whose wife had been treated at Yale–New Haven Hospital twenty years ago and died soon after. His debt climbed to $40,000, though over time he had paid the hospital $16,000, about the amount of the original bill; but interest and attorneys' fees caused it to balloon. Yale–New Haven, according to Lagnado, counted among the hospitals that "now rank[ed] as America's most aggressive debt collectors" and resorted to jailing debtors. So too did a teaching hospital of the University of Illinois and nonprofits in Indiana, Michigan, Kansas, and Oklahoma. Nonprofit hospitals also exploited uninsured, low-income patients by charging them more than the discounted rates negotiated, for example, by HMOs. Gouging the poor led to lawsuits against three hundred nonprofits in seventeen states.[13]

The IRS has long required nonprofit hospitals to maintain their tax exempt status by providing community benefits, a category difficult to measure and thus easy to ignore. The Affordable Care Act (Obamacare), however, instituted new rules intended to make evasion more difficult. One rule prohibited charging the needy uninsured their set prices but giving lower negotiated prices to the insured; another called for reasonable efforts to determine if a patient qualifies for its financial assistance before engaging in "extraordinary collection efforts."[14]

Confronted with requests to pay taxes, some large nonprofits complied, but overall the industry's voluntary contributions were paltry. That stood in stark contrast to what many nonprofits, large and small, shelled out to professional fund-raisers.

From 2011 to 2015 state attorneys general exposed widespread instances of charities receiving very little of the funds raised from their donors by professional fund-raisers. In one investigation 90 percent of over $1 million raised for thirteen California charities went to the middlemen. The charities included Amnesty International, Defenders of Wildlife, and Save the Children Foundation. In 2012 a Michigan Veterans of Foreign Wars local kept only 9.4 percent of over $1 million raised by a Canadian firm, Xentel, Inc., with U.S. operations based in Florida. The VFW director called this a "necessary evil," but Xentel over the previous decade had been fined a total of $1.4 million for fraudulent activity in several states. Massachusetts's Coakley reported that during 2010 professionals had gathered $367 million in donations for several organizations, but approximately $166 million or 45 percent went to the charities.[15]

The steady rise in nonprofit executive salaries owes much to their boards of trustees and directors imitating the for-profit sector. The spectacular increase in for-profit CEO compensation on Wall Street and in large corporations is well known. Large nonprofits are doing their best to catch up. Executives and boards now consult websites such as that of the *Nonprofit Times*, "The Leading

Business Publication for Nonprofit Management," to learn about compensation throughout the profession and how to maximize it.[16]

Since 2002 federal law has aimed to prevent "excess compensation" among nonprofits, suggesting they should pay "reasonable compensation," defined as "an amount as would ordinarily be paid for like services by free enterprises under like circumstances." That language hardly seems a deterrent to anything, and when in doubt boards of directors easily find law firms willing to sign off on whatever compensation they propose.

One study of nonprofits' executive compensation found it unrelated to performance but rather to organizational size and primarily to "free cash flow;" it noted the complexity of measuring mission fulfillment, a criterion difficult to use in determining compensation. A study of executives of nonprofit hospitals revealed that their compensation was 10 percent higher when they are voting members of their boards rather than ex officio members or staff. This mirrors the cozy relationships on the boards of large for-profit corporations that produce "extremely high executive pay" that Thomas Piketty found to be detached from "firm performance."[17]

"Free cash flow," or loads of money coming in, can lead nonprofit executives to award themselves excessive salaries and engage in lavish spending. The Wounded Warrior Project, started after 9/11 to aid wounded veterans, became over the next fifteen years a fund-raising juggernaut, taking in $150 million in 2011 and $372 million in 2015. But as money poured in, veterans, including those who worked for WWP, began to question how the top executives spent the money. In 2013 the *Tampa Bay Times* and the Center for Investigative Reporting challenged WWP's claim of devoting 80 percent to veterans and said the figure was actually 58 percent. Charity watchdogs and disillusioned veterans charged that WWP spent more on marketing and "dog and pony shows" and less on help for wounded veterans. In January 2016 current and former employees described excess spending on first-class air travel and expensive retreats. Finally, in March 2016, the project's board fired its two top executives. CEO Steven Nardizzi's compensation had risen to $473,000 in 2014, and a staff meeting at a five-star hotel in Colorado, where he rappelled into a crowd, cost nearly $1 million.[18]

Coakley's efforts to persuade nonprofits to curb excessive pay and perks yielded mixed results. She enjoyed some success in egregious cases involving small nonprofits that received government subsidies,[19] but a *Boston Globe* story on the compensation of cultural and arts executives exposed a tone-deaf lack of sensitivity to appearances on the part of enabling trustees in the New Gilded Age.

In 2013 director Michael Conforti of the Clark Institute in Williamstown earned nearly $923,000 and was given co-ownership of a $1 million home. Malcolm Rogers, outgoing director of the Museum of Fine Arts in Boston, received a $60,000 annual housing allowance in addition to his total compensation of $906,897. Museum of Science president Ioannis Miaoulis took home $509,265, and the museum paid tuition for his two children to attend Tufts University, an expense justified by the museum for having wooed Miaoulis from a deanship at Tufts where if he had stayed his children would have received free tuition, room, and board ($61,000 a year). Mark Volpe's compensation as director of the Boston Symphony Orchestra includes a salary of $698,805, summer housing at Tanglewood, reimbursement for his wife to travel with him to court donors, and significant help with his mortgage.[20]

These institutions receive tens of thousands of taxpayer money; in 2014 the Museum of Science took in grants totaling $610,000. In response to questions from the *Globe*, trustees defended generous compensation as necessary to recruit and retain such unique managers and proclaimed their good fortune at having them. In contrast, Kathy Postel Kretman, director of Georgetown University's Center for Public & Nonprofit Leadership, disagreed: "In a public charity, the work is mission-driven . . . so with that comes a certain sense of accountability to the public—and these, to me, are beyond reasonable."[21]

The argument that nonprofit executives could be making more in the for-profit world overlooks the simple fact that they chose a career in nonprofits; the experience acquired is valuable in that sector. A veteran of thirty years in New Hampshire nonprofits and now a consultant, Alan Caron comments: "A veteran nonprofit executive cannot present himself at Goldman Sachs at age 55 and expect to be made a partner." But the outsize compensation of nonprofit executives is producing demoralizing inequality of rewards in those organizations. As executive salaries "spiral out of control, the rest of the staff is left behind." The freebies of housing allowances, extra travel money, college tuition, luxury cars, sweetheart mortgage deals "only add salt to the wound."[22]

Between 1978 and 2013 compensation for chief executives in for-profit firms soared 937 percent, while the average worker's pay climbed just 10 percent.

CEOs' salaries climbed most rapidly at firms where directors selected highly paid peers as benchmarks to determine compensation, where long tenure meant a cozy relationship with the board, and where *the CEO chaired the board.*[23] But during 2008–9 private-sector corporate/Wall Street packages of stratospheric compensation encountered a populist backlash, especially when American International Group, a major culprit in the financial meltdown, received a $185 billion bailout, reported a record loss of $61.7 billion, and then had the chutzpah to pay out $165 million in bonuses (that may have later reached $450 million or much more) to retain the "talented" executives responsible for the disaster. (Was there a line of headhunters outside AIG's doors waiting to steal them away?) In a February *New York Times/CBS News* poll 83 percent of respondents wanted the government to cap the amount of compensation for executives whose firms were receiving taxpayer assistance. During 2009 several Wall Street CEOs advertised taking a voluntary pay cut and several, along with their wives, informed the media they were cutting back on luxury items. The pay cuts, however, distracted attention from their awarding second-level staff a record collective payday: several big firms paid out $140 billion in compensation and benefits to their associates.[24]

Leading economists—Joseph Stiglitz, Paul Krugman, Thomas Piketty, Robert Reich—have argued that CEO pay hundreds of times greater than the average salary of their employees is a drag on economic growth. Both the International Monetary Fund and the Organization for Economic Co-operation and Development have released reports demonstrating that nations with high levels of inequality have advanced more slowly economically than those with lower levels of inequality.[25]

Wall Street remains immune, however, to any concern for society's welfare as a whole. Although popular outrage over the bailouts and compensation practices remained high, it hardly mattered. Several European countries took unprecedented action to put limits on bankers' compensation, and the 2009 American Recovery and Reinvestment Act imposed limits on the pay of executives at some firms that received substantial government assistance. But as the alleged limits proved fraudulent, end-runs made them wholly ineffective. Political class regulators and financial firm lawyers rendered those caps null and void, successfully appealing for waivers, exploiting loopholes, and in several cases allowing executives at bailed-out firms to receive tens of millions in stocks and options, thus ending up with even larger bonuses.[26]

So business went on as usual. Shareholder opposition to excessive pay sim-
mered but remained "frustratingly rare." In 2011 shareholders rejected pay packages for senior executives at only forty-two of the more than three thousand
companies to hold (nonbinding) votes, so significant compensation limits in
the for-profit sector remained "hard to find."[27]

State-level efforts to rein in executive pay at nonprofit hospitals, museums,
social service agencies, and universities also stalled. Legislators in Massachusetts, California, New York, New Jersey, and Florida introduced pay-capping
bills without result. The SEIU United Healthcare Workers West proposed a
ballot measure to limit hospital CEOs earnings to $450,000 but later dropped it.
The Massachusetts Nurses Association at first campaigned for a ballot initiative
to fine hospitals that paid CEOs more than one hundred times the earnings of
the lowest-paid employee. They then asked for legislation that would require
disclosure of hospital profit margins, executive pay, and overseas investments,
charging that hospital executives were "stashing millions . . . in Cayman Island
accounts." Indeed, the union released a list of forty hospitals with offshore accounts in the Caymans and Bermuda and briefly ran TV and radio ads blast-
ing high hospital CEO salaries and money stored in offshore accounts; one
commercial showed two hospital executives clinking champagne glasses on a
Cayman beach.[28]

Despite their feisty attacks on CEO compensation, the nurses' union eventually settled for legislation setting varying nurse staffing ratios in hospital units.
Across the country, high CEO compensation in the nonprofit and for-profit sectors remained unpopular, but the sporadic attempts at imposing limits yielded
no results.

"The Sun Shines Bright
on My Old Kentucky Home"

Kentucky's political class also includes many nonprofit managers in step with
counterparts elsewhere whose incomes, perks, and One Percent lifestyle comes
often at taxpayer expense and, usually, with immunity from prosecution and
jail time. Perhaps the extraordinarily compensated nonprofit CEOs of the East
Coast think of Kentucky as a frontier where the rewards of nonprofit careers
are meager. They would be wrong.

From 2008 through 2011 scandals in the state's nonprofit taxpayer-supported sector came in rapid succession. The combined investigative work of *Lexington Herald-Leader* reporters and Kentucky state auditor Eugenia Crittenden ("Crit") Blackburn Luallen treated the public to a stunning series of exposures of corruption. The newspapers' series of reports on abuse of taxpayer money won it a Public Service Award from the Associated Press Managing Editors Association.

Luallen had held administrative positions in state government under six governors when she was elected state auditor in 2003. A Democrat, she earned a reputation for nonpartisanship in uncovering millions of dollars in fraud in local governments, in board-governed nonprofits getting taxpayer money, and in entities contracting with government. Reelected in 2007 by a landslide, in eight years she sent up an unprecedented 120 cases to law enforcement resulting in the prosecution of thirty-four public officials, most of them members of her party.[29]

The focus here is on nonprofit excesses, although Luallen's successor, Adam Edelen, and the *Herald-Leader* continued to uncover financial mismanagement and corruption in public agencies and state government through 2014.

"A Sense of Entitlement"

The first episode emerged in spectacular fashion as the result of an investigation by the *Lexington Herald-Leader* of spending by the executive director and several administrators of the Blue Grass Airport (BGA), a scandal that riveted the city's and state's attention for months and even, a rarity, resulted in criminal charges.[30]

On November 23, 2008, the *Herald-Leader* ran a story titled "A Sky-High Expense Account," and reporter Jennifer Hewlett informed readers that BGA director Michael Gobb in the past few years had spent more than $200,000 on trips, luxury hotel rooms at first-class hotels, business-class airline tickets, and a catalog of expensive consumer items including gourmet foods and alcohol. He traveled to St. Petersburg, Russia, to give a presentation at a conference on air-cargo security, a trip that cost, including a reception, nearly $13,000; BGA, however, has no commercial international flights. During the period checked Gobb had traveled to at least thirty-three cities in the United States and abroad.

Gobb's spree also included "thousands on meals, rental cars, sightseeing tours, clothing, taxis, limousine services, and tickets to cultural and sporting events." By early January Luallen's team issued a 256-page audit detailing how Gobb and three other airport executives had racked up a grand total of over $500,000 for a mind-boggling array of purchases: thousands for Godiva chocolates; $700 at a Las Vegas nightclub for one bottle of champagne; $14,000 for holiday hams; 400 DVDs; $800 on cigars; $4,000 at a Dallas strip club; and $2,300 for four shotguns, with Gobb himself making "the most questionable purchases."[31]

The airport is a public, nonprofit corporation run by a board appointed by the mayor and is "a component unit of Lexington city government" owned by the Lexington-Fayette Urban County Airport Corporation. Fernita Wallace, a former member of the Urban County Council and former chair of the airport board, told Hewlett that whether the airport's budget comes from passenger and other fees or private or public funds, "it's the people's money."

Gobb made a hefty salary of $220,000 a year, with benefits not usually available at other airports that included unrestricted use of an airport SUV (a 2009 Ford Expedition that cost $29,000), unlimited gas, home Internet and cell-phone service costing more than $6,000 a year, and club memberships worth thousands of dollars. His partners in excess included operations director John Coon, administration and finance director John Rhodes, and director John Slone. Those men also traveled frequently on the airport's dime, approved their own credit card purchases, and could charge purchases to departments not their own without prior approval. Rhodes and Coon both violated BGA nepotism policy: Coon employed a daughter in his department, and Rhodes two sons in his.[32]

The chairman of the airport board with the responsibility of approving Gobb's expenses, Lexington lawyer Bernard Lovely, told Hewlett that the travel and related expenses were justified. He asserted that the expenditures went for airport marketing, public relations, and training (the strip club visit had been justified as "training"). But a *Herald-Leader* survey of expenses of top officials at airports with passenger usage similar to Blue Grass showed that Gobb's sums exceeded them all; indeed, in some cases his spending dwarfed those of entire airport staffs. Heads of some much larger airports, noted Hewlett, traveled far less. Lovely insisted, however, that Gobb had brought new airlines and success to the airport, and that the board was "more than satisfied [with Mike's performance], we are extremely satisfied."

In early December the Urban County Council, clearly not satisfied, voted 11 to 4 to ask State Auditor Luallen to examine the airport's finances. Meanwhile the mayor, Jim Newberry, a conservative lawyer with ties to local corporations, remained silent on the scandal. The board suspended Gobb with pay; he resigned in early January.[33]

Luallen's audit, released in February and covering the period from January 2006 to December 2008, condemned a "shameful" culture of wasteful spending and contained additional details of the egregious indulgence of Gobb and his deputies at taxpayer expense. They had given themselves generous raises: Gobb's salary increased by 108 percent from 2000 to 2008, while the others "enjoyed large increases in their salaries ranging from 42 to 92 percent." The executive director, too, in a three-year period, gave out generous bonuses to employees while management collected over $82,000 in vacation payouts. The audit found no discussion in board minutes of approvals for spending. Luallen referred the audit to law enforcement agencies; in October a grand jury returned indictments against Gobb, Coon, Rhodes, and Sloane (management director Brian Ellestad was not charged).[34]

During 2010 the four executives, after reimbursing the airport piddling amounts compared to the scale of their thefts, all received plea deals, with Coon and Sloane pleading guilty not to felony but misdemeanor charges; Rhodes pleaded guilty to felony theft, and Gobb pleaded guilty to two felony charges. The Fayette Circuit Court Judge Pamela Goodwine, the first female African American judge in Fayette County, sentenced all to probation. In sentencing Rhodes she said that his Christian faith, which she shared, meant that he was fundamentally a good person.[35]

But the sentences outraged many who concluded they proved once again that white-collar criminals received different justice from poor jerks who stole from a convenience store. *Herald-Leader* columnist Tom Eblen expressed frustration in a blog comparing the probation to a recent sentence given to a former University of Kentucky basketball star, Ed Davender, an African American, found guilty of a $100,000 ticket scam, of eight years in prison. "These recent cases left me scratching my head, and I wasn't alone. No wonder people question the fairness of our judicial system and speculate that punishment is influenced by wealth, race, class, the skill of your attorney and the whims of your judge."[36]

Reading between the lines of the audit, the complicity of the airport board emerged loud and clear. They participated often in the festivities, attending

Christmas parties and other events when gifts, prizes, and alcohol flowed. Board chairman Lovely benefited most: he owned a share of a new local restaurant, Azur, where airport staff and board members dined often and ran up big checks. During early January 2008 three airport officials and two board members attended the annual American Association of Airport Executives meeting in Hawaii, including Bernard and his wife, Sylvia Lovely, and board member James Boyd. Entertainment expenses included horseback riding ($1,499), water sports ($591), a helicopter tour, and "other" charges ($5,576). Total cost, over $36,000.[37]

In 2012 a chastened and contrite Michael Gobb, his career and life severely damaged, told the *Business Lexington* staff of abuse of alcohol and drugs and health problems during his tenure as airport director. That behavior helped explain "why" he behaved as he did. So too did his feeling that success in managing the airport in his first years on the job gave him a "sense of entitlement to be rewarded for achievements."[38]

"Someone Else Used My Laptop"

The next scandal of nonprofit extravagance with taxpayer money in Lexington surfaced within weeks of the revelation of criminal activity at the airport. It also involved a sense of entitlement and a complacent board that preferred to look the other way.

In early 2009 suspicion arose that spending by Kathleen Imhoff, director of the Lexington Public Library, might be out of control. In 2007 outside auditors had warned the library board that there was a problem, but it took no action. On April 6 information about the director somehow came to Kentucky state auditor Crit Luallen, who brought it to the attention of the mayor, and within two weeks Newberry requested an internal city audit of the library. By then the *Herald-Leader* had reported that in a five-year period Imhoff had spent more than $134,000 on travel, meals, gifts, and other items. Her trips included travel to Canada, across Europe, and Africa, the latter itself costing $5,874, for which she and "a friend" reimbursed the library $1,807.[39]

The institution, a modern building on Lexington's Main Street, is legally an independent nonprofit dependent on public money. Its budget increases continuously because of a 1979 lawsuit that ended up requiring 5 cents of every $100 in property taxes to go to the library. Imhoff had been hired in 2003 from Fort Lauderdale, Florida, and by 2009 was earning $130,035 a year (plus a bonus in

2008 of $1,600), more than the mayor's salary of $120,574, and more than her counterpart in Louisville, who was then paid $118,224. By 2005 the sixty-three-year-old Imhoff had developed a regal approach to running the library, indulging herself and dispensing raises and bonuses to employees, and gifts and parties to staff, board members, and friends.

The city audit found that from January 17, 2003, to April 20, 2009, the Lexington Public Library was credit card heaven for Imhoff and staff, though apparently many of her subordinates used their cards to pay vendors at her direction. During that period credit card purchases totaled $897,411.21. From January 2006 through April 2009 the audit found that 35 different employees with credit cards bought $547,538.56 of goods and services from no less than 965 different vendors. The audit was complicated by the "sheer volume of activity," the lack of supporting evidence, and the "problematic legitimacy" of the transactions.[40]

Burgess Carey, the forty-four-year-old board chairman, a local businessman born into the city's elite, defended Imhoff and said she was doing an "outstanding job." As the first reports of spending surfaced, Imhoff declared: "Corruption or personal gain, there was none of that." Indeed, as the scandal unfolded, Imhoff dug in her heels, maintaining that she had done nothing wrong, and, according to the *Herald-Leader*, "fiercely defended herself."[41]

After the auditors found 1,522 "images of adult material" on her laptop, she adamantly claimed that someone else must have used her computer to access pornography. Someone addicted to pornography, it appeared, had somehow gained access to her office computer. A forensic software specialist recovered the images for the auditors but was unable to retrieve, to the auditors' barely concealed anger (or disappointment?), more than 14,000 files deleted from her computer immediately after the auditors specifically requested that she preserve all records.[42]

Neither did the auditors' finding of conflict of interest faze her, notably a payment of a $4,666 consulting fee from a company doing $145,000 worth of business with the library. The director's generosity with taxpayer money extended well beyond herself: over the audit period the library distributed $870,392.91 in Variable Pay bonuses to some two hundred employees beyond regular salary increases, although this practice is not allowed at "taxpayer funded entities."[43]

In July 2009 Mayor Newberry appointed a new chair; shortly afterward the board fired Imhoff, but without citing the cause of her dismissal. Her lawyer complained that she was "rushed out the door." In July 2010 Imhoff sued the library for $5 million in damages for violating the terms of her contract and being "publically defamed." In May 2013 arbitrators voted 2–1 to award her $927,191, but a year later a Fayette Circuit Court judge threw out over half of that, deciding that the arbitrators exceeded their authority and retaining the $256,490 she would have earned finishing her contract. Both sides appealed.[44]

A League of Their Own

The Kentucky League of Cities (KLC) offers legal, financial, and developmental advice as well as lobbying, insurance, and loans to most of the state's 382 cities. In 2009 as the recession deepened in Kentucky, Sylvia Lovely, the executive director of the League, declared: "Make no mistake. Cities are in a full-blown financial crisis," as municipalities laid off workers and cut vital services as they coped with falling revenues. The belt-tightening, however, did not extend to the KLC, its top executives, and dozens of its employees.

The public, conscious of lost jobs in a depressed economy, had just been shocked by revelations of taxpayer money wantonly squandered for personal use at the airport and public library. Now came another bombshell from *Herald-Leader* investigative reporter Linda B. Blackford: "League Prospers As Kentucky Cities Struggle." Above all, Lovely, KLC deputy executive director Neil Hackworth, and chief insurance services officer William Hamilton personally suffered no "financial crisis." The details of their princely lifestyles astounded readers of the paper. The public reeled at the sums involved for travel with spouses, expensive hotels and hundreds of meals costing many thousands at upscale restaurants, thinly disguised vacations with spouses, and personal items. But one perk stuck in the public's craw. At KLC expense Lovely drove a $64,000 BMW SUV instead of an American car or, better, a midrange Toyota produced at the plant just outside Lexington in Georgetown, Kentucky (though the reporter for the *Bowling Green Daily News* was more impressed by "questionable bonuses, lots of alcohol and a trip to a Las Vegas strip club").[45]

Blackford followed with more stories based on KLC records obtained under the state's Open Records Act; in July State Auditor Luallen decided on an audit of KLC, which appeared in early December 2009. After referring her report to the state attorney general, the U.S. Attorney's Office, and the IRS, Luallen commented that she was amazed at how people she had known for many years could create a culture of such excess. "I was shocked. I was outraged on behalf of the public, which has supported this organization through their tax dollars."

Most of KLC revenue came from its insurance and financial programs, 87 percent in 2008, and in the previous ten years its income increased by 155 percent from $4.3 million to $11 million. Again, loads of money lying around and a sense that achievement equals entitlement. Old-time ward politicians called cash for personal spending (or bribing voters) "walking around money" or "street money." Lovely & Co. had access to plenty of driving, dining, hoteling, eating, and flying around money.

Luallen on cash flowing in to KLC: "KLC should have found ways to return increases in revenue . . .to their member cities . . .instead of spending it on personal gain." The executive staff could have provided more services to member cities, she said, or reduced their insurance fees.[46]

Salaries and perks: Lovely's salary went up by 95 percent from $170,000 in 2002 to $331,186 in 2009; Hackworth's by 80 percent from $141,753 to $255,258; Hamilton's by 93 percent from $123,909 to $238,867. Nineteen other employees at KLC had salaries over $100,000. In 2008, some 72 percent of expenses went to salaries, retirement, employee benefits, and payroll taxes. Perks included a box at Churchill Downs, Ryder Cup tickets, season tickets to University of Kentucky football and basketball games, vehicles, these items together costing over a two-year period $314,000, and thousands in gas money. Ticket purchases totaled $50,000.[47]

Retirement bonuses: "KLC provided $533,998 to six employees in the form of a bonus, contribution, and forgivable loans for rewarding loyalty [used primarily to increase retirement accounts]." The auditor rejected claims by KLC staff that they repaid the loans. Lovely's platinum-plated retirement package was one most Kentucky's citizens could have only in their dreams.[48]

Twenty-six employees enjoyed the use of credit cards with no oversight or need to provide supporting documents, resulting in charges of $1,046,702. Of that sum senior staff alone accounted for $523,261 without board review or approval; and of that sum $56,000 was spent on meals at local restaurants, with the lion's share disbursed at—where else?—Azur, co-owned by Bernard Lovely, which took in $28,000. Sylvia Lovely said that she was "flabbergasted" that anyone would question KLC staff dining at such a well-known, fine restaurant, also favored by BGA staff. The biggest item in the conflict of interest category went beyond food: Bernard Lovely's law firm also provided $1.4 million worth of legal services to KLC. That, too, hit a nerve with the public.[49]

Frequent flyers: The auditor found no justification for KLC executives' frequent out-of-state travel of 162 trips, costing $431,354, including vacations in Europe and the Caribbean. In the previous three years KLC had paid $19,000 for spouses' travel. Lovely's comment: "I go to a lot of events I'm expected to be at. . . . It's like a university president. Spouses play a major role."[50]

Lovely may have envisioned herself as university president also when she set up a think tank in 2002, the New Cities Institute. Auditors decided, however, that the $7,239,378 the league spent on the institute over eight years had "no quantifiable results." The money went to cover overhead, such as rent and the salaries of three employees, but KLC was "pretty vague" about New Cities' mission. Supported by in-kind contributions from the League, the operation recorded a net loss of $603,507 over the period.[51]

The audit made clear in numerous ways that the concept of conflict of interest was unknown in the fashionable offices of KLC headquarters at 100 Vine Street in Lexington, a building purchased in 2000 for $7 million. Insurance director Hamilton's wife earned $14,413 for decorating services and a $1,000 trip to New York City to select artwork. Indeed, the Hamiltons never saw a conflict of interest in anything related to their advantage. He rented office space in a Georgetown building to Collins & Co., a Tennessee firm that was paid $6.6 million over three years for processing insurance claims for KLC. The CEO of Collins made available to the Hamiltons and other KLC couples housing he owned on a Dutch Island in the Caribbean. The couple also accepted trips to Naples, Florida, and Munich, Germany, from a reinsurance vendor. Hamilton was not fired until June 2010.[52]

The audit's itemization of credit card charges made by Lovely, Hamilton, and Hackworth goes on for pages. Lovely used her credit card for small purchases of personal items such as cosmetics and newspapers, frequent buys of expensive leather goods, and thousands for hotel rooms "for no purpose" according to the audit; the largest sum in that category was $6,336; Lovely's total charges for 2007–9: $273,199.41.[53]

Hackworth's credit card charges included dozens of meals at top restaurants in Lexington and others across the country: $1,157.32 for a meal at Galatoire's in New Orleans; $1,201.65 for five nights and bar charges in San Antonio; $585.05 for a meal at Sardine Factory in Monterey, California; $410.28 at Morton's in San

Juan, Puerto Rico. These bills probably ran up because of alcohol, but the auditors could not determine what part of the bills went for booze. They did identify specific buys for alcohol totaling $12,349. The many items apart from dining included $858 for "golf supplies" (one critic quipped: "that's a lotta balls").[54]

But neither Lovely nor Hackworth came close to the thousands Hamilton spent dining, especially at Bernard Lovely's co-owned Azur. Six of his meals during 2007 reached a grand total of $5,069.69. All other employees' credit card charges for 2007–9 added up to $523,441.80.[55]

An item in the audit of Sylvia Lovely's credit card transactions connected the spending at Blue Grass Airport, where Bernard Lovely chaired its board, and his spouse's League expenses. In 2007 she attended a "storytelling workshop" in Colorado Springs, charging $4,200 to KLC. The result was a book, "The Little Red Book of Everyday Heroes: How Ordinary People Can Become Community Patriots." For a March 2008 airport board meeting, chaired by Bernard Lovely, Michael Gobb instructed his marketing manager to buy fourteen copies of the book ($296) and had a copy placed at every seat around the table.

The book suggests something of Lovely's self-image. From a tiny city, Frenchburg, in Menifee County, one of Kentucky's poorest, she rose from her "Appalachian background" through college at Morehead State and University of Kentucky Law School to become what she termed a "community patriot." Ambitious, energetic, and a tireless speaker at public events, by 2008 she had been named one of Kentucky's Top Women of Influence and won numerous awards, including Appalachian Woman of the Year and the 2006 Vic Hellard Award, the state's highest honor for public service.[56]

As the scandal broke, Lovely had defenders. A few mayors pointed to help the League had given various cities, but the critics were numerous and vociferous. As with airport and library spending, KLC board members had seen excess firsthand and benefited from it at expensive dinners, parties, and receptions.[57]

Less than a year after the auditor's report and her resignation, Lovely had launched a comeback and was again involved in public service and speaking around the country. She had formed a consulting firm to advise executives and organizations how to manage "reputational risk." In an interview with *Herald-Leader* columnist Tom Eblen, who wanted to know what lessons she had learned from the scandal, she admitted that she had not "run a perfect organization," but said that the full story was unknown: "I should have spoken out sooner." She suggested the auditor had treated her unfairly, judging KLC as a governmental organization rather than a private trade group. On those grounds her salary and perks were justified. She added: "there were a lot of shades of gray in that stuff." Eblen told his readers that her wounded feelings perhaps were soothed by eligibility for an annual state pension of $165,000, boosted by an extra five years bought with a KLC $125,000 forgivable loan. He concluded, though, that she seemed unaware of what had caused her setback.[58]

Shameless in Kentucky

Two weeks later readers of the *Herald-Leader* might have had a sense of, in the immortal words of Yogi Berra, "déjà vu all over again." Reporter Ryan Alessi began his account of the next scandal, hard on the heels of the last one:

> When the Kentucky Association of Counties sent six people to Washington, D.C., in March 2008 to attend a conference and lobby officials, the $31,700 trip included two dinners totaling $4277 and a $10,000 cancelation fee for hotel rooms that weren't used. . . . In all, the associations' top five executives racked up nearly $600,000 in travel, entertainment and other expenses over the last two years. More than half was charged on the credit card of Executive Director Bob Arnold.[59]

Once more the *Herald-Leader* exposed a "sickening" recital of wanton spending of taxpayer money, self-enriching, and, plainly speaking, greed and gluttony. Thousands spent on travel and hotels, lofty restaurant tabs, sports tickets, Ryder Cup and Derby tickets, Christmas and retirement gifts, parties, expensive hotels when the conferences attended were held at less expensive venues, large payments to officials and board members not in accord with "industry standards," blatant padding of retirement packages, rampant conflicts of interest, complete lack of oversight by a board some of whose thirty-four members participated in the gravy train, familiar transparent rationalizations, and flat-out lies. The five officials investigated by the newspaper were Arnold, deputy director Denny Nunnelly, director of insurance Joe Greenhouse, director of financial services, Grant Slattery, and general counsel Tim Sturgill. They, and others who surfaced later in additional stories and the auditor's report, served in town and county offices, politicians by trade latching on to a "good thing." Sylvia Lovely, while no stranger to self-dealing, at least professed ideals and a sense of purpose to improve society. The Kentucky Association of Counties (KACo) crew resembled nothing more than small-time grafters with big-time opportunities. Rural people call their breed "the Main Street gang."

KACo was created in 1974 to lobby state government, and like KLC it had expanded its services to include selling insurance and providing financing to some 120 dues-paying counties. Its help to counties ranged from roof repairs after storm damage to hospital services. In the five years before 2008 revenue increased by 75 percent, rising to almost $6 million in 2008.[60] The temptation of available money, a sense of entitlement, and willful ethical myopia created another culture of reckless excess.

Bob Arnold's costly dinners fell short of the League's Bill Hamilton, but even Hamilton did not tip 47 percent on a $816 check in New York City. Arnold's compensation of $178,000 also included a vehicle and a country club membership. Aware of the disastrous impression Lovely had made by driving a $64,000 BMW, as exposure mounted he pointed out that his BMW was a "low-end" BMW SUV at $38,000.[61]

But KACo's BMW moment was perhaps the $20,000 Arnold signed off on for strip club and "escort services." The official reputed to have incurred these expenses, David Jenkins, Spencer County judge-executive, denied they were his and claimed someone else must have used his credit card. Unfortunately for Jenkins, the state auditor's report insisted that "the cardholders were present when the charges were made . . . and likely signed all receipts."[62]

The state audit made other disclosures: from 2007 to 2009 $334,300 paid to board members and affiliates just to attend meetings; bonuses totaling $140,000 over three years for the director of insurance and director of financial services; $219,144.89 for 77 restaurant charges, each costing over $1,000; tens of thousands spent on alcohol from July 1, 2006, to June 30, 2009; over $28,000 for tickets to various events, mostly sports; $48,426 on *two* annual Christmas dinners; $11,593,77 for staff birthday meals over three years; $247,944 spent on advertising over three years directed at sports events attended by the general public and not public officials, partially in exchange for season tickets to basketball and football games; and, not finally, no supporting documentation was provided as required by policy for over $800,000 of credit card charges and reimbursement requests.[63]

Crit Luallen described KACo as pursuing a "self-serving culture" that abandoned its primary mission. In contrast, Chris Harris, an association vice president and magistrate of economically depressed Pike County, said he was "unaware" of spending problems and that "there are always going to be mistakes in every organization." Among those "mistakes," perhaps, were circumstances that led to KACo spending over $2 million, as the *Herald-Leader* revealed that August, on employees who were fired or had their contracts terminated, spending not covered in the audit.[64]

Alessi finished his principal story on KACo by pointing out to readers that, as with KLC and the Lexington Public Library, "the money they spend comes from you, the taxpayer."[65]

The *Herald-Leader*'s editors made a blunter comparison of KLC and KACo: "The KACo audit suggested one long on-going party for good ol' boys, including strip clubs and escort services. The KLC audit is more suggestive of greed."[66]

Self-Dealing

The KACo stories and audit did not bring to an end either investigative reporting by the *Lexington Herald-Leader* nor audits by the state of nonprofits and government organizations. If KACo exemplified the theme of "shameless in Kentucky," the top executives at the nonprofit Bluegrass Mental Health–Mental Retardation Board followed in their footsteps. Serving seventeen counties and thirty thousand adults and children, the organization had experienced rapid growth in revenue while reducing charity giving and services but spending plentifully on executive pay, political lobbying, and real estate. In early June 2012 John Cheves of the *Herald-Leader* exposed another set of self-serving nonprofit executives enriching themselves and violating any standard of conflict of interest.[67]

Shannon Ware, CEO since 2008, earned $250,016 in 2010 plus a $25,002 bonus. The former CEO and Ware's husband, Joseph Toy, took home $877,777 that year, a sum boosted by a large one-time deferred compensation payout; Toy remained a paid consultant at Bluegrass and since 1999 had collected a state pension of $96,395. In 2006 Toy bought a $295,000 house (and $32,000 worth of furnishings) near Cumberland Lake for KACo's "senior management team" to use while working in Somerset. Since 2008 the agency spent close to $500,000 to retain four lobbyists in the state capitol. In December 2012 the new state auditor, Adam Edelen, reported that since 1997 Bluegrass had paid more than $2.8 million in executive benefit compensation at the discretion of the president with no scrutiny by board members; the organization received 68 percent of its money from taxpayers.[68]

Board chair Scott Gould defended the agency's expenses and compensation as in line with the private sector. But Cheves reported the Toy/Ware compensations to be considerably higher than those at the state's other regional mental health groups. Some workers who dealt directly with patients from 2000 to 2010 had made less than $30,000 a year, while their annual pay raises were often skipped because they were told the agency was struggling financially. Former employees interviewed by Cheves also cited austere working conditions and mediocre food provided to staff and patients while the board's annual dinner featured entertainment, an open bar, and steak dinners. Meanwhile, the lunch budget for some twenty mentally handicapped adults in Harrison County was a "closely watched" $100 a week.

Within two weeks of publication of the *Herald-Leader* stories, the Bluegrass board acknowledged "a bad morale problem" among its 2,300 employees and awarded a round of bonuses and pay raises. Ware retired in December to the two $600,000 homes she and Toy owned in a swank Lexington neighborhood.[69]

Later that same month another nonprofit came under the paper's scrutiny for financial activities best described as *"you scratch my back and I'll scratch yours."* In June John Cheves revealed that Hospice of the Bluegrass, a nonprofit with a 2010 income of more than $66 million coming from private and public sources such as Medicare, had spent more than $1.82 million since 2005 on business deals involving several board members and spouses of its executives. Its CEO, Gretchen Marcum Brown, received $334,198 in compensation in 2010, its chief medical officer Todd Cote $251,665, and six other officials $100,000 or more. The executives also engaged in business activities that the Internal Revenue Service labels "self-dealing" or "insider transactions," but that are loosely regulated. These included $837,999 for insurance to a firm whose managing director, John Milward, was a Hospice board member; $540,000 for political lobbying and legal representation to a law firm with partners connected to the board by former member Lisa English Hinkle and member James Frazier; and $392,042 for printing to a company owned by the husband of Deede Byrne, Hospice's chief clinical officer. When asked to produce documents disclosing the arrangements for these contracts, Hospice could not or would not provide them. Cheves informed readers that of the forty nonprofits in Lexington with revenue above $10 million, only two other than Hospice reported a deal with an insider.[70]

Two years later the organization began to lay off and not replace workers who left, resulting in a 20 percent reduction in staff between January and May 2013, affecting a total of 121 persons. Hospice also cut back sharply on inpatient beds and announced the closing of a palliative care clinic in Lexington; the reductions were necessary, it said, because of an 11 percent decline in reimbursements since 2009.[71]

The *Herald-Leader* and auditor Edelen continued to deal with abuse of taxpayer money in the following years. In an editorial on June 6, 2013, the *Herald-Leader* editors called on Edelen to "take a very close look at . . . the Bluegrass Area Development District." Their concern grew out of the inability of the Riverpark Neighborhood Association to learn about the ADD's plans for a building it had paid $600,000 to buy and $500,000 to renovate. The ADD spent over $1 million on something that never opened and that it had no authority to buy; much of the money went to an associate on a no-bid contract. The state created ADDs to help local governments plan local economic growth, and they funnel federal funds and technical services, in Bluegrass's case, to seventeen counties around Lexington. By the time Edelen issued his "blistering" audit, the agency's executive director, Lenny Stolz II, had been forced to resign months before.[72]

The audit found egregious conflicts of interest, too numerous to recount here, and spending rivaling the frat boys of KACo, including $513,770 worth of credit card expenditures from 2011 to 2014 that were excessive or without documentation: for expensive meals ($62,830.36); airline tickets, many for non-agency persons ($168,505.88); and hotels ($207,155.45). Stolz exited with an $8,000 consulting contract in addition to a $128,000 severance package. While criticizing Stolz for "rogue management," Edelen did not censure the ADD board, consisting of seventy-seven political class members, mostly elected officials. One wonders how all those public servants were not "paying close attention to its [the ADD's] activities" that led Edelen to refer the case to the state's attorney general, Kentucky State Police, and FBI.[73]

To follow the abuse of taxpayer money in Kentucky one need only search through the reports of the state's auditor, such as Edelen's 2013 report regarding millions spent in "waste and abuse" at the Kentucky Emergency Management Agency overseen by National Guard Brigadier General John W. Hertzel.[74]

Many other instances of corruption in state government agencies could be added to the dreary account above. But for brevity's sake, just one must be mentioned. It involved Richie Farmer, a popular former University of Kentucky basketball star whose iconic status won him election as commissioner of agriculture in 2003. Farmer's spending and use of his position for his own and friends' purposes did not approach the scale of KACo millions, but given the importance of basketball in Kentucky, it attracted considerable publicity. The gregarious Farmer seemed to lose his way in "a toxic culture of entitlement." The unusual aspect of the case was that in 2012 he was sentenced to jail for twenty-seven months.[75] This writer's check with the communications director of the state auditor found that during this period Farmer was the only government or nonprofit official who went to jail.

Kentuckians in executive positions in nonprofits and state government who use their access to money to live the high life are emulating many of their representatives in Congress, who use their "Leadership PACs" to fund a posh lifestyle. Rep. Andy Barr, for example, spent $32,000 on tickets to the Kentucky Derby and Breeders' Cup, plus $300 to hire a handicapper to give betting tips to his racetrack guests. Hal Rogers dispersed $21,504 for a golf outing at California's scenic Pebble Beach, $10,168 at the Ritz-Carlton Golf Resort in Naples, Florida, thousands for dining in D.C. and for limos and cigars, and $2,000 to his wife for "event planning." Kentucky's exceptions to such spending are Republican Thomas Massie and Democrat John Yarmuth, who use much of their smaller PAC treasuries to actually contribute to colleagues' campaigns.[76]

Kentucky political scientists and historians have suggested that "a high degree of tolerance for political corruption exists in the Commonwealth of Kentucky," and respectable members of the business and political classes often tend to look the other way in the face of unethical and even criminal behavior.

Countless Kentuckians from Louisville to the mountains toil tirelessly for the public interest. But many Kentuckians involved in public office at the local and state levels think of government jobs as a reward for campaign work or contributions and for political loyalty; once in office many elected officials or political appointees see their positions "as a trough" to distribute favors. Nepotism is rampant and often approved at the local level by voters; seventy-five counties allow some form of nepotism, fifty have full-time family hires. Kim Davis, the county clerk who became a national lightning rod by refusing to grant marriage licenses to gay couples, served as deputy clerk from 1991 to 2012 to her mother, who was the Rowan county clerk for thirty-seven years;

Davis then ran for the office and won when her mother retired. Her son works in the office.[77]

In Kentucky, corruption, nepotism, and inequality march together arms linked at all levels of the political and business class, from small towns and the poorest counties to corporate suites in Lexington and Louisville and the corridors of the state capitol in Frankfort.

Conclusion

While some states are more corrupt than others, and Kentucky falls into the "more" category, in many ways its political culture and political economy resemble other states and mirror on a smaller scale Washington, D.C., where the stakes are much higher, but the game is often the same: monetize your public service.

Money is said to be the mother's milk of politics. During the first Gilded Age, Republican industrialist, politico, and McKinley campaign manager Mark Hanna famously said that just two things mattered in politics: the first was money, and he could not remember the second. In our time Rahm Emanuel, currently mayor of Chicago, after being elected to Congress, explained to his staffers the facts of campaigning: "The first third of your campaign is money, money, money. The second third is money, money, and press. And the last third is votes, press and money."

Recall the secretly recorded conversation reported by New York's Moreland Commission between politicians involving the exchange of cash to obtain a gubernatorial nomination: "That's politics, that's politics, it's all about how much. Not about whether or will, it's about how much, and that's our politicians in New York, they're all like that because of the drive that the money does for everything else. You can't do anything without the f*****g money."

Money, to rephrase the old axiom, is the mother's milk of the permanent political class. What most threatens the American republic, however, is not merely the self-enrichment of the political class, but rather our rulers enabling the formation of a powerful aristocracy of inherited wealth. Any illusion that these pluto-aristos (*aristos* was often used derisively by the founders instead of *aristocrats*; in Greek it means "best") are benign rulers should be dispelled by their reckless, immoral, and cutthroat accumulation of wealth over the past few decades.

Unprecedented quantities of money flow in and out of politics and corporate America. The financial sector now sets the pace for a wide range of institutions, undeterred by repeated scandals and criminal activity for which high-level executives are not held accountable. The drive for money has undergirded corporate scandals from Enron to Lehman Brothers to LIBOR. Until recently the fraudulent accounting that caused the bankruptcy and implosion of the Houston-based energy company Enron was then the biggest corporate scandal of recent years. Exposed in October 2001, it also brought down Arthur Andersen, one of the five largest audit and accountancy partnerships in the world. Sherron Watkins, a vice president and accountant at Enron, tried to warn its executives that the company was headed for a crash because of conflicts of interest, fraudulent accounting, and forging of documents. In the aftermath Watkins became a hero—one of *Time* magazine's three persons of the year in 2002, all whistle-blowers. Though she rejects that title because she did not take her protests outside the company, she did later testify before a congressional committee.

In a 2007 interview with *Fraud Magazine* Watkins said that what went wrong at Enron could be accurately summarized "using two words, greed and arrogance," but she added it was also a case of a company's culture breeding "disreputable behavior from the outside [including] auditors, lawyers, consultants, and lenders."[1]

She described Enron CEO Ken Lay as not "walking the walk" when it came to his professed commitment to "respect, integrity, communication, and excellence." In a classic case of petty self-dealing, "He always had us use his sister's travel agency. Trouble was that it was neither low cost nor good service," and it screwed up international travel. Watkins "was stuck in Third World countries where I didn't speak the language without a hotel room or with an insufficient airline ticket home." When she used a different agency, Watkins would be reminded to use Lay's sister's Travel Agency in the Park. "We called it The Travel Agency in the Dark."

Watkins interpreted this signal from Lay as indicating to his managers that "once you get to the executive suite," you can start self-dealing with the company's assets. She connected it also to the firm's board enabling Chief Financial Officer Andrew Fastow to engage in massive conflicts of interest and fraud. Each board director "received nearly $350,000 per year for serving on Enron's board . . . double the high end of normal large public company director fees." Money induced the board, company executives, and professionals to go along with "questionable—and, in some cases, fraudulent—off-balance-sheet vehicles. . . . Their judgement was clouded by high salaries, bonuses, and stock-option proceeds." Given Watkins's new occupation as a professional ethicist advising corporations on not becoming the "new Enron," she should not lack for clients in the New Gilded Age.

Just after Enron's collapse, WorldCom went bankrupt, and a Niagara Falls followed of one financial and accounting fraud after another. WorldCom inflated its assets by $11 billion, resulting in 30,000 lost jobs and $180 billion in losses to investors. CEO Bernard Ebbers received a long jail sentence. Two sharp executives at Tyco, Dennis Kozlowski and Marc Swartz, misrepresented the company's income by $500 million, and they rewarded themselves with $150 million. Kozlowski gave his wife a birthday party on a private island costing $1–2 million and charged it to the company; he spent $14 million on renovating his Fifth Avenue apartment, including a $2,200 wastebasket and a $6,000 shower curtain. Both men were sentenced to 8 ½ to 25 years in prison. In 2004 the SEC brought charges against Richard M. Scrushy, founder of Health South, regarding inflated earnings of $1.4 billion, but Scrushy was acquitted, only to go to jail for bribing the governor of Alabama. Next the scandals of Freddie Mae and Freddie Mac with millions of investors losing retirement accounts, AIG, Lehman Brothers, and Bernard Madoff's Ponzi scheme bilking investors of $64.8 billion.

Madoff went to jail, and before him Fastow, Ebbers, Kozlowski, and Swartz, but while their fraudulent activity was egregious, none of them were the architects of the financial meltdown of 2007–9. None of those men, reviled by an angry public as "banksters," have ever worn an orange jumpsuit.

Take Richard M. Fuld, one of those regarded as most responsible for the crisis, who presided over the collapse of Lehman Brothers, still the largest bankruptcy in U.S. history. When Lehman, a financial services firm, crashed in 2008, it set off a global economic meltdown. Known as the "The Gorilla" of Wall Street for his aggressiveness, Fuld gained notoriety for using $1.22 million of the firm's money to furnish his office with items such as a $16,000 umbrella stand. Fuld took about $529 million out of Lehman while running it into bankruptcy. He left "tens of thousands of people and institutions to which Lehman owed money—from foreign orphanages to the city of Long Beach, California—high and dry." Lehman's twenty-six thousand employees lost their jobs, along with thousands of others such as those at Merrill Lynch (bought by Bank of America). Fuld walked away from the deluge disgraced but unrepentant, still owning several palatial residences, including a mansion in Greenwich, Connecticut, and a large home on Jupiter Island, Florida; reports of his net worth of $160 million were probably too low. In 2009 he sold his Park Avenue apartment for $26 million and in 2015 auctioned off his Sun Valley, Idaho, estate worth $30–50 million. He was never prosecuted.[2]

Fuld's reckless deals, along with his self-indulgent excess, typified the new normal on Wall Street. Sheila Bair served as head of the Federal Deposit Insurance Corporation from 2006 to 2011 and was one of the few regulators who labored to correct what she saw as the dangerous behavior of large banks. Although President George W. Bush appointed Bair, a moderate Republican, Obama kept her in office for her competence and dedication to protect Main Street. In 2012 she published a memoir of her immersion in the financial crisis and in closing surveyed an "egregious parade of horribles," financial firms' misconduct causing billions of losses to customers. With weak regulation continuing, she observed, "a culture of greed and shortsightedness also continues to permeate our financial system."

Bair explained the ongoing risk-taking, law breaking, and lack of punishment on timid regulators confusing "their regulatory mandate with maintaining bank profitability," fearful of crashing the banks and damaging the economy. Members of Congress, too, protect "the profitability of large financial institutions that fund the campaigns that help them stay in office and represent a potent source of lucrative jobs and consulting contracts once they leave." Matt Taibbi, the investigative journalist who has provided unparalleled exposure of Wall Street fraud and greed, extended Bair's analysis. When it comes to Wall Street, he wrote in *Rolling Stone*, "the justice system not only sucks at punishing financial criminals, it has actually evolved into a highly effective mechanism for protecting financial criminals. This institutional reality has absolutely nothing to do with politics or ideology—it takes place no matter who's in office or which party's in power."[3]

In 2013 a *Washington Post* blogger published "a complete list of Wall Street CEOs prosecuted for their role in the financial crisis": although several "small fish" such as mortgage brokers who lied went to jail, the number of CEOs was zero. Their apparent "immunity" fed an existing impression that there is one justice system for the rich and powerful and another for everyone else.[4]

The Obama Justice Department's inaction contrasted sharply with the aftermath of the 1980s' savings and loan debacle, which was one-seventieth the size of 2007–10. Regulators made over 30,000 criminal referrals that led to over 1,000 felony charges and 839 convictions. Since 2008 one executive "several rungs from the corporate suite at a second-tier financial institution" has gone to jail, but none of the top perpetrators. Apologists describe the Justice Department as recoiling from overreaching in financial prosecutions and losing in the courtroom and also having courts taking away key prosecutorial tools. Nor did Congress provide adequate funding to investigate the causes of the financial crisis. Further, federal prosecutors and regulators argue that finding evidence to prosecute individuals is difficult and prefer the certainty of big fines.[5]

The nonprosecution of corporate financial criminals can be traced, however, to the rise of deferred-prosecution and nonprosecution agreements, which have virtually the same result. These deals between the Justice Department and companies accused of crimes became more common under the Bush administration and increased during Obama's. The companies avoid criminal charges and prosecution if they pay substantial fines, promise to improve their business and compliance practices, and sometimes change personnel or revamp corporate governance. In the states they are known as settlement agreements. At the federal level between 1993 and 2001 there were 11; from 2002 to 2005 there were 23; and from 2004 to 2012 Justice offered 242 deferred-prosecution and nonprosecution agreements.[6]

This development has essentially turned prosecutors into regulators of errant companies. But prosecutors are not trained to regulate companies, so this raises many questions, not least of which is the competence of prosecutors to regulate, in contrast, say, to actual regulatory agencies such as the Securities and Exchange Commission. And sometimes the nonprosecution agreements contain small print allowing the firms to pay far less than reported to the media as well as tax benefits reducing the amount further.[7]

Some of these agreements involved egregiously criminal behavior, notably a deferred prosecution with HSBC in 2012 in which the bank agreed to pay a $1.9 billion fine. But the bank's laundering of over a trillion dollars included bulk movements of cash from Mexican drug cartels as well as cash from Iran, a country the U.S. regarded as a "state sponsor of terrorism." (Credit Suisse and LIBOR-tainted Barclays and Royal Bank of Scotland [see below] also provided services to rogue nations such as Libya, Iran, Sudan, and Myanmar.) The HSBC agreement indicated that "too big to fail" had morphed into "too big to jail." Taibbi recounted the long list of such settlements and concluded that the "'not enough evidence defense' [is] either a total lie or the most unbelievable coincidence in history." Moreover, Obama's attorney general, Eric Holder, and his assistant attorney general in charge of the Criminal Division, Lanny A. Breuer, came into office with a policy of prosecuting firms, not individuals. Holder defended his policy by citing his concern for "collateral consequences" or a "negative impact on the national economy, perhaps even the world economy." This amounted to a "get-out-jail-free policy . . . for the too-big-to-fail mega-firm."[8]

In 2015 Holder left Justice for his former job defending corporate criminals at Covington. The firm where his partnership had paid him $2.5 million in his last year eagerly welcomed back him and his expertise in prosecuting corporate criminals, having left his eleventh-floor corner office empty awaiting his return. The *National Law Journal* headlined the move as "Six Years in the Making." Taibbi, irreverently as ever, saw the reunion as "Eric Holder, Wall Street Double Agent, Comes in from the Cold."[9]

The LIBOR crisis impacted "the whole world," according to no less an authority on finance Warren Buffett. LIBOR—the London Interbank Offered Rate—is the benchmark calculated from banks' interest rates around the world; it was set daily by sixteen banks, including Barclays, UBS, Rubobank, and the Royal Bank of Scotland. In July 2012 the world learned that executives at the banks had conspired to manipulate the rates to earn profits from derivatives trades for over two decades by falsely inflating or deflating the rate to profit from their own trades. They also had submitted fraudulent daily submissions to make their banks look as if they were in healthier financial condition than other banks shaken by the recession. Barclays paid a $450 million fine, and UBS, the most egregious manipulator, $1.5 billion. Top executives of several of the big banks allegedly "stepped down," but no one went to jail.[10]

Print and electronic media uniformly labeled it "the crime of the century." The financial press and media repeatedly observed that *something*, somewhere was wrong with the culture of banking and finance. An early report of the scandal published in the conservative magazine *The Economist* bore the headline "The Rotten Heart of Finance" and asserted that it was not just, as Barclays claimed, a few "rogue traders," but collusion carried on openly and brazenly throughout several of its trading floors. Liberal journalist Robert Scheer described modern international bankers "as a class of thieves the likes of which the world has never before seen. . . . The modern day robber barons pillage with a destructive abandon totally unfettered by law or conscience and on a scale that is almost impossible to comprehend." A pithier comment came from Eliot Spitzer, who prosecuted criminals as attorney general of New York for eight years: "I think the mob learned from the banks."[11]

But outrage from across the political spectrum has not ended the drumbeat of criminal behavior by financial institutions, despite promises from the Justice Department, the Federal Reserve, the SEC, and other regulators that they intend to crack down on big banks. The perpetrators seem to know these are empty threats meant to pacify the public, a powerless citizenry held to a different standard of justice. The fines may have gone up, but no one goes to jail, even when they plead guilty to felony. For average citizens a felony conviction means most will lose their jobs, go to prison, and lose their voting rights.

Copyright Joel Pett. Reprinted with permission.

In 2015 the giant banks Citigroup, JPMorgan Chase, and again Barclays and the Royal Bank of Scotland pleaded guilty to an array of antitrust and fraud charges; prosecutors tore up a 2012 nonprosecution agreement with UBS regarding LIBOR manipulation, with the bank agreeing to plead guilty to wire fraud. The criminal activity began in 2007 when traders at the banks used a chat room—they called it "The Cartel"—to fix daily foreign exchange currencies to tilt currency fluctuations in their favor. The various fines for the five banks totaled about $9 billion, but none of the convicted felons faced jail time. Instead of prosecuting individuals, the banks were placed on corporate probation, "a sweet deal," said critics, "for a scam that lasted for at least five years . . . during which time the banks revenue from foreign exchange was some $85 billion." "Banks as Felons, or Criminality Lite," commented the *New York Times* editorial board.[12]

Reckless and criminal behavior continues because of the power that financial institutions possess over the economy and government. Finance now has a larger share of the economy than ever: total compensation to the sector in 2012 was 9 percent of GDP: that's about $1.4 trillion, a rise since 1970 of 70 percent, while the number of employees has remained about the same. Thomas Phillippon and other economists estimate that what society gets in return is not much; "shadow banking" has increased rent-taking, that is, profit for nothing. Financialization has promoted inequality by skimming off an inordinate share of national wealth, devaluing and depressing the nation's workforce to concentrate solely on shareholder value and reducing by about half labor's share.[13]

Economists who argue that a hyper-inflated financial sector damages the entire economy have received support even from that conservative voice of business, *Forbes* magazine. Reporter Steve Dunning accepts the conclusion of an International Monetary Fund study that a financial sector that grows too large slows economic growth, and "a smaller financial sector . . . would perform more efficiently and the economy would grow more quickly." The IMF study demonstrated that "excessive financialization of the U.S. economy reduces GDP growth by 2% every year . . . a massive drag on the economy—some $320 billion per year." If the financial sector shrank to an optimum size, the U.S. economy would experience a normal recovery of 3 to 4 percent per year instead of the anemic 1 to 2 percent of the past few years.

An overgrown financial sector "loses interest in the 'boring" returns from financing the real economy and instead devotes itself to using money to make money, "rather than making real goods and services," thus leading to "wealth for the few, and overall national economic decline." Denning criticized the Dodd-Frank attempt to reform Wall Street as complicated and unwieldy and missed the fact that it at least partially succeeded in reigning in banks' risky behavior. But his basic point was on target: ending financial corruption as usual is not a matter of drafting new, simple rules, but "a matter of finding political will to treat admitted criminality as criminal."[14]

As billionaire financiers and super-rich inheritors increasingly dominate the political process and public policy, inherited wealth is accumulating to an unparalleled degree. Chilling evidence comes from the Annual Survey by the U.S. Trust of wealthy Americans: the survey predicted that over the next two decades "more than $15 trillion will be passed across generations in high-net worth families." That is an estimate of the wealth that is known about. Gabriel Zucman, an economist at the University of California who collaborates with Piketty and Emmanuel Saez, has published a book examining "The Scourge of Tax Havens." He estimates that about 8 percent of the world's wealth, or $7.6 trillion, is hidden in tax havens; the probable tax loss to the United States is $35 billion; some estimates put the tax loss closer to $100 billion. The Tax Justice Network, a nonprofit watchdog group, has estimated that the "black hole" of offshore wealth could be as high as $21 to $32 trillion. The TJN says this estimate does not take into account real estate, yachts, racehorses, gold bricks, and many other valuables. Whatever the amount, much of that wealth will wind up with a generation of wealthy inheritors. What portion of the offshore wealth is owned by Americans is not known, but Goldman Sachs is one of three banks holding most of the money, along with JPMorgan Chase and Bank of America.[15]

The loopholes in the U.S. tax code also permit wealth to accumulate through legal tax avoidance by multinational corporations and billionaire hedge fund managers. Corporations shift their profits to tax-friendly countries claimed as their base of operations; in 2014 Google parked $13 billion in profit in Bermuda. Billionaires simply route their money to Bermuda and back. The *New York Times* described this as "a kind of private tax system, catering to only several thousand Americans." Jared Bernstein, a former chief economic advisor to Vice President Joe Biden, commented that it's not so much that "the wealthy use their money to buy politicians; more accurately, it's that they buy policy, and specifically, tax policy."[16]

In early April 2016 the enormity of offshore wealth hidden in tax havens for the rich and powerful received sensational exposure as articles appeared in media outlets based on 11.5 million documents secretly leaked from the Panama law firm Mossack Fonseca. After receiving the documents in 2015 from a German newspaper, an international team of investigative journalists spent six months analyzing the data, and media outlets, notably the *Guardian*, began publishing reports showing how billions of dollars were hidden in shell accounts and naming 140 politicians and public officials in different countries as clients. The scope of the law firm's activities, with dozens of offices around the world, was staggering: over 14,000 clients and more than 214,000 offshore entities involved. Not all such accounts are illegal, but many criminals and wealthy individuals use these only-on-paper companies to hide money and illicit traffic and to avoid taxes. Wealthy Americans ranging from a former Citibank executive to a former All-Star baseball player have used the Panama firm to avoid tens of millions in taxes.[17]

Yet Mossack Fonseca is just one of hundreds of such firms globally specializing in hiding assets. Zucman observed that the Panama Papers uncovered one small corner of tax avoidance, perhaps 5 percent of it. There are "hundreds of thousands of offshore companies," he said, in tax havens "creating shell companies." Bankers in Switzerland, Luxembourg, and elsewhere are also creating shell companies, trusts, and foundations.[18]

Both of 2016's major presidential candidates, Hillary Clinton and Donald Trump, make use of the onshore tax haven of Delaware, at an address used by 285,000 companies. When the Panama story broke, Clinton denounced the use of such havens as "outrageous," but several of Clinton's financial backers turned up in the Panama Papers. Trump boasted regularly that not paying taxes is "smart." (Mossack Fonseca's headquarters are located just a few blocks from the Trump International Hotel in Panama City.)[19]

Four of ten big banks most heavily involved in this global industry have operations in the United States, which itself is a major tax haven for hidden billions. The Panama Papers revealed that thousands of shell companies exist in states in addition to Delaware, notably Wyoming and Nevada, where banks can hire fronts, known as nominees, to lawfully pose as owners. U.S. laws requiring banks to know their customers and comply with tax codes are wholly ineffective.[20] Thus tens of billions in tax revenue are lost to the U.S. Treasury.

More billions have been lost over the past twenty years, and increasingly since 2010, as Congress has cut the Internal Revenue Service's budget, resulting in a sharp drop in auditors and in auditing of large corporations. Audits of partnerships in finance and insurance has declined to less than 1 percent, so that, according to Sen. Carl Levin (D-MI), the IRS is "failing to audit where the big money is." IRS director John A. Koskinen calls the budget cuts "tax cuts for cheaters," running into the billions.[21]

Corporate and financial firms' tax avoidance creates a gigantic drain of revenue, increases inequality, and is subsidized by U.S. taxpayers who do not cheat, who indeed cannot cheat, since their taxes are collected automatically. Shortly after the bombshell of the Panama Papers, Oxfam released a report finding that the fifty largest U.S. corporations are also hiding vast wealth in offshore tax havens like Bermuda and the Cayman Islands: $1.4 trillion in all, costing the federal government $111 billion in tax revenue; the Fortune 500 saved $695 billion in taxes on $2.4 trillion held offshore. The biggest tax dodger was Apple with $181 billion stashed offshore: CEO Tim Cook's salary was $9.2 million while his stock awards have increased in value to $681 million. Oxfam commented that tax dodging by multinational corporations "contributes to dangerous inequality that is undermining our social fabric and hindering economic growth."[22]

The super rich also enlarge their fortunes because of the low federal rates on capital gains and dividends. The estate tax exemption since 2001 has risen from $650,000 per person to $5.43 million, or $10.86 million per couple. Few estates actually pay the full tax, often just one-sixth of their value. Republicans claim that the estate tax hurts small businesses and farms: in 2013 roughly 20 such small entities nationally owed an estate tax. On the high end, if repealed, the 316 estates worth at least $50 million would each receive a tax windfall of $20 million, another gift for a looming aristocracy of wealth.[23]

Then there are "dynasty trusts," probably unknown to most Americans. Since the 1980s, according to Boston University law professor Ray D. Madoff, dynasty trusts have allowed wealthy families to transfer huge amounts of money and assets to succeeding generations that can hold them in perpetuity. These trusts, according to Madoff, "operate largely outside public view, like spores in a horror movie, [and] are poised to fundamentally transform the face of the United States by creating a new aristocracy made up of individuals who have access to large amounts of untaxed wealth to meet their every need and desire while being immune to the claims of creditors."[24]

Twenty-eight states and the District of Columbia, lobbied by bankers seeking to attract investments, have abolished their perpetuity rules that existed for centuries limiting the length of time a property owner could control the use of his or her property after death. Repeal or opt-out provisions have allowed wealthy Americans to set property aside for heirs forever; grantors need not even live in those states but simply hire a trustee in one of them. In 1986 Congress enabled this process when it revised the Generation Skipping Tax, creating "a marketing bonanza for banks and trust companies" and furthering mass avoidance of taxes. Madoff believes that dynasty trusts impose "considerable social harm" and bestow advantages for their beneficiaries who constitute an aristocracy in the making.[25]

Immunity from the justice meted out to other Americans reinforces the financial class's sense of entitlement. A best-selling book (2003) and then a film documented the rise and fall of Enron, *The Smartest Guys in the Room*. A mentality of "smartness" pervades the culture of Wall Street, as Karen Ho demonstrated in a revealing ethnography based on firsthand experience. Investment bankers and managers regard themselves as "the smartest people" *anywhere*, and the most prestigious firms like Goldman Sachs recruit exclusively at Princeton, Harvard, Yale, and a few other elite institutions. They tell eager undergraduates that because these are the only pools they target, those students are already certified by their presence there. Ho described the "culture of smartness" as meaning much more than individual intelligence: "it conveys a naturalized and genetic sense of 'impressiveness,' of elite, pinnacle status and expertise, which is used to signify, and even prove, investment bankers' worthiness as advisor to corporate America and leaders of the global financial markets."[26]

Ho's description of changes in Wall Street recruiting practices over the past decades echoes the transition from E. Digby Baltzell's WASP exclusivity to a meritocracy that has devolved into oligarchy. Traditionally Wall Street did not practice "open" recruiting but relied on kinship and the "old boys' network" operating through wealthy families and the Ivy League. But in the 1980s, as Wall Street solidified its expert influence over many U.S. corporations, it began to recruit "in droves at elite East Coast schools." Exclusive recruiting has created a new kind of caste system that Baltzell would recognize.[27]

Although the share of Harvard and Princeton graduates going to Wall Street has fallen since pre-2008 "droves," their numbers are still disproportionately high, close to 40 percent some years. Sheila Bair is one of those who "bemoan the fact that so many of our best and brightest are drawn to the financial services sector," and she asks, "what kind of message does the tax code send? Go get a job and find the cure for cancer, we will tax you at 35 percent. But go manage a hedge fund, and you will have to pay us only 15 percent."[28]

The train of financial wrongdoing recounted here and the immunity from prison for criminals who use money to make money substantiates as much as any other indicator the emergence of a privileged aristocracy. Our political class has already transformed our polity from a democratic representative government into a plutocracy and simultaneously increases inequality and enables the formation of a new aristocracy of wealth.

Rising economic inequality is global and is regarded as a threat to the world's economic stability even by the super rich who gather annually at the World Economic Forum in Davos, Switzerland (though what the "Davos class" is willing to sacrifice to address the threat is unclear). Also global is the spreading consolidation of oligarchical political classes in many nations.[29]

In Europe and the United States populist reaction against oligarchies has spawned protest, discontent, and frustration with the established political classes and their corruption, self-dealing, and nepotism. Together with anti-immigrant reaction, alienation from the democratic process has bolstered the influence of neopopulist right-wing parties. In the spring of 2014, as the European Union elections approached, the *Guardian* saw across Europe "sullen anger and frustration with a mainstream political class seen as detached and remote, incompetent and venal, and often illegitimate."[30]

In June 2016 Britain voted on a referendum on whether to leave or stay in the European Union. The stunning vote to "Leave" fueled by people left behind by globalization and decades of rising inequality rocked the political establishment. The Centre for Social Justice and Legatum Institute reported that voters in the middle and upper classes were the only income groups in which majorities voted "Remain," while "the people with little or nothing to lose—as they saw it—backed 'Leave.'"[31]

In the 2016 presidential campaign the American permanent political class and the professional politicians of the Democratic and (especially) Republican Parties reaped what they have sowed. Voters angry with the "establishment" and Washington politicians went into ballot boxes and registered anger and frustration with the economic damage the political class has inflicted on them. The unexpected strength of Vermont Senator Bernie Sanders's populist challenge to Hillary Clinton forced the presumptive Democratic heir to echo Sanders's focus on economic inequality, on poverty, and on the financial havoc created by Wall Street and billionaires. Angry voters fueled the extraordinary success of Donald Trump in blustering his way to repeated victories and the Republican presidential nomination.

Trump and Sanders appealed to voters with unfiltered populist rhetoric, though Trump's reactionary, white nationalist populism scapegoated immigrants, Muslims, and the vulnerable. He launched his campaign with a diatribe against Mexican immigrants, promising to "build a wall," and consistently appealed to a significant portion of voters reacting against our first African American president and an ethnically and racially more diverse population. Sanders concentrated on economic issues, crusading against inequality and the Wall Street money power reminiscent of the People's Party of the 1890s. Sanders's economic populism—and to a degree even Trump's—followed in the footsteps of protest movements of the past that have challenged political and economic systems tilted in favor of corrupt elites.[32] (In office, Trump has pursued an economic policy far from populist.)

In the primaries Trump and Sanders drew strong support from those who have experienced economic insecurity and pain, with their voters describing themselves as "financially falling behind." Sanders overwhelmingly attracted young voters from a generation with over a trillion dollars in student debt and facing bleak prospects in an economy offering few good jobs. Many union members also gravitated to "The Bern" because they saw themselves let down by conventional Democrats represented by Hillary Clinton. In towns across the country where trade deals have shuttered factories, devastated their economies, and sapped the sinews of community life, people backed Sanders and Trump.[33]

Both "outsiders" vigorously denounced free trade treaties, favorite bipartisan projects of the political class, maintaining that such deals have exported manufacturing jobs to Asia, China in particular. Research by economists supports their claims: one study estimated that job losses from import competition from China during 1999–2011 ranged from 2.0 to 2.4 million. Both Trump and Sanders echoed populist predecessors who have traditionally emphasized that fairness for American workers comes first.[34]

Two of Trump's strongest cohorts were those without college and with income under $50,000, groups that have lost wages or slid into lesser jobs. With Sanders the economic divide was even sharper. In various primaries he drew as much as 72 percent of those with incomes under $30,000 and 60 percent of those making $49,999 or less. Some surveys registered majorities of truck and motorcycle drivers preferring Sanders. A geopolitical survey of Trump country identified West Virginia, ravaged by unemployment and opiate addiction, as his strongest state.[35]

The downwardly mobile have lost jobs to offshoring, trade deals, consolidation, and technology, and they have slipped often into work that robs them of dignity. If not insecure themselves, many members of the electorate in both parties probably know of relatives, neighbors, or coworkers afflicted by the "epidemic of pain" raging though the cohort of middle-aged whites described in the disturbing report by economists Anne Case and Angus Deaton on morbidity and mortality. It suggests the toll taken by lost jobs and status: midlife white Americans are killing themselves at record rates by drug and alcohol poisoning, suicide, chronic liver diseases, and cirrhosis.

Despite a media narrative attributing disaffection and Trump support as located largely among the "white working class," economic stagnation extended across the middle class. The typical household has a net worth 14 percent lower than the typical one in 1984. Though Republican voters tend to be more affluent than the rest of the electorate, they too have recoiled from an economy—and Republican obsession with tax cuts for the rich—that has been producing enormous rewards at the top—for the One Percent and the 0.1 percent—and not for the vast majority. Over the past several decades the economy has produced one of the lowest-wage labor forces among developed countries. The middle class has literally shrunk; those falling out of it or in danger of doing so rallied to Trump and Sanders.[36]

A 2015 Pew Research Center poll found that Americans' attitude to their government was "BEYOND DISTRUST." Just 19 percent said they trust the government always or most of the time, and 55 percent believe that "ordinary Americans" would do a better job of running the government than elected officials. For several years Congress's favorability rating has been at an all-time low, 12 percent in 2016, and disapproval of the Supreme Court has reached a record high of 50 percent.[37]

Business and corporate leaders fare no better. The public relations firm Edelman has conducted a trust survey for the past thirteen years. It found that just 15 percent of Americans trust business leaders to tell the truth when confronted with a difficult problem; with regard to government leaders the level dropped to 10 percent. In surveying American trust in different industries, banks and finance services cratered to the bottom. Although nongovernmental organizations received a higher trust rating, trust in charities has declined sharply, and 41 percent believe leaders of nonprofit charities are paid too much.[38]

Shortly before the 2016 election another survey of attitudes to government and leaders found "astonishing" cynicism about government. "Vast majorities" lacked confidence in government solving problems, believed most politicians were more interested in winning elections than doing what's right, and thought most elected officials do not care what voters think. Dissatisfaction extended to almost all institutions and sectors of American life. Large majorities believed that the economic system was rigged in favor of the wealthiest, that leaders in corporations, media, universities, and technology cared little about ordinary citizens, and that people running the government do not tell the truth; 75 percent said you "can't believe" the "mainstream media."[39]

The report from the Institute for Advanced Studies in Culture at the University of Virginia presented disturbing evidence that the supporters of the two major party nominees, Hillary Clinton and Donald Trump, held two starkly different views of the world, virtually "tribal." The authors pointed to a "Vanishing Center" and declining "shared civic culture that made for compromise, limited partisan disagreements, and made possible [a] broad governing consensus." On a range of issues Clinton and Trump loyalists stood poles apart. Yet for all the emphasis on these "two nations," opposed on most issues relating to race or ethnicity, the "greatest social distance" revealed was not "along racial or ethnic lines, but along lines of class, with the wealthiest Americans and its cultural elite seen as furthest removed from the values and benefits of the majority."[40]

Two findings stood out: 84 percent said Wall Street and big business often profit at the expense of ordinary Americans; and *62 percent believed "the most educated and successful people ... are more interested in serving themselves than the common good."* Corruption, said the authors, could be found in all sectors of society.[41]

"The Vanishing Center" observed that alienation from government has been building for decades, but "what is new is the absence of a balance of a thoughtful, political engagement by a seasoned and knowledgeable political class."[42] *American Oligarchy* provides ample evidence that the behavior of the political class, and the examples it sets, have created the current intense wave of cynicism, distrust, and alienation of ordinary citizens across the political spectrum that the report so ably documents. Muckraking books like this one, along with investigative journalists exposing corruption on numerous websites, are among the steps needed to advance the long fight ahead to bring about reform. "Throwing out the rascals" has been shown not to work. A corrupt political culture simply breeds more rascals.

The political class almost predictably added to voters' alienation by delivering two candidates with historically high unfavorability ratings, higher than any in seven decades of presidential elections moreover, and two quintessential members of the political class. Clinton's political class attributes: a foundation, Bill's collecting $17.5 million over five years from for-profit Laureate International University to serve as honorary chancellor, coziness with Wall Street CEOs who paid her outlandish amounts for speeches, and more. A Democratic Party preferring to play it safe with a centrist—despite Sanders demonstrating the appeal of a strong progressive agenda in the party's base and among Independents—gave Clinton to voters ready for a change.

Despite her experience and glowing résumé, Clinton had not just been around for many years but was perceived as entrenched in the political class and associated with policies that helped bring about the Great Recession that brought pain to so many, including people normally inclined to vote Democratic. Her coziness with what Naomi Klein has called "the Davos class, a hyper-connected network of banking and tech billionaires, elected leaders who are awfully cozy with their interests, and Hollywood celebrities who made the whole thing seem unbearably glamorous. . . . People such as Hillary and Bill Clinton are the toast of the Davos party. In truth, they threw the party."[43]

Trump too typifies the political class with wealth qualifying him for the Davos class; and after he gained the nomination, the reactionary billionaire and climate change denier Robert Mercer (see above) shifted his support from Cruz to Trump. Trump arrived due to the economic decline and disaffection mentioned above, and what John Nichols and Robert W. McChesney term the money-media-election complex dominated by a handful of large corporations who mightily helped boost his candidacy. In 2015 he benefited from 327 minutes of nightly broadcast news coverage compared with Clinton's 121 and Sanders's 20. By March 2016 Trump had received $2 billion worth of "earned" or free media, compared to $746 million for Clinton and insignificant amounts for his Republican rivals. The previous month Lesley Moonves, CEO of CBS News, told an investors' conference, "It [covering Trump] may not be good for

America, but it's damn good for CBS." It was a "good thing" because Republican presidential rivals were "not discussing issues, they're throwing bombs at one another." One wonders what Moonves was thinking when several weeks into his administration the president of the United States repeatedly accused the news media of being "the enemy of the people." Yet over the course of the campaign, with CNN leading the chorus, candidate Trump received the equivalent of $5.8 billion in free media, $2.9 billion more than Clinton.[44]

The liberal media depicted Trump often as a political class deviant. But in proposing a tax system to benefit himself and claiming deductions to pay no federal tax for eighteen years, in participating in the gift economy by using campaign donations to get future favors from officeholders, and in undermining trust in representative institutions, Trump represents an extreme version of the political class.

Conservative commentator Andrew Sullivan has described the United States as a "late empire," entities "known for several things: a self-obsessed, self-serving governing class, small over-reaching wars that bankrupt the Treasury, debt that balloons until retreat from global power becomes not a choice but a necessity, and a polity unable to address reasonably any of these questions—or how the increasing corruption of the media enables them all."[45] Sullivan might have added a citizenry much of which has lost faith in the empire's governing institutions.

Not many Americans are thinking in terms used in this book: oligarchy, ruling class, aristocracy of inherited wealth. Not many citizens pay attention to congressional travel, fund-raising, lobbyists' influence, think tanks, the self-dealing in nonprofits, and all the rest. They vastly underestimate the extent of inequality of wealth and "think they live in Sweden": they are way off the mark in estimating CEO pay and the hundreds of times more the executive suite is paid than their average workers. They seldom really see or encounter the incredible wealth and opulent lifestyle of the super rich, the yachts growing ever larger, the multicar garages filled with cars worth hundreds of thousands, the helicopters to mansions on Long Island, and multiple private fortress-like retreats.

But more and more ordinary Americans are waking up to the self-dealing of leaders in government and large institutions with high-salaried executives, the nepotism that looks at them from their television screens, and, above all, the closing of opportunity and diminished rewards for hard work. The hollowed-out middle class knows the rising cost of college tuition, if not the bloated salaries of university administrators as tuition soars, student debt tops $1 trillion, and universities increasingly employ adjunct faculty whose average salary is under $20,000. On the Internet and in print the rigged tax system had come to the attention of millions before presidential candidate Senator Bernie Sanders made it a staple of his campaign speeches delivered for months to audiences of tens of thousands. Billionaire investor Warren Buffet has told the world he paid lower taxes than his secretary, union members know of stagnant wages, clawed-back benefits, and the Koch network's campaign to have state legislatures pass "right-to-work" laws that equal "right-to-work-for-less" laws. In short, millions are informed by the diminishing quality of their lives and the experience of economic insecurity. They live in a world created by the permanent political class that does very well for itself but not for them or the public good. Slowly, maybe, they are catching on.

Afterword

The history of this country is not a continuous narrative of wealth and power always winning, always greedy, and never limited. Yes, money has always "talked," sometimes responsibly for the public good. From colonial times to the present, control of economic resources meant access to political power and government policy, but at times, both inside and outside of electoral politics, those disadvantaged or oppressed by a rigged system have mobilized episodically to check or limit the power of money.

In the latter decades of the nineteenth century, the First Gilded Age, the rise of industrial capitalism concentrated economic and political power in the hands of a corporate-political plutocracy. Then, as now, throughout the country millions of people in all walks of life, but particularly in the agrarian Midwest and South, believed that the two major parties and all government had become subservient to the grandees of industrial and financial capitalism. Building on farmers' organizations established to contest the power of railroads and to improve the lives of rural people, the discontented mobilized in the 1890s in the People's Party, a broad coalition of farmers, labor leaders and wage workers, professionals, and middle-class reformers, to restore political and economic fairness and equal opportunity.

One sympathetic historian called them a "grand coalition of outsiders," but they were much more than that. Populists launched a formidable challenge to corporate power and constituted "one of the most powerful independent movements in American history." Their radical 1892 party platform called for government regulation or ownership of railroads and the telegraph, direct election of U.S. senators by popular vote (state legislatures had elected them since 1789), currency inflation to help debtors, a universal secret ballot system, a graduated income tax, and other measures to address the imbalance of power between "the people" and "millionaires."[1]

Since the Populists included many small rural businessmen, large farmers, and middle-class reformers, they were hardly anticapitalist. Rather, they aimed to preserve their property—farms and businesses—by securing legislation to check corporate power, reverse extreme inequality of income and wealth, and extend democratic representation. A key economic proposal asked the government to establish a subtreasury that would provide credit for farmers, not welfare, and storage for their crops when prices were low. Wage earners in the Populist coalition wanted better pay and working conditions.

The Populists saw a nation suffering under the heel of a plutocratic elite, with the result, as their platform preamble thundered: "Corruption dominates the ballot-box, the Legislatures, the Congress, and touches even the ermine of the bench. . . . The fruits of the toil of millions are boldly stolen to build up colossal fortunes for a few, unprecedented in the history of mankind; and the possessors of these, in turn, despise the Republic, and endanger liberty. From the same prolific womb of governmental injustice we breed the two great classes—tramps and millionaires."

The Populist demand "that the power of government—in other words of the people—should be expanded" was radical for its time. In proposing government intervention to end "oppression, injustice, and poverty," the Populists realized that the Jeffersonian classical-liberal tradition of limited government left them at the mercy of consolidated corporate power, so they engaged in a wholesale reorientation of the republican tradition.

As the Progressive Era intellectual Herbert Croly explained in *The Promise of American Life* (1909), the Jeffersonian tradition had assumed that the guarantee of equal rights would lead automatically to the fulfillment of the American Promise. But the liberation of self-interest from all restraint led to "extreme individualism" and the oppression and injustice that the Populists challenged. "The existing concentration of wealth and financial power in the hands of a few irresponsible men is the inevitable outcome of the chaotic individualism of our political and economic organization . . . inimical to democracy, because it tends to erect political abuses and social inequalities into a system." Croly thus fused Jefferson's doctrine of equal rights with the Hamiltonian program of a strong, regulatory American state to ensure "a morally and socially desirable distribution of wealth."[2]

Croly described well what the Populists had already done, and Progressive Era presidents continued with policy, in synthesizing the Jeffersonian and Hamilton traditions. At the time Croly wrote, his hero, Theodore Roosevelt, and after him William Howard Taft, both Republicans, and Democrat Woodrow Wilson, successively enacted substantial parts of the Populist program and brought into existence, in historian Elizabeth Sanders's words, "a rudimentary interventionist state that limited corporate prerogatives in ways that seemed genuinely frightening to capitalists at the time." Progressive presidents and congressional representatives after them continued the Populists' struggle to bring into being a regulatory state "to restrain rapacious corporations, [and] prevent excessive concentration of wealth and market power"[3] In the 1930s a Great Depression that crippled the country led Franklin D. Roosevelt and Progressive congressional majorities to expand the power of the federal government to an unprecedented level, once again for Jeffersonian ends.

The Progressives and New Dealers freed themselves from the past, as Americans have done since at least the American Revolution. They need once again to reorient their thinking about the economy and government and to discard the bankrupt fictions of a permanent political class that is neither meritocratic nor democratic. *American Oligarchy* has been written, not to propose a path out of the New Gilded Age, but to discredit the political class by raking its muck between covers in black and white.

The "Populist Tsunami" of 2016 exposed how vulnerable the permanent political class has become. A self-described "democratic socialist" almost unseated the Democratic establishment's anointed champion. In the Populist platform preamble above substitute for *tramps* and *millionaires* the words *the poor* and *billionaires*, and Bernie Sanders's populist rhetoric is approximated. More importantly, he proposed to check the power of concentrated wealth and to restore fairness to a rigged economy. Many Trump voters, according to polls, were willing to vote for Sanders, suggesting that those middle-class and working-class whites should not be written off as bigots or unready for the right kind of change. Populist upheavals often have tended to be ephemeral, but the millions of Sanders's supporters, and many of Clinton's and Trump's, appear to have had their fill of the self-dealing, immunities, and fraudulence of the political class.

If the political shocks of 2016 proved anything, it's that millions of Americans want their government to provide opportunity and protect them from economic insecurity. They thirst for fairness in the distribution of benefits and social goods, for fairness in the legal and justice system, for social justice, and for actions that match talk. The yearning for a government that serves the people leads many of the disillusioned to listen to the wrong voices. They disengage or vote for "none of the above," or follow the buncombe of a Pied Piper leading them nowhere and to further disillusionment. They live in a culture of artifice, of "truthiness" (in Stephen Colbert's famous word coinage) and self-indulgence, in which the satisfaction of individual desires (wants advertised into needs) supplants all concern for the common good. Thus are they taught by example from above, by the political class and the din of consumerism. They need to see clearly what goes on there, "up above," with veils of pretense, rhetoric, and falsehood stripped away.

Notes

Preface

1. On the hostility of populist movements to traditional elites, John Abromeit, Bridget Maria Chesterton, Gary Marotta, and York Norman, introduction to Abromeit et al., eds., *Transformations of Populism in Europe and the Americas: History and Recent Tendencies* (London: Bloomsbury Academic, 2016), xiv. The formal concept of "the political class" is derived from the theory of Gaetano Mosca (1848–1941) that societies inevitably tend to develop a ruling elite. Journalists, citizens, and even members of *la classe politica* find it a useful villain to hold responsible when things go wrong. (Think of American politicians who have spent their lives in politics railing against "Washington.")

2. Joseph LaPalombara, *Democracy, Italian Style* (Binghamton, NY: Vail-Balou Press, 1987), 152–60, quotations 157, 160.

3. Joan Didion, *Political Fictions* (New York: A. A. Knopf, 2001), quotation 9; Alan M. Dershowitz, *Supreme Injustice: How the High Court Hijacked the Election of 2000* (New York: Oxford University Press, 2001), 81.

4. Didion, *Political Fictions*, 15.

Introduction. Beyond Plutocracy: Becoming an Aristocracy

1. Emmanuel Saez, "Striking It Richer: The Evolution of Top Incomes in the United States (Updated with 2014 Preliminary Estimates)," UC Berkeley, June 25, 2015, http://eml.berkeley .edu/~saez/saez-UStopincomes-2014.pdf; "Income Inequality," 2014, Inequality.org, Institute of Policy Studies, http://inequality.org/income-inequality/.

2. Chris Matthews, "Wealth Inequality in America: It's Worse Than You Think," *Fortune*, October 31, 2014, http://fortune.com/2014/10/31/inequality-wealth-income-us/.

3. From a 2002 column reprinted in Paul Krugman, *The Great Unravelling: Losing Our Way in the New Century* (New York: W. W. Norton, 2005), 258.

4. Quotation from Michael Massing, "Reimagining Journalism: The Story of the One Percent," *New York Review of Books*, December 17, 2015; see also the website created and edited by David Callahan, *Inside Philanthropy*, http://www.insidephilanthropy.com/.

5. Barney Frank, *Frank: A Life in Politics from the Great Society to Same-Sex Marriage* (New York: Farrar, Straus and Giroux, 2015), 33–34. White later promoted Lewis to be one of his top political aides.

6. Robert G. Kaiser, *So Damn Much Money: The Triumph of Lobbying and the Corrosion of American Government* (New York: Alfred A. Knopf, 2009), 21.

7. Kaiser, *So Damn Much Money*, quotations 18, 19.

8. Adam Bellow, *In Praise of Nepotism: A Natural History* (New York: Doubleday, 2003).

9. Eric Pace, "E. Digby Baltzell Dies at 80; Studied WASPs," *New York Times*, Aug. 20, 1996; Edith Kurzweil, "Changing of the Guard in Digby Baltzell's 'The Protestant Establishment,'" *New York Sun*, May 7, 2008, http://www.nysun.com/arts/changing-of-the-guard-in-digby -baltzells/75945/.

10. E. Digby Baltzell, *The Protestant Establishment: Aristocracy and Caste in America* (New York: Vintage Books, 1964), x, x–xi.

11. Baltzell, *Protestant Establishment*, 382.

12. Freeland referred to the work of historians Daron Acemonglu and James Robinson, who argued that Venice in adopting exclusivity came to exemplify unsuccessful "extractive states" that fail because they "are controlled by ruling elites whose objective is to extract as much wealth as they can from the rest of society and to maintain their own hold on power." Chrystia Freeland, *Plutocrats: The Rise of the New Global Super-Rich and the Fall of Everyone Else* (New York: Penguin Press, 2012), 277–87, quotation 284.

13. Freeland, *Plutocrats*, 283.

14. Thomas Piketty, *Capital in the Twenty-First Century*, trans. Arthur Goldhammer (Cambridge, MA: Harvard University Press, 2014), 422–24.

15. Ronald P. Formisano, *Plutocracy in America: How Increasing Inequality Destroys the Middle Class and Exploits the Poor* (Baltimore: Johns Hopkins University Press, 2015), 122–45.

16. Jonathan Martin and Maggie Haberman, "Back to the Future: Clinton vs. Bush?" *Politico*, November 8, 2012, http://www.politico.com/story/2012/11/back-to-the-future-clinton-vs -bush-083550; Jeff Jacoby, "A Clinton vs. Bush Race? Again? Democracies and Dynasties Don't Mix," *Boston Globe*, October 29, 2014, http://www.jeffjacoby.com/15559/a-clinton-vs-bush -race-again; Winter Trebax, "Aristocracy 2016: Jeb Bush vs. Hillary Clinton," *Voices of Liberty*, March 16, 2015, http://www.voicesofliberty.com/article/aristocracy-2016-jeb-bush -vs-hillary-clinton/.

17. Peter Olsen-Phillips, Russ Choma, Sarah Bryner, and Doug Weber, "The Political One Percent of the One Percent in 2014: Mega Donors Fuel Rising Cost of Elections," *Open Secrets*, April 30, 2015, http://www.opensecrets.org/news/2015/04/the-political-one -percent-of-the-one-percent-in-2014-mega-donors-fuel-rising-cost-of-elections/; Daniel

L. Davis, "America 2015: Democracy, Republic or Aristocracy?" *National Interest*, May 19, 2015, http://nationalinterest.org/blog/the-buzz/america-2015-democracy-republic-or -aristocracy-12921. In October 2015 the *New York Times* reported that thus far just 158 families and their corporations had given nearly half of all campaign contributions for 2016, largely to Republican candidates; most of the donors had made their money in energy or finance. Nicholas Confessore, Sarah Cohen, and Karen Yourish, "The Families Funding the 2016 Presidential Election," *New York Times*, October 10, 2015.

18. Rage against Obama and the popular reaction began early: Gabriel Sherman, "The Wail of the 1%," *New York* magazine, August 19, 2009; Paul Krugman, "Plutocrats Feeling Persecuted," *New York Times*, September 26, 2013; Mark Gongloff, "AIG CEO: Bonus Uproar 'Just as Bad' as Racist Lynch Mob," *Huffington Post Business*, September 24, 2013, http://www .huffingtonpost.com/2013/09/24/aig-bonuses-benmosche-deep-south_n_3981911.html; James Surowieki, "Moaning Moguls," *New Yorker*, July 7, 2014.

19. Quotation from Tim Donovan, "Clueless Rich Kids on the Rise: How Millennial Aristocrats Will Destroy Our Future," *Salon*, July 21, 2014, http://www.salon.com/2014/07/21/ clueless_rich_kids_on_the_rise_how_millennial_aristocrats_will_destroy_our_future/; "Millenials: The Politically Unclaimed Generation," The Reason-Rupe Spring 2014 Millennial Survey, July 10, 2014, 5, 6, 25, 39–41, 65, https://reason.com/assets/db/2014-millennials -report.pdf.

20. Michael J. Sandel, *What Money Can't Buy: The Moral Limits of Markets* (New York: Farrar, Straus and Giroux, 2012).

21. This paragraph paraphrases Harry Stein, "How the Government Subsidizes Wealth Inequality," Center for American Progress, June 25, 2014, https://www.americanprogress.org/ issues/tax-reform/report/2014/06/25/92656/how-the-government-subsidizes-wealth -inequality/; Stein points out that the decline in the tax rate on capital gains since 1992 has benefited most "the richest of the rich"; the four hundred wealthiest taxpayers in 2009 "claimed a full 12 percent of all capital gains that result from reduced tax rates"; Paul Buchheit, "5 Ways Rich People's 'Entitlements' Cheat You and Me," *Alternet*, February 9, 2014, http://www.alternet.org/economy/5-ways-rich-peoples-entitlements-cheat-you-and-me; in 2011 the wealthiest four hundred paid an average tax of 17 percent.

22. Adrienne Koch and William Peden, eds., *The Life and Selected Writings of Thomas Jefferson* (New York: Random House, 1944), 51–52; Jefferson to Adams, October 28, 1813, in Lester J. Cappon, ed., *The Adams-Jefferson Letters: The Complete Correspondence between Thomas Jefferson and Abigail and John Adams* (Chapel Hill: University of North Carolina Press, 1959), 2:389. Adams also held no love for aristocracy and wealth accumulation. To Jefferson he described it as "a subtle venom that diffuses itself unseen, over Oceans and Continents, and triumphs over time. If I could prevent its deleterious influence I would put it all into 'The Hole' of Calcutta [a notorious prison] but this is impossible, as it is a Phoenix that rises again out of its own Ashes." Adams to Jefferson, December 19, 1813, in Cappon, *Adams-Jefferson Letters*, 2:409.

23. Saul Cornell, *The Other Founders: Anti-Federalism & the Dissenting Tradition in America, 1788–1828* (Chapel Hill: University of North Carolina Press, 1999), 34, 69, 72, 79, 205; defenders of a natural aristocracy tended to fear an excess of democracy and demagogues who

swayed public opinion, 151, 152; Jefferson to Adams, October 28, 1813, in Cappon, *Adams-Jefferson Letters*, 2:388.

24. Cornell, *Other Founders*, 97, 107.

25. Adams to Jefferson, November 15, 1813, in Cappon, *Adams-Jefferson Letters*, 2:400.

26. Christopher Hayes, *Twilight of the Elites: America after Meritocracy* (New York: Crown, 2012), 32–40, 54–60, quotation 40; on meritocracy producing unequal and opportunity-blocking outcomes, Leslie McCall, *The Undeserving Rich: American Beliefs about Inequality, Opportunity, and Redistribution* (New York: Cambridge University Press, 2013), 11, 204n19, 263–64.

Chapter 1. Meet the Political Class

1. Mark Leibovich, *This Town: Two Parties and a Funeral—Plus Plenty of Valet Parking!—in America's Gilded Capital* (New York: Penguin, 2013), 1–2.

2. Editors, "Congress Rushes to Aid the Powerful," *New York Times*, April 26, 2013.

3. Erik Ose, "Congress Secretly Voted Themselves a Cromnibus Luxury Car Perk," *Huffington Post*, February 15, 2015, http://www.huffingtonpost.com/erik-ose/after-congress-secretly-v_b_6330644.html.

4. Joshua Green, "The Pampered World of Congressional Air Travel," *Bloomberg Business*, April 30, 2013, http://www.bloomberg.com/bw/articles/2013-04-30/the-pampered-world-of-congressional-air-travel; Katie Pavlich, "Why Are Members of Congress Using Your Money to Fly First Class?" *Townhall.com*, March 21, 2014, http://townhall.com/tipsheet/katiepavlich/2014/03/21/why-are-congressman-flying-first-class-n1812655; Glenn Kessler, "First-Class Travel for Lawmakers: A 4-Pinocchio Falsehood Pops Up Again," *Washington Post*, October 21, 2014, http://www.washingtonpost.com/blogs/fact-checker/wp/2014/10/21/first-class-travel-for-lawmakers-an-silly-falsehood-pops-up-again/.

5. John Parkinson, "Exclusive House, Senate Gyms Remain Open during Shutdown," *ABC News*, October 18, 2013, http://abcnews.go.com/blogs/politics/2013/10/exclusive-house-gym-remains-open-during-shutdown/; Jennifer Steinhauer, "Capitol Portraits, a Perk of Access, Become a Symbol of Excess Instead," *New York Times*, February 5, 2016.

6. Charles Babbington and Lourie Kellman, "Income Inequality Pronounced at Capitol," *Lexington Herald Leader*, May 3, 2015.

7. Quotation from Melanie Batley, "Lawmakers Get First-Class Service to Ease Pain of Obamacare Enrollment," *Newsmax*, November 20, 2013, http://www.newsmax.com/Newsfront/obamacare-exchanges-lawmakers-healthcare/2013/11/20/id/537635/; Robert Pear, "Perks Ease Way in Health Plan for Lawmakers," *New York Times*, November 19, 2013; J. D. Harrison, "More than 12,000 Congressional Staffers Have Enrolled in Health Plans through Obamacare," *Washington Post*, February 20, 2013.

8. Jennifer Senior, "Generous Republican Benefits," *New York Times*, January 25, 2015.

9. Sean Williams, "10 Perks Congress Has That You Don't," *Motley Fool*, October 20, 2013, http://www.fool.com/investing/general/2013/10/20/10-perks-congress-has-that-you-dont.aspx.

10. Jonathan Martin, "Lacking a House, a Senator Is Renewing His Ties in Kansas," *New York Times*, February 7, 2014; Jonathan Martin, "National G.O.P. Moves to Take Over Campaign of a Kansas Senator," *New York Times*, September 4, 2014.

11. Luke Rosiak, "Exography: Some Senators, Including Harry Reid, Rarely Go Home; Other Senators Do It Constantly," *Washington Examiner*, July 23, 2014, http://www.washington examiner.com/exography-some-senators-including-harry-reid-rarely-go-home-other -senators-do-it-constantly/article/2551156; debate quoted in David McCabe, "Roberts, Orman Exchange Blows in Debate," *The Hill* (Washington, DC), October 15, 2014, http://thehill.com/ blogs/ballot-box/senate-races/220915-roberts-links-ebola-isis-to-border-security-in-kansas -debate; also, David Helling and Steve Kraske, "Sen. Pat Roberts Survives, Defeating Challenge from Greg Orman," *Kansas City Star*, November 4, 2014, http://www.kansascity.com/ news/government-politics/election/article3565540.html.

12. Tom Daschle, with Michael D'Orso, *Like No Other Time: The 107th Congress and the Two Years That Changed America Forever* (New York: Crown, 2003), 9.

13. Glenn Greenwald, "The Daschles: Feeding at the Beltway Trough," *Salon*, February 1, 2009, http://www.salon.com/2009/02/01/daschle_2/.

14. On Daschle's moderation and pragmatism, Daschle, *Like No Other Time*, 11, 17.

15. Nick Bauman, "The Real Problem with Tom Daschle," *Mother Jones*, February 2, 2009, http://www.motherjones.com/mojo/2009/02/real-problem-tom-daschle.

16. David D. Kirkpatrick, "In Daschle's Tax Woes, a Peek into Washington," *New York Times*, February 2, 2009; Editors, "The Travails of Tom Daschle," *New York Times*, February 3, 2009.

17. *The Hill* staff, "Top Lobbyists 2014: Hired Guns," *The Hill*, October 22, 2014, http://thehill .com/business-a-lobbying/business-a-lobbying/221478-top-lobbyists-2014-hired-guns.

18. Tom Daschle with David Nather, *Getting It Done: How Obama and Congress Finally Broke the Stalemate to Make Way for Health Care Reform* (New York: St. Martin's Press, 2010), 118–20.

19. Jonathan Weisman, Laura Meckler, and Naftali Bendavid, "Obama on Defense as Daschle Withdraws," *Wall Street Journal*, February 4, 2009.

20. "EduCap," *Wikipedia*, http://en.wikipedia.org/wiki/EduCap.

21. Amit R. Paley and Valerie Strauss, "Student Loan Nonprofit a Boon for CEO," *Washington Post*, July 16, 2007.

22. The better-known Clinton Foundation has had a similar problem with a blurred line between the foundation and for-profit spinoffs. Nicholas Confessore and Amy Chozick, "Unease at Clinton Foundation over Finances and Ambitions," *New York Times*, August 13, 2013.

23. Valerie Strauss and Amit R. Paley, "Senate Seeks Student Loan Firm's Data," *Washington Post*, July 24, 2007.

24. Chris Frates, "Lobbyists Call Bluff on 'Daschle Exemption,'" *Politico*, July 26, 2010, http://www.politico.com/story/2010/07/lobbyists-call-bluff-on-daschle-exemption -040207; on Daschle as one of the growing numbers of "strategic advisors" and the type generally, Leibovich, *This Town*, 87, 98–99, 165.

25. James B. Steele and Lance Williams, "Who Got Rich off the Student Debt Crisis?," *RevealNews*, June 28, 2016, https://www.revealnews.org/article/who-got-rich-off-the -student-debt-crisis/; Shahien Nasinpour, "America's Largest Student Loan Firm Abused Borrowers and Broke the Law, Officials Say," *Huffington Post*, April 27, 2016, http://www

.huffingtonpost.com/entry/state-prosecutors-navient_us_57214218e4b01a5ebde47a02; Rana Foroohar, "How the Financing of Colleges May Lead to DISASTER," *New York Review of Books*, October 13, 2016, reviews seven recent books on the topic of student loans and for-profit colleges and universities.

26. "Tom Daschle Net Worth," Celebrity Net Worth, http://celebritynetworths.org/net-worth/tom-daschle-net-worth/.

27. Leibovich, *This Town*, 166–67. Early in the 2004 primaries Gephardt won endorsements from over twenty labor unions. Kevin Bogardus, "Former House Dem Leader Gephardt Hired as Lobbyist by Firm Battling SEIU," *The Hill*, June 15, 2010, http://thehill.com/business-a-lobbying/103411-gephardt-hired-as-lobbyist-by-firm-battling-the-seiu.

28. Sebastian Jones, "Dick Gephardt's Spectacular Sellout," *The Nation*, September 30, 2009, http://www.thenation.com/article/dick-gephardts-spectacular-sellout.

29. Michael Crowley, "Final Resolution: K Street Cashes In on the 1915 Armenian Genocide," *New Republic*, July 23, 2007; "Publisher: Former House Majority Leader Gets Top Hypocrite Prize," PanARMENIAN Network, August 20, 2014, http://www.panarmenian.net/eng/news/181732/.

30. Chris Matthews, "What's Really Outrageous about Eric Cantor's Wall Street Gig," *Fortune*, September 4, 2014; quotations from Laurence Arnold, "Cantor at Moelis Shows Government Can Do Something: Opening Line," *Bloomberg*, September 3, 2014, http://www.bloomberg.com/news/articles/2014-09-03/cantor-at-moelis-shows-government-can-do-something-opening-line.html; Eric Lichtblau, "Lawmakers Regulate Banks, Then Flock to Them," *New York Times*, April 13, 2010.

31. Graham Bowley, "At Brown, Spotlight on the President's Role at a Bank," *New York Times*, March 1, 2010; Joshua Rhett Miller, "Brown University Should Consider Name Change Due to Slave Ties, Critics Say," *Fox News*, April 17, 2009, http://www.foxnews.com/story/2009/04/17/brown-university-should-consider-name-change-due-to-slave-ties-critics-say/.

32. Chrystia Freeland, *Plutocrats: The Rise of the New Global Super-Rich and the Fall of Everyone Else* (New York: Penguin Press, 2012), 284.

33. Quotation from Jacqueline Trescott and James V. Grimaldi, "Smithsonian's Small Quits in the Wake of Inquiry," *Washington Post*, March 27, 2007.

34. James V. Grimaldi and Jacqueline Trescott, "Former IG Says Small Asked Her to Drop Audit," *Washington Post*, March 20, 2007.

35. James V. Grimaldi, "Smithsonian Head's Expenses 'Lavish,' Audit Says," *Washington Post*, February 25, 2007.

36. Quotations from James V. Grimaldi, "Smithsonian Documents Detail Chief's Expenses," *Washington Post*, March 19, 2007.

37. Quotation from Trescott and Grimaldi, "Smithsonian's Small Quits."

38. James V. Grimaldi, "Report Slams Small's Tenure," *Washington Post*, June 20, 2007; Sant quoted in Grimaldi, "Smithsonian Head's Expenses 'Lavish.'"

39. Report quoted in Grimaldi, "Report Slams Small's Tenure"; "Smithsonian's Small Quits"; "SEC and OFHEO Announce Resolution of Investigation and Special Examination of Fannie Mae," U.S. Securities and Exchange Commission, May 23, 2006, http://www.sec.gov/news/press/2006/2006-80.htm.

40. Dennis Hevesi, "I. Michael Heyman, Smithsonian Leader, Dies at 81," *New York Times*, November 27, 2011; "I. Michael Heyman, 1930–2011," Smithsonian Institution Archives, http://siarchives.si.edu/history/i-michael-heyman.

41. "I. Michael Heyman," Smithsonian Archives; Susan Young, "Roger W. Sant, MBA 1960: 2013 Alumni Achievement Award Recipient," *Alumni: Harvard Business School*, January 13, 2013, https://www.alumni.hbs.edu/stories/Pages/story-bulletin.aspx?num=2783; Jacqueline Trescott, "Sants Donate $15 Million to Smithsonian," *Washington Post*, June 27, 2008. Trescott reported that in 2007 Sant objected to a gift of $5 million from the American Petroleum Institute because of the industry's questionable practices in the world's waters.

42. James V. Grimaldi and Jacqueline Trescott, "Indian Museum Director Spent Lavishly on Travel," *Washington Post*, Dec. 28, 2007; Grimaldi and Trescott, "West's Travel Topped Other Smithsonian Directors'," *Washington Post*, February 2, 2008; "Smithsonian Museum Director's Spending Questioned," *Philanthropy News Digest*, January 2, 2008, http://philanthropy newsdigest.org/news/smithsonian-museum-director-s-spending-questioned; Grassley quoted in Grimaldi, "Portrait Cost Indian Museum $48,500," *Washington Post*, January 4, 2008.

43. Grimaldi and Trescott, "Indian Museum Director"; James V. Grimaldi and Jacqueline Trescott, "Ex-Director to Repay Smithsonian," *Washington Post*, October 29, 2008.

44. Henderson quoted in Grimaldi, "Portrait Cost Indian Museum $48,500"; "Rick West Lost Sight of Basic Mission," *Indianz.Com*, January 7, 2008, http://www.indianz.com/News/2008/006496.asp, an editorial that was largely critical, as were Indians closer to tribes and reservations; Jerry Reynolds, "Former NMAI Director's Spending Scrutinized," *Indian Country Today Media Network*, January 11, 2008, part 1, http://indiancountrytodaymedia network.com/2008/01/11/former-nmai-directors-spending-scrutinized-92062.

45. "WEDDINGS; Pilar Frank, William O'Leary," *New York Times*, December 6, 1998.

46. "Pilar O'Leary: Latina Yuppie Disgraces Smithsonian," *S.O.Y. Sick of Yuppies* (blog), April 15, 2008, http://saeberzprime.blogspot.com/2008/04/pilar-oleary-latina-yuppie-disgraces.html.

2. Our One Percent Government, Congress, and Its Adjuncts

1. Russ Choma, "Millionaires' Club: For First Time, Most Lawmakers Are Worth $1 Million-Plus," *Open Secrets*, Center for Responsive Politics, January 9, 2014, http://www.opensecrets.org/news/2014/01/millionaires-club-for-first-time-most-lawmakers-are-worth-1-million-plus/; Peter Whoriskey, "Growing Wealth Widens Distance between Lawmakers and Constituents," *Washington Post*, December 26, 2011, http://www.washingtonpost.com/business/economy/growing-wealth-widens-distance-between-lawmakers-and-constituents/2011/12/05/gIQAR7D6IP_story.html; Eric Lipton, "Half of Congress Are Millionaires, Report Says," *New York Times*, January 9, 2014, http://www.nytimes.com/2014/01/10/us/politics/more-than-half-the-members-of-congress-are-millionaires-analysis-finds.html.

2. Gary DeMar, "Rich Congressmen Keep Getting Richer," *Godfather Politics*, November 11, 2011, http://godfatherpolitics.com/1983/rich-congressmen-keep-getting-richer/; Shane Goldmacher, "Nearly One in Five Members of Congress Gets Paid Twice," *National Journal*,

June 28, 2013, https://www.yahoo.com/news/nearly-one-five-members-congress-gets-paid
-twice-060314402.html.

3. Mark Leibovich, "How Not to Seem Rich While Running for Office," *New York Times
Magazine*, Apr. 8, 2014, http://www.nytimes.com/2014/04/13/magazine/leibovich-rich
-politicians.html.

4. Studies discussed in Chrystia Freeland, *Plutocrats: The Rise of the New Global Super-
Rich and the Fall of Everyone Else* (New York: Penguin Press, 2012), 269–70.

5. Tamara Keith, "How Congress Quietly Overhauled Its Insider-Training Law," *NPR*, April
16, 2013, http://www.npr.org/blogs/itsallpolitics/2013/04/16/177496734/how-congress
-quietly-overhauled-its-insider-trading-law.

6. Freeland, *Plutocrats*, 270.

7. CREW [Citizens for Responsibility and Ethics in Washington], *Family Affair*, 2012, 5, http://
www.crewsmostcorrupt.org/page/-/PDFs/Reports/Family_Affair_House_2012_CREW
.pdf; Bob Norman, "Alcee Hastings' Scandals Collide in Sexual Harassment Lawsuit," *New Times
Blogs*, March 8, 2011, http://blogs.browardpalmbeach.com/pulp/2011/03/alcee_hastings
_scandals_collid.php; Brody Mullins and T. W. Farnum, "Lawmakers Keep the Change:
Cash Left Over from Official Trips Overseas Is Often Used for Personal Expenses," *Wall
Street Journal*, March 2, 2010, http://online.wsj.com/news/articles/SB1000142405274870
3429304575095592193574752.

8. CREW, *Family Affair*, 53–54; "Rep. Maxine Waters Faces Ethics Hearing," *USA Today
on Politics*, September 20, 2012, http://content.usatoday.com/communities/onpolitics/
post/2012/09/20/waters-ethics-hearing/70000789/1#.VDVbf7NATrc; quotations from
Tim Dickinson, "The Ten Worst Members of the Worst Congress Ever," *Rolling Stone*, January 12, 2012, http://www.rollingstone.com/politics/news/the-ten-worst-members-of-the
-worst-congress-ever-20120112?page=2.

9. CREW, *CREW's Most Corrupt 2012*, 157–58, http://www.crewsmostcorrupt.org/most-
corrupt/entry/most-corrupt-members-of-congress-report-2012; Ronald P. Formisano, *The
Tea Party: A Brief History* (Baltimore: Johns Hopkins University Press, 2012), 94.

10. CREW, *Family Affair*, 37; Lee Fang, "Will California Congressman Buck McKeon Go
Down?," *The Nation*, October 26, 2012, http://www.thenation.com/print/article/170863/
will-california-congressman-buck-mckeon-go-down/.

11. CREW, *CREW's Most Corrupt 2013*, 4–9, http://www.crewsmostcorrupt.org/most
corrupt/entry/most-corrupt-members-of-congress-report-2013; Andrews quoted in Jason
Horowitz, "Amid Ethics Inquiry, South Jersey Democrat Giving Up House Seat for a New
Job," *New York Times*, February 4, 2014.

12. CREW, *CREW's Most Corrupt 2012*, 204–5; CREW, *CREW's Most Corrupt 2013*, 9; Elie
Mystal, "Law School Sales Pitch Doubles Down on the 'Getting Rich' Rationale for Law
School," *Above the Law*, May 18, 2012, http://abovethelaw.com/2012/05/law-school-sales
-pitch-doubles-down-on-the-getting-rich-rationale-for-law-school/; "LST Calls for Dean's
Resignation and ABA Investigation," *Law School Transparency*, May 20, 2012, http://
www.lawschooltransparency.com/blog/2012/05/lst-calls-for-deans-resignation-and-aba
-investigation/.

13. Richard Pearsall, "Andrews' Wife Hints at 'Placeholder' Role," *Courier-Post* (Cherry Hill, NJ), April 9, 2008, http://www.courierpostonline.com/apps/pbcs.dll/article ?AID=/20080409/NEWS01/804090367; Steve Kornacki, "When Lautenberg's Age Met Booker's Ambition: An Elegy for the Swamp Dog," *Politico New York*, January 4, 2013, http://www.capitalnewyork.com/article/politics/2013/01/7175915/when-lautenbergs-age -met-bookers-ambition-elegy-swamp-dog.

14. Daniel Wagner, "Congressman Defends Payday Lending Industry: High-Interest Lenders an Alternative to Loan Sharks, Says Rep. Meeks," Center for Public Integrity, July 18, 2014, http:// www.publicintegrity.org/2014/07/18/15118/congressman-defends-payday-lending-industry.

15. Formisano, *Plutocracy in America*, 91–92, 94.

16. Daniel Wagner and Alison Fitzgerald, "Meet the Banking Caucus, Wall Street's Secret Weapon in Washington: Lawmakers Help Industry Donors Beat Back Tougher Rules," Center for Public Integrity, April 24, 2014, http://www.publicintegrity.org/print/14595; "Report Reveals Suspiciously Timed Contributions from Payday Lenders to Key Members of Congress," Allied Progress, September 30, 2015, https://alliedprogress.org/news/ report-reveals-suspiciously-timed-contributions-from-payday-lenders-to-key-members-of -congress/; Isabel Vincent, "'Payday' for Rep. Meeks," *New York Post*, April 28, 2013, http:// nypost.com/2013/04/28/payday-for-rep-meeks/.

17. *CREW's Most Corrupt 2012*, 49–53; *CREW's Most Corrupt 2013*, 77–83.

18. Among the many stories in the fallout from Stanford's scheme, Brent Kendall, "Supreme Court: Stanford's Victims Can Sue Third Parties," *Wall Street Journal Law Blog*, February 26, 2014, http://blogs.wsj.com/law/2014/02/26/supreme-court-rules-allen-stanford -ponzi-scheme-victims-can-sue-third-parties/; but see Reuters, "Court Rules against Victims of Ponzi Scheme," *New York Times*, July 18, 2014, http://www.nytimes.com/2014/07/19/ business/court-rules-against-victims-of-ponzi-scheme.html.

19. Eric Lipton and Raymond Hernandez, "Congressman Cries Poor, but Lifestyle May Disagree," *New York Times*, March 19, 2010.

20. Raymond Hernandez, "What Would You Drive, If the Taxpayers Paid?" *New York Times*, May 1, 2008; Louise Radnofsky and T. W. Farnum, "Lawmakers Bill Taxpayers for TVs, Cameras, Lexus," *Wall Street Journal*, May 30, 2009.

21. CREW, *Family Affair*, 309; Chris Roberts, "Beto O'Rourke Ousts Eight-Term U.S. Rep. Silvestre Reyes in 16th Congressional District Race," *El Paso Times*, May 30, 2012, http://www.elpasotimes.com/ci_20736581/16th-congressional-district-race-beto-orourke -ousts-eight-term-u-s-rep-silvestre-reyes.

22. When Senator Evan Bayh (D-IN) announced his intention to resign from the Senate in 2010 (without giving Democrats ample warning), his valedictory attracted considerable attention. He attributed his departure to Congress's dysfunction, and his list of Washington's ills began and ended with an emphasis on "strident partisanship" and "unyielding ideology." Evan Bayh, "Why I'm Leaving the Senate," *New York Times*, February 21, 2010. Shortly after leaving the Senate he took a job as a Fox News contributor.

23. Ryan Grim and Sabrina Siddiqui, "Call Time for Congress Shows How Fundraising Dominates Bleak Work Life," *Huffington Post*, Politics, January 8, 2013, http://www.huffington

post.com/2013/01/08/call-time-congressional-fundraising_n_2427291.html; Anthony Corrado, "Money and the Permanent Campaign," in Norman J. Ornstein and Thomas E. Mann, eds., *The Permanent Campaign and Its Future* (Washington, DC: American Enterprise Institute and the Brookings Institution, 2000), 75–76.

24. Ayotte quoted in Eric Lipton, "A Loophole Allows Lawmakers to Reel in Trips and Donations," *New York Times*, January 19, 2014. In 2010 Ayotte suddenly resigned as New Hampshire attorney general to run for the Senate just months before a Ponzi scandal broke, costing investors $80 million. A state investigation found that her administration failed to respond to consumer complaints regarding the company, but the scandal failed to prevent her winning a decisive electoral victory. Kevin Landregan, "Ayotte's Ponzi Alerts Called Faulty," *Nashua (NH) Telegraph*, September 1, 2010, http://www.nashuatelegraph.com/news/839399-196/report-ayotte-didnt-have-procedures-to-spot.html. For a list of fundraising events hosted by lawmakers and their cost, "Lucrative Getaways," *New York Times*, January 19, 2014 (a long list compiled by the editors).

25. Jeff Connaughton, *The Payoff: Why Wall Street Always Wins* (Westport, CT: Prospecta Press, 2012), 142–43.

26. Sean Cockerham, "As Panel Chief, Whitfield Gets $1.1 Million from Energy Interests," *Lexington (KY) Herald-Leader*, October 28, 2014. Ed Whitfield advocates humane treatment of animals; it is not known if the Humane Society has contributed to his campaign.

27. John Bresnahan and Anna Palmer, "Ethics Ends Whitfield, Rush Probes," *Politico*, November 11, 2014, http://www.politico.com/story/2014/11/ethics-probe-ed-whitfield-bobby-rush-112754.html.

28. Brody Mullins and T. W. Farnum, "Congress's Travel Tab Swells: Spending on Taxpayer-Funded Trips Rises Tenfold; From Italy to the Galápagos," *Wall Street Journal*, July 2, 2009, http://www.wsj.com/articles/SB124650399438184235; Eric Lipton and Eric Lichtblau, "Rules for Congress Curb but Don't End Junkets," *New York Times*, Dec. 12, 2009.

After extravagant travel, legislators do not overlook using or picking up the change. When using public funds for travel they are allotted up to $250 a day to cover meals and expenses. By rule they are required to return any leftover money from that allotment to the government. Usually they do not, spending it on shopping, spouses, or gifts for constituents, or they keep it. Brody Mullins and T. W. Farnam, "Lawmakers Keep the Change," *Wall Street Journal*, March 2, 2010.

29. Shane Goldmacher, "Congress Took More Free Trips in 2013 Than in Any Year since the Abramoff Reforms," *National Journal*, February 3, 2014, http://www.nationaljournal.com/congress/congress-took-more-free-trips-in-2013-than-in-any-year-since-the-abramoff-reforms-20140203.

30. Quotation from Justin Elliott, "Law Shrouds Details of Congressional Trips Abroad," *ProPublica*, April 11, 2012, http://www.propublica.org/article/details-of-congressional-trips-abroad-a-secret; on the constitutional ban, Zephyr Teachout, *Corruption in America: From Benjamin Franklin's Snuff Box to Citizens United* (Cambridge, MA: Harvard University Press, 2014).

31. The irony deepens in view of Hastert entering Congress with modest net worth and leaving twenty years later worth several millions. He immediately went to work as a lobbyist earning a reputation as "an eclectic lobbyist" because he used his former influence "on all sides of issues" and on controversial issues such as working for Big Tobacco to protect the selling of candy-flavored and electronic cigarettes. Jonathan Weisman, "After Speakership, Hastert Amassed Millions Lobbying Former Colleagues," *New York Times*, May 31, 2015. From 2010 on, Hastert was obsessed with earning money, in part perhaps to finance large, secret payoffs to a victim he had sexually abused while a wrestling coach decades earlier: Eric Lipton, "Hastert Rushed to Earn Money amid Payouts," *New York Times*, June 7, 2015.

32. All quotations from Shane Goldmacher, "How Lobbyists Still Fly through Loopholes," *National Journal*, January 10, 2014, http://www.nationaljournal.com/magazine/how-lobbyists-still-fly-through-loopholes-20140110. Pingree was the only legislator who returned the phone call of the reporter investigating the trip. Legis-Storm's Congressional Travel Database can be accessed at http://www.legistorm.com/trip/about.html.

33. Peter Schweitzer quoted in Steve Kroft, "Washington's Open Secret: Profitable PACS," *60 Minutes*, CBS News, excerpt from "Washington's Open Secret," which aired October 20, 2013, http://www.cbsnews.com/news/washingtons-open-secret-profitable-pacs/.

34. Josh Hicks and Lisa Rein, "In GSA's Las Vegas Scandal, an Indictment," *Washington Post*, September 25, 2014; Sam Stein and Paul Blumenthal, "IRS Spending Scandal Not All It Seems, Other Departments, Agencies Spent Far More," *Huffington Post*, June 4, 2013, http://www.huffingtonpost.com/2013/06/04/irs-spending-scandal_n_3384978.html.

35. Marcus Stern and Jennifer LaFleur, "Leadership PACs: Let the Good Times Roll," *ProPublica*, October 13, 2009, http://www.propublica.org/article/leadership-pacs-let the-good-times-roll-925.

36. Larry Bartels, *Unequal Democracy: The Political Economy of the New Gilded Age* (Princeton, NJ: Princeton University Press, 2008), 267–75, quotation 275; Martin Gilens, *Affluence and Influence: Economic Inequality and Political Power in America* (Princeton, NJ: Princeton University Press, 2012), 9.

37. Stephen Lurie, "Why It Matters That Politicians Have No Experience of Poverty," *The Atlantic*, June 2014, http://www.theatlantic.com/politics/archive/2014/06/why-it-matters-that-politicians-have-no-experience-of-poverty/371857/; Nicholas Carnes, *White-Collar Government: The Hidden Role of Class in Economic Policy* (Chicago: University of Chicago Press, 2013), 16, 25–58, 120–35, quotations 2, 48, 16.

38. Michael W. Kraus and Bennett Callaghan, "Noblesse Oblige? Social Status and Economic Inequality Maintenance among Politicians," *PLOS ONE* 9, no. 1 (2014), http://journals.plos.org/plosone/article?id=10.1371/journal.pone.0085293.

39. *CREW's Most Corrupt 2013*, quotations 1, Rep. Don Young, 100–110. Shelley Berkley made CREW's *Most Corrupt* list in 2011 and 2012 for repeatedly intervening with federal officials to funnel money to her husband's medical practice and the lucrative kidney care industry. *After* she lost a 2012 campaign to move up to the Senate, in part because of ethical issues, the House Ethics Committee released a statement that she had indeed violated

House rules, but it concluded that Berkley had no "intent to duly enrich herself," gave no recommendation for punishment, and did not even issue a letter of "reproval." (The political class deems losing reelection to be "suffering enough.") *CREW's Most Corrupt 2012*, 124–36; Eric Lipton, "Panel Finds Lawmaker Broke Ethics Rules," *New York Times*, December 20, 2012.

40. Thomas B. Edsall, "The Value of Political Corruption," *New York Times*, August 5, 2014, http://www.nytimes.com/2014/08/06/opinion/thomas-edsall-the-value-of-political -corruption.html; Frank Newport, "Americans: My Member OK, Most in Congress Are Not," *Gallup Politics*, October 15, 2014, http://www.gallup.com/poll/178487/americans-member -congress-not.aspx.

41. Editors, "The Court Follows the Money," *New York Times*, April 2, 2014; Nicholas Confessore, "Power Surge for Donors as Terrain Is Reshaped on Campaign Money," *New York Times*. For details of the decision, see Federal Election Commission, *McCutcheon, et al. v. FEC*, Case Summary, http://www.fec.gov/law/litigation/McCutcheon.shtml; Michael Wines, "It Only Seems That Political Corruption Is Rampant," *New York Times*, January 26, 2014. On the evolution of the Supreme Court's decisions getting to "money is speech," see Richard L. Hasen, *Plutocrats United: Campaign Money, the Supreme Court, and the Distortion of American Elections* (New Haven, CT: Yale University Press, 2016).

42. Reity O'Brien and Chris Young, "Majority of Supreme Court Members Millionaires: Ginsburg, Breyer Top List of Wealthiest Justices," *Center for Public Integrity*, June 14, 2013, http://www.publicintegrity.org/print/12827; Richard Wolf, "Nearly All Supreme Court Justices Are Millionaires," *USA Today*, June 20, 2014, http://www.usatoday.com/story/ news/politics/2014/06/20/supreme-court-justices-financial-disclosure/11105985/.

43. Nan Aron, "An Ethics Code for the High Court," *Washington Post*, March 13, 2011, http:// www.washingtonpost.com/opinions/an-ethics-code-for-the-high-court/2011/03/11/ ABILNzT_story.html; Eric Lichtblau, "Advocacy Group Says Justices May Have Conflict in Campaign Finance Cases," *New York Times*, January 19, 2011; Associated Press, "Justices Explain Links to Energy Company," *New York Times*, January 20, 2011.

44. Richard L. Hasen, "Celebrity Justice: Supreme Court Edition," University of California, Irvine, School of Law, Research Paper no. 2015–61, January 12, 2016, http://www .greenbag.org/v19n2/v19n2_articles_hasen.pdf.

45. Eric Lichtblau, "Thomas Cites Failure to Disclose Wife's Job," *New York Times*, January 24, 2011; "Clarence Thomas Is Not above the Law! (Let's Tell Charlie Rangel)," CREDO Action, October 26, 2011, http://markcrispinmiller.com/2011/10/clarence-thomas-is-not -above-the-law-lets-tell-charlie-rangel/.

46. Eric Lichtblau, "Justice Thomas's Wife Sets Up a Conservative Lobbying Shop," *New York Times*, February 4, 2011; Mike McIntire, "Friendship of Justice and Magnate Puts Focus on Ethics," *New York Times*, June 18, 2011; Robert Barnes, "Clarence Thomas Attends Hometown Museum Dedication; Source of Funds for Institution Prompts Questions," *Washington Post*, November 19, 2011. For a detailed examination of Justice Thomas and Virginia Thomas's political thinking and activism, Jeffrey Toobin, "The Partners: Will

Clarence and Virginia Thomas Succeed in Killing Obama's Health-care Plan?," *New Yorker*, August 29, 2011.

47. Joan Biskupic, Janet Roberts, and John Shiffman, "At America's Court of Last Resort, a Handful of Lawyers Now Dominates the Docket," in "The Echo Chamber: A Small Group of Lawyers and Its Outsized Influence at the U.S. Supreme Court," Reuters Special Report, December 8, 2014, http://www.reuters.com/investigates/special-report/scotus/; Janet Roberts, Joan Biskupic, and John Shiffman, "In an Ever-Clubbier Specialty Bar, 8 Men Have Become Supreme Court Confidants," in "Echo Chamber."

48. Quotations from Biskupic, Roberts, and Shiffman, "At America's Court."

49. "A Corporate Court? Tracking the U.S. Chamber of Commerce and the Roberts Court," *Constitutional Accountability Center*, 2014, http://theusconstitution.org/corporate -court; Adam Liptak, "Justices Offer Receptive Ear to Business Interests," *Sunday New York Times*, December 19, 2010; Adam Serwer, "Americans Frustrated with Supreme Court: Poll," MSNBC, May 20, 2014, http://www.msnbc.com/msnbc/americans-frustrated-supreme- court; Justin McCarthy, "Americans Losing Confidence in All Branches of U.S. Gov't," *Gallup Politics*, June 30, 2014, http://www.gallup.com/poll/171992/americans-losing-confidence -branches-gov.aspx.

50. Pamela S. Karlan, "Foreword: Democracy and Disdain," in "The Supreme Court 2011 Term," special issue *Harvard Law Review* 126, no. 1 (2012), quotation 3, and 3n4.

51. First quotation, Teachout, *Corruption in America*, 9, also 267–71, 273–74; Karlan, "De- mocracy and Disdain," quotations 5, 28.

3. Is the Political Class Corrupt?

1. Definition from Patrick Radden Keefe, "Corruption and Revolt," *New Yorker*, January 19, 2015; Lawrence Lessig, *Republic Lost: How Money Corrupts Congress—and a Plan to Stop It* (New York: Hachette Book Group, 2011), xii, quotations 7, 38. For different views regard- ing corruption, see Thomas B. Edsall, "The Value of Political Corruption," *New York Times*, August 5, 2014.

2. Jan Sonnenschein and Julie Ray, "Government Corruption Viewed as Pervasive World- wide," *Gallup*, October 18, 2013, http://www.gallup.com/poll/165476/government-corruption -viewed-pervasive-worldwide.aspx; Zachary Roth, "Fighting Corruption Polls off the Charts," *MSNBC*, December 3, 2013, http://www.msnbc.com/msnbc/fighting-corruption -polls-the-charts.

3. Transparency International, "Corruption Perception Index 2014: Results," http://www .transparency.org/cpi2014/results; quotation from "Corruption by Country/Territory," Transparency International, http://www.transparency.org/country#USA.

4. Caitlin Ginley, "Grading the Nation: How Accountable Is Your State?," Center for Public Integrity, March 19, 2012, http://www.publicintegrity.org/print/8423; Niraj Cokshi, "A State Guide to Political Corruption, according to Reporters Who Cover It," *Washington Post*, De- cember 8, 2014, http://www.washingtonpost.com/blogs/govbeat/wp/2014/12/08/a-state

-guide-to-political-corruption-according-to-the-reporters-who-cover-it/. See also Brennan Center for Justice, "National Survey: Super PACs, Corruption, and Democracy," New York University School of Law, 2012; and Oguzahn Dincer and Michael Johnston, "Measuring Illegal and Legal Corruption in American States: Some Results from the Corruption in America Survey," December 1, 2014, Center for Ethics, Harvard University, http://ethics.harvard .edu/blog/measuring-illegal-and-legal-corruption-american-states-some-results-safra.

5. Zephyr Teachout, *Corruption in America: From Benjamin Franklin's Snuff Box to Citizens United* (Cambridge, MA: Harvard University Press, 2014), quotations 8, 253.

6. Quoted in Carl Hulse, "Is the Supreme Court Clueless about Corruption? Ask Jack Abramoff," *New York Times*, July 5, 2016.

7. Michael Johnston, *Syndromes of Corruption: Wealth, Power, and Democracy* (New York: Cambridge University Press, 2005), 1, 2, 11.

8. Teachout, *Corruption in America*, 72–73, 254–55, quotations 73, 255.

9. Lee Drutman, *The Business of America Is Lobbying: How Corporations Became Politicized and Politics Became More Corporate* (New York: Oxford University Press, 2015), 8, 9, 13–14; for a view of a plurality of interests, see James A. Thurber, "Changing the Way Washington Works? President Obama's Battle with Lobbyists," paper presented at The Early Obama Presidency Conference, Westminster University, London, May 14, 2010, quotations 3, 8, https://www.american.edu/spa/ccps/upload/Thurber-Paper-Obama-and-Lobbyists.pdf.

10. Reid Wilson, "Amid Gridlock in D.C., Influence Industry Expands Rapidly in the States," *Washington Post*, May 11, 2015; Donald Kettl, "Lobbyists Leave Capitol Hill for States," *Governing*, June 2016, http://www.governing.com/columns/potomac-chronicle/ gov-lobbying-states-washington.html; Eric Lipton, "A Bipartisan Push to Limit Lobbyists' Sway over Attorneys General," *New York Times*, December 26, 2014.

11. Tim LaPira, "How Much Lobbying Is There in Washington? It's DOUBLE What You Think," Sunlight Foundation, November 25, 2013, http://sunlightfoundation.com/ blog/2013/11/25/how-much-lobbying-is-there-in-washington-its-double-what-you-think/.

12. Thurber, "Changing the Way Washington Works?"; Dan Auble, "Lobbyists 2012: Out of the Game or under the Radar?," OpenSecrets.org, Center for Responsive Politics, March 20, 3013, https://www.opensecrets.org/news/2013/03/lobbyists-2012-out-of-the-game -or-u/ Thomas B. Edsall, "The Unlobbyists," *New York Times*, December 31, 2013; Lee Fang, "Where Have All the Lobbyists Gone?" *The Nation*, March 10–17, 2014; the huge scale of lobbying is suggested by Frank R. Baumgartner, Jeffrey M. Berry, Marie Hojnacki, David C. Kimball, and Beth L. Leech, *Lobbying and Policy Change: Who Wins, Who Loses, and Why* (Chicago: Chicago University Press, 2009).

13. Edsall, "The Unlobbyists."

14. Robert G. Kaiser, *So Damn Much Money: The Triumph of Lobbying and the Corrosion of American Government* (New York: Alfred A. Knopf, 2009), 43–51, 67–81, quotation 72.

15. Thomas B. Edsall, "The Lobbying Bonanza," *New York Times*, June 10, 2015.

16. Kaiser, *So Damn Much Money*, quotations 94, 95, 97.

17. Ibid., 191, 246–49, 311, 34, 311–12; Michael Cohen, "How For-Profit Prisons Have Become the Biggest Lobby No One Is Talking About," *Washington Post*, April 28, 2015.

18. Peter Schweizer, *Extortion: How Politicians Extract Your Money, Buy Votes, and Line Their Pockets with It* (Boston: Houghton Mifflin Harcourt, 2013), quotations 13, 16.

19. Kaiser, *So Damn Much Money*, 3–24, quotation 17.

20. Ibid., 19, 297, 300; Jack Abramoff, *Capitol Punishment: The Hard Truth about Washington Corruption from America's Most Notorious Lobbyist* (Washington, DC: WND Books, 2011), 65–66, 206; Frank quoted in Andrea Seabrook and Alex Blumberg, "Take the Money and Run for Office," *Planet Money: NPR*, March 30, 2012, http://www.npr.org/blogs/money/2012/03/26/149390968/take-the-money-and-run-for-office. See also the highly creative report in *Mother Jones*: Dave Gilson, "Who Owns Congress? A Campaign Cash Seating Chart," *Mother Jones*, October 4, 2010, http://www.motherjones.com/print/72756. Color-coded charts display answers to the question "What if members of Congress were seated not by party but according to their major business sponsors?" *New York Times* columnist and Nobel Prize–winning economist Paul Krugman once suggested that members of Congress wear jackets emblazoned with the logos of their major business sponsors.

21. D. C. DeWitt, "Ohio Congressman Called Out for Payday Lending Hackery," *Plunderbund*, October 5, 2015, http://www.plunderbund.com/2015/10/05/ohio-congressman-called-out-for-payday-lending-hackery/; Joshua Holland, "Did Predatory Lenders Pay These 12 Lawmakers to Hobble the CFPB?," *The Nation*, October 8, 2013, http://www.thenation.com/article/how-predatory-lenders-paid-a-dozen-lawmakers-to-hobble-elizabeth-warrens-cfpb/.

22. Alan Rosenthal, *The Third House: Lobbyists and Lobbying in the States* (Washington, DC: CQ Press, 1993); quotation from Kathleen Rice, Milton Williams Jr., and William Fitzpatrick, State of New York, The Commission to Investigate Public Corruption, "Preliminary Report," December 2, 2013, 3–4, http://publiccorruption.moreland.ny.gov/sites/default/files/moreland_report_final.pdf; William K. Rashbaum and Thomas Kaplan, "Sheldon Silver, Assembly Speaker, Took Millions in Payoffs, U.S. Says," *New York Times*, January 22, 2015. Governor Cuomo had second thoughts about the corruption probe: see Susanne Craig, William K. Rashbaum, and Thomas Kaplan, "Cuomo's Office Hobbled Ethics Inquiries by Moreland Commission," *New York Times*, July 23, 2014.

23. Glenn Bain, "Exclusive: Top Aide for Disgraced Assemblyman Sheldon Silver Earns More than Gov. Cuomo," *New York Daily News*, March 9, 2015; Yancey Roy, "Judy Rapfogel Sat In on Pork-Barrel Meetings," *Newsday*, September 26, 2013, http://www.newsday.com/long-island/politics/judy-rapfogel-sat-in-on-pork-barrel-meetings-1.6147918; Jacob Finklestein, "Judy Rapfogel; the Link between Silver & the Met Council," *Jewish Voice*, February 4, 2015, http://jewishvoiceny.com/index.php?option=com_content&view=article&id=10030:&catid=112&Itemid=792; Benjamin Weiser, "U.S. Cites Extramarital Affairs as Misuse of Power in Sheldon Silver Case," *Jewish Voice*, April 15, 2016.

24. Rice, Williams, and Fitzpatrick, Commission to Investigate Public Corruption, quotations 5, 3. And on the West Coast, see Norimitsu Onishi, "California Democrats Await Fallout After 3 Are Caught Up in Scandals," *New York Times*, April 3, 2014.

25. Nicholas Kusnetz, "State Legislators' Ties to Nonprofit Groups Provide Fertile Ground for Corruption," Center for Public Integrity, June 12, 2013, http://www.publicintegrity.org/

print/12794; for a defense of New York nonprofits generally, see Rick Cohen, "New York's Nonprofit Culture: 'Corrupt at the Core'?," *Nonprofit Quarterly*, February 7, 2014, http://nonprofitquarterly.org/2014/02/07/new-york-s-nonprofit-culture-corrupt-at-the-core/.

26. Revolving Door Database, Center for Responsive Politics, OpenSecrets.org, http://www.opensecrets.org/revolving/top.php?display=Z. And see the report by the Center for Responsive Politics and Sunlight Foundation, "All Cooled Off: As Congress Convenes, Former Colleagues Will Soon be Calling from K Street," January 6, 2015, https://www.open secrets.org/news/2015/01/coming-out-of-the-cool-as-congress-convenes-former-colleagues -will-soon-be-calling-from-k-street/.

27. Lessig, *Republic Lost*, 246; Lee Drutman and Alexander Furnas, "K Street Pays Top Dollar for Revolving Door Talent," Sunlight Foundation, January 21, 2014, http://sunlight foundation.com/blog/2014/01/21/revolving-door-lobbyists-government-experience/; Drutman and Furnas, "The Rise of the Million-Dollar Lobbyists," Sunlight Foundation, January 24, 2014, http://sunlightfoundation.com/blog/2014/01/24/million-dollar-lobbyist -rise/. Quotation from Eric Lipton and Ben Protess, "Law Doesn't End Revolving Door on Capitol Hill," *New York Times*, February 1, 2014.

28. CRP and Sunlight Foundation, "All Cooled Off"; "Revolving Door: Former Members," Center for Responsive Politics, OpenSecrets.org database, http://www.opensecrets .org/revolving/top.php?display=Z; Abby Ohlheiser, "Former Senators Trent Lott and John Breaux Have New Gigs. As Russian Bank Lobbyists," *Washington Post*, September 2, 2014, http://www.washingtonpost.com/blogs/the-fix/wp/2014/09/02/former-senators-trent -lott-and-john-breaux-have-brand-new-gigs-as-russian-bank-lobbyists/.

29. Abramoff, *Capitol Punishment*, 95.

30. Teachout, *Corruption in America*, 59–67, quotation, 67; also, Lessig, *Republic Lost*, 123.

31. Drutman, *Business of America Is Lobbying*, 31–33; an "engaged public" can be a match for business lobbying, but complexity and "low salience" issues work in favor of corporate lobbyists, 30–31.

32. Jeff Connaughton, *The Payoff: Why Wall Street Always Wins* (Westport, CT: Prospecta Press, 2012), 152; Bara Vaida, "Former Lobbyists Join Obama," *National Journal*, January 24, 2009; Karen Tumulty, "Peter Rouse and Mark Patterson, Former Top Obama Aides, Join Perkins Coie," *Washington Post*, January 24, 2014.

33. Schultz quoted in Byron Tau, "How K Street Beat Obama," *Politico*, August 12, 2014, http://www.politico.com/story/2014/08/obamas-revolving-door-109930; Lipton and Protess, "Law Doesn't End Revolving Door"; Julie Hirschfeld Davis, "Obama Administration Loosens Ban on Lobbyists in Government," *New York Times*, August 12, 2014; Thurber, "Changing the Way Washington Works?," quotation 10.

34. Sheryl Gay Stolberg, "Reaping Profit after Assisting on Health Law," *New York Times*, September 17, 2013; Eric Lipton, "Ex-Lawmaker Still a Friend of Hospitals," *New York Times*, August 2, 2011, Timothy P. Carney, "One Class of Obamacare Beneficiaries: The Public Servants Who Created It," *Washington Examiner*, September 18, 2013, http://www.washington examiner.com/one-class-of-obamacare-beneficiaries-the-public-servants-who-crafted-it/ article/2536012.

35. First quotation from Bill Moyers, "WATCH: Washington's Revolving Door Is Hazardous to Our Health," *Huffington Post*, December 17, 2012, http://www.huffingtonpost.com/bill-moyers/watch-washingtons-revolvi_b_2316245.html; Glenn Greenwald, "Obamacare Architect Leaves White House for Pharmaceutical Industry Job," *Guardian* (Manchester), December 5, 2012, http://www.theguardian.com/commentisfree/2012/dec/05/obamacare-fowler-lobbyist-industry; Wheeler quoted in Greenwald.

36. Moyers, "WATCH."

37. Paul Blumenthal, "The Max Baucus Health Care Lobbyist Complex," Sunlight Foundation, June 22, 2009, http://sunlightfoundation.com/blog/2009/06/22/the-max-baucus-health-care-lobbyist-complex/; Sam Youngman, "Gibbs Takes Shot at Finance Committee," *Hill*, September 8, 2009, http://thehill.com/homenews/administration/57693-gibbs-takes-shot-at-senate-finance-committee.

38. Quotation from Eric Lipton, "Tax Lobby Builds Ties to Chairman of Finance Panel," *New York Times*, April 8, 2013; Timothy P. Carney, "Sen. Max Baucus, Master of Revolving Door, Heads for the Exit," *Washington Examiner*, April 24, 2013, http://www.washingtonexaminer.com/tim-carney-sen.-max-baucus-master-of-revolving-door-heads-for-the-exit/article/2528062.

39. Andrew Ross Sorkin, "Encouraging Public Service, through Wall Street's Revolving Door," *New York Times*, December 1, 2014, defended the banks' practice. Sorkin's cozy relationship with the heads of big banks is suggested in a review by Ruth Sunderland, "Too Big to Fail: Inside the Battle to Save Wall Street by Andrew Ross Sorkin," *Guardian*, December 12, 2009, http://www.theguardian.com/books/2009/dec/13/too-big-to-fail-sorkin.

40. Jessica Silver Greenberg, Ben Protess, and Peter Eavis, "New Scrutiny of Goldman's Ties to the New York Fed after a Leak," *New York Times*, November 19, 2014, http://dealbook.nytimes.com/2014/11/19/rising-scrutiny-as-banks-hire-from-the-fed/.

41. Joseph Lawler, "$20 Million Bonus Draws Fire in Treasury Nomination," *Washington Examiner*, December 27, 2014, http://www.washingtonexaminer.com/20-million-bonus-draws-fire-in-treasury nomination/article/2557902; Peter Schroeder, "Warren Digs In against Obama Pick," *Hill*, December 9, 2014, http://thehill.com/policy/finance/226475-warren-lock-revolving-door-between-wall-street-and-washington; regarding Lew, see Jonathan Well, "Citigroup's Man Goes to the Treasury Department," *Politico*, February 21, 2013, http://www.bloomberg.com/news/articles/2013-02-21/citigroup-s-man-goes-to-the-treasury-department.

42. Jesse Eisinger, "In Turnabout, Former Regulators Assail Wall St. Watchdogs," *New York Times*, October 22, 2014; Ben Protess, "Khuzami, S.E.C. Enforcement Chief Who Reinvigorated Unit, to Step Down," *New York Times*, January 9, 2013, http://dealbook.nytimes.com/2013/01/09/s-e-c-enforcement-chief-khuzami-steps-down/. The federal judge Jed S. Rakoff, who challenged the light punishments of firms and advocated prosecution of individuals, laid out his case in "The Financial Crisis: Why Have No High-Level Executives Been Prosecuted?," *New York Review of Books*, January 9, 2014. See also Glenn Greenwald, "The Untouchables: How the Obama Administration Protected Wall Street from Prosecutions," *Guardian*, January 23, 2013, http://www.theguardian.com/commentisfree/2013/jan/23/

untouchables-wall-street-prosecutions-obama/; Matt Taibbi, *The Divide: American Injustice in the Age of the Wealth Gap* (New York: Spiegel & Grau, 2014), 13–19.

43. Cassandra LaRussa, "Congressmen Become Lobbyists, Charlie Rangel Challenged and More in Capital Eye Opener: April 14," Center for Responsive Politics, Open Secrets.org, April 14, 2010, http://www.opensecrets.org/news/2010/04/congressmen-become-lobbyists -charli/; Eric Lichtblau, "Lawmakers Regulate Banks, Then Flock to Them," *New York Times*, April 13, 2010.

44. "Interest Groups," Center for Responsive Politics, *OpenSecrets.org*, http://www .opensecrets.org/industries/; also, "Wall Street Money in Washington," Americans for Financial Reform, December 11, 2014, http://ourfinancialsecurity.org/wall-street-money -in-washington/.

45. Ahmed Tahoun and Florin P. Vasvari, "Political Lending," Institute for New Economic Thinking, working paper no. 47, August 10, 2016, https://www.ineteconomics.org/uploads/ papers/WP_47_Tahoun.pdf; David Sirota, "Lawmakers Overseeing Wall Street Given Bigger, More Flexible Loans Than Others: Study," *International Business Times*, August 19, 2016.

46. Andrew Ackerman and Siobhan Hughes, "House Republicans Push to Roll Back Wall Street Regulations Fails," *Wall Street Journal*, January 7, 2015; Erika Eichelberger, "This Is How Republicans Plan to Destroy Liz Warren's Greatest Achievement," *Mother Jones*, January 16, 2015; Warren quoted in Mike Moguiescu, "The Speech That Could Make Elizabeth Warren the Next President of the United States," *Huffington Post*, December 13, 2014, http:// www.huffingtonpost.com/miles-mogulescu/the-speech-that-could-make-elizabeth-warren -president_b_6319142.html.

47. Tom Groenfeldt, "Banks, Led by Citi, Lobby House (Successfully) to Limit Dodd-Frank on Derivatives," *Forbes*, October 30, 2013, http://www.forbes.com/sites/tomgroenfeldt/ 2013/10/30/banks-led-by-citi-lobby-house-successfully-to-limit-dodd-frank-on-derivatives/; Dan Roberts, "Democrats Concede to Curb Funds for Wall Street Regulators in Spending Bill," *Guardian*, January 14, 2014, http://www.theguardian.com/world/2014/jan/14/republicans -curb-regulator-funding-bipartisan-budget.

48. Connaughton, *Payoff*, quotations 147, 148.

49. Adam Bellow, *In Praise of Nepotism: A Natural History* (New York: Doubleday, 2003), quotations 11, 22, 9, 469; Klause Kneale, "Is Nepotism So Bad?" *Forbes*, June 20, 2009, http:// www.forbes.com/2009/06/19/ceo-executive-hiring-ceonewtork-leadership-nepotism.html.

50. Chrystia Freeland, *Plutocrats: The Rise of the New Global Super-Rich and the Fall of Everyone Else* (New York: Penguin Press, 2012), quotations 280, 283.

51. Bellow, *In Praise of Nepotism*, quotation 470.

52. First quotation Natasha Hunter, "Dem Relatives," *American Prospect*, March 13, 2002, http://prospect.org/article/dem-relatives; Barbara Ferguson, "Rampant Nepotism in the Bush Administration," *Rense.com*, March 15, 2002, http://rense.com/general21/vac.htm. The original Milbank column is referenced several times on the Internet, but the original seems to be no longer available. See also Andrew Sullivan, "Nepotism Watch, Eight Years Late," *Economist*, January 11, 2010, http://www.economist.com/blogs/democracyinamerica/ 2010/01/nepotism_watch_eight_years_late.

53. Paul Krugman, "The Sons Also Rise," *New York Times*, November 22, 2002; see also the website "All in the Family: America's Feudal Families," 2015, http://prorev.com/family.htm.

54. Rick Moran, "In Obama White House, Nepotism Is Alive and Well," *American Thinker*, May 11, 2009, http://www.americanthinker.com/blog/2009/05/in_obama_white_house_nepotism.html; Paul Farhi, "Media, Administration Deal with Conflicts," *Washington Post*, June 12, 2013.

55. Quotations from Clare Malone, "Get Elected, Get Your Kids Rich: Washington Is Spoiled Rotten," *Daily Beast*, February 27, 2014, http://www.thedailybeast.com/articles/2014/02/27/get-elected-get-your-kids-rich-washington-is-spoiled-rotten.html. In February 2015 ABC News televised a special report by John Stossel on nepotism in Washington, described in Stossel, "Family Ties Run Deep in U.S. Politics: Is Politics a Family Business on Capitol Hill?" *ABC News*, February 6, 2015, http://abcnews.go.com/2020/story?id=124321; Tracy Staton, "Think EpiPen Is Mylan's First Scandal?" *FiercePharma*, September 2, 2016, http://www.fiercepharma.com/pharma/think-epipen-mylan-s-first-scandal-here-s-a-timeline-jet-use-resume-fakery-and-more.

56. Quotations from Joe Coscarelli, "Chelsea Clinton Leaving Her Unbelievably Cushy Fake Job at NBC," *New York*, August 29, 2014, http://nymag.com/daily/intelligencer/2014/08/chelsea-clinton-leaving-her-fake-job-at-nbc.html; Amy Chozick, "Chelsea Clinton to Leave Well-Paid NBC News Job," *New York Times*, August 29, 2014. For a full account of Chelsea's Clinton's exemplary nepotistic career, see Matt Bruenug, "Against Chelsea Clinton," *Jacobin*, March 26, 2017, https://www.jacobinmag.com/2017/03/chelsea-clinton-office-democratic-party-foundation-avenue-capital/.

57. William McGowan, "Nepotism Watch: At NBC News, Having Fancy Parents Brings in the Big Bucks But Corrupts the Journalism," *Coloring the News* (blog), June 14, 2014, http://coloringthenews.blogspot.com/2014/06/nepotism-watch-nbc-news-having-fancy.html.

58. Tim Graham, "Nepotistic Broadcasting Company: NBC's Peter Pan Promotion Reveals 'The Tackiest House on the Street,'" *MRC NewsBusters: Exposing and Combating Liberal Media Bias*, December 8, 2014, http://www.newsbusters.org/blogs/tim-graham/2014/12/08/nepotism-broadcasting-company-nbcs-peter-pan-promotion-reveals-tackiest.

59. Alex Parene, "Our Glorious Golden Era of Nepotism," *Salon*, March 4, 2014, http://www.salon.com/2014/03/04/our_glorious_golden_age_of_nepotism_the_luke_russert_ronan_farrow_epoch/; Noreen Malone, "Luke Russert: Why Does Young Washington Dislike Him?," *New Republic*, August 1, 2013, http://www.newrepublic.com/article/114099/luke-russert-why-does-young-washington-dislike-him.

60. The comment about alumni is from an earlier William McGowan article, "All in the Family," *National Review*, May 22, 2003, http://www.nationalreview.com/article/206997/all-family-william-mcgowan.

61. Ibid. Some apparent media legacies include very able individuals from advantaged backgrounds, such as the talented John Dickerson, host of *Face the Nation* and son of Nancy Hanschman Dickerson, the first woman correspondent for network news.

62. David Brooks, "No, Not Trump, Not Ever," *New York Times*, May 18, 2016.

63. Samuel Goldman, "Mild Nepotism and the Illusion of Meritocracy," *American Conservative*, April 24, 2013, http://www.theamericanconservative.com/2013/04/24/mild-nepotism-and-the-illusion-of-meritocracy/?print=1.

4. The Permanent Campaign and the Permanent Political Class

1. Sidney Blumenthal, *The Permanent Campaign: Inside the World of Elite Political Operatives* (Boston: Beacon Press, 1980), 7.

2. Ibid., 1–2, 4, 9, quotations 8, 10.

3. Regarding the constant hunger for cash, see, e.g., Dave Levinthal, "Can't Stop, Won't Stop: The Permanent Campaign's Desperate, Hungry, and Even Uncouth Hunt for Cash," *Slate*, February 16, 2015, http://www.slate.com/articles/news_and_politics/politics/2015/02/permanent_campaign_the_hunt_for_cash_is_desperate_constant_and_uncouth.html; Derek Willis, "Senators Are Announcing Retirements Earlier, Fund-Raising Plays a Big Role," *New York Times*, February 25, 2015; also, David Karol, "Forcing Their Hands? Campaign Finance Law, Retirement Announcements and the Rise of the Permanent Campaign in U.S. Senate Elections," *Congress and the Presidency* 42 (2015), 79–94.

4. Norman J. Ornstein and Thomas E. Mann, "Conclusion: The Permanent Campaign and the Future of American Democracy," in Ornstein and Mann, eds., *The Permanent Campaign and Its Future* (Washington, DC: American Enterprise Institute, Brookings Institution, 2000), quotations 220, 221.

5. Ibid., 224, 225.

6. Hugh Heclo, "Campaigning and Governing: A Conspectus," in Ornstein and Mann, *Permanent Campaign*, quotation 30; Jason Johnson, *Political Consultants and Campaigns: One Day to Sell* (Boulder, CO: Westview Press, 2012), 5–7.

7. Peter Overby, "Explainer: What Is a Bundler?" *NPR Politics*, September 14, 2007, http://www.npr.org/templates/story/story.php?storyId=14434721; "Bundling for Favors: Open the Books on Bundled Campaign Contributions," Public Citizen, August 10, 2012, http://www.citizen.org/documents/bundling-and-bundlers-background-information.pdf; Michael Luo and Christopher Drew, "Obama and McCain Lag in Naming 'Bundlers' Who Rake in Campaign Cash," *New York Times*, July 11, 2008; Eric Lichtblau, "Obama Backers Tied to Lobbies Raise Millions," *New York Times*, October 27, 2011.

8. Jen Christiansen, "LGBT Donors Back President Obama, Big Time," *CNN Politics*, June 6, 2012, http://www.cnn.com/2012/06/05/politics/lgbt-obama-donors/index.html; quotations from Common Dreams Staff, "Big Money Bundlers as Prominent as Ever in Obama White House," *Common Dreams*, January 19, 2012, http://www.commondreams.org/news/2012/01/19/big-money-bundlers-prominent-ever-obama-white-house.

9. Michael Beckel and Chris Zubak Skees, "Wanna Be Ambassador to Argentina?," *Slate*, February 7, 2014, http://www.slate.com/articles/news_and_politics/politics/2014/02/map_of_ambassador_posts_given_to_obama_s_top_fundraisers_noah_bryson_mamet.html; quotation from Fred Schulte, John Aloysius Farrell, and Jeremy Borden, "Obama Rewards Big Bundlers with Jobs Commissions, Stimulus Money, Government Contracts, and More," Center for Public Integrity, June 15, 2011, http://www.publicintegrity.org/2011/06/15/4880/

obama-rewards-big-bundlers-jobs-commissions-stimulus-money-government-contracts-and. The latter is a comprehensive report on the administration and bundlers.

10. Nicholas Confessore, "The Secret World of a Well-Paid 'Donor Adviser' in Politics," *New York Times*, February 5, 2015; Kenneth P. Vogel, "David Brock Resigns from Hillary Clinton PAC," *Politico*, February 9, 2015, http://www.politico.com/story/2015/02/david-brock-resigns-priorities-usa-action-115028.html; on "donor advisers" for philanthropic investors, see *InvestmentNews* Data and Darla Mercato, "More Advisers Are Turning to Donor-Advised Funds," *Investment News*, December 21, 2014, http://www.investmentnews.com/article/20141221/BLOG18/312219999/more-advisers-are-turning-to-donor-advised-funds.

11. *Common Dreams* Staff, "Big Money Bundlers"; Matea Gold and Tom Hamburger, "In 2016 Campaign, the Lament of the Not So Rich," *Washington Post*, March 25, 2015; "Where the Money Is ... (and Where the Bodies Are Buried)," Bundlers.org—Funding Site, http://www:bundlers.org; Clare O'Connor, "The Election's 40 Biggest Billionaire Donors (And Why the Kochs Are Missing)," *Forbes*, October 8, 2012, http://www.forbes.com/sites/clareoconnor/2012/10/08/the-elections-40-biggest-billionaire-donors-and-why-the-kochs-are-missing/.

12. Michael Massing, "How to Cover the One Percent," *New York Review of Books*, January 14, 2016; Michael Hiltzik, "First PBS, Now Brookings: Has Another Institution Lost Its Soul?," *Los Angeles Times*, February 18, 2014.

13. Kristopher Monroe, "Yes, That Big Media Grant to the Center for Public Integrity Is Sticky. Get Used to It," *Inside Philanthropy*, August 9, 2014, https://www.insidephilanthropy.com/journalism/2014/8/9/yes-that-big-media-grant-to-the-center-for-public-integrity.html.

14. David Callahan, "Which Washington Think Tank Do Billionaires Love the Most? And Why?" *Inside Philanthropy*, February 5, 2015, http://www.insidephilanthropy.com/home/2015/2/5/which-washington-think-tank-do-billionaires-love-the-most-an.html; Michael Massing, "Reimagining Journalism: The Story of the One Percent," *New York Review of Books*, December 17, 2015; Lee Fang, "Venture Capitalists Are Poised to 'Disrupt' Everything about the Education Market," *Nation*, September 25, 2014; Paul Blumenthal, "Hedge Fund Execs Spent Big in New York Elections, Now Likely to Reap Their Reward," *Huffington Post*, December 4, 2014, http://www.huffingtonpost.com/2014/12/04/hedge-funds-charter-schools_n_6269920.html.

15. Alex Kotch, "Inside Charles Koch's Plot to Hijack Universities across America and Spread His Radical 'Free Market' Propaganda," *Alternet*, June 24, 2016, http://www.alternet.org/investigations/inside-charles-kochs-plot-hijack-universities-across-america."

16. "State of the Union 2016: Full Text," *CNN Politics*, January 12, 2016, http://www.cnn.com/2016/01/12/politics/state-of-the-union-2016-transcript-full-text/.

17. Connie Cass, "Congress Is Wildly Unpopular, but Safe in Their Seats," *PBS NewsHour*, *The Rundown*, July 30, 2014, http://www.pbs.org/newshour/rundown/congress-wildly-unpopular-safe-seats/.

18. Sam Wang, "The Great Gerrymander of 2012," *New York Times*, February 2, 2013; on the decline of swing districts, see Nate Silver, "As Swing Districts Dwindle, Can a Divided House Stand?," "FiveThirtyEight," *New York Times*, December 27, 2012, http://fivethirtyeight.blogs.nytimes.com/2012/12/27/as-swing-districts-dwindle-can-a-divided-house-stand/.

On the effects of gerrymandering on congressional dysfunction, see Mark Warren, "Help, We're in a Living Hell and Don't Know How to Get Out," *Esquire*, October 2015, http://www .esquire.com/news-politics/news/a23553/congress-living-hell-1114/. For skeptics who doubt that gerrymandering plays a large role in sustaining incumbency, see John N. Friedman and Richard T. Holden, "The Rising Incumbent Reelection Rate: What's Gerrymandering Got to Do with It?" Massachusetts Institute of Technology, June 26, 2007, http://www.mit.edu/ ~rholden/papers/Incumbents.pdf.

19. Alexander Fouirnales and Andrew B. Hall, "The Financial Incumbency Advantage: Causes and Consequences," *Journal of Politics* 76, no. 3 (July 2014), 1; also Derek Willis, "Assigning a Dollar Value to Being the Incumbent," *New York Times*, July 2, 2014; Trump quoted in Lee Fang, "Donald Trump Says He Can Buy Politicians, None of His Rivals Disagree," August 7, 2015, *Intercept*, https://theintercept.com/2015/08/07/donald-trump-buy/.

20. Peter W. Singer, "Washington's Think Tanks: Factories to Call Our Own," August 13, 2010, Brookings, http://www.brookings.edu/research/articles/2010/08/13-think-tanks -singer. For a recent review of the literature, see James G. McGann, Anna Viden, and Jillian Rafferty, "Introduction: Social Development, Think Tanks, and Policy Advice," in McGann, Viden, and Rafferty, eds., *How Think Tanks Shape Social Development Policies* (Philadelphia: University of Pennsylvania Press, 2014), 11–35; McGann, Viden, and Rafferty, "Conclusion: Recommendations for Think Tanks and Policymakers," in ibid., 349.

21. Sheldon Rampton and John Stauber, *Trust Us, We're Experts!* (New York: Putnam Penguin, 2001), 228–29. 252–55, 275–76, 305–7; see also "Think Tanks," *SourceWatch*, Center for Media and Democracy, http://www.sourcewatch.org/index.php?title=Think_tanks.

22. Singer, "Washington's Think Tanks"; Thomas Medvetz, *Think Tanks in America* (Chicago: University of Chicago Press, 2012), 176–78, quotation 178. In 2014 the United States contained 1,830 think tanks, more than four times as many as the country (China) with the second largest number; see James G. McGann, "2014 Global Go To Think Tank Index Report" (copy of record, February 4, 2015), Think Tanks and Civil Societies Program, Lauder Institute, University of Pennsylvania, http://repository.upenn.edu/cgi/viewcontent .cgi?article=1008&context=think_tanks.

23. Quoted in Rampton and Stauber, *Trust Us, We're Experts!*, 307.

24. Kim Phillips-Fein, *Invisible Hands: The Making of the Conservative Movement from the New Deal to Reagan* (New York: W.W. Norton, 2012); Medvetz, *Think Tanks*, 124–26, quotation 124. On conservatives' use of brains, money, and the expertise of think tanks in shifting this nation's political agenda to the right, see also Jean Stefancic and Richard Delgado, *No Mercy: How Conservative Think Tanks and Foundations Changed America's Social Agenda* (Philadelphia: Temple University Press, 1996).

25. Michael Dolny, "What's in a Label?," *FAIR: Fairness and Accuracy in Reporting*, May 1, 1998, http://fair.org/extra-online-articles/Whats-in-a-Label/.

26. Based on the author's experience, both BBC and PBS *NewsHour* hosts routinely interview "experts" from think tanks without identifying their political leanings.

27. Donald E. Abelson, *Do Think Tanks Matter? Assessing the Impact of Public Policy Institutes* (Montreal: McGill-Queen's University Press, 2009), 127, 128, 129, 132–34, 135–41, quotation 133; Medvetz, *Think Tanks*, 108.

28. Abelson, *Do Think Tanks Matter?*, 141–42.

29. Yochi J. Dreazen, "Obama Dips into Think Tank for Talent," *Wall Street Journal*, November 17, 2008.

30. Quotation from Robin Bravender, "Think Tank New 'Training Ground' for Obama's Green Team," *E&E News*, April 7, 2015, http://www.eenews.net/stories/1060016366/; James Ryan, "John Podesta: The Most Powerful Unelected Democrat," IVN (Independent Voter Network), February 23, 2015, http://ivn.us/2015/02/23/john-podesta-powerful-unelected -democrat/; John Cassidy, "John Podesta's Legacy," *New Yorker*, January 14, 2015.

31. For a survey of the literature and debate, see "How Think Tanks Influence Policy: An Overview of the Current Debate," *Transparify*, March 2014, http://static.squarespace.com/ static/52e1f399e4b06a94cocdaa41/t/53204216e4b04cff12000948/1394622998318/.

32. Quotations from Eric Lipton, Nicholas Confessore, and Brooke Williams, *New York Times*, August 8, 2016; see also Lipton and Williams, "How Think Tanks Amplify America's Corporate Influence," *New York Times*, August 7, 2016.

33. Suzanne Mettler, *Degrees of Inequality: How the Politics of Higher Education Sabotaged the American Dream* (New York: Basic Books, 2014), 1–4, 12; also Alec MacGillis, "Higher Ed Lobby Quietly Joins For-Profit Schools to Roll Back Tighter Rules," *ProPublica*, May 5, 2015, http://www.propublica.org/article/higher-ed-lobby-quietly-joins-for-profit-schools -to-roll-back-tighter-rules.

34. David J. Deming, Claudia Goldin, and Lawrence F. Katz, "The For-Profit Postsecondary School Sector: Nimble Critters or Agile Predators?," working paper 17710, National Bureau of Economic Research, December 2011, www.nber.org/papers/w17710/; Michael Stratford, "Senate Report Paints a Damning Portrait of For-Profit Higher Education," *Chronicle of Higher Education*, July 30, 2012. Mettler agrees that the "problems of the for-profits are not limited to a few bad apples"; see Mettler, *Degrees of Inequality*, 37.

35. Kevin Carey, "Corinthian Colleges Is Closing: Its Students May Be Better Off as a Result," *New York Times*, July 2, 2014; Kevin McCoy, "Suit: Corinthian Colleges Victimized Students," *USA Today*, September 16, 2014. "Students who fell behind or defaulted on their loans," the Consumer Financial Protection Bureau said, "were subjected to bullying collection practices, including requiring them to start repayments while still in school, being pulled out of their classrooms and blocked from returning to their studies and having their computer access terminated."

36. Lee Fang, "Corinthian Colleges Secretly Funded D.C. Think Tanks, Dark Money Election Efforts," *Intercept: Unofficial Sources*, May 4, 2015, https://theintercept.com/2015/05/04/ bankruptcy-filing-shows-corinthian-colleges-secretly-funded-d-c-think-tanks-dark-money -election-efforts/.

37. Fang, "Corinthian Colleges"; David Halperin, "Exclusive: Washington Post's Kaplan and Other For-Profit Colleges Joined ALEC, Controversial Special Interest Lobby," *Republic Report*, April 26, 2012, http://www.huffingtonpost.com/davidhalperin/alec-for-profit -colleges_b_1457181.html; "Dr. Sharon Robinson, President and Chief Executive Officer, American Association of Colleges for Teacher Education (AACTE)," JAG: Jobs for America's Graduates, n.d., http://www.jag.org/board-of-directors/sharon-robinson.

38. Quotation from Halperin, "Exclusive."

39. Robert Shireman, "The Covert For-Profit: How College Owners Escape Oversight through a Regulatory Blind Spot," Century Foundation, October 6, 2015, 1, https://s3-us

-west-2.amazonaws.com/production.tcf.org/app/uploads/2015/10/06134943/Shireman _CovertForProfit-11.pdf.

40. Annie Waldman, "Who Keeps Billions of Taxpayer Dollars Flowing to For-Profit Colleges? These Guys," *ProPublica*, November 3, 2015, https://www.propublica.org/article/accreditors -billions-of-taxpayer-dollars-flowing-to-for-profit-colleges#comments; Patricia Cohen, "For-Profit Colleges Accused of Fraud Still Receive U.S. Funds," *New York Times*, October 12, 2015; Patricia Cohen, "Government Moves to Close a Watchdog of For-Profit Colleges," *New York Times*, September 22, 2016; quotation from Robert Shireman, "The Covert For-Profit: How College Owners Escape Oversight through a Regulatory Blind Spot," Century Foundation, September 22, 2015, https://tcf.org/content/report/covert-for-profit/.

41. David Halperin, "For-Profit College Investor Now Owns Controlling Share of Leading Education Trade Publication," *Huffington Post*, January 14, 2015, http://www.huffingtonpost. com/davidhalperin/for-profit-college-invest_b_6471986.html; David Halperin, "Washington Post Opposes Regulating For-Profit Colleges without Disclosing Publisher's Stake in the Industry," *Republic Report*, May 2, 2014, https://www.republicreport.org/2014/washington -post-opposes-regulating-profit-colleges-without-disclosing-publishers-tie-industry/; David Halperin, "Bezos' Purchase of the Post Leaves Graham with Kaplan For-Profit," *Huffington Post*, October 6, 2013, http://www.huffingtonpost.com/davidhalperin/bezoss -purchase-of-the-po_b_3714431.html.

42. For the full story of billionaires' long-running political warfare, see Jane Mayer, *Dark Money: History of the Billionaires behind the Rise of the Radical Right* (New York: Doubleday, 2016).

43. Quotations from Dan Morgan, "Think Tanks: Corporations' Quiet Weapon; Non-profits' Studies, Lobbying Advance Big Business Causes," *Washington Post*, January 9, 2009.

44. "Americans for Prosperity," *SourceWatch*, Center for Media and Democracy, http:// www.sourcewatch.org/index.php?title=Americans_for_Prosperity; Ashley Parker, "Chastened Republicans Beat Democrats at Their Own Game," *New York Times*, November 8, 2014; Steve Peoples, "Koch Political Network to Spend $300M to $400M over 2 Years," *Washington Times*, January 28, 2017; see also Jane Mayer, "Covert Operations: The Billionaire Brothers Who Are Waging War against Obama," *New Yorker*, August 30, 2010.

45. Eric Lipton, "Think Tank Plays Down Role of Donors," *New York Times*, December 3, 2013; Ken Silverstein, "The Secret Donors behind the Center for American Progress and Other Think Tanks," *Nation*, June 10–17, 2013; Jonathan H. Adler, "When Think Tanks Are in the Tank," *Washington Post*, March 9, 2014. For CAP's response to criticism, see Neera Tandem, "Think That Think Tanks Can Be Bought? Not So Fast," *New Republic*, February 20, 2013. Regarding CAP's disclosure of donors, see Dan Berman, "Liberal Group Claims Transparency but Keeps Some Donors' Names Secret," *National Journal*, January 21, 2015, http://www.nationaljournal.com/white-house/liberal-group-claims-transparency-but -keeps-some-donors-names-secret-20150121.

46. Quotations from Ken Silverstein, "The Great Think Tank Bubble," *New Republic*, February 19, 2013.

47. Eric Lipton, Brooke Williams, and Nicholas Confessore, "Foreign Powers Buy Influence at Think Tanks," *New York Times*, September 6, 2014; Jeffrey Goldberg, "The Obama Doctrine," *Atlantic*, April 2016.

48. *Washington Post* quoted in Michael Massing, "How to Cover the One Percent," *New York Review of Books*, January 14, 2016.

49. Quotations from Lipton, Williams, and Confessore, "Foreign Powers Buy Influence."

50. Bruce Bartlett, "The Alarming Corruption of the Think Tanks," *Fiscal Times*, December 14, 2012, http://www.thefiscaltimes.com/Columns/2012/12/14/The-Alarming-Corruption-of-the-Think-Tanks; Karen Tumulty and Allen McDuffie, "DeMint Marks a New, Sharper Edge for Heritage Foundation," *Washington Post*, December 6, 2012; Bryan Bender, "Many D.C. Think Tanks Now Players in Partisan Wars," *Boston Globe*, August 11, 2013.

51. Ken Silverstein, "The Great Think Tank Bubble."

52. Richard Perez-Pena, "A Senior Fellow at the Institute of Nonexistence," *New York Times*, November 12, 2008.

53. INCITE! Women of Color Against Violence, ed., *The Revolution Will Not Be Funded: Beyond the Non-Profit Industrial Complex* (New York: South End Press, 2009). INCITE! is a self-described "nation-wide network of radical feminists of color working to end violence against women, gender non-conformity, and transgender people of color, and our communities." After a 2004 conference exploring independent social activism, INCITE! published the book of essays cited here.

54. Peter Buffet, "The Charitable-Industrial Complex," *New York Times*, July 26, 2013.

55. Mark Dowie, *Losing Ground: American Environmentalism at the Close of the Twentieth Century* (Cambridge, MA: MIT Press, 1995), 90, 91, 95; quotation from Mark Dowie, *American Foundations: An Investigative History* (Cambridge, MA: MIT Press, 2001), xxiii. On Dowie, see Michael Barker, "Co-opting the Green Movement," New Left Project, August 1, 2010, http://www.newleftproject.org/index.php/site/article_comments/co-opting_greens_the_environmental_foundations_of_capitalism.

56. Daniel R. Faber and Deborah McCarthy, "Introduction: Foundations for Social Change: Critical Perspectives on Philanthropy and Popular Movements," in Faber and McCarthy, eds., *Foundations for Social Change: Critical Perspectives on Philanthropy and Popular Movements* (Lanham, MD: Rowman & Littlefield, 2005), quotation 5; Sally Covington, "Moving Public Policy to the Right: The Strategic Philanthropy of Conservative Foundations," in ibid., 89–114.

57. For an early critique of foundations functioning to protect privilege and capitalism, see Horace Coon, *Money to Burn: What the Great American Philanthropic Foundations Do with Their Money* (New York: Longmans, Green, 1938), esp. 336–37; Paul Kivel, "Social Service, or Social Change?," *Getting Together for Social Justice* (website), 2010, http://paulkivel.com/resource/social-service-or-social-change/; Jennifer Ceema Samimi, "Funding America's Nonprofits: The Nonprofit Hold on Social Justice," *Columbia Social Work Review* 1 (2010), 17, http://academiccommons.columbia.edu/catalog/ac:156455.

58. Jane Roelofs, *Foundations and Public Policy: The Mask of Pluralism* (Albany: State University of New York Press, 2003), quotation 25.

59. Blaire Brody, "10 Insanely Overpaid Nonprofit Execs," *Fiscal Times*, December 20, 2012, http://www.thefiscaltimes.com/Articles/2012/12/20/10-Insanely-Overpaid-Nonprofit-Execs; Ronald D. White, "Not So Nonprofit: 34 Top Charity Execs Earn $1 Million or More," *Los Angeles Times*, September 24, 2013.

60. "GOP Senators Question $1M Salary for Boys and Girls Club CEO," *Fox News*, March 12, 2010, http://www.foxnews.com/politics/2010/03/12/gop-senators-question-m-salary -boys-girls-club-ceo/; Berger and Colburn quoted in Stephanie Strom, "Lawmakers Seeking Cuts Look at Nonprofit Salaries," *New York Times*, July 26, 2010.

61. Spillett quoted in Strom, "Lawmakers Seeking Cuts"; "GOP Senators Question $1M Salary"; Gary Snider, *Silence: The Impending Threat to the Charitable Sector* ([United States]: Xlibris, 2011), 150, 151.

62. Joe Stephens and Mary Pat Flaherty, "Inside the Hidden World of Thefts, Scams and Phantom Purchases at the Nation's Nonprofits," *Washington Post*, October 26, 2013; for the *Post*'s database, see "Millions Missing, Little Explanation," *Washington Post*, October 26, 2013.

63. U.S. Government Accountability Office, "Tax-Exempt Organizations: Better Compliance Indicators and Data, and More Collaboration with State Regulators Would Strengthen Oversight of Charitable Organizations," Report to the Ranking Member, Committee on Homeland Security and Governmental Affairs, U.S. Senate, December 17, 2014, http://www .gao.gov/products/GAO-15-164; Gary Snyder, "The Nonprofit That Blew through Billions of Taxpayer Funds," *Nonprofit Imperative*, March 24, 2015, http://nonprofitimperative.blogspot .com/2015/03/the-nonprofit-that-blew-through.html.

64. Rick Cohen, "Multi-Million Dollar Salaries and Perks for University CEOs on the Rise," *Nonprofit Quarterly*, September 12, 2013, https://nonprofitquarterly.org/policysocial -context/22888-multi-million-dollar-salaries-and-perks-for-university-ceos-on-the-rise. html; Jaeah Lee and Maggie Severns, "Charts: When College Presidents Are Paid Like CEOs," *Mother Jones*, September 5, 2013, http://www.motherjones.com/print/233476; Melissa Korn, "Yale Gives Former Leader $8.5 Million Payout," *Wall Street Journal*, May 19, 2015.

65. David W. Chen, "Dreams Stall as City's Engine of Mobility Sputters," *Sunday New York Times*, May 29, 2016; Isabel Vincent, "CUNY and SUNY Bigs Get Chauffeurs as Tuition Soars," *New York Post*, June 9, 2013.

66. Editors, "U of L Foundation Needs New Scrutiny," *Lexington Herald-Leader*, April 24, 2015; Editors, "Auditors Must Save U of L from Itself," *Lexington Herald-Leader*, January 22, 2016; James McNair, "Amid Education Cuts, Retired Community College President Gets Hefty Financial Gift from Foundation," Kentucky Center for Investigative Reporting, March 10, 2016, http://wfpl.org/amid-education-cuts-retired-community-college-president-gets -hefty-financial-gift-foundation/.

67. Andrew Erwin and Marjorie Wood, "The One Percent at State U," *Institute for Policy Studies*, May 21, 2014, http://www.ips-dc.org/one_percent_universities/; quotation from Frank Bruni, "Platinum Pay in Ivory Towers," *New York Times*, May 20, 2015.

68. Rachel Landen, "Another Year of Pay Hikes for Non-Profit Hospital CEOs," *Modern Health Care*, August 9, 2014, http://www.modernhealthcare.com/article/20140809/ MAGAZINE/308099987. See also Elizabeth Rosenthal, "Medicine's Top Earners Are Not the M.D.s," *New York Times*, May 17, 2014.

69. Karen E. Joynt, Sidney T. Le, E. John Orav, and Ashish K. Jha, "Compensation of Chief Executive Officers at Nonprofit US Hospitals," *Journal of the American Medical Association: Internal Medicine* 174, no. 1 (January 2014): 61–67; quotation from "Hospital CEO's Salary—

How Much More Than Docs?" *Physicians Weekly*, July 8, 2014, http://www.physicians
weekly.com/hospital-ceos-salary-much-docs/.

5. Political Class Adaptation and Expansion

1. On inequality generally, see Joseph E. Stiglitz, *The Price of Inequality: How Today's Divided Society Endangers Our Future* (New York: W. W. Norton, 2013); Ronald P. Formisano, *Plutocracy in America: How Extreme Inequality Destroys the Middle Class and Exploits the Poor* (Baltimore: Johns Hopkins University Press, 2015); on CEO pay, see Thomas Piketty, *Capital in the Twenty-First Century*, trans. Arthur Goldhammer (Cambridge, MA: Harvard University Press, 2014). For a positive view of "citizen groups," see Jeffrey Berry, *The New Liberalism: The Rising Power of Citizen Groups* (Washington, D.C.: Brookings Institution, 1999); Jacob S. Hacker and Paul Pierson, *Winner-Take-All Politics: How Washington Made the Rich Richer—And Turned Its Back on the Middle Class* (New York: Simon and Schuster, 2010).

2. Theda Skocpol, *Diminished Democracy: From Membership to Management in American Civic Life* (Norman: University of Oklahoma Press, 2003), 12, 13, 15, 127.

3. Ibid., 222.

4. Ibid., 180–223, Gans quoted 163.

5. Ibid., 144–45.

6. Ibid., 230, quotation 236. In contrast, Berry optimistically stated that "citizens groups . . . are social movements grown up . . . . [They] represent large constituencies, and their success is the mark of a system that is open, democratic, and responsive to its citizens." Berry, *New Liberalism*, 170.

7. Mark Dowie, *Losing Ground: American Environmentalism at the Close of the Twentieth Century* (Cambridge, MA: MIT Press, 1995), xiv.

8. Ibid., 109–17, Hair quoted 75.

9. Michael Shellenberger and Ted Nordhaus, "The Death of Environmentalism: Global Warming Politics in a Post-Environmental World," *Breakthrough*, January 14, 2005, http://www.thebreakthrough.org/images/Death_of_Environmentalism.pdf; Robert J. Brule and J. Craig Jenkins, "The U.S. Environmental Movement: Crisis or Transition?" *Research Gate*, February 3, 2015, http://www.researchgate.net/publication/228742222_The_US_environmental_movement_Crisis_or_transition; Felicity Barringer, "Paper Sets Off a Debate on Environmentalism's Future," *New York Times*, February 6, 2005. But see Michael Shellenberger and Ted Nordhaus, *Break Through: From the Death of Environmentalism to the Politics of Possibility* (New York: Houghton Mifflin, 2007).

10. For right-wing attacks on the EPA, see William Yeatman, "Regulatory Capture Comes Full Circle at the EPA," *GlobalWarming.org*, May 15, 2014, http://www.globalwarming.org/2014/05/15/regulatory-capture-comes-full-circle-at-the-epa/; and Jeffrey A. Joseph, "Too Close for Comfort: Two Federal Regulatory Agencies Are Filling Their Ranks with Partisan Employees," *Baltimore Sun*, March 3, 2014, http://articles.baltimoresun.com/2014-03-03/news/bs-ed-revolving-door-20140302.

11. First quotation from "The Revolving Door," *Business-Managed Government*, n.d., http://www.herinst.org/BusinessManagedDemocracy/government/national/revolving.html; Craig Collins, *Toxic Loopholes: Failures and Future Prospects for Environmental Law* (New York: Cambridge University Press, 2010), 10–11, quotation 10. In the red state of Texas, state environmental officials regularly leave for high-paying jobs with industry; see Asher Price, "Revolving Door at Texas Environmental Agency?," *Austin American Statesman*, January 18, 2009, available as "Environmental Regulators Find Higher-Paying Jobs in Industry," http://texasnuclearsafety.org/downloads/aas_011809.pdf.

12. David B. Ottaway and Joe Stephens, "Nonprofit Land Bank Amasses Billions," *Washington Post*, May 4, 2003; also, Oliver Burkeman, "Wilderness Bewilderment," *Guardian* (London), May 29, 2003; Gary R. Snyder, *Nonprofits: On the Brink* (New York: iUniverse, 2006), 12–14.

13. Quotation from Ottaway and Stephens, "Nonprofit Land Bank."

14. Joe Stephens and David B. Ottaway, "Nonprofit Sells Scenic Acreage to Allies at a Loss," *Washington Post*, May 6, 2003; David B. Ottaway and Joe Stephens, "Landing a Big One: Preservation, Private Development," *Washington Post*, May 6, 2003; Naomi Klein, *This Changes Everything: Capitalism vs. the Climate* (New York: Simon & Schuster, 2014), 197.

15. Julia Lurie, "Fracking Chemicals, Brought to You by Susan G. Komen," *Mother Jones*, October 9, 2014; Karuna Jagger, "Think Before You Pink: Stop the Distraction," *Huffington Post*, December 1, 2014, http://www.huffingtonpost.com/karuna-jaggar/think-before-you-pink-sto_b_5910696.html/. Jagger is executive director of Breast Cancer Action.

16. Harley D. Nomes, "Birth of the Nature Conservancy Scandal Blog," *The Nature Conservancy Scandals*, February 28, 2008, http://tncscandals.blogspot.com/2008/02/birth-of-tnc-scandal-blog.html; Joe Stephens, "Nature Conservancy Faces Potential Backlash from Ties to BP," *Washington Post*, May 24, 2010; Ron Arnold, "Nature Conservancy Embroiled in Another Land Grab Scandal," *Washington Examiner*, January 10, 2013, http://www.washingtonexaminer.com/ron-arnold-nature-conservancy-embroiled-in-another-land-grab-scandal/article/2518153; Justin Gillis, "Group Earns Oil Income despite Pledge on Drilling," *New York Times*, August 3, 2014; Naomi Klein, "Why Aren't Environmental Groups Divesting from Fossil Fuels?," *Nation*, May 2, 2013; Janet Wilson, "Wildlife Shares Nest with Profit," *Los Angeles Times*, August 20, 2002.

17. First quotation Christine MacDonald, *Green, Inc.: An Environmental Insider Reveals How a Good Cause Has Gone Bad* (Guilford, CT: Lyons Press, 2008), 16; Klein, *This Changes Everything*, 191–201, quotation 199.

18. Chris Long, "WWF Scandal: Part I: Bears Feeding on Toxic Corporate Waste," *Wrong Kind of Green*, July 27, 2011, http://wrongkindofgreen.org/2012/04/12/wwf-scandal-part-1-bears-feeding-on-toxic-corporate-waste/.

19. MacDonald, *Green, Inc.*, 31; Mark Pawlosky, "Green, Inc. Author Says Big Environmental Groups Have Sold Out to Big Business," *Grist*, October 4, 2008, http://grist.org/article/green-inc/. CI's ties to corporations resemble those of TNC, and in 2011 a sting operation by a small British TV magazine embarrassed a charity endorsed by celebrities including Harrison Ford (a vice chair on its board), Julia Roberts, Kevin Spacey, Penelope Cruz, and

the Dixie Chicks. *Don't Panic* sent two reporters to CI posing as executives from Lockheed Martin to seek help in greenwashing the arms maker's image. The CI official they spoke with offered advice about making Lockheed Martin's image more eco-friendly by linking it to an endangered species. Tom Zeller Jr., "Conservation International Duped by Militant Greenwash Pitch," *Huffington Post*, July 17, 2011.

20. MacDonald, *Green, Inc.*, quotation 21–22.

21. First quotation from Arianna Huffington, "The Politics of Populism: In This Year's Most Competitive Senate Races, Suddenly Everyone's a Populist," *Salon*, September 24, 2002, http://www.salon.com/2002/09/24/populism_4/; Paul Krugman, "For the People," *New York Times*, October 29, 2002; "Paul Wellstone's Appeal," *Economist*, October 10, 2002.

22. Mark Leibovich, "Ordinary People," *New York Times Magazine*, June 21, 2015.

23. Karen Ho, *Liquidated: An Ethnography of Wall Street* (Durham, NC: Duke University Press, 2009), 22; on private exchanges, see Hayes, *Twilight of the Elites*, 98–101; Matt Taibbi, "Why Isn't Wall Street in Jail?," *Rolling Stone*, February 16, 2011, http://www.rollingstone.com/politics/news/why-isnt-wall-street-in-jail-20110216.

24. Amy Chozick, "The Clintons' Hamptons Quandry," *New York Times*, June 21, 2015.

25. This account of the 2008 campaign and following paragraphs are based on Ronald P. Formisano, "Populist Currents in the 2008 Presidential Campaign," in Liette Gidlow, ed., *Obama, Clinton, Palin: Making History in Election 2008* (Urbana: University of Illinois Press, 2011), 86–122.

26. For discussion of Obama addressing inequality, see Formisano, *Plutocracy in America*, 12–13, 19–23.

27. Ibid.; Taibbi, "Why Isn't Wall Street," 22–38.

28. Michael D. Sheen, "The Trans-Pacific Partnership: Questions and Answers," *New York Times*, June 16, 2015; David Acemoglu, David Autor, David Dorn, Gordon H. Hanson, and Brendan Price, "Import Competition and the Great Employment Sag of the 2000s," *Journal of Labor Economics* 34, no. 1, pt. 2 (2015), 141–98.

29. For Christie described as a "populist personality," see Sally Kohn, "Warren and Christie Are the Anti-Hillarys," *Daily Beast*, October 14, 2014, http://www.thedailybeast.com/articles/2014/10/14/warren-and-christie-are-the-anti-hillarys.html; also, Jim Newell, "Chris Christie's Dangerous Social Security Demagoguery: Cloaking the Pluotcrats' Agenda in Populist Rhetoric," *Salon*, April 16, 2015, http://www.salon.com/2015/04/16/chris_christies_dangerous_social_security_demagoguery_cloaking_the_plutocrats_agenda_in_populist_rhetoric/; Richard Perez-Pena, "Democrats Pounce on Chris Christie's Blunt Words," *New York Times*, April 15, 2011; quotations from Perez-Pena, "Christie's Talk Is Blunt, but Not Always Straight," *New York Times*, March 9, 2011.

30. Kate Zernike and Michael Barbaro, "Chris Christie Shows Fondness for Luxury Benefits, When Others Pay the Bill," *New York Times*, February 2, 2015.

31. Cindy Boren, "Chris Christie's Trip to Dallas on Jerry Jones's Dimes Raises Ethical Concerns," *Washington Post*, January 6, 2015; Matt Berman, "Cowboys Superfan Chris Christie Spent More Than $80,000 at NFL Games," *National Journal*, May 1, 2015, http://www.national journal.com/2016-elections/cowboys-superfan-chris-christie-spent-over-80-000-at-nfl

-games-20150511; Mark Lagerkvist, "Christie Buys $300K of Food & Booze with NJ Expense Account," *New Jersey Watchdog*, May 11, 2015, http://watchdog.org/217942/christie-nj-expense -account/; quotation from Mark Lagerkvist, "State Secrets: Why Won't Gov. Christie Disclose His Travel Expenses?" *NJ Spotlight: Politics*, December 2, 2014, http://www.njspotlight.com/ stories/14/11/30/state-secrets-why-won-t-gov-christie-disclose-his-travel-expenses/.

32. Lee Fang, "Pensiongate? Christie Campaign Donors Won Huge Contracts," *Nation*, April 7, 2014; Editors, "Gov. Chris Christie's Phony Truth-Telling," *New York Times*, June 30, 2015; Kate Zernike, "New Jersey's Top Court Rules Christie Can Skip Pension Payments," *New York Times*, June 9, 2015; Brad Friedman, "Audio: Chris Christie Lets Loose at Secret Koch Brothers Confab," *Mother Jones*, September 7, 2011.

33. Igor Bobic, "Meg Whitman, Former Chris Christie Campaign Chair, Slams Him over Trump Endorsement," *Huffington Post*, February 27, 2016, http://www.huffingtonpost.com/ entry/meg-whitman-chris-christie-donald-trump_us_56d305e5e4b0871f60ebbb87.

34. Russ Buettner, "Trump's Casinos' Debt Was $30 Million. Then Christie Took Office," *New York Times*, August 16, 2016.

35. John Dickerson, "The Populist Egghead," *Slate*, October 25, 2013, http://www.slate.com/ articles/news_and_politics/politics/2013/10/ted_cruz_is_a_populist_egghead_the_texas _senator_has_elite_credentials_but.html; "Populist Opposites: On Bernie Sanders and Ted Cruz," *Austin American Statesman*, May 4, 2015, http://www.freerepublic.com/focus/ news/3286145/posts; Zach Beauchamp, "Can Ted Cruz's Hawkish Populism Actually Win?" *Vox: Policy & Politics*, April 30, 2015, http://www.vox.com/2015/4/30/8514671/ cruz-populism; for "superman" J. K. Totter, "Populist Hero Forgot about $100,000 Invest- ment," *Gawker*, October 18, 2013, http://gawker.com/populist-hero-ted-cruz-forgot-about -100–000-investment-1447869661; Laura Clawson, "Ted Cruz, Humble Populist, Was Arro- gant by Harvard Law School Standards," *Daily Kos*, March 23, 2015, http://www.dailykos.com/ story/2015/03/23/1372719/-Ted-Cruz-humble-populist-was-arrogant-by-Harvard-Law -School-standards.

36. "Ted Cruz 2016" Official Website; Sen. Marco Rubio (R-FL) called for disman- tling "the cartel of existing colleges and universities" in his campaign for the Republican nomination: see Jeremy W. Peters, "First Draft: Marco Rubio Calls for Overhaul of the 'Cartel' of Colleges," *New York Times*, July 7, 2015 http://www.nytimes.com/politics/first -draft/2015/07/07/marco-rubio-attacks-higher-education-cartel-and-jabs-rivals/.

37. Joe Conason, "Country Music, Tea Party 'Populism,' and Ted Cruz," *Creators*, June 15, 2015, http://www.creators.com/liberal/joe-conason/country-music-tea-party-populism -and-ted-cruz.html.

38. David Greenberg, "We're All Populists Now," *Washington Post*, May 15, 2015; Tory Newmeyer, "Ted Cruz Just Upped the Populist Ante for 2016 Republicans," *Fortune*, June 24, 2015, http://fortune.com/2015/06/24/cruz-attacks-cronyism/.

39. Nick Penzenstalder, "Ted Cruz Blasts Media during Debate," *USA Today*, October 28, 2015, http://www.usatoday.com/story/news/nation-now/2015/10/28/ted-cruz-media -comments/74776260/.

40. First quotation Clawson, "Ted Cruz, Humble Populist"; second Conason, "Country Music"; also Laura Clawson, "Ted Cruz, High-Dollar Lawyer, vs. Ted Cruz, Rising Conserva-

tive Star," *Daily Kos*, March 26, 2015, http://www.dailykos.com/story/2015/03/26/1373458/
-Ted-Cruz-high-dollar-lawyer-vs-Ted-Cruz-rising-conservative-star.

41. Johnson quoted in David Brooks, "The Ted Cruz Establishment," *New York Times*, December 11, 2015.

42. Ashley Parker, "A Wife Committed to Cruz's Ideals, but a Study in Contrasts to Him," *New York Times*, October 23, 2013; Manu Raju, "Some GOP Colleagues Angry with Ted Cruz," *Politico*, October 2, 2013, http://www.politico.com/story/2013/10/ted-cruz -blasted-by-angry-gop-colleagues-government-shutdown-97753.html; Erik Wemple, "Ted Cruz Admits He'll Be Getting Insurance through Obamacare," *Washington Post*, March 24, 2015.

43. David Knowles, "Ted Cruz Knocks Goldman Sachs, Wife's Firm, over 'Special Favors from Government,'" *Bloomberg Politics*, March 24, 2015, http://www.bloomberg.com/politics/ articles/2015–03–24/ted-cruz-knocks-goldman-sachs-employer-of-his-wife.

44. Russ Choma, "Ted Cruz's Corporate Contributors," *Open Secrets*, September 26, 2013, http://opensecrets.org/news/2013/09/ted-cruz; Mike McIntire, "Ted Cruz Didn't Report Goldman Sachs Loan in a Senate Race," *New York Times*, January 13, 2016.

45. Eric Lichtblau and Alexandra Stevenson, "Hedge-Fund Magnate Robert Mercer Emerges as a Generous Backer of Cruz," *New York Times*, April 10, 2015; Betsy Woodruff, "Meet Ted Cruz's Tax-Dodging Sugar Daddy," *Daily Beast*, April 10, 2015, http://www.the dailybeast.com/articles/2015/04/10/meet-ted-cruz-s-tax-dodging-sugar-daddy.html; Molly Redden, "Ted Cruz's Big Money Man Is a Hedge Funder with a $2 Million Train Set," *Mother Jones*, April 13, 2015, http://www.motherjones.com/mojo/2015/04/ted-cruz-super-pac -donor-robert-mercer.

46. Jeremy W. Peters and Maggie Haberman, "Ted Cruz, a Public Firebrand on Social Issues, Is Cooler When Wooing Donors," *New York Times*, February 3, 2016; Mike Allen, "What Ted Cruz Said behind Closed Doors," *Politico*, December 22, 2015, http://www .politico.com/story/2015/12/ted-cruz-gay-marriage-secret-audio-217090; also, Emily Atkins, "Ted Cruz Assures Voters He Will Address 'Crisis' of Gay Marriage," *Think Progress*, January 27, 2016, http://thinkprogress.org/lgbt/2016/01/27/3743336/cruz-gay-marriage-iowa/.

47. Matt Flegenheimer, "Behind Ted Cruz's Campaign Manager, Scorched Earth and Election Victories," *New York Times*, February 23, 2016; Frank Bruni, "The Devil in Ted Cruz," *New York Times*, February 23, 2016.

48. Kenneth P. Vogel, "How the Kochs Launched Joni Ernst," *Politico*, November 11, 2015, http://www.politico.com/story/2015/11/the-kochs-vs-the-gop-215672.

49. Joni Ernst, "Squeal," *YouTube*, March 24, 2014, https://www.youtube.com/ watch?v=p9Y24MFOfFU.

50. Quotation from Michael Hiltzik, "Sen. Joni Ernst Learned to 'Live within Her Means'—on the Taxpayer's Dime," *Los Angeles Times*, January 23, 2015; also, Sam Knight, "Despite Campaigning on Pork-Cutting Family Living 'Within Our Means,' Sen. Ernst's Kin Took over $460,000 in Farm Subsidies," *District Sentinel News Co-op* (Washington, DC), January 12, 2015, https://www.districtsentinel.com/despite-campaigning-pork-cutting -family-living-within-means-sen-ernsts-kin-took-460000-farm-subsidies/.

51. Quotation from Hiltzik, "Sen. Joni Ernst."

52. For "libertarians with benefits," see Ronald P. Formisano, *The Tea Party: A Brief History* (Baltimore: Johns Hopkins University Press, 2012), 86–97.

53. Julia Porterfield, "With a Heavy Dose of Economic Populism, Santorum Launches Second White House Bid," *National Review*, May 27, 2015. For Santorum's earlier ties to "big business," see Mike McIntire and Michael Luo, "After Santorum Left Senate, Familiar Hands Reached Out," *New York Times*, January 3, 2012.

54. Walker quoted in John Fonte, "The Conservative Populist Breakout," *National Review*, April 30, 2015; Jeff Sessions, "America Needs to Curb Immigrant Flows," *Washington Post*, April 9, 2015; Editors, "Senator Sessions, Straight Up," *New York Times*, April 15, 2015. On the rise of anti-immigration parties in Europe, see Carlos de la Torre, ed., *The Promise and Perils of Populism* (Lexington: University Press of Kentucky, 2015).

55. First quotation from Robert Kuttner, "Schumer's Delicate Dance with Wall Street," *Huffington Post*, December 22, 2014, http://www.huffingtonpost.com/robert-kuttner/sly -senator-schumer_b_6370168.html; second from Brian Montopoli, "Charles Schumer's Wall Street Dance," *CBS News*, June 29, 2011, http://www.cbsnews.com/news/charles -schumers-wall-street-dance/.

56. Schumer quoted in Thomas B. Edsall, "Is Obamacare Destroying the Democratic Party?," *New York Times*, December 2, 2014; Robert Borosage, "Chuck Schumer's Populist Concession," *Campaign for America's Future*, December 3, 2014, http://ourfuture.org/ 20141203/schumers-populist-concession.

57. Zoë Carpenter, "Will Phony Populists Hijack the Fight against Inequality?" *Nation*, April 21, 2014, http://www.thenation.com/article/will-phony-populists-hijack-fight-against -inequality/.

58. Gregory Ferenstein, "The Disrupters: Silicon Valley Elites' Vision of the Future," *City Journal* (Manhattan Institute), Winter 2017, https://www.city-journal.org/html/disrupters -14950.html.

59. Carpenter, "Will Phony Populists Hijack"; Hacker and Pierson, *Winner-Take-All Politics*; John Ehrenreich, *Third Wave Capitalism: How Money, Power, and the Pursuit of Self-Interest Have Imperiled the American Dream* (Ithaca, NY: Cornell University Press, 2016); Stiglitz, *Price of Inequality*; Piketty, *Capital in the Twenty-First Century*; Jake Rosenfeld, *What Unions No Longer Do* (Cambridge, MA: Harvard University Press, 2014); Judith Stein, *Pivotal Decade: How the United States Traded Factories for Finance in the Seventies* (New Haven, CT: Yale University Press, 2010); Paul Krugman, "Knowledge Isn't Power," *New York Times*, February 23, 2015.

60. Gabriel Debenedetti, Kenneth P. Vogel, and Ben White, "Clinton's Wall Street Backers: We Get It," *Politico*, April 15, 2015, http://www.politico.com/story/2015/04/hillary -clintons-wall-street-backers-we-get-it-117017.

61. Victor Fleischer, "Hillary Clinton's Attitude toward Wall Street Is Subjective," *New York Times*, February 8, 2016; Matt Taibbi, "Campaign 2016: Hillary Clinton's Fake Populism Is a Hit," *Rolling Stone*, April 26, 2015, http://www.rollingstone.com/politics/news/campaign -2016-hillary-clintons-fake-populism-is-a-hit-20150416.

6. The Political Class in a Poor State

1. Quoctrung Bul, "Actually, Income in Rural America Is Growing, Too," *New York Times*, September 16, 2016.

2. Basic data is available from the U.S. Census Bureau, American Community Survey; or Sarah Baron, *State of the States Report 2014*, December 2014 Center for American Progress Action Fund, https://cdn.americanprogress.org/wp-content/uploads/2014/12/ StateofStates2014-report.pdf; Mike Sauter, "America's Richest (and Poorest) States," *Yahoo Finance*, September 20, 2013, http://finance.yahoo.com/news/america-richest-poorest -states-042117509.html; Christopher R. Bollinger, William H. Hoyt, David Blackwell, Michael T. Childress, and James M. Sharpe, "Kentucky Annual Economic Report 2015," *Kentucky Annual Economic Report*, Paper 20, Center for Business and Economic Research, University of Kentucky, 56; Dan Witters, "Alaska Leads U.S. in Well-Being for First Time," *Gallup*, February 19, 2015, http://www.gallup.com/poll/181547/alaska-leads-states-first-time .aspx; Jacob Ryan, "Kentucky Student Loan Default Rates among Highest in Nation," WFPL (NPR News Station), October 1, 2015, http://wfpl.org/kentucky-student-loan-default-rates -among-highest-nation/; Laura Unger, "Health and Poverty in Kentucky," *Louisville Courier-Journal*, April 14, 2014, http://www.courier-journal.com/story/health-bytes/2014/04/17/ public-health-laura-ungar-kentucky-counties-economic-health-outcomes/7820093/.

3. Quotation from "Income Inequality Has Grown in Kentucky," Economic Policy Institute / Center on Budget and Policy Priorities, 2012, http://www.cbpp.org/sites/default/ files/atoms/files/Kentucky.pdf; Anna Baumann, "Top 1 Percent of Kentuckians Continue to Capture Bulk of Income Gains in Recovery," *KY Policy Blog*, Kentucky Center for Economic Policy, January 26, 2015, http://kypolicy.org/top-one-percent-kentuckians -continue-capture-bulk-income-gains-recovery/; Jason Bailey, "Kentucky among 10 States with Fastest-Growing Income Inequality," *KY Policy Blog*, Kentucky Center for Economic Policy, November 15, 2012, http://kypolicy.org/kentucky-among-10-states-fastest-growing -income-inequality/; Estelle Sommeiller and Mark Price, "The Increasingly Unequal States of America," Economic Analysis and Research Network, January 26, 2015, http://www.the nation.com/wp-content/uploads/2015/04/IncreasinglyUnequalStatesofAmerica1917 to2012.pdf.

4. In 2013 government and community leaders launched an effort to lift Eastern Kentucky's economy and create jobs in keeping with technological change, forming a network called Shaping Our Appalachian Region (SOAR): see SOAR Innovation Summit, 2016, http:// www.soar-ky.org/summit.

5. Bollinger et al., "Kentucky Annual Economic Report 2015," 32; U.S. Department of Labor, Bureau of Labor Statistics, "County Employment and Wages in Kentucky—First Quarter 2016," http://www.bls.gov/regions/southeast/news-release/countyemploymentand wages_kentucky.htm#table2; regarding hunger and food insecurity, see U.S. Department of Agriculture, Household Food Insecurity in the United States in 2013.

6. Kenneth R. Troske, John Green, Devanathan Sudharshan, and Roy A. Sigafus, "Kentucky Annual Economic Report 2007," *Kentucky Annual Economic Report*, Paper 6, Center for

Business and Economic Research, University of Kentucky, 9, http://uknowledge.uky.edu/cber_kentuckyannualreports/6/.

7. "Education Inequality Worsening," *Lexington Herald-Leader*, December 22, 2013; Bollinger et al., "Kentucky Annual Economic Report 2015," 156; Anna Baumann, "Revenue Options That Strengthen the Commonwealth," Kentucky Center for Economic Policy, January 2016, 1, http://kypolicy.org/dash/wp-content/uploads/2016/02/Revenue-Options-2016–2.pdf.

8. "Kentucky Finances in Shambles," *Lexington Herald-Leader*, January 5, 2014; John Cheves, "Gubernatorial Hopefuls Keep Tax Talk Quiet," *Lexington Herald-Leader*, September 13, 2015.

9. Bill Estep, "Coal Baron Justice Owes $4.2 Million in Ky. Back Taxes as He Seeks Office in West Virginia," *Lexington Herald-Leader*, October 10, 2016; Bill Estep, "Audit: Owsley Clerk Failed to Bill for Nearly $400,000 in Taxes," *Lexington Herald-Leader*, September 30, 2016; John Cheves, "Boyle County Clerk Missed $500,000 in Tax Bills, Audit Says," *Lexington Herald-Leader*, September 30, 2016.

10. John Cheves and Linda Blackford, "Tax Relief Intended to Save Kentucky Farms Helps Pave Them Instead," *Lexington Herald-Leader*, February 21, 2016.

11. Ronald D. Eller, *Uneven Ground: Appalachia since 1945* (Lexington: University Press of Kentucky, 2008), 169. Eller's description of the region sadly extends that of Harry M. Caudill a generation earlier: *Theirs Be the Power: The Moguls of Eastern Kentucky* (Urbana: University of Illinois Press, 1983).

12. Ashley Spaulding, "Kentucky Going against National Trend by Failing to Reinvest in Higher Education," Kentucky Center for Economic Policy, May 1, 2014, http://kypolicy.org/kentucky-going-national-trend-failing-reinvest-higher-education/; Michael Mitchell and Michael Leachman, "Years of Cuts Threaten to Put College out of Reach for More Students," Center on Budget and Policy Priorities, Washington, D.C., May 13, 2015, http://www.cbpp.org/research/state-budget-and-tax/years-of-cuts-threaten-to-put-college-out-of-reach-for-more-students; Linda B. Blackford, "State Sees Big Drop in Graduation Rates," *Lexington Herald-Leader*, May 14, 2015; Linda B. Blackford, "Minority, Low-Income Students Lag," *Lexington Herald-Leader*, November 11, 2014.

13. James McNair, "Lucrative Retirement Deal for KCTCS Chief," *Lexington Herald-Leader*, May 9, 2014.

14. Institute of Taxation and Economic Policy, "Executive Summary," *Who Pays? A 50-State Report by the Institute on Taxation and Economic Policy*, 2015, http://www.itep.org/whopays/executive_summary.php; Institute of Taxation and Economic Policy, "Kentucky State and Local Taxes in 2015," *Who Pays?*, http://www.itep.org/whopays/states/kentucky.php; Institute of Taxation and Economic Policy, *Who Pays? A Distributional Analysis of the Tax Systems in All Fifty States*," 5th ed., January 14, 2015, http://www.itep.org/whopays/full_report.php.

15. Oguzhan Dincer and Michael Johnston, "Measuring Illegal and Legal Corruption in American States: Some Results from the Corruption in American Survey," Harvard University, Edmond J. Safra Center for Ethics, December 1, 2014, http://ethics.harvard.edu/blog/measuring-illegal-and-legal-corruption-american-states-some-results-safra; Joe Sonka, "Harvard Study: Kentucky's State Government One of the Most Corrupt in the Country,"

Insider Louisville, December 8, 2014, http://insiderlouisville.com/metro/harvard-study
-kentuckys-state-government-one-corrupt-country/; see also Jacalyn Carfargno, "Kentucky Gets C- Grade in 2012 State Integrity Investigation: Why Kentucky Ranked 19th
of 50 States," *State Integrity Investigation*, March 29, 2012, https://www.publicintegrity
.org/2012/03/19/18180/kentucky-gets-c-grade-2012-state-integrity-investigation.

16. Martin Booe, "ETHICS: Kentuckians Amazed That $400 Can Buy a Lawmaker," *Los
Angeles Times*, April 13, 1993, http://articles.latimes.com/1993-04-13/news/mn-22398_1
_harness-racing-industry.

17. The General Assembly meets for sixty days in even-numbered years and thirty days
in odd-numbered years.

18. Kentucky Legislative Ethics Commission, "Ethics Reporter: Kentucky Derby Issue,"
April 2016.

19. Jack Brammer, "Lobbyist Spending Hits Record for 2013," *Lexington Herald-Leader*,
February 3, 2014; Tom Loftus, "Record $18M Spent Lobbying Legislature," *Louisville Courier-
Journal*, January 23, 2015; John Cheves, "Jack Abramoff Discusses Influence Peddling with
Kentucky Lawmakers," *Lexington Herald-Leader*, January 5, 2012, http://www.mcclatchydc
.com/news/politics-government/article24721507.html; Catalina Camia, "Trade Group
Says Abramoff Shouldn't Teach Ethics," *USA Today*, December 22, 2011, http://content
.usatoday.com/communities/onpolitics/post/2011/12/jack-abramoff-lobbying-kentucky
-ethics-/1#.VbUHULOD7rc.

20. Tom Loftus, "Top Frankfort Lobbyists Make Big Money . . . VERY Big," *Louisville
Courier-Journal*, January 23, 2015. For how lobbying *pays off*, see "Lobbying Dollars Yield
Great Returns," *Lexington Herald-Leader*, June 3, 2016.

21. "State Legislative Incumbent Turnover in 2014," *Ballotpedia*, 2014, http://ballotpedia.org/
State_legislative_incumbent_turnover_in_2014.

22. Detailed information is available in a remarkable report by Lowell Reese, "The Unsustainable: Kentucky's Public Employee Pension," *Kentucky Roll Call*, July 25, 2012, http://
www.toopdf.com/file/the-unsustainable-kentuckys-public-employee-pension-.html; see
also John Cheves, "Group Highlights Six-Figure Government Pensions, Calls for More
Transparency," *Lexington Herald-Leader*, December 20, 2011.

23. John Mauldin, "These States Are Headed for a Death Spiral," *Business Insider*, August
3, 2016, http://www.businessinsider.com/these-states-are-headed-for-a-death-spiral-2016-8;
John Cheves, "Troubled Kentucky Pension System Might Need Billions More Than Assumed," *Lexington Herald-Leader*, February 17, 2017.

24. Darrell Preston and Margaret Newkirk, "Ky. Workers' Pension in Dire Straits; Not So
Lawmakers," *Bloomberg News*, June 28, 2015, http://www.kentucky.com/2015/06/28/3921588/
ky-workers-pension-in-dire-straits.html; James McNair, "KRS Investment Fees Much Higher
than Reported," *Lexington Herald-Leader*, September 16, 2015; Adam H. Edelen, auditor
of public accounts, "Auditor Releases Retirement Systems Audit, Finds 19 Deficiencies,"
press release, December 11, 2013, http://apps.auditor.ky.gov/Public/Audit_Reports/
Archive/2013KYRetirementSystems-PR.pdf; John Cheves, "State Pension Assets Fall to 19
Percent," *Lexington Herald-Leader*, November 20, 2015; see also Chris Tobe with Ken Tobe,
Kentucky Fried Pensions (privately printed, 2013), 47.

25. Matt Taibbi, "Looting the Pension Funds," *Rolling Stone*, September 26, 2013, http://www.rollingstone.com/politics/news/looting-the-pension-funds-20130926; Ira Stoll, "The Latest Public-Sector Pension Scandal," Reason.com, July 14, 2014, http://reason.com/archives/2014/07/14/the-latest-public-sector-pension-scandal; Jim Waters, "BIPPS Op-ed: Pension Transparency Does Not Violate Privacy Laws," *Bluegrass Institute*, May 23, 2016, http://www.bipps.org/tag/pension-transparency/.

26. Reese, "Unsustainable"; Kevin Quealy and Margot Sanchez-Katz, "Obama's Health Law: Who Was Helped the Most," *New York Times*, October 29, 2014.

27. Matt Klesta, "Comings and Goings in Eastern Kentucky," *Forefront*, Federal Reserve Bank of Cleveland, August 1, 2016, https://www.clevelandfed.org/newsroom-and-events/publications/forefront/ff-v7n02/ff-20160801-v7n0209-comings-and-goings-in-eastern-kentucky.aspx; Lyman Stone, "Kentucky's Migration Story: How Migration Data Can Help Answer Local Questions," *Medium*, November 24, 2014, https://medium.com/migration-issues/kentuckys-migration-story-begins-in-the-bluegrass-d16606dad696#.rjp02gkqx.

28. "Percent of Total Population in Poverty, 2015," U.S. Department of Agriculture, Economic Research Service, http://www.ers.usda.gov/Data/povertyrates/.

29. Annie E. Lowrey, "What's the Matter with Eastern Kentucky?" *New York Times*, June 26, 2014; Bill Estep, "Coal: Statewide, Production and Jobs Fell Sharply in 2015," *Lexington Herald-Leader*, February 2, 2016.

30. Eller, *Uneven Ground*, 129–76, 213–14, quotation 221–22; on local political structures shaped by outside elites, see John R. Burch Jr., *Owsley County, Kentucky, and the Perpetuation of Poverty* (Jefferson, NC: McFarland, 2008).

31. Bill Estep, "Eastern Ky. Worst in National Well-Being," *Lexington Herald-Leader*, April 6, 2014; "State of American Well-Being: 2013 State, Community, and Congressional District Analysis," Gallup-Healthways Well-Being Index, 2014, 33, http://cdn2.hubspot.net/hub/162029/file-610480715-pdf/WBI2013/Gallup-Healthways_State_of_American_Well-Being_Full_Report_2013.pdf; Sarah Burd-Sharps and Kristen Lewis, "Geographies of Opportunity: Ranking Well-Being by Congressional District," Measure of America series, Social Science Research Council, 2015, 10, http://ssrc-static.s3.amazonaws.com/wp-content/uploads/2015/04/Geographies-of-Opportunity-4.22.2015.pdf.

32. John Cheves, "Prince of Pork: Hal Rogers Hauls Home Tax Dollars by the Billions," *Lexington Herald-Leader*, February 6, 2005; "The Pork Parade: Mr. Rogers' Neighborhood," Citizens for Responsibility and Ethics in Washington, December 9, 2010, http://www.citizensforethics.org/mr-rogers-neighborhood/.

33. Bill Estep, "Toll of Eastern Kentucky's Drug Epidemic: Violence and Heartache," *Lexington Herald-Leader*, December 1, 2013; Trust for America's Health, "Kentucky Has the Third Highest Drug Overdose Mortality in the United States, *Prescription Drug Abuse: Strategies to Stop the Epidemic*, http://www.healthyamericans.org/reports/drugabuse2013/release.php?stateid=KY.

34. U.S. Congressman Hal Rogers, press release, "ICYMI: Rogers, Congressional Caucus on Prescription Drug Abuse Urges FDA to Act to Reduce Rx Drug Abuse," August 1, 2012, https://halrogers.house.gov/press-releases?ID=09D40C3A-9F12-4D54-B68F-4CFFE3F47145, one of the many Rogers's press releases on the subject.

35. Eric Lipton, "In Kentucky Hills, a Homeland Security Bonanza," *New York Times*, May 14, 2006.

36. G. W. Shultz, "Kentucky," May 2, 2010, Center for Investigative Reporting, http://cironline.org/reports/kentucky-2358.

37. "A Disgrace," *National Review*, May 17, 2006; Tim Dickinson, "The Ten Worst Congressmen," *Rolling Stone*, October 19, 2006; Citizens for Responsibility and Ethics in Washington (CREW), *CREW's Most Corrupt 2013*, http://www.crewsmostcorrupt.org/mostcorrupt/entry/most-corrupt-members-of-congress-report-2013.

38. Eric Lichtblau, "Earmark Puts $17,000 Pans on Army Craft," *New York Times*, May 18, 2012; CREW, *CREW's Most Corrupt 2013*, 92; Anu Narayanswamy, "Earmarks Boost Small Kentucky Businesses," Sunlight Foundation, December 18, 2007, http://sunlightfoundation.com/blog/2007/12/18/earmarks-boost-small-kentucky-businesses/; John Bresnahan, "$17K Drip Pans Bring Ethics Complaint," *Politico*, June 11, 2012, http://www.politico.com/news/stories/0612/77289.html.

39. David S. Fallis, Scott Higham, and Kimberly Kindy, "Congressional Earmarks Sometimes Used to Fund Projects near Lawmakers' Properties," *Washington Post*, February 6, 2012; John Cheves, "Rogers Wants Taxpayer Help for Cheetahs," *Lexington Herald-Leader*, July 20, 2012.

40. Brett Barrouquere and Dylan T. Loval, "Food Stamp Cut Hits Owsley County Harder than Most," *Lexington Herald-Leader*, January 20, 2014. Owsley took another hit when the state auditor revealed that the recent county clerk, Sid Gabbard, left office with a deficit of $307,000. Gabbard was sentenced to eight years in prison, but a judge probated the sentence after a plea deal with Gabbard repaying just $61,118 in restitution. Bill Estep, "$307,000 Deficit in Owsley Audit," *Lexington Herald-Leader*, April 16, 2014.

41. John McCormick and Gregory Giroux, "Food Stamp Cut Backed by Republicans with Voters on Rolls," *Bloomberg Business*, August 14, 2013, http://www.bloomberg.com/news/articles/2013-08-14/food-stamp-cut-backed-by-republicans-with-voters-on-rolls; "County-by-County Review of SNAP/Food Stamp Participation," Food Research and Action Center, January 5, 2010, http://frac.org/wp-content/uploads/2010/07/ny_times_snap_poverty_formatted.pdf. A Pew Research Center Study found that more Democratic identifiers received food stamps in the course of their lives: Rich Morin, "The Politics and Demographics of Food Stamp Recipients," *Fact Tank: News in the Numbers*, Pew Research Center, July 12, 2013, http://www.pewresearch.org/fact-tank/2013/07/12/the-politics-and-demographics-of-food-stamp-recipients/.

42. Alec MacGillis, "Who Turned My Blue State Red?" Sunday Review, *New York Times*, November 22, 2015.

43. David Sutton, "The 2008 Presidential Election in Appalachia: Reading from the Margins," *Appalachian Journal* and *Appalachian State University* 56, no. 3/4 (Spring/Summer 2009), 188–98.

44. Eller, *Uneven Ground*, 32, 33. The coal industry not only took wealth out of eastern Kentucky. The state tax on severed coal goes mostly into the General Fund, and what is returned to counties has not been adequate to fund economic development. In some western states the coal severance tax is 7 to 9 percent gross value per ton; in Kentucky it's roughly

4.5 percent or not less than 50 cents per ton; only half is returned to the county. In addition, most severance funds stay mostly in the county seat with very little dispersed to the smaller coal towns to finance development or infrastructure. See Stephanie McSpirit and Shaunna Scott, "E. Ky. Also Suffered as It Subsidized Goal of 'Cheap' Electricity," *Lexington Herald-Leader*, December 1, 2013.

45. Carol Jouzaitis, "Still Poor, Appalachia Faces the New Welfare," *Chicago Tribune*, November 11, 1996, http://articles.chicagotribune.com/1996-11-11/news/9611110180_1_new-welfare-cautious-hope-ghost-towns; Luke Mullins, "How Kentucky's Struggling Miners View the Country's Most Expensive Senate Race," *Yahoo News*, October 2, 2014, http://news.yahoo.com/how-kentucky-s-struggling-miners-view-the-country-s-most-expensive-senate-race-203703048.html; Bill Estep, "Decades of Poverty and Vote-Buying Led to Widespread Corruption in Clay County," *Lexington Herald-Leader*, November 30, 2013; Bill Estep, "Jury Convicts All 8 Defendants in Clay Vote-Buying Case," *Lexington Herald-Leader*, March 26, 2010; "Vote-Buying Reported in 19 Kentucky Counties," *Washington Times*, May 20, 2014.

46. Eller, *Uneven Ground*, 33; "Updated: Southeastern Kentucky Political Corruption; More of a Tradition than a Rarity," *Rural Democrat* (Sandy Hook, Elliott County, Kentucky), March 15, 2008, http://theruraldemocrat.typepad.com/the_rural_democrat/2008/03/southeastern-ke.html. For a history of the deep roots of poverty in Clay County that de-emphasizes the role of coal, see Dwight Billings and Katherine Blee, *The Road to Poverty: The Making of Wealth and Hardship in Appalachia* (New York: Cambridge University Press, 2000).

47. Eller, *Uneven Ground*, 34–35, 35.

48. "Social Security Disability Insurance Works for Kentucky," 2015, http://www.socialsecurityworks.org/wp-content/uploads/2015/03/SSDI-Works-for-Kentucky_2015.pdf.

49. Social Security Office of Retirement and Disability Policy, Congressional Statistics, December 2014, "Kentucky: Social Security," http://www.ssa.gov/policy/docs/factsheets/cong_stats/2014/ky.html; Stan Parker, "DOL Cracks Down on Coal Cos. with Black Lung Benefits Rule," *Law360*, April 25, 2016, http://www.law360.com/articles/788386.

50. Stephen Ohlemacher, "Congressional Report: Social Security Backlog May Add to Agency Financial Woes," *Washington Post*, September 4, 2012.

51. Damian Paletta, "Disability Claims Judge Has Trouble Saying 'No,'" *Wall Street Journal*, May 19, 2011; quotations from U.S. Senate, Committee on Homeland Security and Governmental Affairs, "Staff Report: How Some Legal, Medical, and Judicial Professionals Abused Social Security Disability Program's for the Country's Most Vulnerable: A Case Study of the Conn Law Firm," October 7, 2013, Hearing, 1–4, quotations 2, http://media.kentucky.com/smedia/2013/10/07/14/52/10QT2P.So.79.pdf. This is the executive summary.

52. U.S. Senate, Committee on Homeland Security and Governmental Affairs, "Staff Report"; see also John Cheves, "Eastern Kentucky Lawyer Earned Millions in Fees through Disability 'Scam,' Investigators Say," *Lexington Herald-Leader*, October 7, 2013.

53. U.S. Senate, Hearing before the Committee on Homeland Security and Governmental Affairs, "Social Security Disability Benefits: Did a Group of Judges, Doctors, and Lawyers Abuse Programs for the Country's Most Vulnerable?" 1st Sess., October 7, 2013, http://www.gpo.gov/fdsys/pkg/CHRG-113shrg85499/html/CHRG-113shrg85499.htm. This transcript

of the hearing indicates that several Huntington SSA officials in addition to Andrus enabled Conn and Daugherty.

54. Levin quoted in U.S. Senate, Hearing before the Committee on Homeland Security and Governmental Affairs, "Social Security Disability Benefits."

55. U.S. House, Hearing before the Committee on Oversight and Government Reform, "Social Security Administration Oversight: Examining the Integrity of the Disability Determination Appeals Process," June 10, 2014 (Serial no. 113-128), http://www.gpo.gov/fdsys/pkg/CHRG-113hhrg89597/html/CHRG-113hhrg89597.htm; Andrew Wolfson, "'Mr. Social Security' Faces Lawsuits," *Louisville Courier-Journal*, July 7, 2015.

56. John Cheves, "Much of Fraud Case against E. Ky. Lawyer Dismissed," *Lexington Herald-Leader*, July 31, 2015; Lambert is mentioned in other accounts of court hearings. Ned Pillersdorf, "'Mr. Social Security' Conned Us All, Got Rich," *Lexington Herald-Leader*, October 18, 2015.

57. Linda B. Blackford, "State Struggles to Pay for New Courthouses," *Lexington Herald-Leader*, January 31, 2010; "OP-ED: Herald Leader Op-ed Piece Takes Close Look at AOC and Hiring and Building Issues," *Kentucky Law Review*, November 13, 2008, http://kentuckylaw.typepad.com/blog/2008/11/op-ed-herald-le.html.

58. "OP-ED"; quotation from "Forum Flashes: Good Moves, Bad moves," *Louisville Courier Journal*, February 17, 2009. The AOC's reputation incurred further damage in an unrelated—except for the players—scandal. In November 2008 the *Herald-Leader* reported that the AOC promoted Judge Scott's son Andrew to a position monitoring criminals, including drug offenders, despite his facing a felony drug charge in Virginia. He was also allowed to keep a raise in an earlier demotion. Scott resigned after the newspaper's reporter inquired into his record, but the AOC refused to answer questions regarding Scott's history with the agency. Brenden Ortiz, "Justice's Son Resigns AOC Post," *Lexington Herald-Leader*, November 6, 2008.

59. Bill Estep, "Social Security Disability Payments Restored for Hundreds in Eastern Kentucky Facing Eligibility Review," *Lexington Herald-Leader*, June 4, 2015.

60. John Cheves, "'Mr. Social Security' Charged with Fraud," *Lexington Herald-Leader*, April 6, 2016; John Cheves, "Disability Lawyer to Stay in Jail for Now," *Lexington Herald-Leader*, April 8, 2016.

61. Bill Estep, "Disability Lawyer Conn Pleads Guilty to Fraud," *Lexington Herald-Leader*, March 25, 2017. Sentencing was set for July. Bill Estep, "Conn Ordered to Pay $31 Million to Government, Whistle Blowers," *Lexington Herald-Leader*, April 6, 2017.

62. "After a Decade Conn Finally Indicted," *Lexington Herald-Leader*, April 7, 2016; U.S. House, Committee on Oversight and Government Reform, "Staff Report: Systemic Waste and Abuse at the Social Security Administration: How Rubber-Stamping Judges Cost Hundreds of Billions of Taxpayer Dollars," 113th Congress, June 10, 2014, 4, 8, 11, https://oversight.house.gov/report/systemic-waste-abuse-social-security-administration-rubber-stamping-disability-judges-cost-hundreds-billions-taxpayer-dollars/; see also Jillian Kay Melchior, "SSA Scandal," *National Review*, June 12, 2014.

63. Hal Rogers, "Rogers Opening Statement at Prescription Drug Hearing," Washington, DC, March 7, 2012, House Judiciary Committee Subcommittee on Crime, Terrorism and

Homeland Security: "The Prescription Drug Epidemic in America," http://halrogers.house
.gov/news/documentsingle.aspx?DocumentID=283706. Meanwhile the Pepsi Company
was taking away children's teeth and health, with its aggressive marketing in Appalachia of
its high-caffeine, high-sugar "soft drink" Mountain Dew: see the ABC special editions of
20/20 hosted by Diane Sawyer, "A Hidden America: Children of the Mountains," February
10, 2009. Dentists in the area treated children with rotting teeth and a condition they called
"Mountain Dew Mouth."

64. Quotations from Bill Estep, Dori Hjalmarson, and Halimah Abdullah, "OxyContin
Abuse Spreads from Appalachia across U.S.," *McClatchy DC*, March 13, 2011, http://www
.mcclatchydc.com/news/crime/article24616228.html; Bill Estep, "Ex-Owner of Fla. Pill
Mill Says It Ran like a Factory," *Lexington Herald-Leader*, February 9, 2015.

65. Laura Unger, "Lawsuit Seeks to Make Drugmaker Pay for OxyContin Abuse," *USA
Today*, December 20, 2014.

66. Nick Redding, *Methland: The Death and Life of an American Small Town* (New York:
Bloomsbury, 2009), 115–16, 161, 163. Pharmacists and drugstore chain lobbying recently
defeated stricter controls on prescription drugs; see Robert Pear, "Lobbying Effort Is Said
to Sink New Controls on Painkillers," *New York Times*, June 18, 2012.

67. Marianne Skolek, "Eric Holder Negotiated an OxyContin Settlement in West Virginia—Working for Purdue Pharma," *Salem-News* (OR), June 1, 2011, http://www.salem
-news.com/articles/june012011/holder-purdue-ms.php; Marianne Skolek, "West Virginia
Uses OxyContin Settlement Money to Build a Gym," *Choopers Guide*, April 30, 2012, http://
www.choopersguide.com/article/purdue-pharma-articles-west-virginia-uses-oxycontin
-settlement-money-to-build-a-gym.html. Over half of the $10 million paid for a new gym
and remodeling of buildings at the West Virginia State Police Academy.

68. Amy Goldstein and Carrie Johnson, "U.S. Attorney Became Target after Rebuffing
Justice Department," *Washington Post*, August 1, 2007; Dan Eggen and Amy Goldstein,
"Voter-Fraud Complaints by GOP Drove Dismissals," *Washington Post*, May 14, 2007.

69. Rogers quoted in Unger, "Lawsuit," *USA Today*; "Kentucky Lawsuit against Oxycontin Makers Stalled by Deadline Dispute," *Insurance Journal*, April 1, 2015, http://www
.insurancejournal.com/news/southeast/2015/04/01/362736.htm.

70. Gregory W. Bee, "New Kentucky 'Pill Mill Bill' Places New Restrictions on Pain Management Facilities and Controlled Substance Prescribing," *Taft Law*, May 8, 2012, http://
www.taftlaw.com/news/publications/detail/941-new-kentucky-pill-mill-bill-places-new
-restrictions-on-pain-management-facilities-and-controlled-substances-prescribing;
"Study Shows Prescription Drug Abuse Declining in Kentucky," *WLKY* (Frankfort), July
27, 2015, http://www.wlky.com/news/study-shows-prescription-drug-abuse-declining
-in-kentucky/34380884; Laura Ungar and Chris Kenning, "Special Report: Heroin Surges
as Kentucky Cracks Down on Pain Pills," *Louisville Courier-Journal*, May 16, 2014.

71. Alex Morrell, "The OxyContin Clan: The $14 Billion Newcomer to Forbes 2015 List
of Richest U.S. Families," *Forbes*, July 1, 2015, http://www.forbes.com/sites/alexmorrell/
2015/07/01/the-oxycontin-clan-the-14-billion-newcomer-to-forbes-2015-list-of-richest-u-s
-families/.

72. First quotation, Mike Mariani, "How the American Opiate Epidemic Was Started by One Pharmaceutical Company," *Week*, March 4, 2015, http://theweek.com/articles/541564/how-american-opiate-epidemic-started-by-pharmaceutical-company; second quotation, Kate Eban, "OxyContin: Purdue Pharma's Painful Medicine," *Fortune*, November 9, 2011, http://fortune.com/2011/11/09/oxycontin-purdue-pharmas-painful-medicine/; "Dollars for Doctors: How Industry Money Reaches Physicians," *ProPublica*, https://www.propublica.org/series/dollars-for-docs.

73. Art Van Zee, "The Promotion and Marketing of OxyContin: Commercial Triumph, Public Health Tragedy," *American Journal of Public Health* 99, no. 2 (February 2009): 221–27, https://www.ncbi.nlm.nih.gov/pmc/articles/PMC2622774/; Lisa King, "OxyContin Continues to Devastate Appalachia," *Communities Digital News*, March 11, 2014, http://www.commdiginews.com/life/oxycontin-continues-to-devastate-appalachia-11986/.

74. "Drug Use and Overdose," Washington State Department of Health [2012], updated March 4, 2014, http://www.doh.wa.gov/Portals/1/Documents/5500/RPF-Drg2014.pdf.

75. Van Zee, "Promotion and Marketing"; Zachery Siegel, "The OxyContin Cartel: Billionaire Family 16th Richest in the U.S.," *Fix*, July 3, 2015, https://www.thefix.com/content/oxycontin-cartel-billionaire-family-16th-richest-us-according-forbes; Eban, "OxyContin"; Estep, Johnson, and Abdullah, "OxyContin Abuse Spreads."

76. King, "OxyContin Continues to Devastate."

77. "Heroin Use and Prescription Drug Abuse in Kentucky," 2014 Kentucky Health Issues Poll, February 15, 2014, http://www.healthy-ky.org/site/default/files/KHIPdrugmisuse FINAL.pdf; King, "OxyContin Continues to Devastate."

78. Phil Galewitz, "The Pharmacies Thriving in Kentucky's Opioid-Stricken Towns," *Atlantic*, February 2017, https://www.theatlantic.com/health/archive/2017/02/kentucky-opioids/515775/.

79. Beth Musgrave, "Special Report: The 'Invisible' Children," *Lexington Herald-Leader*, August 30, 2015; Annie E. Casey Foundation, "A Shared Sentence: The Devastating Toll of Parental Incarceration on Kids, Families and Communities," April 18, 2016, http://www.aecf.org/resources/a-shared-sentence/.

80. Centers for Disease Control and Prevention, "New Data Show Continuing Opioid Epidemic in the United States," December 16, 2016, press release, https://www.cdc.gov/media/releases/2016/p1216-continuing-opioid-epidemic.html.

81. Wayne Barrett and Dan Collins, "Cashing In on Catastrophe," *Nation*, September 25, 2006, http://www.thenation.com/article/cashing-catastrophe/; Barry Meier and Eric Lipton, "Under Attack, Drug Maker Turned to Giuliani for Help," *New York Times*, December 28, 2007; "Interview with Mary Jo White, Partner, Debevoise & Plimpton, LLP, New York, New York," *Corporate Crime Reporter* 19, no. 48, December 23, 2005, 11, http://www.corporatecrimereporter.com/maryjowhiteinterview010806.htm; Barry Meier, "3 Executives Spared Prison in OxyContin Case," *New York Times*, July 21, 2007; Peter Eavis, "S.E.C. Approves Rule on C.E.O. Pay," *New York Times*, August 5, 2015; David Dayen, "Democrats Are Fed Up with the SEC's Weak Financial Crimefighting," *New Republic*, June 18, 2015.

82. David Corn, "Why Eric Holder Represents What's Wrong with Washington," *Mother Jones*, January 14, 2009, http://m.motherjones.com/mojo/2009/01/why-eric-holder-represents -whats-wrong-washington.

83. Christopher Lane, "America's Opioid Epidemic," *Psychology Today*, October 28, 2016, https://www.psychologytoday.com/blog/side-effects/201610/america-s-opioid-epidemic.

84. First quotation, Lauren McCauley, "Big Pharma's 'Stranglehold' on Congress Worsening Opioid Epidemic," *Common Dreams*, October 31, 2016, http://www.commondreams .org/news/2016/10/31/big-pharmas-stranglehold-congress-worsening-opioid-epidemic; second quotation, Democratic Staff of the Senate Committee on Finance, "Dying Waiting for Treatment: The Opioid Use Disorder Treatment Gap and the Need for Funding," October 2016, https://www.finance.senate.gov/imo/media/doc/101116%20Opioid%20Treatment %20Gap%20Report%20Final.pdf; Gardiner Harris and Emmarie Huettman, "Actions by Congress on Opioids Haven't Included Limiting Them," *New York Times*, May 18, 2016.

85. Lenny Bernstein and Scott Higham, "How Drugs Intended for Patients Ended Up in the Hands of Illegal Users: 'No One Was Doing Their Jobs,'" *Washington Post*, October 22, 2016; Eric Eyre, "Drug Firms Poured 780M Painkillers into WV amid Rise of Overdoses," *Charleston Gazette-Mail*, December 16, 2016, http://www.wvgazettemail.com/news -health/20161217/drug-firms-poured-780m-painkillers-into-wv-amid-rise-of-overdoses.

86. Scott Higham and Lenny Bernstein, "Investigation: The DEA Slowed Enforcement While the Opioid Epidemic Grew out of Control," *Washington Post*, October 22, 2016; Transactional Records Clearinghouse, "Convictions Decline from Drug Enforcement Investigations," December 16, 2016, http://trac.syr.edu/tracreports/crim/450/; Scott Higham and Lenny Bernstein, "Senators Ask for DEA Data in Wake of Washington Post Investigation," *Washington Post*, October 26, 2016.

87. National Physicians Alliance, "Conflicts of Interest with Pharmaceutical Industry," http://npalliance.org/integrity-trust-in-medicine/conflicts-of-interest-with-pharmaceutical-industry/; for an overview of the many enablers, see Ronald Hirsch, "The Opioid Epidemic: It's Time to Place Blame Where It Belongs," *Observer*, May 23, 2016, http:// observer.com/2016/05/the-opioid-epidemic-its-time-to-place-blame-where-it-belongs/.

88. Robert Gebelhoff, "The Opioid Epidemic Could Turn into a Pandemic If We're Not Careful," *Washington Post*, February 9, 2016.

7. The Profitable World of Nonprofits

1. "CharityWatch Hall of Shame," CharityWatch, https://www.charitywatch.org/charity watch-articles/charitywatch-hall-of-shame/63.

2. Gary Snyder, *Silence: The Impending Threat to the Charitable Sector* (Bloomington, IN: Xlibris, 2011), 15, 29–72, 75–85.

3. Raymund Flandez, "Charities and Watchdog Groups Clash over Monitoring Systems," *Chronicle of Philanthropy*, September 1, 2010, https://www.charitywatch.org/home; quotation from Chuck Grassley, U.S. senator from Iowa, "Charitable Sector Abuse Outlined by IRS," July 23, 2007, http://www.grassley.senate.gov/news/news-releases/charitable-sector -abuse-outlined-irs.

4. Quotation from Eric Lipton, "'Breathtaking' Waste and Fraud in Hurricane Katrina Aid," *New York Times*, June 27, 2006; Jacqueline L. Salmon, "Red Cross, Humane Society under Investigation," *Washington Post*, March 26, 2006; Alan Chernoff, "Is the American Red Cross Worthy of Our Donations?" *CNN Money*, February 2, 2010, http://money.cnn.com/2010/02/01/news/economy/red-cross-donations/; Janet Greenlee, Mary Fischer, Teresa Gordon, and Elizabeth Keating, "An Investigation of Fraud in Nonprofit Organizations: Occurrences and Deterrents," *Nonprofit and Voluntary Sector Quarterly* 36, no. 4 (December 2007): 676–94, http://journals.sagepub.com/doi/pdf/10.1177/0899764007300407; Deborah L. Rhode and Amanda K. Packel, "Ethics and Nonprofits," *Stanford Social Innovation Review*, Summer 2009, http://ssir.org/articles/entry/ethics_and_nonprofits.

5. Robert Weisman, "After a Rich Severance Deal, Insurer Issues Refunds," *Boston Globe*, October 21, 2011, http://www.boston.com/business/articles/2011/10/21/blue_cross_blue _shield_issues_refunds_averaging_3_after_42_million_severance_pay_for_ex_ceo _killingsworth/; Office of the Attorney General, Commonwealth of Massachusetts, letter to board of directors of four charitable health insurers, April 14, 2011, http://www .mass.gov/ago/docs/nonprofit/findings-and-recommendations/director-compensation -report-4-14-11.pdf; "AG Coakley Determines That Compensation of Board Members at Non-Profit Health Insurers Is Not Justified," press release, April 14, 2011, http://www.mass.gov/ ago/news-and-updates/press-releases/2011/ag-determines-comp-of-board-members-not -justified.html.

6. Rosetta Thurman, "Nonprofit CEOs Who Want For-Profit Salaries Should Work at For-Profit Companies," *Chronicle of Philanthropy*, March 17, 2010, https://philanthropy.com/ article/Nonprofit-CEOs-Who-Want/195859; Rick Cohen, "Massachusetts AG Coakley Examines High Nonprofit Salaries," *Nonprofit Quarterly*, December 24, 2013, http://nonprofit quarterly.org/2013/12/24/massachusetts-ag-coakley-examines-high-nonprofit-salaries/.

7. Mike Keefe-Feldman, "Cuomo Unveils N.Y. Nonprofit Reform Plan," *Nonprofit Quarterly*, May 18, 2012, http://nonprofitquarterly.org/2012/05/18/cuomo-unveils-ny -nonprofit-reform-plan/; Maine Association of Nonprofits, "Executive Compensation," http:// www.nonprofitmaine.org/about-nonprofits/nonprofit-faqs/executive-compensation/; New Hampshire Center for Public Policy Studies, "Executive Compensation at New Hampshire's Non-Profit Hospitals," June 2012, http://doj.nh.gov/charitable-trusts/documents/20120702 -nh-public-policy-report.pdf.

8. Lee Ann O'Neal, "Health CEOs Top Nonprofit Pay Listing," *San Diego Union-Tribune*, December 16, 2013. The paper has traditionally done a survey of executive compensation.

9. Michael Cooper, "Squeezed Cities Ask Nonprofits for More Money," *New York Times*, May 11, 2011; Michael Rezendes, "City Sends 'Tax' Bills to Major Nonprofits: Aims to Triple Voluntary Payments within 5 Years," *Boston.com*, April 24, 2014, http://www.boston.com/news/ local/massachusetts/articles/2011/04/24/boston_sends_tax_bills_to_major_nonprofits/; Jim Doyle, "Nonprofit Hospitals' Huge Tax Breaks under Increasing Scrutiny," *St. Louis Post-Dispatch*, October 23, 2011; Jean Hopfensperger, Tribune News Service, "Cities Ask Tax-Exempt Nonprofits to Pay for Services," *Governing*, January 28, 2013, http://www .governing.com/news/local/mct-cities-ask-tax-exempt-nonprofits-to-pay.html.

10. "IRS Revokes Tax-Exempt Status of 275,000 Organizations," Bea & VandenBerk, http://www.beavandenberk.com/tax-exempt-organizations/irs-revokes-tax-exempt-status-of-275000-organizations/; Rick Cohen, "Tacoma, Wash. to Tax Nonprofit Health Systems Like Businesses," *Nonprofit Quarterly*, November 30, 2012, http://nonprofitquarterly.org/2012/11/30/tacoma-wash-to-tax-nonprofit-health-systems-like-businesses/; Adam H. Langley, Daphne A. Kenyon, and Patricia C. Balin, "Payments in Lieu of Taxes by Nonprofits: Which Nonprofits Make PILOTs and Which Localities Receive Them?," Lincoln Institute of Public Policy Working Paper, September 2012, http://www.lincolninst.edu/sites/default/files/pubfiles/langley-wp12al1-full_0.pdf.

11. Congressional Budget Office, U.S. Congress, "Nonprofit Hospitals and the Provision of Community Benefits," December 2006, http://www.cbo.gov/sites/default/files/cbofiles/ftpdocs/76xx/doc7695/12-06-nonprofit.pdf; quotation from M. Gregg Bloche, "Tax Preferences for Nonprofits: From Per Se Exemption to Pay-for-Performance," *Health Affairs* 25, no. 4 (July 2006): 304, http://content.healthaffairs.org/content/25/4/W304.full; Lisa Kinsey Helvin, "Caring for the Uninsured: Are Non-Profit Hospitals Doing Their Share?" *Yale Journal of Health Policy, Law, and Ethics* 8, no. 2 (2008): 423–70; Melanie Evans and Joe Carlson, "Out in the Open: Not-for-Profit Hospitals' Charity Spending Revealed, but Finding a Standard Measure May Not Be So Simple," *Modern Healthcare*, December 19, 2011, http://www.modernhealthcare.com/article/20111219/MAGAZINE/312199972.

12. Paul Kiel, "From the E.R. to the Courtroom: How Nonprofit Hospitals Are Seizing Patients' Wages," *ProPublica*, December 19, 2014, http://www.propublica.org/article/how-nonprofit-hospitals-are-seizing-patients-wages. Mount Carmel Hospital (Catholic) in Columbus, Ohio, from 2009 to 2011 sued over 1,500 patients.

13. Lucette Lagnado, "Jeanette White Is Long Dead But Her Hospital Bill Lives On," *Wall Street Journal*, March 13, 2003, http://www.wsj.com/articles/SB104750835516087900; Lucette Lagnado, "Hospitals Try Extreme Measures to Collect Their Overdue Debts," *Wall Street Journal*, October 30, 2003, http://www.wsj.com/articles/SB106745941349180300; Leonard Post, "Hospitals Hit with Plague of Lawsuits: Unfair Billing Practices Alleged against Nonprofits," *National Law Journal*, July 19, 2004, 1.

14. Lisa English Hinkle, "The ACA's Effect on Nonprofit Hospitals Re: Affordable Care Act," *National Law Review*, December 29, 2013, http://www.natlawreview.com/article/aca-s-effect-nonprofit-hospitals-re-affordable-care-act.

15. Columbia Law School, National State Attorneys General Program, "AGs and the Charitable Sector: In the News," http://web.law.columbia.edu/attorneys-general/ags-news/ags-and-charitable-sector-news. This remarkable website lists dozens of news items involving state attorneys general activities in the nonprofit sector. Some of the details in previous paragraphs are drawn from it.

16. "Nonprofit Organizations Salary and Benefits Report," Executive Summary, *NonProfit Times*, 2014, http://www.thenonprofittimes.com/wp-content/uploads/2014/04/1.12.14-2014-NPT-Executive-Summary.pdf.

17. Jan Masaoka, "How Much to Pay the Executive Director?" *Blue Avocado: A Magazine for American Nonprofits* [2012], http://blueavocado.org/content/how-much-pay-executive

-director; Elizabeth R. Keating and Peter Frumkin, "What Drives Nonprofit Executive Compensation?" *Nonprofit Quarterly*, July 27, 2011, http://nonprofitquarterly.org/2011/07/27/what-drives-nonprofit-executive-compensation/; James A. Brickley, R. Lawrence Van Horn, and Gerard J. Wedig, "Board Structure and Executive Compensation in Nonprofit Organizations: Evidence from Hospitals," (draft), October 1, 2003, William E. Simon Graduate School of Business Administration, http://citeseerx.ist.psu.edu/viewdoc/download?doi=10.1.1.196.1192&rep=rep1&type=pdf; Piketty, *Capital in the Twenty-First Century*, 334.

18. Kris Hundley, "Wounded Warrior Project Spends 58% of Donations on Veterans Programs," *Tampa Bay (FL) Times*, July 21, 2013; Tim Mak, "Wounded Warrior Project under Fire: Is Much-Touted Charity for American Veterans Everything It Says It Is?," *Daily Beast*, September 26, 2014, http://www.thedailybeast.com/articles/2014/09/26/wounded-warriors-project-under-fire.html; Dave Philipps, "Wounded Warrior Project's Board Fires Top Two Executives," *New York Times*, March 10, 2016.

19. Brian Jordan, Kristina Finn, and Walter V. Robinson, "A Tiny Tax-Exempt School Gives President a Lavish Life," *Boston Globe*, April 26, 2012, http://www.boston.com/news/local/massachusetts/articles/2012/04/26/tiny_tax_exempt_falmouth_school_lavishes_salary_perks_on_president/.

20. Beth Healey and Sacha Pfeiffer, "Leading Nonprofit Jobs Hold Big Perks," *Boston Globe*, January 24, 2015.

21. Kretman quoted in ibid.; Drew Johnson, "Agency Uses Tax Payer Dollars to Subsidize Rich Museums, Schools," *Washington Times*, November 6, 2014.

22. Alan Cantor, "CEOs and Everyone Else," Alan Cantor Consulting, January 29, 2015, http://alancantorconsulting.com/tag/ceo-salaries/. Cantor wrote this in response to the *Boston Globe* story regarding cultural nonprofit executive pay and perks.

23. Michael W. Faulkender and Jun Yang, "Inside the Black Box: The Role and Composition of Compensation Peer Groups," Social Science Research Network, May 1, 2010, http://papers.ssrn.com/sol3/papers.cfm?abstract_id=972197.

24. Katie Johnson and Adam Nagourney, "Bracing for a Backlash over Wall Street Bailouts," *New York Times*, March 15, 2009; Stephen Grocer and Aaron Lucchetti, "Traders Beat Wall Street CEOs in Pay," *Wall Street Journal*, April 6, 2010.

25. Ronald P. Formisano, *Plutocracy in America: How Increasing Inequality Destroys the Middle Class and Exploits the Poor* (Baltimore: Johns Hopkins University Press, 2015), 3, 18; Susan Holmberg and Michael Umbrecht, "Understanding the CEO Pay Debate: A Primer on America's Ongoing C-Suite Conversation," Roosevelt Institute, October 23, 2014, http://rooseveltinstitute.org/sites/all/files/Susan_Holmberg_Michael_Umbrecht_Understanding_the_CEO_Pay_Debate_Web.pdf.

26. Matt Taibbi, "Secrets and Lies of the Bailout," *Rolling Stone*, January 4, 2013, http://www.rollingstone.com/politics/news/secret-and-lies-of-the-bailout-20130104.

27. Edmund L. Andrews and Vikas Bajaj, "U.S. Plans $500,000 Cap on Executive Pay in Bailouts," *New York Times*, February 3, 2009; "Executive Pay Curbs Go Global," *Wall Street Journal*, October 21, 2008; Ben Protess and Susanne Craig, "SEC Proposes Crackdown on Wall Street Bonuses," *New York Times*, March 2, 2011; quotations from Mark R.

Reiff, *Exploitation and Economic Justice in the Liberal Capitalist State* (New York: Oxford University Press, 2013), 206.

28. Katie Johnston, "Efforts to Regulate CEO Pay Gain Traction," *Boston Globe*, October 26, 2014; "States Nationwide Seek to Limit Non-Profit CEO Pay," CBIZ, May 24, 2012, http://www3.cbiz.com/page.asp?pid=10098; "Is a One Million Dollar Nonprofit Salary As Bad As It Sounds?" *Forbes*, January 23, 2013, http://www.forbes.com/sites/investopedia/2013/01/23/is-a-one-million-dollar-nonprofit-ceo-salary-as-bad-as-it-sounds/; Ron Shinkman, "MA Nurses Union Pushes for Pay Curbs, Financial Disclosures at Hospitals," *Fierce Healthcare*, June 12, 2014, http://www.fiercehealthcare.com/finance/ma-nurses-union-pushes-for-pay-curbs-financial-disclosures-at-hospitals; Katie Sullivan, "Mass. Nurses' Union Reveals Offshore Accounts at 40 Hospitals," *Fierce Healthcare*, April 30, 2014, http://www.fiercehealthcare.com/finance/mass-nurses-union-calls-hospital-fiscal-transparency/2014-04-30; Gintauntas Dumcius, "With Aim of Avoiding Ballot Question on Nurse Staffing Ratios, Massachusetts House Passes Bill," *Mass Live*, June 28, 2014, http://www.masslive.com/politics/index.ssf/2014/06/with_aim_of_avoiding_ballot_qu.html.

29. Crit Luallen, "Kentucky Voices: A Kentucky Corruption Fighter's Report after Eight Years on the Job," *Lexington Herald-Leader*, January 15, 2012, http://www.kentucky.com/opinion/op-ed/article44150199.html; Tom Eblen, "Auditor Crit Luallen a Tough Act to Follow," *Lexington Herald-Leader*, November 13, 2014.

30. On the impact of the story in Lexington, see Patrick Crowley, "Uncovering Extravagance," *American Journalism Review*, April/May 2009, http://ajrarchive.org/Article.asp?id=4743. Jennifer Hewlett, who investigated and broke the airport story, spent twenty-two years as the paper's writer of extraordinary obituaries.

31. Jennifer Hewlett, "The Story That Sparked the Investigation: A Sky-High Expense Account," *Lexington Herald-Leader*, November 23, 2008, http://www.kentucky.com/2008/11/23/602751/the-story-that-sparked-the-investigation.html.

32. Hewlett, "Story That Sparked"; Jennifer Hewlett, "Gifts, Other Purchases Add Up," *Lexington Herald-Leader*, November 23, 2008; Crit Luallen, Auditor of Public Accounts, "Examination of Certain Financial Transactions, Policies, and Procedures of the Lexington Bluegrass Airport," February 25, 2009, http://www.kentucky.com/latest-news/article41005173.ece/BINARY/Read%20the%20Blue%20Grass%20Airport%20audit, iii, iv, v.

33. Beverly Fortune, "State Auditor to Check Airport Records," *Lexington Herald-Leader*, December 3, 2008; Michelle Ku, "Mayor, Vice Mayor Differ on Scandal," *Lexington Herald-Leader*, January 11, 2009; Jennifer Hewlett, "Airport Director Michael Gobb Resigns," *Lexington Herald-Leader*, January 3, 2009.

34. Jennifer Hewlett and Ryan Alessi, "Gobb, Three Former Airport Executives Indicted," *Lexington Herald-Leader*, October 21, 2009, http://www.kentucky.com/2009/10/21/984884/gobb-three-former-airport-leaders.html.

35. Jennifer Hewlett, "Former Blue Grass Airport Executives Accept Plea Deal," *Lexington Herald-Leader*, March 20, 2009; Goodwine comment reported in "Blue Grass Airport Sentencing Nightmare," Page One Kentucky, June 17, 2010, https://pageonekentucky.com/2010/06/17/blue-grass-airport-sentencing-nightmare/.

36. Tom Eblen, "Gobb, Davender Give Reasons to Rethink Justice," *Bluegrass and Beyond* (blog), August 21, 2010, http://tomeblen.bloginky.com/2010/08/.

37. "Trip to Hawaii," *Lexington Herald-Leader*, March 2, 2009.

38. "Q & A with Michael Gobb," *Business Lexington*, April 27, 2012, http://smileypete.com/business/2012-04-27-qa-with-michael-gobb/; in 2013 he was working as a sales representative for local businessman Alan Stein when he was found dead in his apartment at age fifty. Jim Warren, "Former Lexington Airport Director Michael Gobb Found Dead," *Lexington Herald-Leader*, September 11, 2013.

39. John Cheves, "Library Finances: Checking Out the Books," *Lexington Herald-Leader*, April 26, 2009; "Internal Audit Report," Lexington-Fayette Urban County Government, Office of Internal Audit, December 3, 2009, http://www.lexpublib.org/sites/misc/resources/pdf/Lexington_Public_Library_Internal_Audit_Report.pdf.

40. Quotation from "Internal Audit Report," 10.

41. First quotation Cheves, "Library Finances"; second from John Cheves, "Lexington Library Board Fires Chief Executive Kathleen Imhoff," *Lexington Herald-Leader*, July 16, 2009.

42. "Internal Audit Report," 15, 18.

43. Ibid., 10, 12–13.

44. John Cheves, "Fired Chief Sues Lexington Public Library for Millions in Damages," *Lexington Herald Leader*, July 15, 2010, John Cheves, "Judge Throws Out Much of the Money Awarded to Kathleen Imhoff, Former Lexington Library CEO," *Lexington Herald-Leader*, May 13, 2014.

45. Linda B. Blackford, "League Prospers As Ky. Cities Struggle," *Lexington Herald-Leader*, June 7, 2009; Andrew Thomason, "KLC Audit: Booze, Strip Club Visit," *Bowling Green (KY) Daily News*, December 18, 2009.

46. Linda B. Blackford, "Auditor Blasts Ky. League of Cities," *Lexington Herald-Leader*, December 18, 2009, http://www.kentucky.com/news/special-reports/article44017845.html; Crit Luallen, Auditor of Public Accounts, "Examination of Certain Financial Transactions, Policies, and Procedures of the Kentucky League of Cities," December 17, 2009, http://www.kentucky.com/latest-news/article40963038.ece/BINARY/Read%20the%20auditor%27s%20executive%20summary.

47. Blackford, "League Prospers"; "Long-Awaited Kentucky League of Cities Audit," *Page One*, December 17, 2009, http://pageonekentucky.com/2009/12/17/long-awaited-kentucky-league-of-cities-audit/.

48. Luallen, "Examination of Kentucky League of Cities," ii–iii.

49. Ibid., iv–v, viii; Lovely quoted in Blackford, "League Prospers."

50. Luallen, "Examination of Kentucky League of Cities," vii; Lovely quoted in Blackford, "League Prospers."

51. Luallen, "Examination of Kentucky League of Cities," ix; Ryan Alessi and Linda B. Blackford, "Changes May Be Coming for New Cities," *Lexington Herald-Leader*, December 20, 2009.

52. "Long-Awaited Audit," *Page One*; Jack Brammer and Cheryl Truman, "KLC Insurance Director Fired," *Lexington Herald-Leader*, June 25, 2010.

53. Luallen, "Examination of Kentucky League of Cities," 20–22; "Long-Awaited Audit," *Page One.*

54. Luallen, "Examination of Kentucky League of Cities," 24, 25.

55. Ibid., 26–27.

56. Sylvia Weixler, "Sylvia Lovely Will Speak at LWC on Community Patriots," *Columbia Magazine,* March 14, 2008, http://www.columbiamagazine.com/index.php?sid=22170.

57. Ronica Shannon, "Richmond Mayor Called Out in KLC Scandal," *Richmond Register,* June 9, 2009, http://www.richmondregister.com/news/local_news/richmond-mayor -called-out-in-klc-scandal/article_2b001a0d-20ed-5782-99f0-5b9e7c0ec5c2.html.

58. Tom Eblen, "Sylvia Lovely Tries for a Comeback after KLC Scandal," *Bluegrass and Beyond* (blog), December 11, 2010, http://tomeblen.bloginky.com/2010/12/11/sylvia-lovely -tries-for-a-comeback-after-klc-scandal/.

59. Ryan Alessi, "The High Cost of Doing the Counties' Business," *Lexington Herald-Leader,* June 28, 2009, http://www.kentucky.com/news/special-reports/article44002431.html.

60. Alessi, "High Cost"; Ryan Alessi, "Help from Roof Repair to Hospital Services," *Lexington Herald-Leader,* June 28, 2009.

61. Arnold quoted in Alessi, "High Cost."

62. Alessi, "Official Disputes Charges to Strip Club, Escort Service," *Lexington Herald-Leader,* June 28, 2009, http://www.kentucky.com/2009/06/28/843195/official -disputes-charges-to-strip.html; Crit Luallen, Auditor of Public Accounts, "Examination of Certain Financial Transactions, Policies and Procedures of the Kentucky Association of Counties, Inc." October 29, 2009, iii–iv, https://omiopinion.files.wordpress.com/ 2009/10/2009kacoexamination.pdf.

63. Luallen, "Examination of Kentucky Association of Counties," ii–v, vii–viii, x, xi.

64. "Employee Lawsuits Cost Kentucky County Group Millions, Report Says," *Claims Journal,* August 21, 2009, http://www.claimsjournal.com/news/southeast/2009/08/21/103192 .htm. The lawsuits were brought by former employees who claimed they were fired in retaliation for blowing the whistle on a "hostile workplace."

65. Alessi, "High Cost"; Blackford, "League Prospers."

66. "KLC: A Mess of Conflicts, Excess," *Lexington Herald-Leader,* December 18, 2009.

67. John Cheves, "Kentucky Mental Health Agency Spends Big on Executive Pay and Political Lobbying," *Lexington Herald-Leader,* June 3, 2012, http://www.kentucky.com/ 2012/06/03/2210440/kentucky-mental-health-agency.html.

68. Ibid.; John Cheves, "State Auditor to Examine Bluegrass Mental Health-Mental Retardation Board," *Lexington Herald-Leader,* June 8, 2012, http://www.kentucky.com/news/ local/watchdog/article44363763.html.

69. John Cheves, "CEO of Mental Health Agency Retiring; State Audit Due Soon," *Lexington Herald-Leader,* December 3, 2012, http://www.kentucky.com/news/politics-government/ article44393145.html; quotation from "Edelen Releases Examination of Bluegrass MH/MR, Questions Executive Benefits, Certain Expenditures; Recommends Board Strengthen Controls," The Mountain Wolf (website), December 20, 2012, http://www.tmwolf.com.

70. John Cheves, "Hospice of the Bluegrass Does Business with Firms Connected to Board, Executives," *Lexington Herald-Leader,* June 23, 2012, http://www.kentucky.com/ news/local/watchdog/article44365653.html.

71. Mary Meehan, "Hospice of the Bluegrass Cuts More Jobs, to Close Palliative Care Center in Lexington," *Lexington Herald-Leader*, May 13, 2014.

72. "Editorial: Scrutiny Overdue at Regional Agency; Bluegrass ADD's Odd Secrecy, Spending," *Lexington Herald-Leader*, June 6, 2013, https://riverparkassociation.wordpress.com/2013/06/06/editorial-scrutiny-overdue-at-regional-agency-bluegrass-adds-odd-secrecy-spending/.

73. Payne quoted in Linda B. Blackford, "Auditor: Lexington-Based Bluegrass Area Development District a Wayward 'Octopus,'" *Lexington Herald-Leader*, March 4, 2014, http://www.kentucky.com/2014/03/04/3120573/auditor-lexington-based-agency.html; Adam H. Edelen, Auditor of Public Accounts, "Examination of the Bluegrass Area Development District," March 4, 2014, http://apps.auditor.ky.gov/Public/Audit_Reports/Archive/2014 bluegrassareadevelopmentdistrictexam.pdf, see 44 regarding spending.

74. Quotation from John Cheves, "Auditors: Employees Intimidated, Millions Misspent at Ky. Emergency Management," *Lexington Herald-Leader*, August 6, 2013; John Cheves, "Head of Ky. Emergency Management Agency Resigns Following Scathing Audit," *Lexington Herald-Leader*, August 8, 2013; Adam H. Edelen, Auditor of Public Accounts, "Examination of the Kentucky Emergency Management, August 6, 2013; the full report can be found at http://www.pageonekentucky.com/wp-content/uploads/2013/08/kyemaudit.pdf.

75. Janet Patton, "Auditor Details a 'Toxic Culture of Entitlement' While Richie Farmer Was Ag Commissioner," *Lexington Herald-Leader*, April 30, 2012, http://www.kentucky.com/2012/04/30/2169892/auditor-details-spending-by-richie.html; Tom Loftus, "Ex-Kentucky Star Richie Farmer Sentenced to 27 Months in Prison," *USA Today*, January 14, 2014, http://www.usatoday.com/story/sports/ncaab/2014/01/14/richie-farmer-kentucky-basketball-sentenced-more-than-two-years-in-prison/4478635/.

76. John Cheves, "How Kentucky's Congressmen Let Others Pay for Their 'Political Lifestyle,'" *Lexington Herald-Leader*, May 27, 2016.

77. FBI Louisville, "FBI Louisville Seeks the Public's Assistance in Identifying Public Corruption within the Commonwealth of Kentucky," press release, July 31, 2015, https://www.fbi.gov/louisville/press-releases/2015/fbi-louisville-seeks-the-publics-assistance in -identifying-public-corruption-within-the-commonwealth-of-kentucky; paraphrases and quotations from Steven G. Koven, "Hiring Practices in the State of Kentucky: The Ethical Conundrum," in James C. Clinger and Michael W. Hair, eds., *Government, Politics, and Public Policy* (Lexington: University Press of Kentucky, 2013), 281, 288. James McNair, "When Hiring, Kentucky's County Officials Often Turn to Relatives," *Lexington Herald-Leader*, November 21, 2015.

Conclusion

1. Dick Carozza, "An Interview with Sherron Watkins," *Fraud Magazine*, January/February 2007, http://www.fraud-magazine.com/article.aspx?id=583.

2. William D. Cohan, "Dick Fuld's Return to Wall Street Was Hard to Watch," *Vanity Fair*, June 3, 2015, http://www.vanityfair.com/news/2015/06/dick-fuld-return-to-wall-street-speech; "25 People to Blame for the Financial Crisis," *Time*, n.d., http://content.time.com/time/specials/packages/completelist/0,29569,1877351,00.html.

3. Sheila Bair, *Bull by the Horns: Fighting to Save Main Street from Wall Street and Wall Street from Itself* (New York: Free Press, 2012), quotations 362, 363; Matt Taibbi, "Why Isn't Wall Street in Jail?" *Rolling Stone*, February 16, 2011, http://www.rollingstone.com/politics/news/why-isnt-wall-street-in-jail-20110216.

4. Neil Irwin, "This Is a Complete List of Wall Street CEOs Prosecuted for Their Role in the Financial Crisis," *Washington Post*, September 12, 2013, https://www.washingtonpost.com/news/wonk/wp/2013/09/12/this-is-a-complete-list-of-wall-street-ceos-prosecuted-for-their-role-in-the-financial-crisis/.

5. Joshua Holland, "Hundreds of Wall Street Execs Went to Jail during the Last Fraud-Fueled Crisis," *Moyers & Company*, September 17, 2013, http://billmoyers.com/2013/09/17/hundreds-of-wall-street-execs-went-to-prison-during-the-last-fraud-fueled-bank-crisis/; Jesse Eisinger, "Why Only One Top Banker Went to Jail for the Financial Crisis," *New York Times Magazine*, April 30, 2014.

6. Daniel M. Uhlmann, "Prosecution Deferred, Justice Denied," *New York Times*, December 13, 2013 (Uhlmann was chief of the environmental crimes section at the Justice Department from 2001 to 2007; he is a law professor at the University of Michigan.); Nathaniel Popper, "In Settlement's Fine Print, Goldman May Save $1 Billion," *New York Times*, April 11, 2016.

7. Rachel E. Barkow and Anthony S. Barkow, eds., *Prosecutors in the Boardroom: Using Criminal Law to Regulate Corporate Conduct* (New York: New York University Press, 2011).

8. Marc L. Ross, "HSBC's Money Laundering Scandal," *Investopedia*, January 29, 2013, http://www.investopedia.com/stock-analysis/2013/investing-news-for-jan-29-hsbcs-money-laundering-scandal-hbc-scbff-ing-cs-rbs0129.aspx; Matt Taibbi, *The Divide: American Injustice in the Age of the Wealth Gap* (New York: Spiegel & Grau, 2014), 13–19, 404–9, quotations 19, 407.

9. *National Law Journal* quoted in David Dayen, "Why Eric Holder's New Job Is an Insult to the American Public," *Salon*, July 7, 2015, http://www.salon.com/2015/07/07/why_eric_holders_new_job_is_an_insult_to_the_american_public/; Matt Taibbi, "Eric Holder, Wall Street Double Agent Comes in From the Cold," *Rolling Stone*, July 8, 2015, http://www.rollingstone.com/politics/news/eric-holder-wall-street-double-agent-comes-in-from-the-cold-20150708.

10. Bonnie Kavoussi, "Warren Buffett: Libor Scandal Involves 'The Whole World,'" *Huffington Post*, July 12, 2012, http://www.huffingtonpost.com/2012/07/12/warren-buffett-libor-scandal_n_1668649.html; "The LIBOR Scandal," *Forbes*, July 26, 2012, http://www.forbes.com/sites/investopedia/2012/07/26/the-libor-scandal/.

11. "The Rotten Heart of Finance," *Economist*, July 7, 2012; Robert Scheer, "Libor: The Crime of the Century," *Nation*, July 6, 2012; Christopher Matthews, "LIBOR Scandal: The Crime of the Century?" *Time*, July 9, 2012, http://business.time.com/2012/07/09/libor-scandal-the-crime-of-the-century/.

12. Antoine Gara, "Four Banks Plead Guilty to Foreign Exchange Collusion, UBS Pleads Guilty to Wire Fraud," *Forbes*, May 20, 2015, http://www.forbes.com/sites/antoinegara/2015/05/20/four-banks-plead-guilty-to-foreign-exchange-collusion-ubs-pleads-guilty-to-wire-fraud/; Editorial Board, "Banks as Felons, or Criminality Lite," *New York Times*, May 22, 2015.

13. See Thomas Phillippon, "Finance versus Wal-Mart: Why Are Financial Services So Expensive?," in Alan S. Blinder, Andrew W. Lo, and Robert M. Solow, eds., *Rethinking the Financial Crisis* (New York: Russell Sage Foundation, 2012), 235–46; Robin Greenwood and David Scharfstein, "The Growth of Modern Finance," July 2012, Harvard Business School, http://www.people.hbs.edu/dscharfstein/Growth_of_Modern_Finance.pdf; Gerald F. Davis and Suntae Kim, "Financialization of the Economy," University of Michigan, June 13, 2015, http://webuser.bus.umich.edu/gfdavis/Papers/Davis_Kim_financialization_revised .pdf; also, Benjamin Landy, "Graph: How the Financial Sector Consumed America's Economic Growth," Century Foundation, February 25, 2013, http://www.tcf.org/blog/detail/ graph-how-the-financial-sector-consumed-americas-economic-growth. For a view that finance grew inadvertently from the state's attempt to solve other problems, see Greta R. Kreppner, *Capitalizing on Crisis: The Political Origins of the Rise of Finance* (Cambridge, MA: Harvard University Press, 2011).

14. Steve Denning, "Wall Street Costs the Economy 2% of GDP Each Year," *Forbes*, May 31, 2015, http://www.forbes.com/sites/stevedenning/2015/05/31/wall-street-costs-the -economy-2-of-gdp-each-year/; Ratna Sahay et al., "Rethinking Financial Deepening: Stability and Growth in Emerging Markets," International Monetary Fund, https://www.imf.org/external/ pubs/ft/sdn/2015/sdn1508.pdf. This paper built on Stephen G. Cecchiti and Enisse Kharroubi, "Why Does Financial Sector Growth Crowd Out Real Economic Growth?," Bank for International Settlements, BIS Working Papers No. 490, February 2015, http://www.bis.org/ publ/work490.pdf. On Dodd-Frank, see Paul Krugman, "Obama's Other Success," *New York Times*, August 3, 2014.

15. Gabriel Zucman, *The Hidden Wealth of Nations: The Scourge of Tax Havens* (Chicago: University of Chicago Press, 2015); "2015 U.S. Trust Insights on Wealth and Worth: Annual Survey of High-Net-Worth and Ultra-High-Net-Worth Americans," U.S. Trust, Bank of America Private Wealth Management, http://www.ustrust.com/publish/content/application/ pdf/GWMOL/USTp_AR3FPDKC_2016-05.pdf; James S. Henry, "The Price of Offshore Revisited: New Estimates for 'Missing' Global Private Wealth Income, Inequality, and Lost Taxes," Tax Justice Network, July 2012, http://www.taxjustice.net/wp-content/uploads/ 2014/04/Price_of_Offshore_Revisited_120722.pdf.

16. Jared Bernstein quoted in Noam Schreiber and Patricia Cohen, "For the Wealthiest, a Private Tax System That Saves Them Billions," *New York Times*, December 29, 2015; Josh Barro, "Thanks Obama: Highest Earners' Tax Rates Rose Sharply in 2012," *New York Times*, December 30, 2015.

17. Michael E. Schmidt and Steven Lee Myers, "Panama Firm's Leaked Files Detail Offshore Accounts Tied to World Leaders," *New York Times*, April 3, 2016; Editorial Board, "The Panama Papers' Sprawling Web of Corruption," *New York Times*, April 5, 2016; Eric Lipton and Julie Creswell, "Panama Papers Show How Rich Americans Hide Millions Abroad," *New York Times*, June 5, 2015.

18. Alex Rusbridger, "The Big Stash of the Big Rich: What Can We Know?" *New York Review of Books*, November 10, 2016.

19. Nomi Pris, "When It Comes to Taxes, Donald Trump and Hillary Clinton Have 1 Thing in Common," *Nation*, May 5, 2016.

20. David Cay Johnson, "Panama Papers Expose Regulation Farce," *USA Today*, April 15, 2016; John Christensen and James Henry, "The Offshore Trillions," *New York Review of Books*, March 10, 2016.

21. "IRS Auditing of Big Corporations Plummets," TRAC (Transactional Records Access Clearinghouse, Syracuse University), March 15, 2016, http://trac.syr.edu/tracirs/latest/416/; Gregory Korte, "IRS Audits Less than 1% of Big-Business Partnerships," *USA Today*, April 17, 2014.

22. Oxfam America, "Broken at the Top: How America's Dysfunctional Tax System Costs Billions in Corporate Tax Dodging," April 14, 2016, http://www.oxfamamerica.org/static/media/files/Broken_at_the_Top_4.14.2016.pdf; the International Finance Corporation loaned money to 68 multinational companies to finance investments in sub-Saharan Africa, although 51 of these companies use tax havens "with no apparent link to their core business"; "Oxfam: The International Finance Corporation and Tax Havens—New Report," Tax Justice Network, April 11, 2016, http://www.taxjustice.net/2016/04/11/15578.

23. This paragraph paraphrases Harry Stein, "How the Government Subsidizes Wealth Inequality," Center for American Progress, June 25, 2014, https://www.americanprogress.org/issues/tax-reform/report/2014/06/25/92656; Stein pointed out that the decline of the capital gains tax since 1992 has benefited most "the richest of the rich."

24. Ray D. Madoff, *Immortality and the Law: The Rising Power of the American Dead* (New Haven: Yale University Press, 2010), 76–85, quotation 76.

25. Ibid., 82, 83–84.

26. Bethany McLean and Peter Elkind, *The Smartest Guys in the Room: The Amazing Rise and Scandalous Fall of Enron* (New York: Portfolio Penguin Group, 2003); Karen Ho, *Liquidated: An Ethnography of Wall Street* (Durham, NC: Duke University Press, 2009), 39–42, quotations 39, 40.

27. Ho, *Liquidated*, 58–62, quotations 58–59, 60.

28. For an insightful analysis of motivation beyond the money, see Ezra Klein, "Wall Street Steps In Where Ivy League Fails," *Washington Post*, February 16, 2012; Bair, *Bull By the Horns*, 350–51.

29. On global inequality see Thomas Piketty, *Capital in the Twenty-First Century*, trans. Arthur Goldhammer (Cambridge, MA: Harvard University Press, 2014), 430–67.

30. First quotation, Jack Hayward, "The Populist Challenge to Elitist Democracy in Europe," in Hayward, ed., *Elitism, Populism, and European Politics* (New York: Oxford University Press, 1996), 10; Samuel Gregg, "Downfall: Europe's Failed Political Class," Acton Commentary, Acton Institute, July 20, 2011, http://www.acton.org/pub/commentary/2011/07/20/downfall-europes-failed-political-class; Ian Traynor, "European Elections: Union Left Sullen by Fury and Frustration with Political Class," *Guardian* (London), May 19, 2014, http://www.theguardian.com/politics/2014/may/19/european-elections-fury-frustration-extreme-right-far-left-union.

31. Christopher Hope, "Britain's Ruling Classes Were Only Group to Vote to Stay in EU, Major New Report Finds," *Telegraph* (London), September 30, 2016; Jonathan Freedland, "A Howl of Rage," *New York Review of Books*, August 18, 2016.

32. Ron Formisano, "2016's Populist Moment," National Constitution Center Blog, February 29, 2016, http://blog.constitutioncenter.org/2016/02/2016s-populist-moment/.

33. David Autor, David Dorn, Gordon Hanson, and Kaveh Majlesi, "Importing Political Polarization? The Electoral Consequences of Rising Trade Exposure," September 5, 2016, http://www.ddorn.net/papers/ADHM-PoliticalPolarization.pdf.

34. Daron Acemoglue, David Autor, David Dorn, Gordon H. Hanson, and Brendan Price, "Import Competition and the Great US Employment Sag of the 2000s," *Journal of Labor Economics*, 34, no. S1 (Part 2, January 2016): 141.

35. Nate Silver, "Stop Comparing Donald Trump and Bernie Sanders," *FiveThirtyEight* (blog), September 9, 2015, http://fivethirtyeight.com/features/stop-comparing-donald-trump-and-bernie-sanders/.

36. David Leonhardt, "A Great Fight of Our Times," *New York Times*, October 11, 2016.

37. Pew Research Center, "Beyond Distrust: How Americans View Their Government," September 25, 2015, http://www.people-press.org/2015/11/23/beyond-distrust-how-americans-view-their-government/. Leonhardt also reported a remarkable study by a team of economists led by Raj Chetty revealing that those born in 1980 have significantly less chance to make as much money as their parents as those born in 1940, 1950, 1960, and 1970. Thirty-six-year-olds inhabit "an economy that disappoints a huge number of people who have heard they live in a country where life gets better, only to experience something quite different." David Leonhardt, "The American Dream, Quantified at Last," *New York Times*, December 8, 2016.

38. Susan Adams, "New Study: Trust in Business and Corporate Leaders Plummets," *Forbes*, October 2, 2015, http://www.forbes.com/sites/susanadams/2013/01/22/new-study-trust-in-both-business-and-corporate-leaders-plummets; see also Pew Research Center, "Beyond Distrust"; Suzanne Perry, "1 in 3 Americans Lacks Faith in Charities, Chronicle Poll Finds," *Chronicle of Philanthropy*, October 5, 2015, https://philanthropy.com/article/1-in-3-Americans-Lacks-Faith/233613.

39. James Davison Hunter and Carl Desportes Bowman, "The Vanishing Center of American Democracy," The 2016 Survey of American Political Culture, Institute for Advanced Studies in Culture, University of Virginia, 2016, 17, 24–25, http://www.iasc-culture.org/survey_archives/VanishingCenter.pdf.

40. Ibid., 53–54, 48.

41. Ibid., 20.

42. Ibid., 13, 58.

43. Naomi Klein, "It Was the Democrats' Embrace of Neoliberalism That Won It for Trump," *Guardian* (London), November 9, 2016, https://www.theguardian.com/commentisfree/2016/nov/09/rise-of-the-davos-class-sealed-americas-fate.

44. Jane Mercer, "The Reclusive Hedge-Fund Tycoon behind the Trump Presidency: How Robert Mercer Exploited America's Populist Insurgency," *New Yorker*, March 27, 2017; John Nichols and Robert W. McChesney, *Dollarocracy: How the Money and Media Election Complex Is Destroying America* (New York: Nation Books, 2013), 4; Victor Pickard, "When Commercialism Trumps Democracy," *Common Dreams*, April 1, 2016; Nicholas Confessore

and Karen Yourish, "$2 Billion Worth of Free Media for Donald Trump," *New York Times*, March 15, 2016; David Jackson, "Trump Again Calls Media 'Enemy of the People,'" *USA Today*, February 24, 2017; Jonathan Mahler, "'That Is Great Television': Inside the Strange Symbiosis between the CNN President Jeff Zucker and Donald Trump," *New York Times Magazine*, April 9, 2017.

45. Andrew Sullivan, "The Rotten Core," Daily Dish, *Atlantic*, August 31, 2009, http://www.theatlantic.com/daily-dish/archive/2009/08/the-rotten-core/197019/.

Afterword

1. Michael Kazin, *The Populist Persuasion: An American History* (New York: Basic Books, 1995), 28; Charles Postel, *The Populist Vision* (New York: Oxford University Press, 2007), 4.

2. Herbert Croly, *The Promise of American Life*, ed. Arthur M. Schlesinger Jr. (1909; Cambridge, MA: Harvard University Press, 1965), 21, 23.

3. Elizabeth Sanders, *The Roots of Reform: Farmers, Workers, and the American State, 1877–1917* (Chicago: University of Chicago Press, 1999), 4, 5.

Index

Ron Formisano is the William T. Bryan Chair of American History and professor emeritus of history at the University of Kentucky. His books include *Plutocracy in America: How Increasing Inequality Destroys the Middle Class and Exploits the Poor, The Tea Party: A Brief History,* and *For the People: American Populist Movements from the Revolution to the 1850s.*